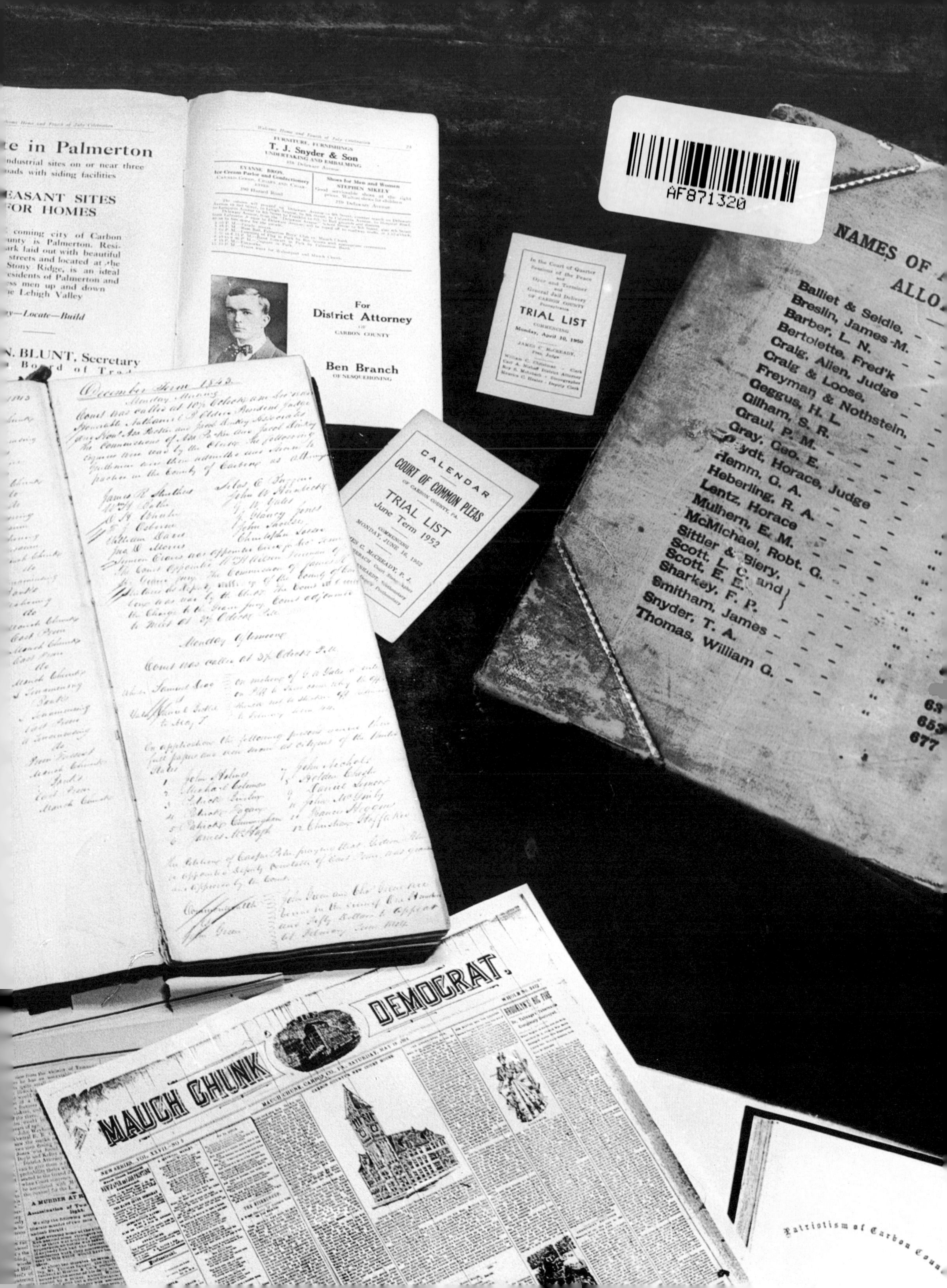

AF871320
...te in Palmerton
...ndustrial sites on or near three ...oads with siding facilities
...EASANT SITES FOR HOMES
...N. BLUNT, Secretary
T. J. Snyder & Son
FURNITURE, FURNISHINGS
UNDERTAKING AND EMBALMING
For District Attorney
OF CARBON COUNTY
Ben Branch
OF NESQUEHONING
In the Court of Quarter Sessions of the Peace and Oyer and Terminer and General Jail Delivery OF CARBON COUNTY Pennsylvania
TRIAL LIST
COMMENCING Monday, April 10, 1950
JAMES C. McCREADY, Pres. Judge
CALENDAR
COURT OF COMMON PLEAS
OF CARBON COUNTY, PA.
TRIAL LIST
June Term 1952
COMMENCING MONDAY, JUNE 16, 1952
December Term 1843
NAMES OF ...
ALLO...
Balliet & Seidle,
Breslin, James M.
Barber, L. N.
Bertolette, Fred'k
Craig, Allen, Judge
Craig & Loose,
Freyman & Nothstein,
Geggus, H. L.
Gilham, S. R.
Graul, P. M.
Gray, Geo. E.
...ydt, Horace, Judge
Hemm, G. A.
Heberling, R. A.
Lentz, Horace
Mulhern, E. M.
McMichael, Robt. G.
Sittler & Biery,
Scott, L. C. and
Scott, E. E.
Sharkey, F. P.
Smitham, James
Snyder, T. A.
Thomas, William G.
MAUCH CHUNK DEMOCRAT.
Patriotism of Carbon Coun...

The Hard Coal Docket

ONE HUNDRED AND FIFTY YEARS OF THE BENCH AND BAR OF CARBON COUNTY

(1843-1993)

John P. Lavelle

Time present and time past
Are both perhaps present in time future
And time future contained in time past.
-- T. S. Eliot

Printed by Times News, Lehighton, Pennsylvania
THE HARD COAL DOCKET
ISBN 0-9658188-0-2
Library of Congress Catalog Card Number: 94-96143
10 9 8 7 6 5 4 3 2

COVER
Herman Herzog "Mauch Chunk, 1872"
Courtesy of William B. Mollard & Family, West Orange, New York

DEDICATION

TO MY FAMILY

To
Dr and Mrs. Conrad W. Raker
With warmest personal regards
John P. [illegible]
December 15, 1997

COURT OF COMMON PLEAS
CARBON CO. PENNA.
1843

CONTENTS

PREFACE

The history of the Bench and Bar of Carbon County has been both a mirror and a motor of the times. Court cases reflected current mores and morals, as well as prevailing interests and issues. Judges' decisions affected people's lives and property. Lawyers' advice suffused many public and private activities. No extant historical work has recorded the course of the legal system in Carbon County for the last century and a half. This volume endeavors to fill that void.

We have drawn data primarily from local newspaper reports, court records, interviews with bar members, bar association minutes and a wide variety of historical treatises and books. Unfortunately, none of these materials is easily accessible, and, for the most part, exist only in microfilm form. Our purpose here is to collect, compress and distill the existing important information about Carbon County lawyers, judges and cases into one published book for easy reference in the next 150 years and thereafter.

This volume seeks to accomplish four goals: (1) to chronicle the growth and development of the Carbon County Judicial System from its beginning, (2) to look back at some of the interesting trials and court proceedings in the last 150 years, (3) to provide in brief biographies an insight into the professional lives and community contributions of those who sat on the bench and some of those who practiced at the bar, and (4) to assess from a due process perspective the "Mollie Maguire" trials of 1876 -- the most famous trials in the history of Carbon County.

Much of what was written about the Carbon Bench and Bar from the mid-twentieth century flowed from the talented and prolific typewriter of Joseph L. Boyle, the court reporter for the *Times News*. His thorough knowledge of the legal system and his ability to turn an elegant phrase in print made us all look and sound better. A chapter in this volume is devoted to him because the Court was his "beat" and his reports were a major resource for this book. Kathleen McBride of Jim Thorpe (an aspiring reporter who was encouraged and inspired by "Joe" to be a journalist) wrote his biography.

As we researched Carbon's legal community over its 150 years, it became apparent that judges and lawyers played significant roles in weaving the richly hued historical tapestry of this county. Among them were towering war heroes, creative legislators, astute businessmen, sensitive church and community leaders, caring bankers and wise counselors to elected officials. We hope that this memorial to their lives and activities adequately reflects our indebtedness to them and inspires future generations to follow in their footsteps.

John P. Lavelle - 1994

ACKNOWLEDGMENTS

Like a petitioner in bankruptcy, I herein acknowledge, albeit cheerfully, my indebtedness to my many creditors in producing this book.

First and foremost, I am truly grateful to Joseph Frendak who was my principal researcher and word processor for the manuscript. He reviewed numerous histories and ancient court documents, painstakingly scanned and copied hundreds of microfilmed pages of newspapers in the Dimmick and various other libraries and constantly directed my attention to historical data and sources which proved to be most helpful. His command of the computer was masterful. He unfailingly kept me current with hard copy, made countless revisions with remarkable equanimity and was able to get the computer to somehow produce a print ready book. Without his invaluable assistance this history could not have been written.

My secretary, Roberta Brewster, who uses the computer like a virtuoso, processed the early portions of the manuscript in her spare time. Because she has so little of that in her life, I particularly value her help.

Sophie Kozuch and Linda Gardner, both aspiring lawyers, played important roles in the difficult jury research and statistical analyses which the chapter on the Mollie Maguire trials required. Their willingness to undertake much of the legwork and unremitting enthusiasm were indispensable to bringing this work to fruition.

A number of librarians responded to my requests. None gave more generously and enthusiastically than Gwen Gillespie of the Dimmick Memorial Library in Jim Thorpe. She was always ready to assist and I am grateful to her for giving me the help I sought and some that I did not. Frances Navin and John Faust, the dedicated preservers of Carbon County records, were most helpful in digging out for me many old legal records in the archives.

Many current members of the bar provided me with information and materials which found its way into this book. I am especially indebted to my father-in-law George A. Shutack and bar members Martin H. Philip and George T. McKinley for sharing their memories of the profession and the bench, especially those covering the early 1930s and into the late 1950s.

I am profoundly thankful to Professor T. Robert Milligan whose enormous learning and love of the language was reflected in his editing of a substantial part of the manuscript. I hope I have incorporated his wise advice and sensitivity. My daughter Marianne and my sons John and James read portions of the manuscript and made helpful suggestions.

Lehighton realtor, Gene Durigan, and Fred Masenheimer, publisher of the *Times News,* contributed immeasureably to this book by giving me access to volumes of old Lehighton and Mauch Chunk newspapers. I also wish to add a special thanks to John Gunsser, George Harvan, Thomas McBride and Kathleen McBride who graciously provided help in gathering and producing photographs and materials for this book. To Conrad Sthare and Beth Yaroseufski of the *Times News*, my undying gratitude for their special expertise in getting this book into print.

Last, first and always, I thank my wife, Marianne, for her unwavering support, encouragement and help in gathering historical data. What she has given to the author in many other ways can never be repaid but I think she knows that I am eternally grateful.

For the good in this book, I thank those mentioned above. Any errors or omissions are mine.

CHAPTER I

WILLIAM PENN AND THE FIRST PENNSYLVANIA COURTS

The courts of Carbon County, as all courts of Pennsylvania, are rooted in the centuries-old judicial system of England. Born of and dominated by English kings, nurtured by the ancient precedents of Greek and Roman law, strengthened in the resolution of disputes since 900 A.D., the judge-made, common-law system represented a whole new way of dispensing justice. During the turbulent political and social upheavals of the seventeenth century, among many longstanding English traditions to fall was monarchical control of the court system.

William Penn brought with him to this country not only the English system but also many fundamental civil rights which he found lacking in the English courts. A scion of a powerful and wealthy family, Penn converted to the outlawed Quaker religion during a stay in the south of Ireland while he was still in his teens. As a result of teaching and preaching his religious beliefs, he soon came to be regarded as a radical and a troublemaker. By 1670, the English Government, fearful that the Quakers were a threat to the established Church of England, closed all Quaker meeting houses and made it a crime to hold any religious gathering other than a meeting of the Church of England. Nonetheless, William Penn, at the age of twenty-six, chose to preach to a small group of Quakers on the street in London and, as expected, he was arrested for the crime of "tumult". Today, Penn's conduct would be protected by the First Amendment of the United States Constitution and by Article I of the Pennsylvania Constitution, but in the England of 1670, Penn's only protection was his unshakable belief that, as an English citizen, he had the inherent right to speak his mind freely.

William Penn
Chalk Portrait by Francis Place

Penn's trial on September 1, 3, 4 and 5 in the year 1670 in the Old Bailey was intriguing courtroom drama with a heady mix of pathos and humor. Articulate and bright, Penn represented himself and opened his case by refusing to plead guilty or not guilty. This infuriated John Starling, the presiding judge, and he warned Penn that he would be found in contempt of court if he did not enter a plea. Penn retorted saucily:

> *"I desire you would let me know by what law you ground my indictment," said Penn.*
>
> *"Upon common law," the judge replied.*
>
> *"Where is that common law?"*
>
> *"You must not think that I am able to run up so many years, and over so many adjudicated cases which we call common law, to answer your curiosity," the judge said.*
>
> *"If it [be] so common, it should not be hard to produce," Penn said.*
>
> *"Sir, will you plead your indictment?"*
>
> *"Shall I plead to an indictment that hath no foundation in law?"*
>
> *"You are a pestilent fellow," the judge said. Whereupon he ordered Penn removed from the court room to the bale dock.*[1]

Later when he was returned to court, Penn exhorted his jury to "mind your privilege as Englishmen and resist dictation from the bench." Judge Starling's charge inferred that the King wanted the jury to find him guilty. But Penn's eloquent defense of individual rights -- his own rights and the rights of his jurors -- led the jury to disregard the judge's instructions, even though the judge had ordered them to be locked up without food, water, light or tobacco until they changed their minds. Their verdict was "Not Guilty". Both Penn and his jury went to jail anyway -- Penn's jury for refusing to find him guilty, and Penn for refusing, as a matter of religious belief, to take his hat off in court.

But the case was not over. On appeal by members of the jury (which English law permitted at that time), Chief Justice John Vaughn of the Supreme Court, in a landmark decision upholding their verdict, ruled that an English jury, like a judge, was free and independent and may never be fined or imprisoned for their verdicts. See 6 Howell's State Trials 999, 1026, Vaughn's Reports 35, 124 Eng. Rep. 1006 (1670).

Eleven years later, when Penn was building his ideal society in the New World, he preserved for all the citizens of this Commonwealth in his "Frame of Government" the right to trial by an independent jury for which he had argued at his trial.

---

[1]*Penn & Mead's Case (Eng), 6 Howell's State Trials, 951, 958 (1670).*

William Penn publishes his Frame of Government -- the first laws of Pennsylvania

King Charles II, by Letters Patent dated March 4, 1681, granted to William Penn, his heirs and assigns, as Absolute Proprietaries, the "Province and Seigniorie" to be called "Pennsylvania, . . ." to make laws "by and with the advice, assent and approbation of the freemen of the said country and to appoint Judges, Magistrates and other Officers . . . and to do all and every other thing and things which the complete establishment of justice, into Courts and tribunals, forms of judicature and manner of proceedings do belong."
Charles II made this grant to Penn in order to satisfy a debt he owed to Penn's father, Admiral Sir William Penn, for back pay and outstanding loans.

In 1682, pursuant to this grant of power, Penn published his "Frame of Government," Pennsylvania's first constitution and a remarkable testament to human rights and individual freedom. With his personal experiences of English justice to guide him, Penn's Charter guaranteed not only freedom of conscience to all inhabitants -- including Indians -- but also an absolute right to trial by jury, bail for all non-capital offenses and humane conditions for prisoners. Mirroring the language of the historic Magna Carta, it boldly declared that "all courts shall be open and justice shall neither be sold, denied or delayed." In 1701, ahead of England and all other colonies, Penn's Declaration of Rights added the guarantee of the right to employ counsel for every purpose in presenting a defense to a criminal charge.

Penn's "Frame of Government" called for an elected General Assembly and an appointed Provincial Council. The Council advised the Governor; the Governor and Council wrote all legislation and ran the government. The Assembly was supposed to either ratify or reject the proposed laws, without debate.

First Courts in Pennsylvania

The Seventeenth Article of Penn's Charter provided "that the Governor and Provincial Council shall erect from time to time, standing Courts of Justices in such places and number as they shall judge convenient for the good government of the province." Penn gave to the Council the privilege of nominating judges, and to the General Assembly the privilege of nominating a double number of justices, from which number the Governor or his deputy was to make a choice and issue commissions for a term of one year.

Under Penn's Charter, litigants could plead their own case or be represented by "friends" before the courts. Legal proceedings were to be short and in English. Appointed justices of the peace sat on the bench. They had no legal education or training and had a deep-seated disdain for lawyers. They concentrated on settling disputes between their neighbors by using common sense and experience and often ended up getting jostled by the litigants. Swearing, drunkenness and lying were punishable by a minimum of five days of hard labor and a bread and water diet. A jury of twelve from the neighborhood was to be used for civil cases and twenty-four men for capital offenses. None of these courts were approved by the king, but this rudimentary judicial system remained in effect well into the eighteenth century.

After several futile attempts between 1701 and 1721 to establish a court system, all of which were disallowed by the Crown, the Governor and the General Assembly on May 22, 1722 passed an act establishing courts of judicature: a state Supreme Court, as well as county courts of common pleas, courts of oyer and terminer, orphans' courts and courts of quarter sessions. These courts became the foundation for the present courts of common pleas and Supreme Court. The Crown approved the Act of 1722 and a duly recognized court system came into being in Pennsylvania.

This judicial system was two-tiered. At the top, there was a Supreme Court, with a chief justice and three associate justices. The high court had general appellate jurisdiction and exclusive original jurisdiction in capital cases and certain civil matters. One or more of the justices went on the circuit twice a year into the several counties to hear cases. Arrayed in a red robe and a white wig, the judge was accompanied to court by the local sheriff with his sword drawn. At the base, there was a court of quarter sessions in each county for criminal cases and a court of common pleas for civil suits involving an amount under forty shillings, over which justices of the peace presided. These justices or "squires" as they were called by the local gentry also conducted business in the orphans' court. The court of quarter sessions had jurisdiction of all offenses except capital crimes. These local courts usually convened four times a year for two days to handle the criminal and civil cases. Appeals might be taken to the Supreme Court from any decision of the court of common pleas involving the titles to land, without regard to the amount involved. It appears that other cases involving any amount might also be removed to the Supreme Court, but if the amount involved was less than fifty pounds, the plaintiff recovered no costs and the defendant was "mulcted in double costs."

English Common Law Adopted

The Act of 1718, approved and confirmed in King's Council in 1719, provided "it is the settled point that as the common law is the birthright of English subjects, so it ought to be their rule in British dominions."

And so it was that English common law became the settled law in Pennsylvania. The common law was actually judge made law. Its outstanding feature was that it was based not on specific laws and statutes or on a code of such laws, but on principles enunciated by judges in their decisions recorded in the reports of decided cases. Judges were supposed to administer "the law and custom of the realm," but in practice they developed their own set of principles and rules, relying on precedents established

Blackstone's Commentaries -- The Common Law

by decisions in previous cases. A stable legal system evolved which had flexibility because it was in a continuous process of change, founded on general custom as reflected in the decisions of generations of judges.

The common law in written form was found in collections, which were privately owned, and consisted primarily of commentaries in book and pamphlet form. The most influential standard legal reference books for lay judges and pioneer lawyers were the *Commentaries on the Law of England* by the revered British jurist Sir William Blackstone. Published in four volumes between 1765 and 1769, they described the essentials of the Common Law of England. They are still often referred to and cited as authority by the Pennsylvania Supreme Court. Published books of decisions made by American courts did not exist until 1790, when Alexander Dallas's "Reports of Cases Ruled and Adjudicated in the Courts of Pennsylvania" appeared.

Lay Lawyers

Charles Warren, an early historian of Pennsylvania courts and lawyers, describes colonial and revolutionary times as an era of "law without lawyers." Royal Governors did not encourage what they regarded as a craft of troublemakers, and the powerful clergy was inclined to regard attorneys as secular rivals teaching law not found in the Scriptures. The Quakers had their own system of arbitrating disputes by "common peacemakers," or lay referees. During the Revolution there was considerable hostility to lawyers. Success of the Revolution propagated an egalitarian philosophy that all careers were open to any man and a true democracy did not need experts and specialists.[2]

John Adams, although speaking of pre-Revolutionary New England, precisely portrayed the legal environment in Pennsylvania counties when he wrote:

> *Looking about me, in the country, I found the practice of law was grasped into the hands of deputy sheriffs, pettifoggers, and even constables, who filed all the writs upon bonds, promissory notes, and accounts, received the fees established for lawyers, and stirred up many unnecessary suits . . . .*

To stem this tide of predatory litigators, Adams proposed regulations not only for confining the practice of law to those who were educated to it, and sworn to fidelity in it, but to introduce more regularity, urbanity, candor and politeness, as well as honor, equity and humanity.[3]

---

[2]Warren, Charles. *History of the American Bar.*

[3]Bowen, Catherine Drinker. *John Adams and The American Revolution.* Boston: Little, Brown and Company., 1950.

Call for Professionalism

Adams' call for change in having trained ethical legal professionals representing litigants had a slow acceptance. There were no law schools in colonial America. Only those from wealthy families could afford to obtain legal training by attending the Inns of Court in England.[4] The usual method by which a young man qualified to practice law was to "read law" as an apprentice in the office of a local practitioner. To be invited to study law, a young man had to come from the proper social strata or have a family relationship to a practicing lawyer. It was strictly a matter of who you were and whom you knew that opened the doors to the legal profession.

In 1759, the Pennsylvania Supreme Court issued an order which was designed to professionalize the practice of law. It provided "that for the future no persons be admitted attorneys of this Court without being previously examined as to their qualifications to practice, nor without having taken the oaths or affirmations of allegiance to His Majesty and subscribed the usual Declaration."

It then became the established practice in most counties for a member of the bar known as a "preceptor" to move in open court for the admission of the candidate who had "read law" in his office. The court would then appoint a special committee of three members of the bar to test his knowledge of law and procedure and if the applicant passed the examination, he was admitted and sworn.[5] On the surface, this system looked like it should produce qualified professionals. In actual practice, these committees performed perfunctory testing and generally passed all of the candidates for admission.

---

[4]According to Loyd's "Early Courts of Penna," p. 117 the following Pennsylvanians studied at the Inns of Court in London from 1760 to the end of the Revolution: Andrew Hamilton, John Kinsey, Edward Shippen, Benjamin Chew, Edward Tilghman, William and Richard Tilghman, Jared Ingersoll, William Rawle, Thomas McKean, John Dickinson, Jasper Yeates. Most of them became leading judges and lawyers.

[5]*Ibid.*, p. 119.

CHAPTER II

BENCH AND BAR BEFORE CARBON COUNTY (1776-1842)

When the American Revolution began, the proprietary government of William Penn ended, and with it fell the laws and the system of courts established under him. The State Constitution of 1776 purported to establish a new judicial system for Pennsylvania. A close reading of the constitution and the acts passed pursuant to it, however, reveals that the changes were minimal. The same judicial system which had existed under Penn was continued except there was no acknowledgement of the authority of the King of England.

Northampton County Courthouse, built in 1754.

From 1752, the territory which is now Carbon County was a part of Northampton County, and Northampton's Bench and Bar served the area's legal needs. On June 3, 1777, the Supreme Executive Council in whom the Constitution of 1776 vested executive power chose twenty-one justices of the peace to serve Northampton County. None of these judges were trained in the law. On June 17, 1777, eleven of the commissioned judges assembled to conduct the first session of the court of quarter sessions (criminal court) and on June 19, 1777, six of the judges held the first session of the court of common pleas (civil court). The continuance dockets of Northampton County for this period show suits for trespass, slander, replevin and assumpsit. The civil caseload averaged about 150 cases per year. Two lawyers were involved in most of the law suits: Samuel Sitgreaves, a Philadelphia lawyer trained in the office of James Wilson,[6] was the more prominent of the two; Robert Trailer, of Easton, not only practiced in the courts, but also served as prothonotary of Northampton County.

The most common criminal offense was assault and battery, and sentences imposed were harsh. Public whipping, branding and cutting off ears awaited a defendant

[6]James Wilson, a native of St. Andrews, Scotland, was the first member of the United States Supreme Court to be appointed from Pennsylvania in 1789.

found guilty of crimes considered minor by today's standards. Debtors could be imprisoned if the creditor paid the cost of his upkeep in the county jail.

While these early courts were serving Northampton County, national events were shaping important reforms in the Commonwealth. Cornwall surrendered at Yorktown in 1781, and the British recognized American independence in 1783. The United States Constitution was ratified by Pennsylvania and went into effect on March 4, 1789. Within just three weeks, the Pennsylvania General Assembly called for a convention to amend the Constitution of 1776. This convention brought forth the Pennsylvania Constitution of 1790, and launched a new era for the administration of justice in Pennsylvania.

Constitution of 1790

The most important changes brought about by the 1790 Constitution were the replacement of laymen with president judges "of knowledge and integrity, skilled in the laws" and a provision for associate judges, who were not required to be trained in the law. Justices of the peace could no longer sit in the county courts. The 1790 Constitution also grouped the counties into judicial districts and provided president judges for the common pleas courts in these districts. It also gave the Governor the power to appoint judges. Supreme Court justices had a life term. Judges of the county courts were also appointed for life and were given authority to try capital cases, which had been previously entrusted exclusively to Supreme Court justices. The Act of April 13, 1791 placed Northampton, Berks, Luzerne and Northumberland counties in the Third Judicial District or Circuit. Jacob Rush of Reading was appointed president judge, and with him three associate judges, Peter Rhoads, William Henry and Daniel Wagener.

In keeping with the spirit of the 1790 Constitution to train and professionalize the bench and bar, many county courts adopted rules and requirements for admission to the bar. Northampton County Court entered such an order at the June Term of 1793. Essentially, it required:

> *(1) Service of a clerkship to "some practicing attorney or gentleman of known abilities" known as a preceptor for three years; or*
>
> *Study of the law "with assiduity" under the direction of a practicing attorney or "Gentleman of the Law" for two years after attaining the age of twenty-one years; or*
>
> *Service of a clerkship in a neighboring state for two years and a final third year in Pennsylvania;*

(2) Certification by the preceptor as to such service or study and to the integrity and good behavior of the applicant;

(3) In order to study in the County if the preceptor was not a native of Northampton County:

Two years of residence in Pennsylvania was required of applicants who came from another state;
Residence in the state for four years and the Oath of Fidelity to the State were required of a foreigner;

(4) The applicant had to submit to an examination by "three Gentlemen of the Law . . . in the fullest manner" in the presence of a judge of the Court;

(5) And if it be unanimously certified by the Gentlemen so appointed that the preceptee is well qualified to practice he may be admitted.

Associate Judges

The 1790 constitutional provision for the appointment of lay associate judges theoretically had a sound purpose. At a time when two or more counties formed most judicial districts, it was important to have people with local knowledge to assist the president judge who was from a distant county in resolving questions relating to the values of property, appointments of minor officers, selection of viewers, setting bail and appraising assets in the orphans' court. In early colonial times, the governor appointed men of integrity and high morals, but as new counties were created the quality of these appointments eroded abysmally.

Men of dubious character were often appointed associate judges and many of them became an embarrassment to the bench and bar. McMaster, in his *History of the People of the United States*, described the associate judges of the late 1790s and early 1800s in unflattering terms:

The president judges were men of ability and well read in the law. But no such qualifications were thought necessary in the county judges (associate judges), who were in general laymen, and the worst kind of laymen, small politicians. The drunkenness, the brawling, the neglect of duty, the airs which these men assumed, and the petty spite they exhibited toward such political opponents as came within their power, made them more hateful to the people than the excise collector of the assessors of the direct tax. They were all Federalists. To complain of them to a Federal Governor and a Federal senate would have been useless. But the moment Thomas McKean was chosen Governor, the moment the Senate passed into Republican hands, complaints and demands for relief came up from every part of Pennsylvania. Two lay judges, during the heated campaign of 1800, had sat quietly on the bench while a clerk of quarter sessions was well pummelled by a political enemy. On another occasion a judge had quit the bench, gone down into the crowd, and engaged in a fist fight with a man he claimed had insulted him. Two others had prevented the sitting of a court by staying away. Still another had forged a name to the acknowledgment to a deed. In Wayne county a judge had, by main strength, dragged a colleague from the bench and kept him from attending Court. As a class, they were well described in a petition to the Legislature, which declared them to be destitute of all legal knowledge, burdensome and expensive. The justices of the peace seem to have been worse yet. Many were tavern-keepers. A few were charged with keeping houses of ill-fame. That they were grossly ignorant and grossly unjust cannot be doubted.[7]

As the eighteenth century drew to an end, Thomas Jefferson established the first law school in the United States in 1779 at William and Mary College in Williamsburg, Virginia. But the general level of legal education in America, obtained for the most part by "reading law" in law offices, was haphazard and rudimentary. (It was not until 1834 that Dickinson College opened the first law school in Pennsylvania.) Legal literature was scarce and foreign. The courts to which the lawyer might look for development of law had little strength or credit. There were not many lawyers and the layman frequently drafted his own instruments, contracts, deeds and wills without professional assistance. The United States Supreme Court was an untried institution recently superimposed upon the state systems. It had no courthouse, no jurisprudence and virtually no business. Its first official session had to be postponed because a quorum of the justices was not present.

In the early 1800s, several abortive attempts to impeach three justices of the Pennsylvania Supreme Court led to a constitutional amendment to take away the life tenure of judges. On March 22, 1804, articles of impeachment were approved against Chief Justice Edward Shippen and Associate Justices Jasper Yeates and Thomas Smith charging them with arbitrarily fining and imprisoning Philadelphia lawyer Thomas Passmore for contempt of court. Cesar Rodney of Delaware had to be retained to prosecute the charges because local lawyers refused to become involved. Jared Ingersoll and Alexander J. Dallas represented the judges. In 1805 after a twenty-day trial before the House of Representatives in Lancaster, the three justices were acquitted. The prosecution came up short by only three

[7]Eastman, Frank M. *Courts and Lawyers of Pennsylvania.* New York: The American Historical Society, Inc., 1922, Vol. II, 1623-1923, 499.

A View of Mauch Chunk in 1845
From the ***History of Northampton, Lehigh, Monroe, Carbon and Schuylkill Counties*** *by I. Daniel Rupp.*

votes in obtaining the two-thirds vote required for conviction. The failure to impeach the justices triggered calls for reform and a public clamor for a constitutional convention to change the life term of judges. The Convention of 1837 responded to the outcry by reducing the terms of Supreme Court justices to fifteen years, common pleas court judges to ten years and associate judges to five years.

During this period, court proceedings for the Third Judicial District were conducted in Easton, Wilkes-Barre, or Sunbury. In making the long journeys from their homes to these locations, the judges and lawyers of the district had to go by roads that were always difficult and dangerous. Usually they traveled on horseback, carrying their law books and briefs in their saddlebags. Overnight stays were in small towns with limited sleeping accommodations. The life of the lawyer -- like that of the itinerant country doctor -- was harsh, produced little income and attracted only a dedicated few.

In the territory which is now Carbon County, the American Industrial Revolution began to heat up during the 1830s with breathtaking technological advances and a heavy influx of cash and business entrepreneuers. The Lehigh Coal and Navigation Company led by Josiah White, Erskine Hazard and E. A. Douglas completed an engineering marvel by designing and building high-lift locks on the upper Lehigh Canal. White conceived and built the five mile Room Run gravity railroad, later called the Switchback, for hauling coal from the mines in Nesquehoning to Mauch Chunk. The Old Company, as it was popularly called, with its monopoly over transportation from the upper Lehigh Valley to Easton, ammassed enormous profits carrying coal in its canal boats from the mines in Northeast Pennsylvania to Easton where connections could be made to Philadelphia and New York City.

In 1833, a tall, raw-boned thirty four year old carpenter, born in Mystic, Connecticut, came to Mauch Chunk and began hauling coal by canal boat to Philadelphia. Within a few years he expanded his business to include construction, merchandising and coal mining. Reputedly, he was the first to send coal in unbroken cargoes from Pottsville to New York City. As money poured in from his many business ventures, he bought large tracts of land in and around Mauch Chunk. A man of large plans and boundless energy with a spirit emboldened by the prospect of huge financial returns, Asa Packer was soon to change the face and the character of this remote and underdeveloped region. If he did not exactly invent Carbon County, more than any other he would define it. In doing so, Asa Packer would dramatically impact its courts and legal community more than any other individual of his time.

CHAPTER III

EARLY CARBON COUNTY COURTS AND LAWYERS (1843-1900)

1843 was a year of economic distress and violence in Pennsylvania. A declining export market and stiff competition from Europe had caused the Panic of 1837, the most serious financial collapse to rock America until the 1929 Wall Street crash. Still reeling from the Panic, the Commonwealth was unable to pay the interest on its debts. Banks began to fail or suspend their operations across the state. A new party, calling itself the Supreme Order of the Star Spangled Banner, had emerged and was insisting that only native-born Protestants be elected to public office. They were called "Know-Nothings" because, when members were asked about their secret oaths and rituals, they would reply "I know nothing." The movement caused deep resentment in the Irish communities, and confrontation between this Native American party and Irish-Americans erupted into rioting, shooting and burning across the Commonwealth. Governor David Porter had to call out the state militia to quell riots in Philadelphia, Kensington and Southwark to restore law and order.

Asa Packer

It was not the best of times to erect a new county. But in Mauch Chunk, Asa Packer, a bold, shrewd business man saw it as a time of opportunity and aspiration. He had already concluded that prosperity would only return when domestic markets were developed to absorb the products of America's farms, mines and factories and he was already thinking about building a railroad to take coal from the mines in Carbon County to Easton and the eastern industrial market.

Elected to the Pennsylvania House of Representatives in 1841, Asa Packer quietly introduced in the Legislature a bill to separate Carbon County from Northampton County. It was not given much chance to succeed. For thirty years various groups and legislators had intermittently but unsuccessfully tried -- through agitation, petition and cajolery -- to persuade the State Legislature to separate Carbon from Northampton and Monroe counties. Between 1837 and 1843, petitions were presented to the Legislature for separation every year only to be met with rejection or silence. In Packer, however, the separatist movement found a leader with wealth, prestige and political clout. Packer had both a personal as well as a civic interest in getting this bill passed. He had invested heavily in the town of Mauch

Chunk and the surrounding area. Mauch Chunk was not only his home, it was the center of his industrial empire. Packer realized that if Carbon became a separate county with Mauch Chunk as its new county seat, his business prospects as well as his property values would escalate. Asa Packer lobbied vigorously for the separation of Carbon County and, as he did in most of his business ventures, he succeeded. On March 13, 1843 Pennsylvania Governor David Rittenhouse Porter signed the historic Act which made the County of Carbon a separate and independent county:

THE ACT (IN PART)

> *Erecting parts of Northampton and Monroe counties, into a separate county, to be called Carbon.*
>
> *SECTION 1. Be it enacted by the Senate and House of Representatives of the Commonwealth of Pennsylvania in General Assembly met, and it is hereby enacted by the authority of the same,*
>
> *That all those parts of the counties of Northampton and Monroe, lying within the following bounds, viz: Beginning at the north-west corner of Northampton county, thence southwardly along the said county line till it intersects the northern line of Lehigh county, thence eastwardly along the top of the Blue mountain to the south-west corner of Monroe county, thence northwardly along the Monroe county line and continue the same point of compass in a direct line through Tobyhanna township, in Monroe county, to such point as may strike the Luzerne county line, thence westwardly along the Luzerne county line to the place of beginning, shall be, and the same is, according to the foregoing lines, declared to be erected into a separate county, to be called Carbon: Provided, That the territory taken from Monroe county, shall only embrace the township of Penn Forest, and that the said township of Penn Forest shall constitute the whole of the territory taken from Monroe county, by the provisions of this act.*

Reports from Harrisburg on the passage of the "Carbon" Act did not reach Mauch Chunk until the evening of March 14. From the top of Chute Hill, the unloading depot for coal trains on the gravity railroad, a loud cannon blast roared the official announcement of this long awaited news. Celebrations and merrymaking broke out like Fourth of July fireworks throughout the new born county.

Joseph H. Siewers and Orville H. Wheeler, who both became members of the Carbon Bar, marked the beginning of Carbon County by changing the name of their newspaper. The *Lehigh Pioneer and Mauch Chunk Courier* became the *Carbon County*

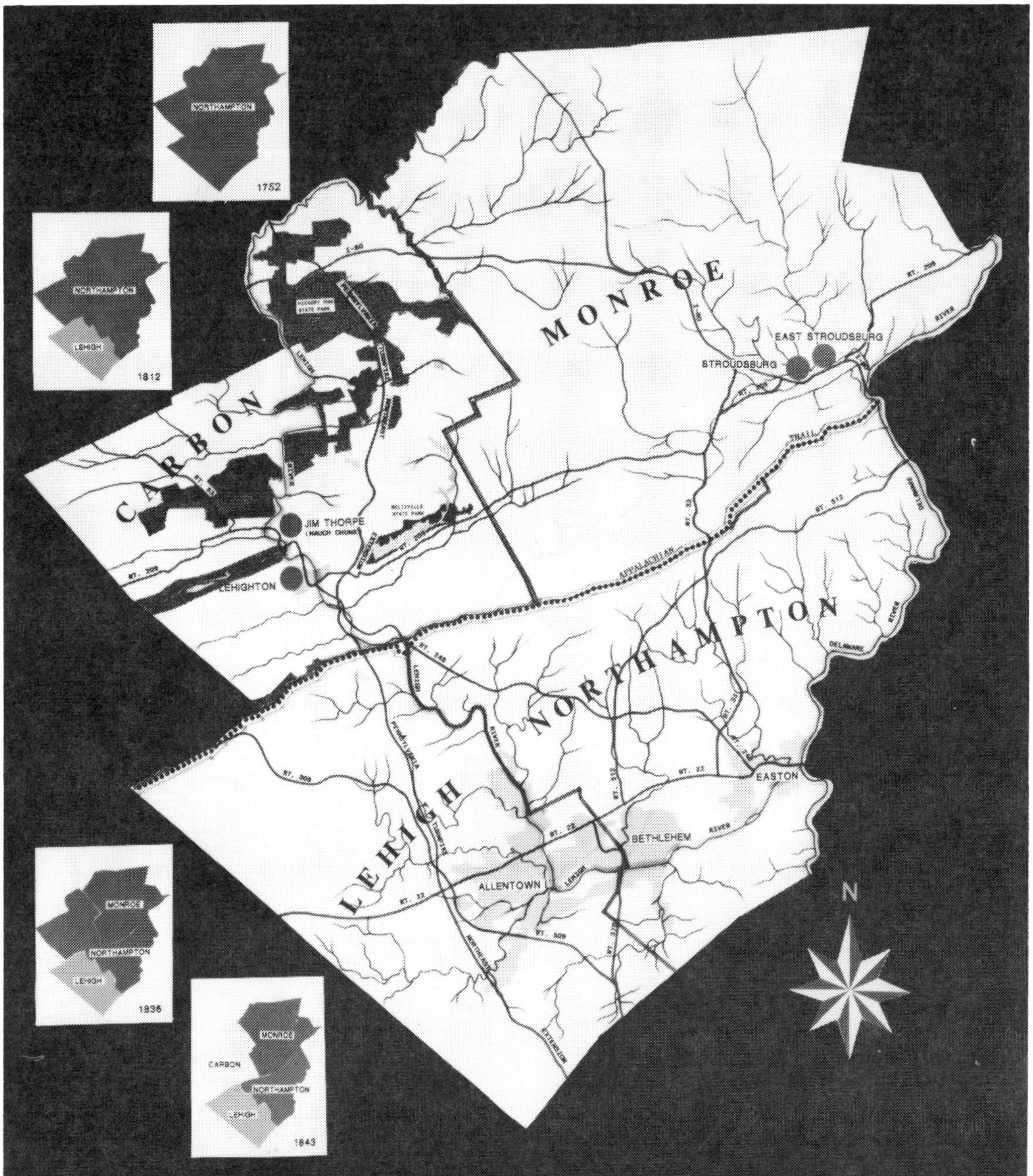

Northampton County was the mother county of Lehigh (1812), Monroe (1836) and Carbon (1843) counties. This photo shows the original layout of Northampton County when it was created in 1752.

Transit on March 21, 1843 with the following intrepid but almost incomprehensible paraphrase of Hamlet's soliloquy:

> ***Birth-Night Celebration***
>
> *Gentlemen:*
> *Allow us to introduce to you Carbon County!*
> *To be or not to be? that is the question*
>
> *"For twice ten tedious years" this has been the burden of our aspirations and now the question has been triumphantly answered. Old Northampton literally notwithstanding, and we have once and for all made our "Transit" over the disk of the Political State Orb, to revolve about its central influence, we certainly may be allowed to felicitate ourselves upon the result. But to sit down passively would be to do injustice to the importance as well as the good humor inspired by the event, and accordingly the news of the Division, circulating rapidly produced a general disposition to testify our joy.*

Selection of County Seat

Governor Porter quickly appointed a committee of prominent non-residents to undertake the difficult task of selecting the best and most central site for the new county seat: J. H. Brodhead of Pike County, W. J. B. Andrews of Clearfield County and Charles W. Hegins of Northumberland County.

Lehighton and Mauch Chunk contended for the seat. Lehighton offered to erect new county buildings "at least equal to those in Monroe County." To show their enthusiasm, the citizens of Mauch Chunk raised $4,000 to purchase the Lehigh Coal and Navigation Company's "Old Store" on the corner of Broadway and Susquehanna in Mauch Chunk together with a lot to the rear. They promised to refurbish it for use as a courthouse and to build a jail with no expense to the new county.

While the committee pondered its decision on the county seat, and no doubt with some prodding by Asa Packer, the Lehigh Coal and Navigation Company agreed to donate its "Old Store" to the county. This trading center, built in 1827 on the land where the courthouse is today, was the most prominent building in Mauch Chunk. The promise of this gift proved to be pivotal to the decision. On June 19, 1843 the Governor's commission recommended Mauch Chunk for the erection of a courthouse, a prison and county offices. The announcement quickly set off unprecedented revelry in Mauch Chunk. People danced up and down Broadway, and the roar of cannons resonated through the surrounding mountains.

"Mauch Chunk, From the Opposite Side of the Lehigh," John Collins' topographical view of the LC&N Company's Mauch Chunk canal operations, including the gravity railroad on Mt. Pisgah, circa 1846.

Establishment of Carbon Courts and First Session

The Act of March 13, 1843 creating the County of Carbon also provided for the formation of the Carbon County court system. Section 9 specified that ". . . from and after the first day of September Carbon County shall be entitled to, and at all times thereafter, have all and singular *the courts, jurisdictions, offices,* rights and privileges to which the inhabitants of the counties of this state are entitled by the Constitution and laws of this Commonwealth." Section 10 of the Act annexed Carbon County to the Twelfth Judicial District, which at that time comprised Dauphin, Schuylkill and Lebanon counties. The statute further directed that court proceedings be held on the third Monday of February, May, September and December, and that the court open for business on the third Monday of December 1843.

Earlier that year, Judge Calvin Blythe of the Twelfth Judicial District resigned to accept the office of collector of customs in Philadelphia, and Governor David Porter appointed Judge Nathaniel B. Eldred, who had presided over several other judicial districts since 1835, as president judge of the district.

Carbon County's first court session took place on Monday, December 18, 1843 in the refurbished LC&N Company building located on the corner of Susquehanna and Broadway in Mauch Chunk. Sheriff Charles Snyder subpoenaed the first criminal jury panel and first grand jury. Judge Nathaniel B. Eldred and Associate Judges Asa Packer and Jacob Dinkey called the court to order at 10:30 A.M. According to the sessions docket, part of the morning session was

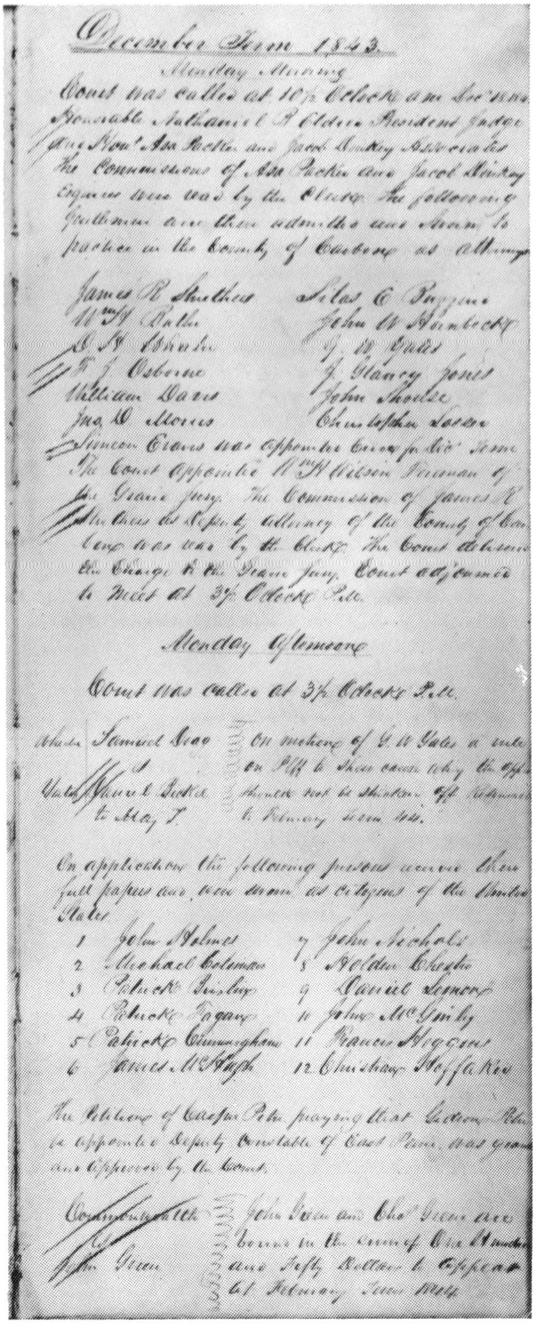
December Term 1843.
Monday Morning
Court was called at 10½ O'clock a.m. [illegible]
Honorable Nathaniel B. Eldred President Judge
and Hon. Asa Packer and Jacob Dinkey Associates
The Commissions of Asa Packer and Jacob Dinkey
Esquires were read by the Clerk. The following
Gentlemen were then admitted and sworn to
practice in the County of Carbon as Attorneys

James R. Struthers — Silas E. Burrows [illegible]
W. H. Potts — John W. Hornbeck
[illegible] — G. W. Yates
[illegible] Osborne — J. Glancy Jones
William Davis — John Shoulse [illegible]
Jno. W. Morris — Christopher Loeser [illegible]

Monday Afternoon
Court was called at 3½ O'clock P.M.

Minutes of First Session of Carbon County Court
December 18, 1843

devoted to the formalities of setting up a justice system. Judge Eldred began the proceedings by reading Section 9 of the Act of March 13, 1843 which created a separate and independent court system for Carbon County. The clerk then read the commissions of Asa Packer and Jacob Dinkey as associate judges.

Formal admission of lawyers to practice law in the courts of Carbon County followed. James R. Struthers, William H. Butler, Orville H. Wheeler, Francis J. Osborn and Silas E. Buzzard, all of whom were residents of Mauch Chunk, were the first to take the official oath. William Davis, John D. Morris, John W. Hornbeck, George W. Yates, J. Glancy Jones, John Shouse and Christopher Loeser, members of the Northampton County Bar, also became charter members of the Carbon Bar.

Sheriff Charles Snyder and Prothonotary and Clerk of the Court William H. Brown were officially sworn in. When he took his oath as deputy attorney general, James R. Struthers became Carbon County's first prosecuting attorney. With all of the principal players in place, Judge Eldred launched the Carbon justice system by instructing the first grand jury on their duties and functions. The morning session adjourned at noon.

The afternoon session of court began at 3:30 P.M. Bail bonds were set in the amount of $50 for defendant John Green[8] on the charge of keeping a tippling house and in the sum of $450 for witnesses Joseph Rach and John Grear to appear to testify against Green at the February 1844 Term of Court. Later, the following individuals were naturalized, and Judge Eldred swore them in as new United States citizens: John Holmes, Michael Coleman, Patrick Brislin, Patrick Fagan, Patrick Cunningham, James McHugh, John Nichol, Holden Chester, Daniel Semen, John McKinley, Francis Hogan and Christian Hoffaker. At 5:00 P.M. court adjourned.

The five local lawyers were a mixed and colorful group. Struthers, an erudite, well-spoken lawyer from Paisley, Scotland, with a classic education in Latin, Greek and German; Butler, a dashing young man from Union County looking for a political career; and Wheeler, Osborn and Buzzard, three wily entrepreneurs. None were native sons of the county. They came to Mauch Chunk because they envisioned lucrative opportunities in a new county in Pennsylvania. Because they could not survive on the income from their law practices, all of them engaged in other business enterprises. Sadly, the fires of hope and ambition which first brought them to Carbon County faded into ashes of disillusionment and failure. By 1860 all five charter members of the bar had left the county to seek their fame and fortune elsewhere.

---

[8] *Commonwealth v. John Green*, December Term 1843.

In 1844, the Carbon courts' first full year of operations, the county had a population of about 7,365 citizens. There were four terms of court -- February, June, September and December. Each term lasted a week or less. Judge Eldred would travel by horseback and stay in one of the hotels in Mauch Chunk while he presided. Court dockets show seventy-eight filings: twenty-seven civil cases, twenty-four criminal cases, twenty-two motions and five petitions. Five civil jury trials for debts, and one criminal jury trial -- a murder case -- made up the annual court caseload.

First Murder Trial

Commonwealth v. William McKay[9] was the first murder trial in Carbon County. It had the scenario of a best-selling crime novel. On January 1, 1844, William McKay of Summit Hill came home from the mines early, peered through the window of his home and saw his wife Bridget locked in a passionate embrace with his friend Henry McCloskey. Crashing through the window, knife in hand, he stabbed McCloskey twice in the stomach causing his death. Charged with first degree murder his trial began before President Judge Nathaniel B. Eldred, Asa Packer and Jacob Dinkey, associate judges, and a jury on June 25, 1844. James R. Struthers, the prosecuting attorney, was seeking the death penalty. Defense counsel James M. Porter, William H. Butler and O. H. Wheeler invoked the classic provocation defense that a husband is justified in killing a man he finds in bed with his wife. The *Mauch Chunk Gazette* on July 3, 1844, acknowledging "special obligations" to Joseph H. Siewers, Esquire for condensing testimony and arguments of counsel for publication, provided extensive and graphic coverage of the trial. Four prosecution witnesses testified that McKay had complained to them about his wife's relationship with McCloskey and admitted to them that he stabbed McCloskey after he saw them together in the kitchen. McKay never mentioned that he saw the couple in an act of adultery. Although the defendant did not testify, eleven witnesses appeared on his behalf. They painted a picture of McKay as a hard-working, peaceable man whose wife would not allow him liquor in the house, and was herself drinking and having romantic trysts with his friend McCloskey while he was at work; that McKay stabbed McCloskey after he caught him on the kitchen floor with his wife.

James M. Porter in his summation speech stressed that McKay did not have to witness the adulterous act to have the benefit of the defense:

> *To be taken in the act is not alone essential. If there can be no other inference drawn, as when a man finds the adulterer and his wife in bed, this is all sufficient. The idea seems to be if there be sufficient reason to induce a*

[9] 1 June Term 1844.

> *conviction that intercourse has taken place-- as where they are secretly lying together as in this case, or locked in each others arms-- this provocation is deemed sufficient. The drunkenness of the wife makes the probability almost if not quite a certainty for, if a woman will expose herself thus completely, -- who will judge her other than she means to be. Nor will the law require deliberation and reflection in an infuriated husband beside himself with the feeling of revenge.*

The Commonwealth contended that the killing was not committed while the couple were in flagrante delicto; that McKay carefully planned to dispatch his wife's lover at a time he could claim the "adultery defense." James R. Struthers, in his summation for the prosecution emphasized that the murder was not a crime of passion, but one of cold, calculated revenge:

> *The expressions used by McKay in the presence of the witness immediately after the murder argues a mind, discriminating, self-possessed, and fatally bent upon mischief, rather than defined by passion, for it must be remembered that no illicit intercourse was seen by McKay or said in the fullness of his confession after his arrest and on his way down to the prison he would have reiterated the fact, would have insisted upon the act, the manner, -- all of which are without the least shadow of evidence. The garments of neither were discomposed, and if the victim had been stabbed in the act, the wounds would not have been inflicted where they were, and the whole defence is therefore grounded upon supposition throughout. If then every element of murder in the first degree, wilful, deliberate and premeditated murder has been committed upon the body of McCloskey, his blood cries for vengeance at the high hand of heaven and the law of this country.*

The jury found McKay guilty of second degree murder. He was immediately sentenced by Judge Eldred to ten years of solitary confinement in the Eastern Penitentiary. The entire proceedings consumed three days.

First Non-Support Proceeding

Under an old and venerable law which remained on the books in Pennsylvania until the late 1960s, when an unwed mother wanted to obtain support payments for her child the district attorney had to file criminal charges of "fornication and bastardy" against the alleged father. Carbon County's first support order was entered on February 19, 1844 when Joseph Ruch was convicted by a jury of "Fornication and Bastardy on the body of Elizabeth Nunnemacher."[10] The following entries in the court docket of *Commonwealth v. Joseph Ruch* show that justice was swift and certain, even if, by today's standards, somewhat inexpensive for the defendant:

---

[10]*Commonwealth ex rel Elizabeth Nunnemacher v. Joseph Ruch, 1 January Term 1844.*

February 19, 1844. Returned by the Grand Inquest "A True Bill."

February 19, 1844. Defendant being arraigned pleads "Not Guilty."

*February 19, 1844. Whereupon a Jury being called come, to wit, A. A. Douglas, Charles Mensing, Pearce Haney, John Bowman, Nathan Heilman, Solomon Snyder, Isaac Quin, Reuben Dinkey, Amos Fegley, Daniel Wentz, and Simpson McCoy, twelve good and lawful men of the County of Carbon, who being severally sworn or affirmed to say the truth of and upon the premises do say that they find the Defendant guilty in manner and form as he stands indicted. Whereupon the same day, the Sentence of the Court is, That Joseph Ruch the Defendant pay a Fine of five Dollars to the Commonwealth of Pennsylvania, for the use of the County of Carbon, that he pay to Elizabeth Nunnemacher the sum of **fifteen Dollars for her lying-in expenses and the Maintenance of her child** up to this time, and the further Sum of **fifty-cents per Week until the child shall arrive at the age of five years**, which will be on the twenty-sixth day of January A.D. one thousand eight hundred and forty nine, if the child shall live so long, the weekly allowance to be paid.*

Like an orphaned child, Carbon County as a judicial entity was bounced around quite a bit in its formative years. Judge Eldred complained that it was too much for him to preside over Dauphin, Schuylkill, Lebanon and Carbon counties and threatened to resign unless the Legislature provided him with some relief. On April 10, 1844, the Legislature passed a bill introduced by Senator Luther Kidder of Luzerne County moving Carbon from the Twelfth to the Twenty-First Judicial District with Schuylkill and Monroe. Five years later, the Legislature organized the Twenty-Second Judicial District with Carbon joining the counties of Monroe, Pike and Wayne.

During its first decade, Carbon's courts had from three to five sessions a year, each one lasting about a week. Charges of assault and battery, larceny, fornication and bastardy, and keeping a tippling house[11] kept the criminal courts busy. Actions for non-payment of bills, the laying out of roads by "Viewers" and several divorce cases made up the civil docket. The court also conducted naturalization hearings for the large influx of foreign born citizens moving into Carbon County.

[11]From 1682 it was a criminal offense to operate a public inn, tavern or tippling house without a license and it carried a fine of five pounds.

Local newspapers notified the public and parties about the scheduling of court cases. They were happy to provide this service because it increased subscribers. The *Mauch Chunk Gazette Courier* of May 10, 1849 pointed out to its readers the importance of having a subscription if they were involved in litigation:

> *At the last session of the Courts of Carbon County, a suitor made application to the Court for the continuance of his cause, upon the ground that he did not know it was on the Trial List. Judge Kidder enquired if the list had been published and, upon being informed that it had, decided that the ignorance of the suitor was no ground for the continuance of his cause, because every man who had business at Court should be a subscriber of the county papers. We have no doubt the new Judge Eldred will confirm so rightous [sic] a judgment.*
>
> *In connection with this we would say that we have room on our list for a great many more subscribers.*
>
> *All kinds of eatables are welcome from farmers for subscriptions.*

Grand Jury

The grand jury, commonly referred to in legal circles as the "prosecutor's puppet," met each term of court in closed session to decide what bills of indictment were true, i.e. which defendants should go to trial. Its use and function could be traced back to the early days of the English courts. The only witnesses to appear before the grand jury were Commonwealth witnesses, and the jury was supposed to decide if the Commonwealth had sufficient evidence to support the charges against the defendant. In reality, the grand jury almost always followed the recommendations of the district attorney who was the only official allowed to appear before them. If the district attorney did not want to prosecute a case, for whatever reason, he would simply tell the grand jury the evidence was weak and tell them not to return a true bill. When they announced to the court that they ignored a bill of indictment, it appeared to the public that the grand jury and not the district attorney had thrown out the case. This is what happened when four men were charged by District Attorney Chester Setzer with the stabbing murder of Frank Jacobs of Hauto at a wedding reception on January 23, 1916. When their cases went before the grand jury in February of 1916,[12] Setzer had no eye witnesses to the knifing in the dark and crowded room and the victim's eleven-year-old son Joseph only saw a man dropping a knife to the floor after his father went down. The grand jury, after hearing all the witnesses, ignored murder indictments against all four men and that ended the matter.

---

[12]*Commonwealth v. Steve Vaggak et al., 25 April Sessions 1916.*

One of the judge's principal duties was to instruct these grand juries before they went into session in the law of the cases before them, the evils which he perceived were afoot in the county and how they were to perform their functions. The grand jury also had power to make recommendations concerning the county buildings, roads and operations. Over the years, the grand jury gradually became a powerful voice in the administration of county government. Typical of the grand jury reports is the following brief excerpt from its "Presentment" of September 8, 1849:

> *The Grand Jury think that there has been a very great dereliction of duty on the part of the proper officers of the County in allowing Taverns and Ale houses to be kept open on the Sabbath, which they deem a very great evil, which evil if allowed to continue will be at the expense of the morals of the community. They would therefore recommend that the proper officers be requested to attend more strictly to their duty.*

When the grand jury made recommendations, county officials usually paid attention and took action, but in their own good time. Local newspapers religiously printed their reports and they were widely read. The court and the district attorney frequently used them to obtain public support for improvements to the court facilities and enforcement of laws. In 1973, the Legislature gave counties the authority to abolish local grand juries. Carbon County discontinued their use in 1976 and replaced them with district attorney approval of all criminal complaints.

Election of Judges

Legislation proposed by citizen groups to have judges elected rather than appointed and to rid the bench of associate judges reached the Legislature in the early 1800s but like most bills relating to the judiciary, it had a slow bumpy road to passage. Not until mid-century was the bill called out of committee for a vote. In 1851, after a long and stormy debate, the Legislature took the judicial appointive power from the Governor and placed the selection of the judges in the hands of the electorate.[13] President judges were to be elected for ten-year terms; associate judges were to be elected for five-year terms, and there were to be two in each county. In Carbon County, as in the other counties, the associate judges sat on the bench flanking the president judge. During jury trials, they usually said nothing. Although they were referred to by lawyers as "flower pot judges" or "wing judges," they seemed to have exercised as much authority as the president judge. We find them overruling the decision of Judge Craig in granting a liquor license to the Hazard Hotel in 1900 and outvoting Judge Heydt in refusing to grant a change of venue in the volatile

[13]Act of April 15, 1851, P.L. 648.

"Mauch Chunk and Mount Pisgah," Henry Fenn engraving, 1872

Commonwealth v. William Ronemus[14] murder trial in 1902. The names of Carbon County's associate judges and their terms of office appear in **Appendix E**, page 412.

In 1873, a constitutional convention assembled in Harrisburg and drafted a new constitution for Pennsylvania. Section 5 of Article V of the 1873 Constitution abolished the office of associate judges not learned in the law in counties forming separate judicial districts.[15] This section also provided that whenever a county contained 40,000 inhabitants it could become a separate judicial district and that the General Assembly could provide for additional judges "as the business of the districts may require." The number of Supreme Court justices was increased from five to seven which is the composition of the high court today.

The combustible mix of poverty, oppressive conditions in the mines, alcoholism and suppression of trade unions by the coal barons produced a soaring criminal docket in Carbon County. Judge Dreher, who lived in Stroudsburg, told the Legislature he could not handle the heavy caseload in Carbon and three other counties.

In 1874, the Legislature divided the Twenty-Second Judicial District. Wayne and Pike counties stayed in the Twenty-Second Judicial District. Monroe and Carbon formed a new judicial district designated as the Forty-Third Judicial District.

The 1870s were turbulent years for Carbon County -- filled with mine strikes, riots, train derailments and murder. The entire decade seemed consumed with the investigation and prosecution of the "Mollie Maguires" who were generally believed to be responsible for this stormy period. During the mid-1870s, arrests were made and the cases were tried in the Mauch Chunk courthouse before large crowds. People talked about little else. Portents of violence hung heavy over the town. Troops marched up and down Broadway with fixed bayonets. Rumors of attempts to free the jailed "Mollies" were rampant. Carbon lawyers General Charles Albright, Allen Craig, Daniel Kalbfus and Edward Mulhearn, seemingly undismayed by the tensions around them, played prominent roles in these cases on both sides of the docket (See **Chapter XV**, page 267). A graphic summarizing the "Mollie" trials in Carbon County appears on pages 324 and 325.

During the 1880s and 1890s, civil and criminal cases dropped dramatically. Court sessions were limited to a few weeks out of the year. Although court was scheduled for two week sessions five times a year, often the terms did not last that long. The criminal

---

[14]6 October Term 1902.

[15]Because Carbon County did not become a separate judicial district until 1901, lay judges continued on the Carbon bench until 1905 when the term of Edwin R. Enbody terminated.

Hotel Row on Hazard Square across from the Courthouse included (from L to R) the Armbruster House, the Switzerland Hotel, and the Central Hotel. A number of lawyers had offices in the upper floors of the Central Hotel which was demolished in the 1950s.

list for a term rarely exceeded twenty cases. The average number of prisoners in the county jail during this period was about seven. Liquor law violations and liquor license applications and renewals dominated the docket. The Brooks High License Law, which went into effect in Pennsylvania in 1887, gave to the court of quarter sessions the power to license the sale of liquor. The law prohibited the sale of liquor to minors, to people affected by liquor, to people with intemperate habits, and prohibited liquor sales on Sundays, election days, or on credit. Enforcement of the Brooks High License Law was in the hands of the constables who had to report to the judge four times a year on the first day of criminal court session and file a sworn statement on the number of offenses in their areas.

Judge Craig repeatedly lectured grand juries and constables about illegal stills, speakeasies, retail businesses where "the aid of women was invoked to increase liquor sales" and other flagrant abuses of the license law. He served notice that constables who ignored these violations would be jailed and that he would carefully scrutinize all applicants for liquor licenses.

Illustrative of court business during this period is the January 1900 term docket of cases before President Judge Allen Craig and Associate Judges Eugene P. Williams and Edwin R. Enbody as reported in the January 9, 1900 edition of the *Mauch Chunk Gazette*:

> *The first business transacted was the naming of successful new applicants at the Liquor License Court. Frank Geist, new house at Palmerton; Charles Wernet, new house at Lehighton; Thomas McGinley, new Hotel at Hazard and James McGill, new house at Lausanne were granted licenses to sell liquor at retail. The remonstrance against Barney Hoffman failed in its purpose and Long Run stays "wet" accordingly.*
>
> *A considerable stir was caused when Judge Craig announced that he had been overruled by Associate Judges Williams and Enbody on the McGinley license for the Hazard Hotel. His Honor said that he was opposed to the granting of the license for the following three reasons: the applicant is not a fit person to conduct a hotel; the place is unnecessary; the house is located too near the zinc works.*

Lawyers who did not live in Mauch Chunk or in the near vicinity would travel by train, trolley or carriage to the county seat. If they had to stay several days to try cases, they would obtain a room in one of the hotels. Mauch Chunk had four hotels in the 1880s which provided a temporary home for out-of-town lawyers and witnesses -- the Mansion House, the New American Hotel, the Mauch Chunk Hotel and Columbia House. The Mansion House was used by the court during the "Mollie" trials to house the jurors who were sequestered during the trials.

Judge Dreher traveled from Stroudsburg to Mauch Chunk on the Central Railroad. He stayed at either the Mansion House or the American Hotel for the court sessions in Carbon County. Judge Craig travelled by carriage or sleigh from his home in Lehigh Gap to the courthouse for the four terms of court.

County Commissioners' Criminal Trials

Politically inspired leaks to the press that the county commissioners took kickbacks from contractors doing business with the county in the late 1890s led to fraud charges being filed against them. The two criminal trials which followed revealed abundant evidence of loose practices and looser tongues in the executive offices but, according to the two jury verdicts, no criminal conduct. The criminal process against ex-Commissioners L. W. Koons, R. H. Bowman and John J. O'Donnell started uncertainly in January of 1900. District Attorney Daniel Sitler made two presentments to the January grand jury charging the commissioners with malfeasance in office and fraud by taking kickbacks from a contractor on a repair job to the Lehighton-Weissport Bridge and for overpaying Herman Riebe for repairs to a county bridge over the Poho Poco Creek in Penn Forest Township. The grand jury after hearing the Commonwealth's witnesses refused to return "true bills." When Judge Craig received their report he angrily asked each grand juror if he had been approached by anyone outside the jury room. When they all replied "No," he gave the panel a blistering lecture charging them with "a wrong on the taxpayers and a failure in justice." He directed District Attorney Sitler to resubmit the charges to the April grand jury. This time they returned true bills against the commissioners. The first trial[16] in April of 1900 pitted District Attorney Sitler against Horace Heydt of Freyman Heydt & Nothstein and James M. Breslin, representing the former commissioners. W. H. Reber and Levi Horn, the Commonwealth's key witnesses, testified that their firm was interested in the bridge repair job although they knew nothing about bridge work; that they would have done the repair work for $2200; that Commissioner Bowman promised to disclose to them what bids were received and that Commissioner O'Donnell told them to go to the majority commissioners and "offer them $500 to get the job."

All three commissioners took the witness stand and denied that they took any kickbacks in awarding the repair contract to Pittsburgh Bridge Company for $3900. They also denied that they talked to Reber and Horn about the bridge repairs work. O'Donnell testified that his remarks were made in jest. By the time the defense ended their case, District Attorney Sitler told Judge Craig that he would not seek a conviction but ask the jury

[16]*Commonwealth v. Lewis W. Koons, Robert H. Bowman and John J. O'Donnell*, 29 October Sessions 1899.

to assess costs against the defendants.[17] On April 17, 1900, after wrestling with the issue of costs for an hour, the jury acquitted the commissioners and placed the costs on the county.

The second corruption trial[18] began on June 19, 1900 with the same cast of characters, but a different jury. The uncontroverted Commonwealth's evidence was that the contract price for the bridge repair was $310 but the commissioners paid Herman Riebe, the contractor who later built the courthouse, $955 to do the work; that there were no specifications for the work and there were no payments to Riebe reflected in the minutes of the commissioner's meetings. The commissioners testified that Riebe was an honest citizen and a first class builder and they paid him in good faith on the basis of the bills he submitted after his work was approved by their bridge inspectors. The jury deliberated for two days before returning a verdict of "Not Guilty" and the costs were again placed on the county.

The trials which lasted eight days were the last high-profile cases tried by Judge Craig. They also had a profound effect on the political careers of the lawyer adversaries. Horace Heydt, who made no secret of the fact that he wanted the judgeship, vaulted into the political limelight and a judicial appointment. District Attorney Daniel Sitler was defeated by Frank Sharkey in the 1901 election.

Visiting judges, lawyers and witnesses often stayed at the Mansion House in the late 1800s and early 1900s.

[17] The criminal laws at this time provided that the court and the jury could find a criminal defendant "Not Guilty" but return a verdict requiring the payment of costs by the defendant or the county. A verdict of "Costs on the defendant" was regarded as a Pyrrhic victory for the prosecution.

[18] *Commonwealth v. Lewis W. Koons, Robert H. Bowman and John J. O'Donnell*, 16 January Sessions 1900.

CHAPTER IV

FIFTY-SIXTH JUDICIAL DISTRICT (1901-1943)

As the year 1901 dawned on the Courts of Common Pleas of Carbon County, a movement to give Carbon its own judge was well underway in the State Legislature. The 1873 Constitution provided that when a county's population reached 40,000 it could be formed into an independent judicial district. By 1900 Carbon's population had reached 44,510.[19] On July 18, 1901, Act 339 of 1901 separated Carbon from Monroe County and erected Carbon County as the Fifty-Sixth Judicial District with its own president judge. James Monroe Dreisbach, a founder and first president of the Mauch Chunk Trust Company and an influential Republican leader, took an active role in securing this legislation. Simultaneously, he successfully persuaded the Legislature that the volume of legal business in Carbon County required separate offices for the prothonotary, clerk of courts, register of wills and recorder of deeds. Governor William Stone appointed Lehighton attorney Horace Heydt to be president judge of the new judicial district.

Although the row office facilities were new, the method of filing and docketing of legal papers had not changed much since the 1850s. Docketing of pleadings and court orders was by pen and ink in huge, heavy docket books. Indexing was minimal and trying to find filings difficult. Court filings were now being typewritten in some of the law offices and by the judge and a mimeograph was used to duplicate copies of court opinions. All court papers were double-folded, wrapped with rubber bands, and stored in steel boxes identified with a confusing court term and number. If the judge wanted to review a file, it was a time-consuming process. He had to unfold and flatten each of the pleadings and then arrange them according to filing date.

At this time, the law required residents to register their cars and stallions with the county prothonotary. Doctors also had to file of record copies of their diplomas and statements of their training and qualifications to practice medicine. There were thirty-eight automobiles and one motorcycle registered between April 23, 1903 and August 24, 1905. Eugene O. Nothstein, a prominent Mauch Chunk attorney, was the first to register his International Motor Company sedan with William J. Zerby, who was then prothonotary.

Law Practice in the First Half of the Twentieth Century

At the turn of the twentieth century, America was a land of optimism and

[19] **Reports of the Twelfth Census: 1900, Table 1.**

bright promises. Ignited by the Industrial Revolution, the economy was booming, the employment rate was at an all-time high and the spending was free-wheeling. No one in their wildest imagining could foresee that this was a prelude to the most killing century in the history of mankind. There were more lawyers in the United States than in any other country in the world. The lawyer was perceived as an absolute necessity to the healthy life of any business or enterprise, small or large.

In Carbon County, the number of lawyers went from sixteen in 1890 to about twenty-six in 1901, an increase of sixty percent. A large leather bound receipt docket in the prothonotary's office exemplified the extravagance of the times. The names of all the members of the bar and the law firms were emblazoned in alphabetical order on the book's cover and on its bright red leather tabs:

Balliet & Seidle
Breslin, James M.
Barber, L. H.
Bertolette, Fred'k
Craig, Allen, Judge
Craig & Loose
Freyman & Nothstein
Geggus, Harrison L.
Gilham, Samuel R.
Graul, P. M.
Gray, Geo E.
Heydt, Horace, Judge
Hemm, Gustave A.
Heberling, R. A.
Lentz, Horace
Mulhearn, E. M.
McMichael, Robt G.
Sittler & Biery
Scott, L. C. & Scott, E. C.
Sharkey, F. P.
Smitham, James
Snyder, T. A.
Thomas, William G.

The use of this elaborate receipt docket which required the lawyer to sign his name when he filed and paid for a pleading ended in 1911. No more entries appear after that date. Undoubtedly either the cost of continuing an obviously expensive receipt system or the struggle to pull the docket book off the shelf every time a pleading was filed led to its disuse.

There was a significant increase in violent crimes in Carbon County after the turn of the century. The criminal dockets were suddenly filled with robberies, assaults with knives and murders. When these cases came into court, you could be sure that James M. Breslin, Frank P. Sharkey, Edward M. Mulhearn and William G. Thomas would be counsel for the defense and more often than not they won acquittals for their clients. Breslin and Thomas often collaborated on criminal cases and they were a formidable team. In April of 1905, they defended John Brinkosh and Martin Pavlish who were charged with the murder of Simon Fuchilla[20] near the No. 5 colliery in Lansford and won their acquittal. When Charles Huber was indicted in 1908 for the first degree murder of William B. Kauffman[21] in Mauch Chunk, it was not surprising that he retained the services of Breslin and Thomas. No one actually saw who threw the rock that killed Kauffman. District Attorney George Gray, not relishing the prospect of facing the dynamic duo alone, brought in trial veteran Edward Mulhearn and a young lawyer from Tamaqua, John O. Ulrich to assist him with the prosecution. John Balliet was the key prosecution witness. He testified that he heard Huber threaten Kauffman just before Kauffman was fatally struck by a large rock. In a dazzling bit of derring-do, Thomas called Breslin as a witness for the defense to rebut Balliet's testimony. Breslin testified that he interviewed Balliet in his office and in response to his plea: "For God's sake, tell us all you know about this case." Balliet replied "I have told you all I know. I don't know that Huber threatened Kauffman." The rest of the case was anticlimactic and the jury quickly returned a verdict of "Not Guilty."

The entire civil caseload for the year 1905 consisted of 125 cases, 17 of which were divorce cases and 19 collection cases. Non-support cases were still criminal in nature and made up the bulk of the caseload. A surprising number of rape cases and adultery cases also appeared on the dockets. Judge Heydt's sentences reflected the prevailing morality of the day and the low esteem of women and children. Liquor law violators were not severely punished. A man and a woman found guilty of adultery were fined $100 and sentenced to six months in jail. Conviction of fornication and bastardy brought a standard support order for the victim of $1 per week for the support of the child to be paid quarterly until seven years of age and $30 for lying in expenses. Seven years in the penitentiary was Judge Heydt's usual sentence for robbery.

Older bar members lamented the fact that courtroom advocacy and brief writing were becoming "lost arts." The new twentieth century lawyer focused more on the prophylactic aspects of lawyering -- problem solving and counseling clients on how to stay out of court. Most of the twenty-six lawyers in Carbon County at the beginning of the twentieth century were sole practitioners.

Law Partnerships

But five law partnerships provided a wider base of service to the legal community: Balliet & Seidle in Lehighton, Freyman & Nothstein, Bertolette & Barber, Craig & Loose, and Mulhearn & York in Mauch Chunk. The firm of Balliet & Seidle was typical of the Carbon partnerships. Family, social or political relationships brought the

[20]*Commonwealth v. John Brinkosh and Martin Pavlish*, 23 & 24 January Sessions 1905.

[21]*Commonwealth v. Charles Huber*, 4 October Sessions 1908.

lawyers together and the firm terminated upon the death of one of the partners. Nathan Balliet was the brother-in-law of Ira Seidle who was married to Balliet's sister. They formed a partnership in 1896 focusing on building and loan business, real estate and estates. After thirteen years on the bench, Judge Horace Heydt, in January of 1914, joined the firm. He became the lead name of Heydt Balliet & Seidle. Heydt left to join a firm in Allentown in 1920 and the firm of Balliet & Seidle engaged in the general practice of law until Seidle died in 1943.

Testimonial Dinner Honoring Nathan Balliet and Ira Seidle
Lehighton Elks Club -- June 27, 1941
*Front Row: **Nathan Balliet, Esq., Judge James C. McCready** (Principal Speaker), **Ira Seidle, Esq.***
*Second Row: Earl Koons of New York City, **Albert Prutzman, Esq.**, W. Franklin Snyder of New York City, William Niehoff, Assistant Attorney General of Maine, **Carl Niehoff, Esq.***

The firm of Freyman & Nothstein is particularly notable because of its longevity. Although the name and its location changed several times and partners came and went, the firm can be traced into the 1990s. It was founded in 1873 by William G. Freyman and General Charles Albright. Albright was the principal "rainmaker" and managing partner of Albright & Freyman. The partners were complementary and compatible but not comparable. Albright was outspoken and charismatic; Freyman was reserved and shunned the limelight. When General Albright died in 1880, Freyman asked James Keifer to join the firm at his new offices at 76 Broadway in Mauch Chunk and then Horace Heydt of Lehighton. When Keifer departed in 1888, Freyman and Heydt took in Eugene O. Nothstein, who was Freyman's nephew. Freyman Heydt & Nothstein achieved a great deal of notoriety and a large following of working class clientele in taking on and winning cases against large corporations. When Heydt went on the bench in 1901 and Nothstein died in 1912, Freyman brought into the firm William G. Thomas and Ben Branch to replace them. They practiced law under the firm name of Freyman Thomas & Branch until 1928 when Freyman died and Thomas went on the bench. Ben Branch took over the firm's large practice in 1928, kept the firm shingle in front of his office, and continued as a sole practitioner until his death in 1952. Albert Heimbach succeeded to Branch's practice moving it to his office at 57 Broadway and hiring Branch's secretary, Rose Watkins. In 1954, Heimbach formed a partnership with Roger Nanovic. When Heimbach became judge in 1960, Nanovic took over Heimbach's law practice. Over the years he developed and expanded it into what is currently the county's largest law firm with five lawyers, all Nanovics practicing under the rubric of "Nanovic Law Offices."

The following are the law partnerships of Carbon County from 1843 to 1993:

Partners	Firm Name	Formed-Dissolved
Horace B. Burnham Joseph H. Siewers	**Burnham & Siewers** **Mauch Chunk**	1856-1859
Orville H. Wheeler P. R. Weitzel	**Wheeler & Weitzel** **Mauch Chunk**	1857-1858
Joseph H. Siewers N. F. Handy	**Siewers & Handy** **Mauch Chunk**	1859-1863
James R. Struthers Stephen E. Sites	**Struthers & Sites** **Mauch Chunk**	1859-1863
Horace B. Burnham Wesley B. Leonard	**Burnham & Leonard** **Mauch Chunk**	1863-1866
Charles Albright William G. Freyman	**Albright & Freyman** **Mauch Chunk**	1873-1880

John D. Bertolette James S. Loose	**Bertolette & Loose** **Mauch Chunk**	1875-1877
Allen W. Craig James S. Loose	**Craig & Loose** **Mauch Chunk**	1879-1892
Francis P. Longstreet Samuel R. Gilham	**Longstreet & Gilham** **Lehighton**	1880-1880
Frederick Bertolette Laird H. Barber	**Bertolette & Barber** **Mauch Chunk**	1882-1913
William G. Freyman Horace D. Heydt	**Freyman & Heydt** **Mauch Chunk**	1885-1888
William G. Freyman Horace D. Heydt Eugene O. Nothstein	**Freyman Heydt & Nothstein** **Mauch Chunk**	1888-1901
William M. Rapsher Michael Cassidy	**Rapsher & Cassidy** **Lehighton**	1888-1897
Nathan M. Balliet Ira E. Seidle	**Balliet & Seidle** **Lehighton**	1896-1943
James S. Loose Allen W. Craig Jacob C. Loose	**Loose Craig & Loose** **Mauch Chunk**	1897-1898
Douglas S. Craig Jacob C. Loose	**Craig & Loose** **Mauch Chunk**	1899-1913
Leighton C. Scott Ellsworth E. Scott	**Scott & Scott** **Lansford**	1902-1919
Theodore A. Snyder Charles A. Hauck	**Snyder & Hauck** **Lehighton**	1903-1907
William G. Freyman Eugene O. Nothstein	**Freyman & Nothstein** **Mauch Chunk**	1901-1912

William G. Freyman William G. Thomas Ben Branch	**Freyman Thomas & Branch** **Mauch Chunk**	1912-1928
Edward M. Mulhearn Frank X. York	**Mulhearn & York** **Mauch Chunk**	1918-1923
Jacob C. Loose Alan S. Loose	**Loose & Loose** **Mauch Chunk**	1925-1942
Frank X. York Daniel P. Dougherty	**York & Dougherty** **Mauch Chunk**	1927-1954
Martin H. Philip Jacob Philip	**Philip & Philip** **Palmerton**	1936-1954
Alan S. Loose George Kerestes	**Loose & Kerestes** **Jim Thorpe**	1951-1953
John Deutsch Albert P. Leonzi	**Deutsch & Leonzi** **Lehighton**	1954-1956
Albert H. Heimbach Roger N. Nanovic	**Heimbach & Nanovic** **Mauch Chunk**	1954-1960
William Z. Scott Robert Lazorchick	**Scott & Lazorchick** **Lansford**	1955-1966
Albert Prutzman William B. Quinn	**Prutzman & Quinn** **Lehighton**	1956-1973
John Deutsch William A. Wyatt	**Deutsch & Wyatt** **Lehighton**	1956-1960
Jacob Philip James A. Wimmer	**Philip & Wimmer** **Palmerton**	1959
Michael L. Ozalas George T. McKinley	**Ozalas & McKinley** **Jim Thorpe**	1978

Roger N. Nanovic Roger N. Nanovic II Thomas S. Nanovic James R. Nanovic Susan J. Nanovic	**Nanovic Law Offices** **Jim Thorpe & Palmerton**	1979
David B. Shulman Barry C. Shabbick	**Shulman & Shabbick** **Palmerton**	1987
Cynthia A. Dyrda Christie Schaffer-Bower	**Dyrda & Schaffer** **Lehighton**	1989
Richard W. Webb William Z. Scott, Jr.	**Webb & Scott** **Lansford, Palmerton**	1989-1991
Charles C. Hansford Gerald F. Strubinger, Jr.	**Hansford & Strubinger** **Palmerton**	1992

From 1910 to 1929, Carbon County enjoyed remarkable growth and prosperity. The mines of the Panther Valley were producing and selling more coal than ever before. The Hauto Power Plant began its commercial operation in 1917 and became the major power source for the newly formed Pennsylvania Power and Light Company. The New Jersey Zinc Company in Palmerton and Wagner Electric in Weatherly became new major players in the local economy. Even World War I failed to slow down the building boom and the population growth.

The annual civil court caseload spiraled with the economy, increasing from 99 cases in 1910 to 188 in 1925. Divorce cases and debt collections dominated the docket but after 1915 as car ownership increased, automobile accident cases came to the forefront. Mauch Chunk's hotels which did a brisk business serving jurors, witnesses and out-of-town lawyers, like the court system, was hard hit by the increased use of automobiles.

The case of *Commonwealth v. Francis Thomas*[22] put James Breslin and William Thomas back on the front pages of the local newspapers. James McHugh, a game warden from Weatherly, was killed by a single shot from the hunting rifle of eighteen-year-old Drifton resident Francis Thomas at the Hazle Creek Bridge in November of 1915. After an investigation by Luzerne County detectives, District Attorney Chester Setzer charged the young man with first degree murder. Breslin and Thomas, both of whom had close ties to

[22] 1 January Sessions 1916.

Drifton, were retained by the boy's parents. Their defense of Thomas would be long remembered not just as a successful day in court but as a work of art.

When the trial played out before Judge Barber and a Carbon jury in January of 1916, there was standing room only in the courtroom and the gallery for the entire week-long trial. Breslin completely undermined the prosecution's case by his deft cross-examination of the Commonwealth witnesses. The defense contended that the shooting was accidental and presented expert witnesses to support its theory. By the time the evidence closed Fred Lewis, who was assisting D.A. Setzer as a deputy attorney general, created confusion in the courtroom by asking the jury to return a second degree murder verdict after Setzer in his closing argued for a first degree murder verdict. The judge angrily summoned both lawyers to sidebar and demanded that the prosecution let him know what verdict they were seeking. Setzer, dazed and confused, responded "second degree murder." Breslin and Thomas both gave masterful summations carefully analyzing the evidence, stressing the fact that accidents will happen and closing with a favorite defense quotation that "it were better that one hundred guilty men go free than one be unjustly convicted." Judge Barber gave the case to the jury at 10:40 on a Saturday night. Just before midnight, the jury filed into the courtroom and announced a "Not Guilty" verdict. The gallery, which was filled with relatives, friends and supporters of Thomas, exploded with shouts, applause and foot stomping. Even Judge Barber's gavelling the courtroom to order had no effect. In an unprecedented move, Judge Barber ordered the tipstaves to bar the gallery doors, held all occupants of the gallery in contempt and ordered that they be brought before him in groups. As each group appeared before him, Judge Barber threatened them with jail, relented and then administered a severe reprimand. The case ended with young Thomas, no doubt prompted by his attorneys, going up to the bench and thanking Judge Barber for his fairness and impartiality in conducting the trial. Knowledgeable court observers lauded the trial strategy as another defensive gem by Breslin and Thomas.

Prohibition and its mindless regulations became the law of the land in 1919. Shortly after its adoption, it became clear that the prohibition laws were unworkable and unenforceable. Carbon County provided compelling evidence that they were honored more in their breach than in their observation. Drinking hard liquor was a rite of male comradeship and an act of rebellion. During the 1920s and early 1930s, just about every hotel, tavern, and restaurant clandestinely served bootleg liquor. Many farmers had their own stills which they used to supply their friends and relatives. The Mauch Chunk Brewery continued to produce its normal output. Local law enforcement authorities simply looked the other way. From time to time, large numbers of federal agents would swoop in on a still or a tavern which was serving liquor and make arrests. Most of the criminal cases resulting from these arrests never survived the grand jury which simply returned "No true bills." Those defendants who were indicted by the grand jury were not too concerned. Judge Barber and Judge Thomas never sent any of the commercial violators to jail. Their usual sentence was a small fine and costs. Only full-time bootleggers, who were making large profits, received jail time. When the Volstead Act was finally repealed in 1935, it drew little notice in Carbon County and had virtually no effect on the volume of alcohol consumption.

Last Death Sentence

On April 7, 1924, Judge Barber sentenced Martin Matalovack and Walter Grymkowski, both from Pittsburgh, to death in the electric chair. It marked the last death sentence imposed in Carbon County. The time between the date of their trial and their execution was five months, a shockingly short period by today's standards.

On September 11, 1923 the pair had robbed James G. Heintzelman, a butcher, in broad daylight as he was selling his meat products in Millport (now Aquashicola). A posse of local police and citizens pursued the robbers and as they closed in on them under cover of darkness and glare of flash bombs there was an exchange of gunfire. Constable Elmer P. Anthony of Palmerton was killed in the crossfire. Their joint trial in January of 1924 lasted four days.[23] Judge Barber appointed Frank York to represent both defendants while District Attorney David Davis was assisted by his predecessor Ben Branch. Both defendants testified that they were intoxicated and fired their pistols to defend themselves. After forty minutes of deliberation the jury convicted both men of first degree murder. At their sentencing Judge Barber directed that the defendants be taken to the Western Penitentiary in Centre County for their execution. Astonishingly, there were no appeals and both men were electrocuted on June 16, 1924.

As the Roaring Twenties came to a close, the country's economic center seemed to fall out. The Dow Jones Industrial average which reached a high of 381 on September 3, 1929 fell to 261 on October 28. (It reached a low of 31 in 1932.) The Wall Street crash marked the end of good times in Carbon County and the beginning of the Great Depression.

Young lawyers starting out in the Depression and post-Depression years, unless they had family and social contacts, had to devise innovative ways to find legal work or clients. To build their practices, they often offered their services free of charge or in return for food products. George Shutack opened his law office in Nesquehoning in 1929 and in his first year of practice he earned a total income of $250. Almost all new lawyers started as sole practitioners and took appointments from the court or referrals from their relatives and friends to survive. In every community there was a struggling lawyer or two. To produce income in these hard economic times, lawyers, such as Fred Lewis, Raymond Smith, Joseph Greco, Sidney Webb, and Joseph Engler, started insurance businesses which they operated from their law offices. David Davis, James McCready, George Gray, Raymond Smith, Albert Heimbach and George Shutack became politically active in the hope that their

[23] *Commonwealth v. Martin Matalovack and Walter Grymkowski*, 7 January Sessions 1924.

campaigning for public office would bring them, if not victory, at least some legal business. The rigid restraints on lawyer advertising in effect at this time were lifted and the lawyer-candidate could publish his name, qualifications and community contributions as often as his funds allowed. There was yet another incentive to seek public office. It provided the lawyer with a regular paycheck.

Real estate transactions, decedent's estates, motor vehicle accident cases, preparing bank loan documents, and title searching made up the bulk of the typical Carbon law practice. It was during this period that Carbon lawyers began to take on negligence cases on a contingent fee basis.[24] Lawyers took just about anything that came into their offices. The New Jersey Zinc Company, the PP&L Company, the LC&N Company and liability insurance carriers generated most of the lucrative legal work in the county. The Loose firm represented the Zinc Company and about half of the insurance firms doing business in the county. Ben Branch represented the LC&N Company, the PP&L Company, and the other half of the insurance companies. From time to time they referred some of their business to other members of the bar. The earnings of most lawyers during this period were modest at best and nonexistent at worst.

Title searching and deed writing produced the bread and butter and potatoes for lawyers' tables in the first half of the twentieth century and, often, payment of legal fees took that form. Attorneys spent many hours carefully crafting and drafting the deeds which would transfer the homes and farms which were the principal possessions of most citizens. Popular at the time among the Pennsylvania Dutch farmers was the unusual "Hausbehalt" clause which required the grantee of property (usually a son or daughter) to not only maintain the house and farm for the grantor during his or her lifetime, but also to provide their food and health care. Carbon lawyers were among the few in the Commonwealth who knew how to draft this curious provision. Lawyers prided themselves on their ability to go into the recorder of deeds' office and do their own real estate searches back to 1843 and beyond. Some practitioners, less inclined to throw the heavy docket books around and scan the indices and legal descriptions, would terminate their search if they found a deed in the chain of title from the LC&N Company. They assumed "The Coal Company", as it was popularly called, had good and marketable title to all its lands and if it did not, no one was going to challenge its title.

The Coal Company

This kind of thinking reflected the domination of LC&N over the county economy and the political arena. Founded in 1822 by Erskine Hazard and Josiah White, it was the principal employer in the county. As late as 1948, the company was sending

[24] A contingent fee is a fee based on a percentage of the recovery in a lawsuit. If there is no money obtained, there is no fee.

4,425,000tons of anthracite to market and was paying $25 million in wages to 6200 Panther Valley miners. There were relatively few court cases against LC&N. Although mine accidents were frequent and often resulted in devastating injuries to miners, laws passed in coal's heyday and a benevolent settlement policy insulated it from lawsuits. Two members of the Carbon Bar were beneficiaries of this policy. Frank Riordan of Summit Hill lost both hands in a mine accident as a young man. LC&N provided him with funds for both a college and legal education and then gave him a lifetime job handling its workman's compensation claims. Samuel R. Gilham, a well known lawyer and justice of the peace from Lehighton, lost his leg in the mines in the late 1860s. LC&N underwrote his college education and after he was admitted to practice in Carbon County the company politically supported him for the office of justice of the peace from 1889 until his death in 1908. Through control of its employees and the Republican Party, LC&N elected its candidates into nearly all of the row offices and commissioners' offices from the 1920s through the 1940s. Its power and prestige began to wane as coal sales declined after World War II. In June of 1954, the Coal Company closed down its coal operations.

Toy Gun Murder Case

On June 5, 1939, at 9:00 P.M., Corporal Ben Franklin of the Pennsylvania State Police fired eight bullets into the body of fourteen-year-old Joan Stevens while she was in the rear seat of his police car parked in Nesquehoning. The sheer brutality of the killing electrified the county. It also galvanized both the local print and broadcast reporters who were incensed by what they perceived as a cover-up news blackout designed for defensive purposes. The state police did not notify the girl's parents of the tragedy until the day following her death and refused to discuss the case with the press for almost twenty-four hours. A belated terse statement by Major William Clark, who was conducting the state police investigation, that Franklin shot the girl in self-defense because she had a gun aimed at him was greeted by public disbelief and indignation. These feelings heightened into outrage when it was revealed that the girl's "gun" turned out to be a toy pistol.

Commonwealth v. Ben Franklin[25] became a political lightning rod. Candidate-for- judge James McCready volunteered his legal services to the dead girl's family and publicly vowed that he would thoroughly investigate the case and make sure that Franklin was vigorously prosecuted. He accused District Attorney Albert Heimbach, who was running for re-election, with letting Franklin out on bail after charging him with homicide and dragging his feet on the case. Heimbach responded that Judge Thomas set the bail on Franklin and that he was appointing a special detective to investigate the killing. To diffuse the rumors and speculation that the girl was sexually molested before her death, Heimbach also had the body of the girl exhumed and an autopsy revealed "no sexual contact." Mrs.

[25] 18 June Sessions 1939.

MAUCH CHUNK TIMES-NEWS

NK, PA., TUESDAY, JUNE 6, 1939 NO. 55

SELF DEFENSE IS CLAIM OF STATE TROOPER WHO KILLED NESQUEHONING GIRL

Citizens of Nesquehoning ... pages of whose histo... with fatal mine d... fully recovered from ... the killing of Joan St... Corporal Ben Franklin ... 9.30 P. M., and indi... high among them ...

DISTRICT ATTORNEY DIRECTS THAT BODY OF JOAN STEVENS BE EXHUMED

District Attorney Albert H. Heimbach announced at 1.00 P. M. today ... to have the body ...

Awards For Im...

SLAIN GIRL'S MOTHER COLLAPSES DELAYING PLEAS TO THE JURY

FOURTEEN-YEAR-OLD NESQUEHONING GIRL KILLED BY STATE TROOPER

14. Nesquehoning, was ... her home by ... Franklin, of the ... last night, at ... agner's store. ... immediately put the ... and it was difficult ... ic particulars concern... police officers said that ... dged not to reveal ... case until officially re...

FRANKLIN GOES ON TRIAL FOR MURDER OF JOAN STEVENS

...Court in Carbon county ... 10 A. M. today with the ... poral Ben Franklin, of ... tor Police, charged with ... Joan Stevens, 14, Nes... the first called, ... ing held at the same ... place, Judge Sam... county, assigned ... rt, is presiding ... in the ...

Three Injured In Nearby Accident

Three persons were injured in ... head-on automobile crash ... road between ... Weatherly ...

BEN FRANKLIN ACQUITTED OF THE MURDER OF JOAN STEVENS

Corporal Ben Franklin, of the State Police, was acquitted of the murder of Joan Stevens, 14, Nesquehoning, yesterday at 4:45 P. M. The Court House bell proclaimed the announcement of the verdict by the tolling of the bell 15 times.

VERDICT READ IN COURT

As Deputy Clerk of the Courts, Morris Nothstein received the verdict from Brinley Richards, foreman of the jury, he passed it to Judge Shull. Mr. Nothstein

TROOPER ACQUITTED IN (

Stevens, the girl's mother, was not satisfied. She asked the Governor and the Attorney General to investigate the handling of the case by local authorities. Attorney General Reno asked Heimbach to turn over his files for examination. Nothing ever came of it. When McCready won the judgeship in the 1939 fall election, he prevailed on George Shutack to take his place in protecting the interests of the Stevens' family. At the behest of Mrs. Stevens, Shutack petitioned the Attorney General to appoint him as a special deputy attorney general to assist the prosecution and the appointment was made. Ben Branch was retained by the Fraternal Order of Police to represent Franklin and he was assisted by James J. Gallagher of Mahanoy City and Albert Prutzman.

In one of his last decisions before retiring from the bench, Judge Thomas turned down Branch's motion for a change of venue on December 11, 1939 by taking "judicial notice" that heightened feelings against the defendant had subsided:

> *The Court takes notice of the fact that the newspapers named by the Petitioner are no longer engaged in their alleged campaign of hostility towards the Petitioner. Also, with the completion of the recent political campaign, the fires of partisanship have been extinguished, and the question of the guilt or innocence of the Petitioner has ceased to be a subject of controversial discussion amongst the electors of the County. The public clamor has passed its climax, and the high feeling that was present in the locality where the unfortunate happening occurred has subsided with the passage of the intervening months.*

The trial began on January 8, 1940. The state Supreme Court assigned Judge Samuel Shull of Monroe County to preside because McCready recused himself. It was the largest media event in Carbon County since the "Mollie" trials of 1876. Each day reporters from the *New York Daily News*, *Associated Press*, *United Press*, *Philadelphia Inquirer*, *Philadelphia Record* and *Philadelphia Bulletin* crowded into press row in the front of the courtroom. Judge Shull ordered three court sessions a day -- morning, afternoon, and evening. Friends and relatives of Franklin and the victim filled every seat in the courtroom including the balcony. Radio station WZAL set up a special broadcast booth in the American Hotel lobby so it could send hourly reports on the progress of the trial to its listeners.

Heimbach called Edward Swatji, a twenty-four-year-old state trooper who was with Franklin at the time of the shooting, as his key witness. He testified that he and Franklin had picked up Joan Stevens in Nesquehoning because she had written to the state police that she knew about some bank robberies which were being planned by members of her "gang" and wanted to give the information to the police; that after they interrogated her they determined that her story was a hoax and were about to take her home when she suddenly whipped out a gun and said; "You bastards, drive me to Lansford or I'll blow your f------ brains out"; that he saw Franklin raise his gun and fire at the girl several times. By the time Franklin took the stand none of the Commonwealth's evidence disputed his self-defense theory. His only problem was to explain why he had to fire eight times to defend himself. Franklin told the jury that when he pulled out his gun he thought the Stevens girl was going to shoot him. He explained that he had borrowed the gun and he was not completely familiar with it even though he did have some instruction in its use. In the excitement of the moment, he said that he just kept fanning the hammer to protect himself and Swatji. Near the end of his testimony the slain girl's mother leaped up from her seat in the courtroom and shouted hysterically, "Why did he kill her; why did he shoot her, she was only fourteen. Oh my poor Joan." Judge Shull refused a defense motion for a mistrial.

After powerful closing arguments by Shutack for the prosecution and Branch for the defense, the jury received the case at 8:00 P.M. on Saturday. During their deliberations telegraphed threats to the jury, judge and district attorney demanding a first degree murder conviction were intercepted. At 4:45 P.M. on Sunday the foreman of the jury announced a "Not Guilty" verdict. The courtroom erupted and sheriff deputies had to be summoned to restore order. The verdict was not a popular one. But according to the *Times News*, in a complete reversal of its original position, the defense had presented a "perfect case of self defense" and "it was the only verdict that could be conscientiously rendered." Ben Branch and the defense team were heralded as "miracle workers."

Komatowski Case - Euthanasia or Murder

Long before the world heard of Dr. Kevorkian and assisted suicide, a Carbon County jury in 1942 heard a confession by a defendant charged with murder that he helped the victim in ending his life. The confession provided the backdrop for the most bizarre murder trial in the annals of the Carbon County Court. On Saturday, June 7, 1941 Fred Komatowski carried his friend Pierce Rehrig, a paralytic, from the porch of his cottage in Franklin Township and threw him into a small swimming pool nearby causing him to drown. Komatowski was the live-in lover of Evelyn Christman, Rehrig's partner in the textile business in Lehighton. Since he was seen with the victim just before the drowning, Lehighton police questioned him and he eventually signed a confession saying that he had, at Rehrig's insistence, assisted Rehrig in committing suicide. Komatowski was arrested and charged with murder.[26]

There were many peculiar aspects to the case. Komatowski repudiated his confession alleging that Lehighton Chief of Police James Yenser beat it out of him using "third degree" methods which he characterized as brutal and inhuman. District Attorney Albert Heimbach requested Justice of the Peace Seip to dismiss the murder charges against Komatowski at a secret midnight hearing. (From Commonwealth's brief filed in the Supreme Court of Pennsylvania.) After the charges were dropped, District Attorney Heimbach petitioned the court to be superseded because he was private counsel for Evelyn Christman and she might be involved in the prosecution. He also alleged that he believed he might be called as a witness for the Commonwealth.

Responding to Heimbach's petition Claude T. Reno, the Attorney General of Pennsylvania, appointed Daniel P. Dougherty as a special deputy to refile the murder charges and prosecute Komatowski. Ben Branch, now Carbon's hottest lawyer after his brilliant defense of Corporal Franklin, was hired to represent the defendant. The trial held before Judge McCready and a Carbon County jury went on for two weeks. Thirty-one witnesses were called by the Commonwealth and twenty-seven for the defense. Two principal factual issues emerged from all of the testimony: (1) whether Rehrig was able to walk without assistance, and (2) whether the defendant's confession was coerced. After hearing all of the conflicting evidence the jury returned a verdict of "Guilty of Murder in the Third Degree," a crime completely unknown to the law at that time. The prosecutor shook his head in disbelief. Ben Branch quickly left the courtroom. Observers noted there was

---

[26] *Commonwealth v. Fred Komatowski, 18 October Sessions 1941.*

a hint of a smile on his face. Judge McCready denied the post verdict motions and sentenced the defendant to the state penitentiary to a term of from six to twelve years for VOLUNTARY MANSLAUGHTER, a crime of which he had not been convicted.

On appeal to the Supreme Court of Pennsylvania, Ben Branch retained the services of A. Evans Kephart, a former chief justice of the Supreme Court to assist him. When Dougherty became ill, the Attorney General appointed Frank York to take his place. After hearing argument, the Supreme Court overturned Komatowski's conviction and sentence. Using harsh, forceful language, the high court also threw out all the charges against him:[27]

> *. . . The most peculiar thing about this case is the verdict, and its irregularity is so at variance with the very fundamentals of "due process of law", that it requires the discharge of the defendant and makes unnecessary the discussion of any other point raised.*[28]
>
> *. . . this case was tried in such a loose and irregular manner as naturally to beget this monstrosity of a verdict which has no "ancestry" known to the law and which we trust will never have any courtroom "posterity". Every member of this court is surprised that the trial judge and the Commonwealth's "special counsel" would apathetically stand by and after hearing this ridiculous and meaningless verdict repeated thirteen times would permit it to be recorded".*[29]

World War II Years

In January of 1940 the bar, now grown to thirty-one, hosted a dinner at the American Hotel and the following members affixed their signatures to a memorial resolution honoring Jacob Loose for his fifty years of practicing law:

---

[27] *Commonwealth v. Komatowski*, 347 Pa. 445, 450, 32 A.2d 905 (1943).

[28] *Commonwealth v. Komatowski, Supra*, at 451.

[29] *Commonwealth v. Komatowski, Supra*, at 454.

Frank P. Sharkey, Nathan M. Balliet, Ira E. Seidle, William G. Thomas, Leighton C. Scott, James Smitham, George E. Gray, Philip M. Graul, Winfred D. Lewis, Ben Branch, Raymond F. Smith, Frank S. Riordan, Eugene Edelstein, Frank X. York, James C. McCready, Alan S. Loose, Daniel P. Dougherty, George A. Shutack, Martin H. Philip, Albert G. Prutzman, Nicholas B. Dobosh, John G. Cipko, George M. D. Richards, John J. Dobosh, Albert H. Heimbach, Jacob Philip, W. Joseph Engler, Donald McCay, Frank D. Llewellyn, Joseph G. Greco, Michael S. Lukish.

By 1942, war clouds were already darkening the country. For the second time in a generation, the youth of the county marched off to a war on foreign soil. Every week, Monsignor Angelini of Nesquehoning blessed a new group of young men at the Mauch Chunk train station as they left for military duty. Many of the middle-aged men of the county stayed at home and contributed to the war effort by producing coal and zinc for the armed forces. Ten members of the bar went into military service: George M. D. Richards, Martin H. Philip, W. Joseph Engler, Donald L. McCay, Frank D. Llewellyn, Joseph G. Greco, Michael S. Lukish, George B. Richards, Albert P. Leonzi and George Kerestes.

On the home front, Jacob Philip served as attorney for the Palmerton draft board; Albert Prutzman became legal advisor to the draft board of appeals, and Alan Loose took his place on the county draft board. These boards supervised the draft lottery and made decisions on applicants' requests for deferments from military service. George Shutack went to work for the Federal Government as a special United States Attorney to help the Army acquire lands for military supply depots.

Centennial Celebration

Judge McCready convened a special session of court on March 13, 1943 to commemorate the one hundredth anniversary of the founding of Carbon County. Mauch Chunk lawyer Ben Branch, a member of the executive board of the Carbon County Historical Society and a devotee of county history was the prime mover for the celebration. An impressive array of local, state, and federal dignitaries filled the courtroom. The Carbon County Historical Society, led by its president Wilbur Warner of Lehighton, arranged the program. Judge Samuel B. Shull, president judge of Monroe County, and Judge Frank McCluskey, president judge of Northampton County, attended the ceremonies. Fred Brenckman, author of the 1913 *History of Carbon County*, was the principal speaker. State Representative Elmer Holmes of Lansford read the Act of the Legislature establishing the county and County Commissioner Homer Kern read the first minutes of the commissioners' meeting in 1843. Minutes of the first court session were read by William S. Williams, clerk of courts, and Thomas Davis, recorder of deeds, read the deed by which the county secured title to the land on which the courthouse was located.

TIM ES-NEWS, MAUCH CHUNK, PA., SATURDAY, MARCH 13, 1943

ROSTER of COUNTY OFFICIALS

Personnel of County Offices

A Lansford, a Summit Hill and a Palmerton man are serving on the board of Carbon County Commissioners at this time when the county is celebrating its centennial.

They are John P. Davis, Lansford, Daniel Bynon, Summit Hill, and Homer Kern, Palmerton. Joseph Bonacci, Treckow, is their deputy.

Albert G. Prutzman is the solicitor.

Other county officials [illegible] the following:

Treasurer: Wm. C. Christman, Lehighton; Mahlon Schoenberger, of Weissport, deputy and Charles Neast, Mauch Chunk, bookkeeper.

Prothonotary: Nathan Drumheller, Lansford; Deputy, Charles Bernhardt, Mauch Chunk.

Clerk of the Courts: William S. Williams, Summit Hill; Deputy, Maurice Heater, Weatherly.

Recorder of Deeds: Thomas Davis, Nesquehoning; Deputy, Mrs. Bertha Davis, Summit Hill.

Register of Wills: Wade M. Burnhauser; Deputy, Jane Decker.

Sheriff: Nathan C. Pollock; Deputy, Harold Richards.

District Attorney: Albert H. Heimbach.

Superintendent of Schools: S. E. Prutzman; assistant, Nan Jenkins.

County Farm Agent: N. M. Rahn.

Probation Officer: Lawrence Campbell, Lansford; Mrs. Sarah Helferty, East Mauch Chunk, assistant.

County Auditors: [illegible] John Herbert, Raymond Kistler; Clerk, Russell Williams.

Jury Commissioners: Ralph Simmons, Nesquehoning; Irvin Snyder, Lehighton. Clerk, John Doak, Nesquehoning.

Court Stenographer: Roy S. Mohrbach, Nesquehoning.

Law Librarian and Court Crier: Theodore Gluck, Summit Hill.

Judge McCready's Secretary: Henry Fitzpatrick.

Institutional Investigator: Stephen Sulek, Lansford.

Janitor: Wm. Walker; Janitress, Mame Dougherty; Engineer, Martin Roth.

Agencies created through the war include:

County Rationing Board Chairman: John C. Tosh.

County Selective Service Boards No. 1 (Lehighton) Dr. Paul N. Roeder, Palmerton, chairman; George Schwartz, E. R. Steigerwalt, Harry Saeger, Lehighton. Atty. Albert Heimbach is appeal agent. No. 2 (Mauch Chunk) A. S. Loose, chairman, E. M. Chunk, Wade Gregory, Weatherly, secretary, and Arthur L. Ulshafer, Beaver Meadows. Atty. Ben Branch is appeal agent. No. 3 (Lansford) Rev. John Pounder, Lansford, chairman; Prof. Elmer McCready, Summit Hill, Isadore Riley, Nesquehoning. Atty. Frank York is appeal agent.

Mary R. Howard is executive secretary of the county chapter of the Red Cross and Rita Schwartz is home secretary.

Harry Fagley, of E. Mauch Chunk, is steward at the County Institution, Laurytown, and Mrs. Fagley is stewardess.

PROBATION OFFICER

Lawrence Campbell

CO. COMMISSIONERS

HOMER KERN

JOHN P. DAVIS
LANSFORD

DANIEL BYNON

DISTRICT ATTORNEY

ALBERT H. HEIMBACH
PALMERTON

PROTHONOTARY

Nathan Drumheller

NATIVE OF SUMMIT HILL
PRESIDENT JUDGE OF COUNTY

Hon. James C. McCready, who became Judge of Carbon County courts four years ago, is a World War veteran. He enlisted in the U. S. Army in May, 1917, following graduation from Dickinson College and was assigned to Pennsylvania State College, to receive instruction in motor mechanics. He was then transferred to Camp Hancock, Ga., and later went overseas with the American Expeditionary Forces. In 18 months service in France he rose to the rank of sergeant. On being honorably discharged April, 1919, he resumed his studies at Dickinson Law School, and received the Bachelor of Laws degree in 1921. He received the Master of Arts degree at the same time.

He received his preliminary education in Summit Hill schools, and [illegible] Hall.

Born in Summit Hill Feb. 13, 1891, he is the son of Mrs. Thomas McCready and the late Mr. McCready.

He is married to the former Margaret Smith and they are the parents of one child, Thomas S. McCready.

COUNTY CORONER

Harry Doll

REGISTER OF WILLS

WADE BURNHAUSER

INSTITUTION STEWARD

Harry Fagley

RECORDER OF DEEDS

Thomas Davis

SHERIFF

Nathan C. Pollock

CLERK OF COURTS

William S. Williams

COUNTY TREASURER

William C. Christman

CO. SUPT. OF SCHOOLS

S. E. Prutzman

COUNTY SOLICITOR

Albert G. Prutzman

COUNTY SURVEYOR

S. K. Evans

County Officials at the Centennial Celebration of the County included three members of the Carbon Bar: Judge James C. McCready, District Attorney Albert H. Heimbach and County Solicitor Albert G. Prutzman.

CHAPTER V

ERA OF TRANSITION AND GROWTH (1944-1993)

By 1946, all ten of Carbon's World War II veteran-lawyers had returned safely to the county. Shortly thereafter William Scott, George McKinley, William Bayer and William Quinn who had also served their country in the war joined them at the bar. They were eager to settle down, practice law and pursue the American dream.

But the county, like the nation, was unsettled and anxious. Returning servicemen were having difficulty finding jobs. Judge McCready gave a great many speeches before civic clubs about the need to get back to the American way of life and the dangers of Communism. There was an uneasy feeling that the war had not brought a true peace. David Halberstan, the incisive journalist and Pultizer prize winning author, observed in his book *The Fifties*: "The nation was ready for witch-hunting." In 1947, Whitaker Chambers shocked the nation by accusing Secretary of State Alger Hiss with being a member of the Communist Party while serving in government. Senator Joseph McCarthy was getting ready to launch his red-baiting campaign of hate and smear in the hallowed halls of the United States Senate. Carbon County had its own witch hunt.

Mystery Building Case

County Commissioner Ambrose O'Donnell publicly charged that the previous board of commissioners had secretly and illegally spent taxpayer's money by constructing a "mystery building" in Weatherly. His no-holds-barred battle to surcharge the former board became the longest running civil court case in county history and tested the talents and patience of many members of the bar.

It all began in March of 1948. Newly elected majority Commissioners Ambrose O'Donnell and Nathan Drumheller through their county solicitor George Kerestes presented a "Memorial" to Judge McCready citing irregularities and illegal expenditures of some $35,000 by the former commissioners in the construction of a building at the Home for the Elderly in Laurytown. Judge McCready immediately ordered a professional audit and directed District Attorney Carl A. Niehoff to investigate the "mystery building" costs. After an eight-month probe, Niehoff reported to the court that he found no evidence of criminal conduct by the former commissioners. Judge McCready strongly disagreed with Niehoff's report and suggested criminal prosecution was warranted. Meanwhile, Controller Ray Kistler audited the county home financial records for 1947 and 1948. When he filed his report in 1949 exonerating the former commissioners from any wrongdoing, County Commissioners O'Donnell and Drumheller, through their special counsel, Frank York, filed numerous exceptions to the controller's audit. These ultimately became the basis for a civil lawsuit against John P. Davis, Steve Pancoe, and Homer B. Kern,[30] the three former commissioners seeking to surcharge them in the sum of $35,587. County Solicitor George Kerestes brought in a lawyer from Harrisburg to represent plaintiffs O'Donnell and Drumheller. Donald McCay became counsel for the former commissioners. Judge John Diefenderfer of Lehigh County was appointed by the Supreme Court to specially preside and the case began in May of 1950 before a Carbon jury. After seven months of intermittent hearings, the jury found in favor of the former commissioners on most of the "irregularity" issues but in a surprising and unusual move Judge Diefenderfer, on January 30, 1951, directed the jury to return a verdict surcharging the ex-commissioners in the sum of $21,231. An appeal to the Supreme Court followed and on January 7, 1952 the Supreme Court reversed the verdict.[31] The high court found that bidding and approval laws were violated but there was no evidence of fraud in the record to support the surcharge. The justices sent the case back to Carbon County for a determination as to whether the building could be used when completed and if not, whether there was any loss to the taxpayers.

Judge Fred Davis of Monroe County was then appointed to preside over the remanded case. Another year of hearings and arguments followed. The case seemed to have taken on a life of its own. But on February 5, 1953, in the middle of a hearing, Judge Davis emerged from an in-chambers meeting with counsel and unexpectedly announced to the print and radio media that the case was settled. The former board of commissioners agreed to pay the sum of $7000 to the county and the county agreed to withdraw its $35,000 claim. Both sides issued statements claiming victory. In April of 1953 a new board of commissioners led by chairman Ralph E. Mooney agreed to complete the "mystery building" and use it as a warehouse and storage building. The settlement, however, did not end the case. Further wrangling erupted over who was to pay the outside lawyers hired by Commissioners O'Donnell and Drumheller to litigate the surcharge case. Only after another lawsuit over the legal fees was filed did the new board of commissioners finally agree to pay.

Falcone Murder Case

Two years before Grace Metalious' *Peyton Place* became a runaway best seller by graphically revealing the dark and steamy secrets of a small factory town that appeared placid on the surface, a double murder tore away Palmerton's bucolic facade revealing a sordid tale of lust and sexual intrigue. *Commonwealth v. Daniel Falcone* became the trial of the Fifties. It was as riveting as a roller-coaster ride. It also provided an interesting insight into what a life sentence can mean in Pennsylvania's criminal justice system.

---

[30]*Davis et al v. Carbon County, 24 April Term 1949.*

[31]*Davis et al v. Carbon County, 369 Pa. 322, 85 A.2d 862 (1952).*

Fifty-one-year-old Daniel Falcone was a former state trooper and borough councilman from Bangor, Pennsylvania. Thirty-four-year-old Mildred Daneker was blond, pretty and married to Matthew Daneker, a Palmerton justice of the peace. In 1951, while working together at the Palmerton Shirt Company factory, Falcone and Mrs. Daneker had become involved in a passionate love affair followed by two years of clandestine trysts and secret exchanges of love letters. Matthew Daneker learned of his wife's illicit romance from Falcone's former girlfriend and urged his wife to end the relationship. In the middle of 1953, an anguished Mildred Daneker told Falcone that she wanted to end the affair. The ardent lover suddenly became a relentless stalker begging her to resume the relationship. For months he followed her, wrote to her and drove by her house, but she refused to see him.

On October 3, 1954 at 7:15 in the evening, Falcone waited outside of Trinity Evangelical Church in Palmerton crouching in the shadows. With the Danekers' son Robert looking on in horror, Falcone shot the couple with a .22 caliber Smith & Wesson pistol at close range as they were leaving church services. Robert and his friends pursued Falcone, but he escaped into the woods. Palmerton police, led by Willard Steigerwalt, combed the lower Carbon County area for fourteen to fifteen hours a day. Three days after the murders, Wind Gap police found Falcone in a drug store in Wind Gap and arrested him. His clothing was torn and his legs were covered with lacerations.

Falcone was charged with two counts of first degree murder and came to trial on January 17, 1955 before Judge James C. McCready and a jury of eight men and four women who were sequestered at the American Hotel in Mauch Chunk.[32] District Attorney Carl A. Niehoff, although weakened and hoarse with a viral infection, prosecuted the case. Edmund P. Turtzo of Northampton County served as lead defense counsel for Falcone. Assisting him were Lehighton lawyers John Deutsch and William A. Wyatt.

Niehoff called ten witnesses who told the jury the numbing details of the double murder and all identified Falcone as the killer. The defense presented Falcone to the jury as the "victim of Mrs. Daneker's hypocrisy and deception" citing love letters to him in which Mrs. Daneker "toyed with Falcone's emotions." Falcone told the jury he was in a zombie-like state over the break-up of his relationship with Mildred Daneker and had no memory of the shooting. He testified that he went to dinner with a woman on the night of the murders and planned to return to his home. The next thing he remembered was waking up in the woods with a gun in his hands. Psychiatrists Dr. Charles Umlauf and Dr. Lesse of Allentown both supported Falcone's lack of intent to kill and testified that Falcone was suffering from "hysterical amnesia" caused by his broken romance when he shot Mildred and

[32] *Commonwealth v. Daniel Falcone*, 4 & 5 January Sessions 1955.

Matthew Daneker. In his three hour closing, Turtzo argued that Mrs. Daneker's letters "were enough to drive any man mad." He portrayed his client as "an honorable and truthful" man who was wronged by the amorous "aggressiveness" of Mildred Daneker.[33]

In his summation, Niehoff called the amnesia defense "smoke and mirrors." He thundered that the evidence showed that Falcone's shooting of the Danekers was an act of revenge for Mildred Daneker telling him she wanted to end their affair. He underlined the fact that Falcone laid in wait for his victims:

> *"If he," pointing to the defendant seated nearby, "walks out of here a free man, it is your responsibility. Live up to the high honor in which you have been placed of serving on a jury. This man has forfeited the right to live in decent society. Those who kill a fellowman, whether out of envy, lust or greed, must be punished. Here before us is a man who had the audacity to say he could recite the Ten Commandments after unleashing his vicious acts upon a woman. Matthew Danker was an honorable man. This man is guilty of having committed a heinous crime."*[34]

On January 29, 1955 after three and one half hours of deliberation, the jury returned two verdicts of guilty of first degree murder. It recommended a sentence of life imprisonment on each murder which Judge McCready immediately imposed. There was no appeal and Falcone began serving his life sentence.

Fourteen years later on February 11, 1969, Thomas S. McCready filed on behalf of Falcone a Post Conviction Hearing Act petition contending that his trial counsel was ineffective because he failed to take an appeal and asked for the right to file post trial motions. After a hearing on May 16, 1969, Judge Heimbach found that Falcone told his lawyer not to file an appeal because he feared that a retrial might result in the death penalty, and ruled he waived his right to appeal. McCready took the case to the Supreme Court of Pennsylvania. It decided that Falcone's waiver was not voluntary and reversed Judge Heimbach's decision. The case was remanded to Carbon County Court for further proceedings.[35] McCready filed post trial motions seeking a new trial, but the motions were never argued.

---

[33]*Jim Thorpe Times-News, Friday, January 28, 1955.*

[34]*Ibid.*

[35]*Commonwealth v. Falcone, 440 Pa. 61, 269 A.2d 699 (1970).*

On April 7, 1972, Governor Milton Shapp, on recommendation of the State Parole Board, granted Falcone a commutation of his sentence changing it from life in prison to life on parole. Then in 1987, Governor Robert Casey granted him another commutation reducing his parole period to thirty-three years and two months, the exact amount of time he was under sentence. At sixty-seven years of age, Falcone became a free man.

First Malpractice Trial

There were no negligence claims filed against doctors, dentists or lawyers in Carbon's first hundred years and there have been very few in recent times. Difficulty in obtaining medical witnesses who will testify against another doctor and the lionization of the medical professional by Carbon citizens have made local lawyers reluctant to sue them for malpractice.

It was not until the early 1950s that Carbon County had its first medical malpractice trials. *Jack Daniel Edinger, a minor by his parents v. Dr. Homer B. Fegley*[36] arose out of the birth of the first baby born in the newly built Gnaden Huetten Memorial Hospital in Lehighton. Dr. Fegley, an obstetrician, was delivering the child when an attending nurse accidently placed the baby on a hot plate in the operating room causing burns to the back. Grounding his case on the "captain of the ship" theory of liability Carl Niehoff filed the claim against Dr. Fegley on behalf of the minor and parents. George Shutack represented the doctor. The case was tried three times. The first trial ended in a verdict for the doctor. Judge McCready granted a new trial and at the second trial there was a hung jury. A third jury returned a verdict for the plaintiff for $680 and the case was finally settled by the payment of the verdict. What makes this case significant is the fact that it was and is today the first and only time a jury ever returned a money verdict against a doctor in Carbon County.

First Criminal Libel Case

Over the years, Carbon's court dockets showed a relatively small number of civil actions for slander and libel. These actions are brought to recover damages for spoken or written words which tend to blacken the reputation or character of an individual in the community. In most of them, the jury returned verdicts vindicating the plaintiff by awarding the nominal "seven cents" which the old common law allowed. Although there was a criminal libel statute on the books since the late eighteenth century, it had never been used in Carbon County -- until 1961.

---

[36]*Edinger v. Fegley, 27 June Term 1952*

On November 20, 1961 Dr. Homer Fegley and George Reich of Lehighton filed criminal complaints in the office of Justice of the Peace Melba Kobal charging Marion A. Morthimer, publisher of the *Lehighton Evening Leader* and her editor Will J. Smith with criminal libel. The charges were based on two critical editorial columns written by Smith on the front page of the *Leader* in November of 1961 concerning the Lehighton Area School District's purchase of a property owned by the Perry Walp Estate to be used for the construction of the new high school. The article stated that Reich who was a Lehighton councilman and had an interest in the property, and Fegley who was a member of the Lehighton school board were close friends and that Reich had arranged to sell the property to the school district for $17,500 and had made a "fast buck" on the deal.

The joint criminal trial began in September of 1962 before Judge Heimbach with John Deutsch as the prosecutor.[37] George Shutack represented Marion Morthimer and John Lavelle was counsel for Will Smith. Because of the First Amendment implications of the cases, many newspapers and news service organizations in the Commonwealth closely monitored the proceedings. Reich and Fegley both testified that they were only remotely involved in the sale; that the property was bought by the school district not for $17,500 but for $10,500 some of which would go to George Reich's wife; that it was a bona fide transaction. They admitted on cross examination that they had both filed civil actions for money damages against both defendants and that Reich had sold four other properties to the school district. Reich denied that he ever told anyone that he made a "fast buck" on the transaction. Will Smith testified that all the information he printed had been given to him by Reich at a wedding reception and two witnesses stated that they heard Reich tell Smith that he made a fast buck and "what are you going to do about it?" Lavelle argued strenuously that the article was inaccurate but not defamatory; that it was simply the kind of rough criticism that every public official has to expect in a free, democratic society. Deutsch told the jury that the editorials were false and malicious and calculated to destroy the reputations of Reich and Fegley. After almost six hours of deliberations the jury found both defendants "Not Guilty." These were the first and last criminal libel trials in Carbon County. In 1972, the Supreme Court of Pennsylvania struck down the Commonwealth's criminal libel statute as unconstitutional because it imposed liability on merely negligent statements.[38]

In February of 1963 the civil libel cases[39] involving the same parties and issues came on for trial. Reich and Fegley had retained the services of Laurence H.

---

[37]*Commonwealth v. Will J. Smith and Marion A. Morthimer*, 11 & 12 April Sessions 1961.

[38]*Commonwealth v. Eugene Armao and Arnold Orsatti*, 446 Pa. 325, 286 A.2d 626 (1972).

[39]*Fegley et al v. Morthimer et al*, 1 September Term 1962.

Eldredge of Philadelphia, the leading libel lawyer in Pennsylvania at the time. The defendants were again represented by Shutack and Lavelle. After a week long trial, a jury returned a split verdict of $4000 for Dr. Fegley and a verdict for the defendants in the Reich case. After Judge Heimbach granted a new trial which was affirmed by the Superior Court,[40] the cases were tried again in 1964. The second jury awarded each plaintiff one dollar in compensatory damages and $2500 in punitive damage. The cases were ultimately settled by payment of the verdicts.

In the mid-1960s, a crime wave of robberies, burglaries and arsons swept over Carbon County. Almost daily there were new reports of break-ins and thefts in various communities which had police scampering for suspects and looking for a common link. A rooftop pursuit and capture of two would-be burglars in Summit Hill in 1964 led to their confessions and some startling revelations. According to their sworn statements to police, a Philadelphia burglary ring led by hairdresser George Bricker had infested Carbon County preying on well-to-do residents and stealing thousands of dollars in cash and valuables. The money was to be used to fund a "mob" takeover of Carbon County by electing a friendly district attorney and judge. Based on their statements, District Attorney Kerestes began an intensive investigation. Many arrests were made and one by one, over a period of two years, Bricker,[41] Frank and Libby Vecchiolli[42] and their cohorts in crime were tried or pled guilty and sentenced to jail.

Eckhart Murder Case

On May 17, 1965 Edward Eckhart bludgeoned to death his girlfriend Carol Juliano on the Maury Road between Weissport and Jim Thorpe in Penn Forest Township. The grotesque details of the murder preoccupied the court during the late 1960s and the first half of the 1970s.

Twenty-one-year-old Carol Juliano, a divorced mother of two, met Eckhart at Zona's Bar in Lehighton and the same day allowed him to move into her home. After several months of living in an abusive alcohol and drug filled relationship, a terrorized Juliano fled from her home. Eckhart, in a drunken rage, tracked her down and after a violent argument, beat her head repeatedly with a rock causing her death. Five days later he surrendered to police and confessed. In January of 1966 a Carbon County jury was

---

[40]*Fegley et al v. Morthimer et al*, 204 Pa. Super. 54, 202 A.2d 125 (1964).

[41]*Commonwealth v. George Bricker*, 38 January Sessions 1965.

[42]*Commonwealth v. Frank Vecchiolli and Libby Vecchiolli*, 26 June Sessions 1965.

empaneled to try the case before Judge Albert Heimbach.[43] Thomas S. McCready, chief public defender, and William B. Quinn represented Eckhart. First Assistant District Attorney John Deutsch prosecuted the case for the Commonwealth. He was assisted by District Attorney George Kerestes and Second Assistant District Attorney Roger N. Nanovic. After five days of trial, the jury convicted Eckhart of first degree murder and fixed the penalty at life imprisonment. On appeal to the Supreme Court, a new trial was granted on April 16, 1968 because the judge permitted the jury to see an autopsy photograph of the corpse of Carol Juliano which the high court found to be "inflammatory and prejudicial."[44]

When his case came up for the retrial, Eckhart told his lawyer Thomas McCready that he did not want to go to trail. On September 16, 1968, he pleaded guilty to a general charge of murder. A three judge panel of Judge Heimbach, Judge Woodring of Northampton County, and Judge Henninger of Lehigh County convicted him of first degree murder and sentenced him to life imprisonment. Eckhart then filed a Post Conviction Hearing Act petition alleging that his plea was not intelligently and voluntarily entered. While this petition was pending, a second appeal was taken to the Supreme Court alleging various errors by the three judge court. This appeal was also rejected.[45] A hearing was held on Eckhart's PCHA petition in October and November of 1973 after which Judge Heimbach denied the petition. The case continued to ping-pong through the court system. For the third time, Eckhart filed an appeal to the Supreme Court and again it was rejected.[46] The longest criminal homicide case in the history of the county had finally ended. Only the sentence remained to be carried out.

While he was serving his life sentence in the state correctional institution at Dallas, Eckhart was assigned to a work detail on a farm outside the walls of the prison. On July 11, 1976 he walked away undetected and made his way back to Carbon County. For over a month local and state police scoured the county looking for him. On the morning of August 19 his former mother-in-law, Doris Gibbons, spotted him slipping into her garage and called the state police. Within minutes twenty police officers and deputy sheriffs surrounded the garage. Eckhart opened fire and police lobbed several rounds of tear gas into the garage. As police closed in Eckhart shot himself in the head with a .22 caliber bullet from a gun owned by Mrs. Gibbons. Ironically, Eckhart had imposed on himself in the garage the death penalty which his lawyers had so skillfully protected him from in court.

---

[43]*Commonwealth v. Edward Eckhart*, 28 June Session 1965.

[44]*Commonwealth v. Edward Eckhart*, 430 Pa. 311, 242 A.2d 271 (1969).

[45]*Commonwealth v. Eckhart*, 436 Pa. 361, 260 A.2d 750 (1970).

[46]*Commonwealth v. Eckhart*, 457 Pa. 483, 326 A.2d 308 (1974).

Court Stenographers

In 1963 the long standing use of pen and ink in the Carbon County courtroom ended. From the beginning, speed writers recorded what witnesses, lawyers and the court said in the courtroom. They wrote down everything in long hand as it was spoken. Two or three of these stenographers were on hand for the longer trials. Early in the twentieth century, court stenographers began to use Gregg shorthand. Roy S. Mohrbach of Nesquehoning was the official court stenographer for Judge McCready and Henry Fitzpatrick of Jim Thorpe was the judge's secretary. Both were skilled practitioners in the art of shorthand. Judge Heimbach used his secretary Rose Watkins for many court proceedings and assigned her as a part-time stenographer for trials. She also performed the stenographic work in shorthand but was uncomfortable in the role. He also used, on a part-time basis, Dundena Groff of Lehighton who was the first to use stenotype equipment in the courtroom. Many members of the bar prevailed upon the judge to abandon this practice and in 1963 Judge Heimbach created the full-time position of court reporter. This decision effectively ended manual reporting in Carbon's courtroom. The court system had the good fortune of having George Repinec of Lansford apply for the job. A skilled stenotypist and a tireless, dedicated worker, Repinec launched the modern era of court reporting and has been a quiet but dynamic performer since 1963. In 1990, Judge Lavelle installed a state-of-the-art recording system in the main courtroom. This equipment permitted the capturing of the words of each participant in the trial or hearing on separate electronic tape tracks for later transcription on word processing computers and ended the use of stenotype machines and typewriters.

1968 Constitution

Repeated calls for judicial reform resulted in the Constitutional Convention of 1968. The Constitution of 1968 produced by the convention reorganized and unified the entire statewide court system under the administration of the state Supreme Court. This set the stage for coordinated management by the Supreme Court of all courts in Pennsylvania as part of a single integrated system. Prior to 1968, judges elected to the common pleas bench also sat as judges of the court of oyer and terminer and general jail delivery and the court of quarter sessions of the peace. Oyer and terminer courts tried felony cases and the quarter sessions court tried misdemeanors. The difference in court names made no difference in court functioning. The 1968 constitutional amendments eliminated these distinctions. In addition, the orphans' court was declared a division of the court of common pleas; the two had previously been separate. The prothonotary was established as the administrative office for civil matters, the clerk of courts for criminal matters. The new constitution also provided for the composition of each court and for the qualifications, election, tenure, and compensation of justices of the appellate courts, judges and district justices.

Although the seventies were relatively serene, during the eighties, greed, sometimes heavily laced with alcohol and marijuana, fueled criminal activity which produced the century's heaviest major criminal trial docket.

After two mistrials, a Carbon County jury, in 1986, found Julian Finsel, a Kidder Township sewage enforcement officer, guilty of taking cash bribes from Lake Harmony real estate agents to issue illegal on-site sewage permits. The trial featured taped conversations between Finsel and a realtor during which corrupt deals were struck and bribe money was passed to Finsel. Judge Lavelle sentenced him to jail for 14 months.

Joseph W. Horn, an unemployed Nesquehoning resident, covered up his lucrative drug dealing operation by obtaining welfare payments as a disabled person. His large cash payment to buy a home triggered a welfare fraud investigation which eventually led state police to search his home and find a huge stash of drugs. His conviction of drug dealing and welfare fraud in 1987 sent him to the penitentiary for three years.

The harrowingly brutal knife murder of sixty-five year old widow Josephine Weiner in the bedroom of her home on February 18, 1987 was a seminal event for Lehighton. It seared the quiet, relatively crime-free community like a red-hot poker implanting a mentality of fear. Edward Lusch, an eighteen year-old with a choir boy face and William "Butch" Moyer, a hulking bear of a man, were both charged with the homicide. When the cases came to trial in August of 1987 and June of 1988, both admitted that they were high on pot and alcohol and entered Weiner's home to look for money to buy drugs. Each accused the other of killing Weiner. District Attorney Webb, in a powerful summation, argued that the injuries to Weiner's body were strong evidence that they both beat her and were involved in the stabbing. Separate juries found Lusch guilty of second degree murder[47] and Moyer of first degree murder.[48] Both received life sentences and were remanded to separate state penal institutions for the remainder of their natural lives.

The Bonnie Leskin murder case in 1985[49] laid bare one of Carbon's dirty secrets - spousal abuse. When the case of the Lower Towamensing housewife who shot her unarmed husband to death came to trial, it looked like an open and shut case of murder one. But Wallace Worth, her wily defense lawyer, and associate Dianne Dickson mounted a stirring "battered spouse" defense which at the time was a brand new concept in the criminal law of Pennsylvania. She testified that her husband had subjected her to

[47]*Commonwealth v. Edward Lusch*, 111 CR 1987.

[48]*Commonwealth v. Wilbur Guy Moyer*, 112 CR 1987.

[49]*Commonwealth v. Bonnie Leskin*, 371 CR 1985.

years of physical and mental abuse and at the time she pulled the trigger, she believed he was going to beat her again. A twelve-woman jury, many shaking and in tears, acquitted the defendant after only two and a half hours of deliberations.

Women at the Bar

Historically, the law has not always been fair in its treatment of women. Denied the right to own property, the right to vote, the right to serve on juries, women have had to fight for what men already had as their birthright. There were no women at the Carbon County Bar for one hundred and sixteen years. Fortunately, it did not take a legal battle to open the doors of the all-male Carbon Bar Association. Marianne Shutack Lavelle of Nesquehoning was the first woman admitted to its membership. Coming from a mining community which had long been associated with the sexist notion that daughters should be bred and prepared for motherhood and the perpetuation of the species, her admission in 1959 signaled the emergence of Carbon women from their traditional role. Other young women, however, did not quickly follow in her footsteps. It was almost twenty years before a second woman joined her at the bar. In 1979, K. Tucker Landon was admitted with Carole Wildoner and Christine Mifkovich following in 1981 and then Holly Heintzelman and Jane Engler in 1982.

Ten women joined the bar in the last decade and have become active in the legal community. In 1980, K. Tucker Landon became the first woman to serve as an assistant District Attorney. The first all-woman law firm in Carbon County was formed in 1989 by Christie Schaffer-Bower and Cynthia Ann Dyrda, under the firm name of Dyrda & Schaffer with law offices located in the Masonic Building in Lehighton. Today, the distaff side make up about sixteen percent of the lawyers in the county.

Second Judge

As the court system moved into the last decade of the twentieth century, it had became obvious that judicial assets were simply not keeping pace with the population and the caseload. According to the United States Census Bureau, the resident population of Carbon County in 1980 was 53,285 and by 1988 had grown to 56,100 for a total increase of 2,815.

A tidal wave of cases particularly criminal and family law cases poured into the court during the 1980s and caused a tremendous strain on the judge and the system. In 1978, the total civil case filings were 1199 cases; in 1988, the total filings were 2,698, a 125 percent increase in ten years. The criminal case volume had grown even more dramatically. In 1978, the court received a total of 228 criminal cases which included both adult and juvenile offenses. By 1988, the criminal case volume had almost tripled in size to a total caseload of 601 cases.

The largest growth in the civil case volume was in cases involving support, custody, divorce, juveniles, and protection from abuse. Of the 2469 civil cases filed in 1988, 1483 or sixty-one percent of those cases were these family law cases.

The breakdown of the family unit was the principle reason for the increase in cases. Half of all Carbon County marriages were ending in divorce and custody disputes were spiraling. More children were being born out of wedlock. The traditional wage-earner/homemaker family of the 1950s gave way to the single parent or blended family of the 1980s. These factors resulted in a much greater need for court intervention to resolve family disputes. A widespread use of hard drugs and the abuse of alcohol spurred the rising criminal caseload. Legislative initiatives at both the state and federal levels also added to the court's workload. These included the new driving under the influence law which resulted in a sharp increase in the number of drunk driving cases. New mandatory sentencing statutes and sentencing guidelines called for harsher penalties and resulted in more pretrial motions and trials. The Pennsylvania statute which had the most significant impact on the family law caseload was the 1980 Divorce Code. This legislation revolutionized the substantive law of divorce in Pennsylvania by providing for no-fault divorce, equitable distribution of property, and alimony after divorce. These were totally new concepts and required lengthy judicial proceedings to resolve the more complex issues. Battered women seeking protection from abusive relationships began to appear more frequently before the Court. Passage of the 1988 amendments to the Protection From Abuse Act which gave easier access to the Courts increased the number of petitions being filed.

In order to hold the burgeoning caseload in check, the Pennsylvania Supreme Court appointed senior judges from other counties to assist Judge Lavelle. Judges Alfred T. Williams, Richard D. Grifo and Michael V. Franciosa of Northampton County, Judge Paul Beckert of Bucks County, Judge Horace A. Davenport of Montgomery County, Judge J. Quint Salmon of Beaver County, Judge James F. Buckingham of York County and Judge John E. Lavelle of Schuylkill County frequently appeared on the Carbon County Bench between 1988 and 1991. Their service was invaluable to keeping the court current.

In September of 1989, Judge Lavelle went to Representative Keith McCall and Senator James Rhoades with a detailed report on the court's workload and enlisted their aid in asking the Legislature to create an additional judgeship for Carbon County. The Pennsylvania Legislature responded favorably. In December of 1990, the Legislature increased to two the number of judges in the Fifty-Sixth Judicial District. In November of 1991, four-term district attorney Richard W. Webb was elected the second judge of Carbon County. On January 6, 1992 he was sworn into office by family friend Judge Albert H. Heimbach.

Judicial Sesquicentennial - 1993

As 1993 drew to a close, the Court and Bar Association celebrated the 150th anniversary of the founding of the courts of Carbon County with a series of events which were memorable, historic and emotional. The two week commemoration began with an historic visit by an Appellate Court. On December 8 and 9, the Superior Court of Pennsylvania, at the invitation of Judge Lavelle, came to Carbon County and for the first time in Carbon's history an Appellate Court sat for official session in the main courtroom. President Judge James E. Rowley, Judge Donald E. Wieand and Judge John G. Brosky presided during the first day of arguments. Judge James R. Cavanaugh, Judge Vincent A. Cirillo and Judge Peter Paul Olszewski conducted the second day session. Students representing all local high schools attended the session held on December 9 and the Superior Court judges took the time to explain to them the procedures and issues involved in the cases coming before the Court.

Superior Court Judges Wieand, Rowley and Brosky hold court in the restored Carbon County Courtroom

The Bar Association hosted an elegant black tie dinner for 125 bar members and their spouses at the Inn of Jim Thorpe (formerly the American Hotel) on the evening

Judge Asa Packer greets President Judge John P. Lavelle and his wife Marianne S. Lavelle, Esquire at the Judicial Sesquicentennial Bar Association Dinner

of December 8 to celebrate the Judicial Sesquicentennial. In a setting of candlelight, flowers and glittering silver, the dinner was filled with light hearted banter, warm camaraderie and nostalgia. Eleven judges of the Superior Court joined in the festivities and heard brief remarks by President Judges James E. Rowley and John P. Lavelle. The evening was highlighted by a surprise visit and some inspiring words to the judges and lawyers from Asa Packer, portrayed by the superb Tamaqua-born actor George C. Miller:

> *The first General Assembly convened by William Penn in December 1682 approved a body of laws that included a number of provisions that covered the Courts in their operations. One of those Court related provisions boldly declared that "all Courts shall be open and justice shall neither be sold, denied or delayed." This provision, enunciating the Court's role in administering the concept of justice, had an historic resonance and it has a contemporary relevance. The Magna Carta, a significant root of our tree of jurisprudence states "to no one will we sell, to no one will we refuse or delay right or justice." The constitution of the Commonwealth of Pennsylvania embraces this age old concept of the Court's and justice in section 11 of article I which states in part that all Courts shall be open and every man shall have a right of justice administered without sale, denial or delay. As we celebrate this Judicial Sesquicentennial of Carbon County and look back with pride we must remain vigilant of our key roles in upholding both the letter and the spirit of the concept of justice embodied in Penn's body of laws and the Declaration of Rights of our present State constitution.*

Joseph J. Matika, Esq., Kathy Matika, Gary F. Dobias, Esq., Judge Donald E. Wieand (Superior Court), Robert P. Yurchak, Esq., Cynthia S. Ray, Esq., Jean A. Engler, Esq.

Several beautiful choral renditions by The Bach & Handel Chorale from St. Mark's Church were performed under the direction of Randall Perry. Prepared and served by The Ballietsville Inn the dinner was a gastronomic delight. It was an evening to savor and one that will be long remembered. Carole Wildoner-Walbert, Richard Abbott and Jean Engler co-chaired the planning and arrangements for the dinner.

Joseph J. Veltisky, Esq., Annette Puchyr, William B. Quinn, Esq., Patricia Quinn, George Brinley Richards, Esq., George A. Shutack, Esq., Judge John G. Brosky (Superior Court)

Alexander Campbell (portrayed by Brian J. Campbell), who did not testify at his trial in 1876, is sworn in at his Mock Trial in 1993 by tipstaff William Zimmerman.

The 150th anniversary of the Common Pleas Court also witnessed a look back at one of Carbon's most intriguing and controversial trials. On December 15, 1993, the "Mock Trial of a Mollie," a re-enactment of the trial of *Commonwealth v. Alexander Campbell* in 1876 was presented in the newly restored main courtroom to an overflow audience of approximately 250 people. The Commonwealth's case was presented by three county prosecutors, District Attorney Gary F. Dobias, and Assistant Prosecutors David Addy and Jean Engler. Three public defenders, Stephen P. Vlossak, Robert T. Yurchak and Gregory Mousseau represented Alexander Campbell. The testimony was taken from the original trial transcripts. Members of the talented Allentown Theatre Group portrayed key prosecution and defense witnesses dressed in late 1800s attire and testified in thick Irish brogues. The trial featured the testimony of Alexander Campbell who did not testify at the original trial. He was portrayed by Brian Campbell, a grandnephew of Alexander Campbell who flew in from his home in Needles, California to portray the role. The day long trial before a rapt audience ended emotionally late in the afternoon when the out-of-county jury who had never heard of the "Mollie Maguires" returned a verdict of "Not Guilty." The courtroom exploded in shouts and applause at the verdict. Many spectators, some of whom were Campbell and "Mollie" descendants leaped from their seats and teary eyed hugged each other.

James McParlan (George Miller) is sworn in at Mock Trial

Defense lawyer Steve Vlossak cross-examines James Kerrigan (Terry Abbott) at Mock Trial

The "Mock Trial" was arranged and directed by Judge Lavelle who said he chose the *Campbell* case because it underscored the class struggle between poor, oppressed Irish miners and the rich, powerful coal barons and railroad magnates that dominated daily life in the hard coal regions in the late nineteenth century. Reporters and media representatives from ten newspapers and five television stations attended the event and gave it widespread coverage. Pioneer Public Television also videotaped the trial for presentation on local cable networks across the Commonwealth.

Exactly 150 years to the day from the first session of the Carbon County Court of Common Pleas, the final event of the Judicial Sesquicentennial took place in the main courtroom on December 18, 1993. It marked the first time the newly restored main courtroom was used for an official court proceeding. The ceremonies began solemnly with a presentation of the Colors by three deputy sheriffs of Carbon County preceded by fifes and a drum from Lehighton Area High School. After welcoming remarks by Judge Richard W. Webb, Judge Asa Packer (portrayed by John Gunsser) reminded the large audience of his involvement in the erection of Carbon County in 1843 and extended his good wishes. Judge Lavelle and Judge Packer symbolically "separated" Carbon from Northampton County using a specially made map reproduction of Carbon and Northampton counties.

Honored during this special session of court was the late Joseph L. Boyle, with his wife Rita Boyle, son Joseph L. Boyle, and sister Gertrude Boyle Apfelbaum in attendance. Marianne S. Lavelle, Esquire eulogized the legendary journalist and presented on behalf of the Carbon County Bar Association to the Court a bronze plaque dedicated to his memory for permanent display in the courtroom.

Commissioner Thomas Gerhard then read a resolution of the Carbon County Board of Commissioners presenting the restored courtroom to the Court for the use of the citizens of Carbon County. In his acceptance, Judge Lavelle rededicated the courtroom "to the pursuit of truth and justice, grounded in respect for individual rights."

In a reprise of Carbon's first court session, Judge Lavelle administered the official oath and admitted five new attorneys to the Carbon Bar. For President Judge Lavelle the day had special significance. He had the singular pleasure of welcoming to the bar his son John P. Lavelle, Jr., and daughter-in-law Colleen F. Coonelly-Lavelle. The motion for their admission was made by Attorney Marianne S. Lavelle. Lynne Kimberly Law, law clerk to Judge Lavelle, on motion of David Addy, Michael S. Greek, on motion of William Schwab and Robin M. Fenick, on motion of Paul Levy, were also admitted to Carbon's legal family.

Newly inducted members of the Carbon County Bar: Colleen F. Coonelly Lavelle, John P. Lavelle, Jr., L. Kimberly Law, Michael S. Greek, Robin M. Fenick

Doctor T. Robert Milligan, associate Professor Emeritus and former Chairman of the Modern Foreign Languages Department at Manhattan College in New York City, composed and read at the ceremonies a special poem which beautifully summarized the court's 150 years:

Family Reunion

The Courts are a quarreling family of five:
The Judge, a parental figure in ruling robes,
Who in presiding keeps disputes on track;
The Jury, a mother hen who late or soon
Must speak as one for her dozen diverse chickens
In a one-or-two word climax -- right out of Dickens.

Next, two siblings, Defense and Prosecution,
Who can engage in argument so wrenching,
The Judge demands they both approach the bench;

And last -- the one the quarrel is all about --
Defendant, who immune from all intent
Till guilt be proved, must be presumed still innocent.

Unlike most families that fight, the Courts
Agree to disagree, that in the end
They might agree again -- closer, one hopes,
To truth and to a kind of lasting peace . . .
What, then, of the Family here today, now free
To mark its century and a half of history?

Its members, looking back, will surely see
Some dark and twisted ways, made light and straight
By those courageous champions of right,
Of different form and face, yet counterparts
Of these today. In spirit, they reunite
With all who care -- and know them all by sight.

And with reunion, now stands renaissance.
One hundred fifty years had much to tell:
A mock trial need not be a mockery,
But makes the path of justice clearer still.
And what of Justice? What will be her way?
Justice should be blind, the ancients say,

But will her blindfold any longer serve?
For Justice sees on earth through human eyes,
And if we are blind to much that is unjust,
How then will Justice see? Now, look up
Into the sky that decks this handsome hall!
There she stands, clear-eyed, with vision free
To weigh her scales -- if need, to use her sword . . .
At this reunion, do we hear her say:
Read and guard the law, and be well-schooled,
That Justice be sustained -- not overruled.

T. Robert Milligan, 1993

County Commissioners
Dean D. W. DeLong
Thomas C. Gerhard
John D. Mogilski

County Administrator
Mortimer L. Smedley

County Solicitor
Roger N. Nanovic II

County Treasurer
Gilbert J. Gerhard

County Coroner
Philip J. Jeffries

Controller
Robert M. Crampsie

Jury Commissioners
Willard C. Hill
Russell J. Zellner, Jr.

President Judge
John P. Lavelle

Judge
Richard W. Webb

Court Administrator
Richard P. Abbott

District Attorney
Gary F. Dobias

County Detective
Joseph V. Pampanin

Sheriff
Peter P. Hoherchak

Prothonotary
William J. O'Gurek

Register of Wills
Margaret C. O'Donnell

Recorder of Deeds
Andrew J. Snoha

Clerk of Courts
William C. McGinley

Carbon County Officials in Sesquicentennial Year

SESQUICENTENNIAL CEREMONIES
OF
THE COURT OF COMMON PLEAS OF CARBON COUNTY

December 18, 1993
10:00 A.M.

Opening of Court	*Court Crier*
Presiding	*Honorable John P. Lavelle*
Advancement of Colors	*Carbon County Sheriff's Color Guard; Fifes and Drum of Lehighton Area High School Band*
Pledge of Allegiance	*Anthony Roberti, Esq., Chancellor, Carbon County Bar Association*
National Anthem	*Josephine Noll, Lehighton*
Invocation	*Rev. Robert McConaghy, Pastor SS. Peter & Paul Church, Lehighton*
Welcoming Remarks	*Honorable Richard W. Webb, Associate Judge, Court of Common Pleas of Carbon County*
Greetings from an Early Judge	*Asa Packer: Portrayed by John Gunsser*
Commemorative Poem	*Dr. T. Robert Milligan*
Presentation of Memorial Plaque to Court Honoring Joseph L. Boyle	*Marianne S. Lavelle, Esq.*
Separation of Carbon From Northampton County	*Presented by: Honorable John P. Lavelle*
Resolution Carbon Co. Commissioners	*Honorable Thomas Gerhard*
Sesquicentennial Commemoration and Dedication of Restored Courtroom No. I	*Honorable John P. Lavelle, President Judge, Court of Common Pleas, Carbon Co.*
Admissions to the Bar - John P. Lavelle, Jr., Colleen Coonelly-Lavelle, L. Kimberly Law, Michael S. Greek, Robin Senick	*Honorable John P. Lavelle*
Benediction	*Rev. Vicki L. Keller, Pastor St. Johns Lutheran Church, Jim Thorpe*
America the Beautiful	*Josephine Noll, Lehighton*
Retirement of Colors	*Carbon County Sheriff's Color Guard; Fifes and Drum of Lehighton Area High School Band*

ADJOURNMENT

Courthouse I

CHAPTER VI

THE COURTHOUSES

Many of life's tragedies and most of society's burning issues eventually find their way to the courtroom. The business of justice is solemn and affects people at all levels of the social strata. In addition to accommodating all participants in the justice system -- litigants, defendants, victims, and witnesses, judges, lawyers, juries, administrators -- a courthouse should express the public interest in justice and reflect the gravity of its proceedings. The Carbon County Courthouse has always been such a building.

Courthouse I
(1843-1849)

One of the most imposing and important structures in Mauch Chunk in 1843 was the Lehigh Coal and Navigation Company's "Old Store" located on the northeast corner of Susquehanna Street and Broadway. To ensure the selection of Mauch Chunk as the county seat, the directors of the LC&N Company had agreed to donate this thirty-six-year-old property as a birthday gift to the newly born county. During the summer months of 1843, contractors employed by the building committee in charge of the county buildings repaired, refurbished and transformed the "Old Store" into Carbon County's first courthouse. The first floor housed the county row offices; the courtroom was located on the second floor; a skylight hung over the jurors' deliberating area. Above the roof towered a cupola with a unique weather vane -- a train of coal cars with a locomotive and engineer beneath a pick crossed with a shovel.

Workers modified a small building to the rear of the "Old Store" for use as a jail. A grand jury found the jail structurally inadequate, but that did not deter county officials from approving it. The editor of the ***Carbon Transit*** described it as "safe as need be, and as comfortable as it ought to be for the violator of law and order."

The first session of court was held on Monday, December 18, 1843.

Mauch Chunk's selection as the county seat had irritated many Lehighton residents who felt their town was better suited to meet the county needs. The celebration over the selection of Mauch Chunk as the county seat had barely subsided when 700 Lehighton citizens petitioned the State Legislature to relocate the county seat to Lehighton. On Valentine's Day of 1844, the petition was filed in Harrisburg. It never reached the floor of the Legislature.

In 1846, the controversy sparked anew. The courthouse was in dire need of repairs and the LC&N Company had not fulfilled its promise to transfer the title to the county. Without the title, the county commissioners were unwilling to make the repairs. Lehighton saw the LC&N Company's reneging on its promise as an opportunity to renew its quest for the county seat by resubmitting a bill to the Legislature titled an "Act for Removal" on February 13, 1846. To be enacted, this bill first had to be passed by the county voters. The bill had a salutary provision for Mauch Chunk. It provided that even if the citizens voted for the transfer, the unseating bill would be revoked should the LC&N convey title to the county or if Mauch Chunk reimbursed the county for the cash value of the building and ground by August 1, 1846.

An act of God actually triggered the LC&N Company's refusal to transfer the courthouse property. In January of 1841, a massive flood of the Lehigh River had wiped out the LC&N Company's canal system. Its mines were still operative, but the anthracite could not be transported to market. Without income from coal sales it was impossible to repair the canals. A cash flow shortage plunged the company into a financial crisis. Creditors demanded payment on overdue loans, and the LC&N Company borrowed money by mortgaging all of its holdings.

On the one hand, the members of the financially hard-pressed LC&N Company's board of directors were naturally reluctant to give up one of their principal assets. On the other hand, they realized that failure to transfer the building would mean that the county seat would probably move to Lehighton and property values in Mauch Chunk would go down. Since it owned most of the lots in Mauch Chunk, the company foresaw a substantial loss of future revenues. LC&N decided to keep its promise by transferring its building and ground to Carbon County. On July 23, 1846, Josiah White, Caleb Cope and James Cox, president of the company, executed and delivered a deed to the County of Carbon. Inexplicably, the deed was not recorded until January 6, 1848 in Deed Book 2, page 302. The deed provided that if the courthouse was ever moved, the property would revert to the LC&N Company.

The LC&N Company's deed of gift killed Lehighton's Act for Removal in the Legislature and its death ended Lehighton's second effort to become the county seat.

The county repaired the buildings, and Commissioners John D. Bowman and William Kern certified that the courthouse and jail were ready for use on December 18, 1845. After a struggling start, the buildings had a brief governmental life because neither was of fire proof construction. The courthouse and the jail behind it burned to the ground in a devastating fire which laid the entire business area of Mauch Chunk in ashes on the afternoon of July 15, 1849. Court records miraculously survived the blaze. When the fire attacked the jail, all prisoners were set free.

The fire again fed Lehighton's desire to attain the county seat and for the third time it petitioned the Legislature. Lehighton borough raised $10,000 as seed money to attract the county seat. Lehighton Borough argued three points in favor of removal. One, the title to the ground for the new county buildings in Mauch Chunk remained in dispute. Two, Mauch Chunk could not support the judicial and administrative needs of an expanding population. Three, the threat of another fire remained. Despite these compelling arguments, Lehighton's third attempt -- and its final one -- also ended in failure.

During the reconstruction period after the fire, court sessions were held in the Public School House in Mauch Chunk. All Carbon County prisoners were placed in the Lehigh County Jail.

Photo of the front of LC&N's 1846 Deed to the County of Carbon for the land and old store at the corner of Broadway and Susquehanna Street.

Courthouse II

Courthouse II
(1850-1893)

Although work began shortly after the fire on the construction of a new jail and "Row Office" building, the commissioners seemed reluctant to build a new courthouse. Successive grand juries and Judge Eldred prodded them to act, reminding them that the thriving economy and increasing county population required the new facility. Early in January of 1850, the commissioners approved a plan drawn by John Root, an architect. It provided for a brick building, Greek revival in design, with forty-five foot frontage on Broadway and sixty foot frontage on Susquehanna Street. The front of the building would have a portico with round columns made of brick, covered with a cement resembling stone. The building would be two stories - the ground floor to be used as a courtroom, the upper story to be divided into jury rooms. The entrance to the jury rooms was to be placed in the rear of the building. Separate buildings to house the commissioners' offices, and "Row" offices and jail would be erected behind the courthouse.

On February 7, 1850 the county awarded Blay & Root the contract for building the new courthouse and county office building. Work began immediately and completion was scheduled for the summer months. The grand jury on April 17, 1850 filed this report:

To the Honorable Court

The Grand Jury would respectfully report that they have examined the County Offices and Jail and are much gratified to find that the buildings have been put up in so substantial a manner, the records of the county they think perfectly secure from fire as the offices are in their opinion fireproof -- The Jail is constructed with a view to convenience, comfort and security of prisoners, much credit is due the commissioners, both for the plan of the Buildings, as well as for the energy with which they found their completion -- The cells of the Jail are of Good size and are kept in good order. The persons who have contracted to build the Court House are at work putting in the foundation and from the character which they, as well the commissioners, sustain for energy and perseverance, we feel warranted in anticipating an early completion.

A shortage of bricks, however, slowed the project. It was not until November of 1850 that the tin roof was installed.

On December 5, 1850, the *Mauch Chunk Gazette and Courier* reported:

There is a probability that the Court House can be used at the coming session of the Courts. The second story is nearly finished, very little remaining to be done, except to put on a second and third coat of plastering. The ceiling of the Court room is plastered with one coat and as soon as it is dry enough, which would be in a day or two of good drying weather, the plasterers can finish their part of the work, after which the carpenters can speedily lay the floor, put in the seats, and hang the doors, when the room will be in a condition to accommodate the Courts. The wood work we believe is all ready to be put in, and can be finished in a few days after the plasterers get out of the way.

It is certainly desirable that if possible the House should be so far finished as to accommodate the courts, at their next sessions.

It cannot of course be completed, but we think it can be so nearly that it can be used on the 30th inst.

The *Gazette* was right. On Monday, December 30, 1850, Judge Eldred convened court for the first time in Courthouse II. Although still in an unfinished state and the plaster in the ceiling damp, the building was a welcome relief for the court and counsel who had endured the cramped quarters in the public school.

Upon completion, Courthouse II not only served as a justice center but it was frequently used for public meetings, lectures and even entertainment. The *Mauch Chunk Gazette* reported to its readers regularly on stormy courtroom meetings of the leading political parties -- the Democrats, the Whigs, and the Know-Nothings. Popular figures in the world of science, health care and religion came to the courthouse to deliver lectures on physiology, hygiene and salvation. The portico provided a stage for all of the outdoor concerts of the Mauch Chunk Brass Band.

Courthouse II -- 1876

Photo of Mauch Chunk in 1850 from Flagstaff Mountain

By 1890 the county's population had grown to 38,624 and the economy was booming. Court activity increased, and Courthouse II's facilities became inadequate to meet the expanding caseload. There were constant complaints about the overcrowded courtroom. Noise from passing horse and carriages and railroad cars interrupted court proceedings. Insufficient space to file the civil, criminal, deed and estate records made conditions in the prothonotary's office chaotic. In 1889 a grand jury recommended that a new courthouse be built where the previous two had stood, but nothing happened. Three years of discussion, and vacillation by the county commissioners followed. There was no disagreement about the need for additional space but there was no consensus on how to provide it. Many groups wanted the courthouse moved to another location on Broadway in Mauch Chunk, removing it from the noise and bustle of the railroad station and busy intersection. The local newspapers favored keeping the original site, demolishing Courthouse II and adding an additional floor to the existing "Row Office" building. They bolstered their position by pointing out the clause in the county's deed which provided that if the courthouse was moved the land would revert to the LC&N Company.

Believed to be the last photo of the building which housed the county offices from 1850 to 1893.

Pictured outside: Associate Judge G. B. Price, Sheriff Henry P. LeVan, Treasurer E. M. Mulhearn,District Attorney Joseph Fisher,Register and Recorder James H. Handwerk, Prothonotary and Clerk of Courts G. W. Esser, and County Commissioners Daniel Cannonand C. J. Sendel. Pictured inside: Attorneys James Breslin and Frank Sharkey. (Photo circa 1892).

James Zellner, Mauch Chunk's professional photographer, took this notable picture of Courthouse II shortly before the structure was razed in 1893.

In March of 1893, when court business and paperwork in Courthouse II and the adjoining buildings had created gridlock, the commissioners voted to build a new courthouse on the same location as the previous ones and selected L. S. Jacoby of Allentown as the architect.

On March 29, 1893 Judge Dreher conducted the last proceedings in Courthouse II listening to a bitter piece of litigation involving the use of houses of worship of the Evangelical Church in Mauch Chunk and Lehighton. The court and the court-related offices temporarily moved to the second, third and fourth floors of the Lehigh Valley Railroad Building (now called the LC&N Company or Navigation Building). Demolition of Courthouse II and the adjoining building began and within five weeks the legal and social center of the county for almost half a century fell to the blows of the contractor's pick axes and sledge hammers.

Courthouse III

Courthouse III
(1894-)

Courthouse III on Hazard Square is an elegant and deliberately proud monument, and it imposes its tone on everything about it. It stands directly across from the red-bricked Navigation Building, the symbolic connection to all old Mauch Chunk power and money. Its lofty clock tower glows at night and dominates views from the top of Flagstaff mountain miles away, from any point on the main street where it is located, as well as from the living quarters of Asa Packer's mansion. In a town whose late nineteenth century prosperity was propelled by coal and railroads, Courthouse III deferentially faces both the old Panther Valley mine fields and the Lehigh Valley Railroad and LC&N company's former headquarters. It is the legacy of artists and artisans who believed that better buildings could make better people. The majestic exterior, the main courtroom - a perfect jewel box of Victorian design -, the intricately hewn woodwork, and the stained glass still speak to us. They say that we can aspire to something better.

In 1892, the county commissioners received fourteen bids for its construction. The lowest was $81,250 from Herman Riebe and the highest was $97,575.75 from Gromen Brothers Brick Mfg., of South Bethlehem, Pennsylvania. The commissioners selected Riebe who razed the old courthouse and began construction of Courthouse III on April 27, 1893.

Mauch Chunk citizens watched in awe as the justice center gradually emerged. Designed by L. S. Jacoby of Allentown, the building suggested a medieval castle featuring a stately tower, vaulted ceilings, turrets and ornate fireplaces. Its Romanesque revival exterior was constructed from a sandstone quarried at Rockport in the northern part of Carbon County.

The use of Rockport stone represented a change order in the original specifications and its first application on a major building. The *Mauch Chunk Democrat* of August 5, 1893 praised the choice of a local stone:

> *The new Carbon County Court House cannot fail to develop and extensively advertise one of the most valuable stone quarries for building purposes in the country, located at Rockport, in this county. . . . When the original contract was made for the erection of the Court House no one seemed to think of the Rockport stone only twelve miles up the Lehigh, and Hummelstown was naturally agreed to on account of its reputation. Then some one called special attention to the beauty and quality of the Rockport stone, and after enquiry as to the capacity of the quarry, the commissioners and contractor mutually agreed to change from Hummelstown to Rockport. The stone is much harder than the Hummelstown and requires more labor to dress, but the cost of transportation is*

> *correspondingly less and therefore the total expense of building is no greater on occount [sic] of the change, whilst the main wall of the building will be far superior both as to durability and beauty. It is already public opinion that our new court house will be one of the most beautiful buildings of its kind in the state, and it will be chiefly the Rockport stone that will make it so. It is a very cheerful purple-brown color.*

A four-sided clock adorned the belfry. French plate illuminated dials, seven feet long, surrounded by ornamental iron frame, provided the time of day. A 2,122-pound bell, cast in 1844 at McShare's Bell Foundry of Baltimore, Maryland, was installed in the clock tower. Two forty-pound striking hammers tolled the bell.

The bell had three uses: it sounded the hours of the day; twelve peals announced the opening of court sessions; thirteen rings preceded a jury's verdict on a murder charge. It has not been used since the early 1940s.

A steam boiler ran the Sturdevant heating system. An air conditioning system, one of the first installed in Carbon County, was constructed in the courthouse basement. The huge unit drew cool air from a shady passage between the walls of the courthouse and the neighboring Mauch Chunk National Bank. The air was drawn into the building and circulated by a huge fan powered by a ponderous electric motor. Before it passed through a labyrinth of sheet metal ducts, the air was filtered and further chilled by a constant stream of water. (The system never worked well. It created moisture problems, made some offices unbearably hot and, on occasion, drew noxious gas into the courthouse. In 1940, it was shut down by order of the county commissioners.)

Inside, Minton tile imported from England graced its imposing hallways. The interior walls were covered with Adamant wall plaster, a finish which was brand new to Northeast Pennsylvania. A multicolor stained glass portrait of the Goddess of Justice looked down regally from the ceiling in the main courtroom. Ornate English oak wainscotting, finely cut and beautifully hued by a Lehighton woodmaking firm, lined the courtroom walls. Lighting was provided by gas burners, chandeliers and over 700 light bulbs. For purely decorative purposes, two oak fireplaces were built into the front corners of the courtroom. Above the judge's bench an ornate wooden spindle peacock fan added to the stately ambience.

Courthouse III was completed in May of 1894, its final costs totaling $125,000. County officials took possession of their respective offices on May 12, 1894. All of the row offices and the sheriff's office were located on the first floor of the new courthouse. The judge's chambers and the library faced the courtroom on the second floor where the district attorney's offices are presently located.

Courthouse III as seen from Mansion House Hill -- 1900

President Judge Allen W. Craig and Associate Judges Samuel B. Price and Daniel Rouse convened the first session of court in Courthouse III on May 15, 1894. Much to the surprise and dismay of all members of the bar who had gathered for the occasion, there were no ceremonies to mark the historic event. Judge Craig merely directed Prothonotary David S. Watkins to make a record of the holding of court in the new building. He then stepped down from the bench and a visiting judge took his place to handle several routine petitions from which Judge Craig had recused himself.

There are two marble markers at the Broadway entrance of the courthouse, one for each of the two board of commissioners elected during the construction of the new courthouse. County Commissioners Henry Miller, Daniel Cannon, and J. C. Sendel were in office when the decision was made to build Courthouse III, and they oversaw the construction. William B. Anthony, Hugh H. McBride, and Morris T. Trexler, who were elected on November 9, 1893, had the responsibility of monitoring the completion of the building and furnishing it. Miller, Cannon and Sendel who planned and built the courthouse were voted out of office because cost overruns angered the county electorate.

Temple of Justice -- 1900

Courthouse III Addition

In 1937, the combination of growth in the county population and the attendant increase in county business and paperwork spurred a move for additional space. The fact that there was federal money available to construct and expand government buildings played a substantial role in the commissioners' decision to erect an annex to the courthouse. The county purchased the home of Robert Klotz, which was located to the rear of the courthouse, and dismantled it. The addition to Courthouse III was undertaken by the Carty Construction Company of Phillipsburg, New Jersey and completed by the end of 1937. The total cost of the building was $113,519 with the Public Works Administration contributing $44,166.

The county commissioners and the election bureau moved their offices to the first floor of the annex early in 1938. The president judge's chambers, the court stenographer and probation offices were relocated on the second floor next to the spacious new law library. A parking lot to the rear of the addition took care of increased parking needs. The architects who designed the annex were H. T. Rinker and M. R. Kiefer. Construction was approved by County Commissioners James W. Bradley, Horace F. Keat, James D. Kistler (who died during construction) and Guerney E. Heiney.

Second Courtroom

Courtroom II

In 1980, in a cooperative effort between County Commissioners Charles E. Wildoner, Albert U. Koch and Bud Angst and President Judge John P. Lavelle, a second courtroom was created on the third floor of the courthouse. Judge Lavelle persuaded the commissioners that a second judge would be needed in the near future and an additional courtroom would be a prudent step in preparing for this inevitable event. Using funds obtained from the sale of the old county home for the elderly in Laurytown and Federal IV D funds, a beautiful cherry wood panelled courtroom designed by Charles F. Kain of Jenkintown was installed and furnished replacing the run down arbitration room. For twelve years, the county commissioners conducted their weekly public meetings there. In 1992 when Judge Richard W. Webb took office, this room became his official courtroom and is known as Courtroom II.

Restoration of Main Courtroom

For more than ten years, Judge Lavelle lobbied the county commissioners to restore the faded beauty of the main courtroom. Time and neglect had taken a heavy toll. The wainscotting had become dark and blistered and the benches and chairs were in dire need of repair. Plaster was falling from the ceiling and the carpeting was frayed and torn. In 1993, Commissioners Dean D. W. DeLong, Thomas Gerhard, and John Mogilski agreed to provide $96,000 in county funds to refurbish the main courtroom. Mark Reda Construction of Easton was the low bidder for the wood and bench restoration. After six months of down-and-dirty grinding and wiping, Jeff Felber and John Blanchfield of Fascination, Inc. artfully stripped down and restained the woodwork and the court benches. By November of 1993, the work was completed. The historical integrity of the courtroom was preserved. Hager Furniture of Palmerton installed new burgundy carpeting throughout the courtroom. William J. Vogt of Kulpmont, Pennsylvania painstakingly took down the 2764 stained glass piece skylight, replaced 852 pieces and installed all new lead binding. With a $10,000 contribution from the Carbon County Bar Association, the jury chairs on both sides of the courtroom were recovered, three new judicial chairs were purchased and eight new chairs for lawyers were added inside the bar of the courtroom. George A. Shutack made a generous contribution of $8250 to restore the balcony benches. Judge Lavelle and his wife Attorney Marianne S. Lavelle filled a long-standing need by providing $2000 to construct and install a mobile lawyers' lectern for the courtroom.

Courthouse III is framed by Navigation Building (L) Asa Packer Mansion and Harry Packer Mansion (R) in 1987 photograph by Walter Kraus.

Stain glass window depicting Lady Justice in Main Courtroom

Main Courtroom after restoration in 1993 evokes Shakespeare's tribute to beauty "Age cannot wither her nor custom stale her infinite variety"[49] *Shakespeare, William. Antony and Cleopatra. Act. II, Scene II, Line 243.*

CHAPTER VII

CARBON COUNTY JAIL

In March of 1853, a Carbon County grand jury examining the Mauch Chunk jail built in 1850 reported that they found it "not safe for the retention of prisoners." They recommended "the building of an additional wall outside the western wall, to be three (3) feet in thickness at the bottom and two and one-half (2½) feet at the top."

In 1855, another grand jury found the jail "filthy and uncomfortable." They went on to report:

> *It is a reproach that such a condition of things should so long have been permitted to exist; that men, some perhaps innocent of crime, are obliged to be incarcerated in a place of which language is inadequate to convey a proper description. Former Grand Juries have presented its condition, its absence of all necessary comforts and decencies, to which apparently no heed has been given.*

For twelve years the movers and shakers in the county seat discussed and debated the unsanitary conditions and lack of security in the jail. In 1865, Mauch Chunk community leaders demanded a safe new jail. The county commissioners responded by negotiating for the purchase of several lots on Broadway. Their action was vigorously opposed by the grand jury which reported to the court at its January 1865 session:

> *[We] have learned with regret that the County Commissioners have either purchased or contracted for the purchase of four (4) lots on Broadway Street in the Borough of Mauch Chunk with the intention to locate and build thereon a new county jail; that they unitedly protest against the said purchase, location and removal of the jail in view of the fact that the County owns the rear part of the lot upon whose front the Mauch Chunk Bank Building is situated and which rear parcel of lot is contiguous and adjoining the present jail and closure; and we protest the more strenuously against such action by the Commissioners because the County has been lately and is at present greatly burdened with extraordinary taxation; and we recommend that the Commissioners suspend any further outlays in reference to such removal, and that they make no more outlays at present than are absolutely necessary upon the present jail or the County offices to keep them in safe or good order.*

Because of this opposition, the county abandoned the new jail project. It was not revived until four years later. On February 17, 1869, the commissioners bought from the LC&N Company lots numbers 90, 92, 94, 96 and 98 on the north side of Broadway as a site

Bastille of Broadway -- Carbon County Jail -- built in 1871

for the new jail. Edward Haviland, a well-regarded Allentown architect, was selected and he promptly prepared plans for a prison that would house forty prisoners. Charles Mendron and Henry Bowman early in 1869 offered the low bid to build the jail for $66,750. Their proposal was accepted. A contract was made on May 18 and construction began. Cost overruns stirred up controversies between the contractors and the commissioners and by early September both contractors quit. Bowman later agreed to carry on the work at a fixed salary until February 1, 1871 when he made a second contract to complete the jail for $25,500. Payments to the time of making this contract were over $102,000. The final cost of the jail was $127,000.

When the jail was completed in 1871, the fortress like building with twenty inch stone walls surrounded by a twenty foot high stone enclosure exuded security. The citizens of Carbon County finally had a place to house criminals and keep their streets safe. What they could not possibly know was that their "Bastille of Broadway" was, within the decade, to be the scene of seven hangings and the recipient of a hand print which has become one of the enduring mysteries of Carbon County history.

Day of the Rope

The largest mass execution in the history of the Commonwealth of Pennsylvania took place on June 21, 1877. In the hard coal regions it is known as the "Day of the Rope." Eleven men were hanged almost simultaneously between the hours of ten in the morning and high noon -- six at the Pottsville jail, four at the Mauch Chunk jail, and one at the Wilkes Barre jail. At Mauch Chunk, Michael J. Doyle, Edward Kelly and Alexander Campbell were executed for the murder of mine boss John P. Jones in Lansford. John "Yellow Jack" Donahue went to the gallows for the killing of Morgan Powell, a mine boss in Summit Hill. Only Campbell was a resident of Carbon County.

A detachment of Easton Greys, eighty strong, in full battle gear and headed by a drum corps, marched up Broadway at about eight o'clock and deployed around the perimeter of the jail. Sheriff J. W. Raudenbush had asked the Governor to send in the militia because he heard rumors of attempts to free the prisoners by their friends. Judge Dreher issued a court order directing that all taverns and saloons be closed for the day. A huge crowd, many of them related to the condemned men, gathered near the entrance steps while several hundred curious onlookers circled the jail. Sheriff Raudenbush, anticipating the huge crowd, had printed up 150 admission passes. At ten o'clock guards admitted fifty reporters, the prosecuting attorneys General Albright, Frank W. Hughes and Edward Siewers, Judge Dreher, who had pronounced the death sentences, defense attorneys Daniel Kalbfus, Edward Jones, the brother of John P. Jones, and citizens with enough political connections to obtain passes. The gallows had been erected in the corridor between the balconies of the jail opposite Campbell's cell. The *New York Graphic* sent their best artist

THE DAY OF THE ROPE - JUNE 21, 1877

The Easton Greys enter Mauch Chunk

Sorrow and solitude: scenes before the hangings

The Jail at Mauch Chunk

Newspaper artist captures the events and the mood in Mauch Chunk from *The Daily Graphic*: New York, Friday, June 22, 1877.

Execution of Thomas P. Fisher in the Mauch Chunk Jail for the murder of Morgan Powell on March 28, 1878

to record the scene at Mauch Chunk. Chairs were strategically arranged along the corridor at ground level for good viewing by the observers.

By 10:30 the preparations were completed and the four prisoners, each accompanied by his priest, were led from their cells and ascended the steps to the gibbet. After praying for the doomed men, the priests departed and Sheriff Raudenbush turned to Alex Campbell:

"Alexander Campbell, do you have anything to say?"

"I forgive everybody." Campbell replied.

"Michael Doyle, do you have anything to say?"

"I beg the forgiveness of God whom I have offended and the forgiveness of all those I have injured."

Donahue was then asked if he had any last words. He shook his head, shrugged his shoulders and said "I have nothing to say."

Nineteen--year-old Edward Kelly was the last to speak. "May God forgive me and grant me mercy." he said. "If I listened to my priest I wouldn't be here today."

Two Coal and Iron policemen handcuffed the men behind their backs, adjusted the ropes around their necks and placed white hoods over their heads. On a prearranged signal, Sheriff Raudenbush pulled on the rope to spring the trap door and in a millisecond the four men were suspended in midair, spinning around wildly. It took a full fifteen minutes before the coroner pronounced the last of them dead. These were the first executions in Carbon County.

Hand on the Wall of Cell No. 17

Throughout his trials and incarceration, Alexander Campbell, the forty-year-old Lansford hotel owner and liquor distributor, vigorously proclaimed his innocence. George Korson, in his *Minstrels of the Mine Patch: Songs and Stories of the Anthracite Industry*, which was published in 1938, wrote:

> *Several months later, when his appeals for a new trial had been denied by the higher courts, Campbell heard the sheriff read his death warrant. Then he rose to his full height -- he was a big, powerfully built man -- and declared: "It's hard to die innocent, but I shall not be the first. God knows that I am innocent of any crime, and the people know it, and the Commonwealth knows it."*

Campbell, according to Korson, continued to deny his guilt right up to the moment when the sheriff came to bring him to the scaffold:

> *As the sheriff approached him, Campbell said brokenly, but with evident deep sincerity -- "I am innocent. I swear I was nowhere near the scene of the crime."*

> *And then, as if to impress the sheriff with the truth of his protest, Campbell bent over, ground his right hand in the dust on the cell floor, and dragging his ball and chain after him, took a long stride towards the wall. Then stretching himself to the full height, he smote the wall with his large hand. "There is the proof of my words" he said. "That mark of mine will never be wiped out. There it will remain forever to shame the county that is hanging an innocent man."*

Campbell's handprint remains on the wall of Cell No. 17 to this day and has become one of the enduring legends of Carbon County.

In 1930, Sheriff Robert L. Bowman decided to put an end to the legend of the "Hand on the Wall." One night he brought the county road gang into the jail and had them tear out the wall that bore the bizarre shadow of a human hand. When the rubble was clear, the workers put in a new wall and covered it with fresh plaster. Sheriff Bowman, who supervised the work, retired for the night confident that he had removed forever the Irish "miracle." When he awoke and visited the cell the next day, he was shocked to see that the fresh plaster was marred by the vague outline of the hand. By evening the palm of a hand was clearly visible on the cell wall.

In 1960, Sheriff Charles Neast, as was the custom up to that time, took up residence in the jail. To test the legend of the hand, he covered it with green latex paint. The shadow hand, however, re-emerged and became clearly visible again. Ferdinand "Bull" Herman, a turn-key at the jail during the painting, observed the reappearance of the hand silhouette and liked to point it out to the many curious visitors of Cell 17. Until recently, when the old prison became overcrowded, Cell No. 17 was a popular tourist attraction in the county, especially for relatives of former miners and Northeast Pennsylvanians of Irish heritage.

Governor's Reprieve Fails to Halt Hangings

The final "Mollie" executions in the Carbon jail on January 14, 1879 produced a riot when the Governor's decision to halt the hangings arrived too late. Charles Sharpe and James "Hairy Man" McDonnell, both miners and members of the Ancient Order of Hibernians, were convicted of participating in the 1871 gang murder of George Smith, superintendent of the Audenried Colliery. Although both men steadfastly denied their guilt, they were both found guilty in separate trials in 1878 and Judge Dreher sentenced both men to death by hanging on January 14, 1879. Francis Longstreet, their youthful defense attorney, obtained a last minute reprieve of six days from Governor John Frederick Hartranft at 9:30 A.M. on the day of the hanging and the Governor sent a telegram to the sheriff of Carbon County notifying him of the stay of execution. Philip Laudenslager, the telegraph operator at the Mauch Chunk Railroad station, received the telegram at 10:37 A.M. and made a mad dash up Broadway to the jail to deliver the telegram. While he was banging on the front door, Sheriff J. W. Raudenbush sprung the trap door and Sharpe and O'Donnell dropped to their deaths. News of the last minute reprieve spread like a flash fire through the county. Angry mobs descended on the jail threatening the life of Raudenbush. Father Bunce, Sharpe's pastor of the Immaculate Conception parish, persuaded the *Mauch Chunk Gazette* to print a public notice exonerating the sheriff from any fault and helped restore order to Mauch Chunk. These hangings closed the era of the "Mollie Maguires" in Carbon County and were emblematic of the violence and dubious justice that accompanied the drive to crush the efforts of some of the members of the Ancient Order of Hibernians to bring trade unionism to the hard coal regions.

Last Execution at Carbon Jail

The final decade of the nineteenth century witnessed the last execution in Carbon County. On March 26, 1891 Oliver William Stangley was hanged in the county jail for the murder of Sybilla Walbert in Weatherly on October 12, 1889.

The crime which brought Stangley to the gallows was a senseless killing by an obviously senseless man. Stangley had a long history of mental illness and retardation and had been confined in a mental hospital for some time. After being disowned and thrown out by his own family, he was befriended by the Walberts and became a tenant in their home. Angered by Mrs. Walberts constant prodding to obtain employment, Stangley shot her in the kitchen of her home during an argument. His trial[50] in April of 1890 drew little public or media attention. District Attorney Joseph Fisher, assisted by William Rapsher and Michael Cassidy, conducted the prosecution. Judge Dreher appointed Edward Mulhearn, Frederick Bertolette and Laird Barber to represent the indigent Stangley without compensation. The prosecution relied on Stangley's confession made to Sheriff Hiram Levan shortly after his arrest. Despite his skeletal appearance and obvious mental instability, the insanity defense presented by Stangley's counsel failed to impress the jury. He was convicted of first degree murder and Judge Samuel Dreher quickly rejected the post trial motions and pronounced the death sentence. There was no appeal.

The hanging attracted far more attention than the trial proceedings. Six hundred people from all parts of Carbon and neighboring counties poured into Mauch Chunk by train and carriage with tickets to see a man legally killed. Sheriff Hiram P. Levan had to turn down another 600 requests for official passes to attend the execution. The *Mauch Chunk Gazette* and the *Mauch Chunk Democrat* told the tale of the rope in minute

[50]*Commonwealth v. Oliver Stangley, 1 January Term 1890.*

detail devoting three full columns to the story from Stangley's last meal to his internment. They pointed out that the scaffold was the same one which was used for the "Mollies," the only other hangings in the history of the county.

The *Mauch Chunk Gazette* of April 3, 1891 concluded its lengthy coverage of the execution with high praise for the sheriff:

> *Sheriff Levan is being highly complimented on the excellent manner in which the execution was carried out. It was a skillful hanging, and justice was tempered with mercy by the law's officers. Everything inside of the jail was all that could be desired, and the best order prevailed throughout the entire proceedings. The desire to see the hanging was great, and the actions of the mob on the outside of the jail could not in any way reflect on the sheriff. Everything attending the execution was carefully arranged, and carried out with out a flaw. Many persons have already notified Sheriff Levan that if they ever get to the scaffold their only wish is to have him hang them with the same skill as he showed when Stangley was swung into eternity.*

Big Martin's Double Escape

The murder of Mary Yanesick by pistol shot in front of her boarding home in Lansford on July 20, 1903 drew a great deal of public attention and outrage. Although "Big Martin" Leskoski, a thirty-three-year-old wanderer, was convicted of the crime, he not only avoided the hangman's noose, he also gained his freedom by escaping twice from the county jail. It is an incredible story and one which red-faced Sheriff James Rothermel and Sheriff William Reber, his successor, had a difficult time living down.

"Big Martin's" trial[51] in January of 1904 before Judge Heydt and a Carbon County jury played out for five days before a packed courtroom. District Attorney Frank P. Sharkey assisted by Edward M. Mulhearn represented the Commonwealth. Nathan M. Balliet, James Breslin, Horace DeYoung Lentz and Robert A. Heberling defended Leskoski. The key witness was a thirteen-year-old boy who said he saw "Big Martin" shoot Mrs. Yanesick from a distance of about fifty feet. Four residents of the boarding home testified that they saw the defendant leave the house with something wrapped in a red handkerchief just before they heard the shooting. The victim positively identified Leskoski as the man who shot her before she died. "Big Martin" denied that he was the shooter and implied that Mrs. Yanesick was shot by a jealous boyfriend. On January 16, 1904, the jury convicted him of first degree murder and Judge Heydt remanded him to the jail while his attorneys filed motions seeking a new trial. His first escape took place two months later.

---

[51]*Commonwealth v. Martin Leskoski, 10 October Sessions 1903.*

On April 1, 1904 at about 2:30 in the morning, Leskoski rang the bell which was used by prisoners when they needed attention. Sheriff Rothermel was out of town. His wife and daughter Belle Rothermel, who lived in the prison with the sheriff were alone at the time. Belle Rothermel answered the ring. Leskoski told her that he wanted two cents worth of coal oil for his lamp. As she opened the door to get the bottle, he pushed her inside the jail corridor, wrestled the keys from her, and made his escape. By the time the shaken Mrs. Rothermel and her daughter could sound the alarm, Leskoski had disappeared into the woods behind the prison.

Typical prisoner's cell in the Carbon County Prison on Broadway in Jim Thorpe.

It was not until February of 1909 that "Big Martin" was located in Butte City, Montana, living under an assumed name with his wife and family. Sheriff James Rothermel and his attorney Eugene O. Nothstein immediately entrained to Montana and arranged for the extradition of Leskoski to Pennsylvania and the Mauch Chunk jail. Within a month, Judge Heydt heard argument on his motion for a new trial, which had been pending since his escape. On March 27, 1909 Judge Heydt refused a new trial and immediately imposed the death sentence. While his appeal to the Supreme Court of Pennsylvania was pending, "Big Martin" escaped from the county jail again. This time he sawed through the lock on his cell door and the bars of one of the jail windows. Somehow he squeezed through the narrow window and slid down a drain pipe to the ground and freedom. During the years that followed, there were many alleged sightings of "Big Martin" and false reports about his death, but he was not actually found until early 1917 living in Arizona. After extraditing him back to Carbon County, the Governor ordered Big Martin's execution on July 19, 1917. The county commissioners had the gallows erected and poised for his execution. But James M.

Breslin, Leskoski's tenacious defense lawyer, came to his rescue by winning a stay of execution from the Board of Pardons. Then to the dismay of D.A. Frank Sharkey, Breslin obtained a commutation of Leskoski's sentence to a life sentence and finally won him a pardon.

The most recent and by far the most implausible escape from the jail occurred in August of 1979. William O. Williams, a 150-pound young man with a penchant for fast cars and an aversion to the motor vehicle laws, was serving a 160-day sentence for failure to pay motor vehicle violation fines when he decided he wanted to visit his girlfriend. Aided and abetted by two fellow inmates who covered his naked body with shaving soap and pulled the window from its frame in his jail cell, Williams slipped his small body through the 5-3/4" x 33" opening and slid down a sheet and blanket to the wall and escaped for almost ten days.

New County Jail

In this year of the Sesquicentennial, 122 years after its construction, the "Bastille of Broadway" is still Carbon County's criminal detention facility. Sheriff Peter Hoherchak discontinued the practice of living in the jail in 1976 because every bit of available space was needed to house the prison population. With a round-the-clock staff of well trained correctional officers and a great deal of ingenuity and hard work, Sheriff Peter P. Hoherchak and Warden William Juracka keep the old fortress running smoothly. It has been found "clean, sanitary, and well operated but overcrowded and unfit for prisoners" by the State Department of Corrections for the past ten years. The prison population has hovered at about sixty since 1985. The tiny cells which were originally designed for men five feet, two inches tall must now accommodate two prisoners in each cell.

Mandated by the Commonwealth to either build a new prison or close the old jail, the county commissioners have purchased a 180 acre tract of land to build a new prison complex in the Borough of Nesquehoning, just off Route 93. Preliminary plans for the new prison have already been drawn and approved. They call for 185 beds: 92 in general population, 20 in maximum security, 42 in a work release unit, 20 in temporary classification cells, 8 in restricted housing cells and 3 in secure medical observation rooms. The estimated cost of the prison buildings is a little over $6 million. In an interesting repeat of history, the commissioners faced the same opposition to the location of the prison as did the commissioners to the present jail in 1865. Citizen groups and officials in Lehighton, Jim Thorpe and Nesquehoning protested the building of a new jail in their towns. Completion of the new corrections complex, according to the commissioners, will be in November of 1994.

CHAPTER VIII

PAST PRESIDENT JUDGES

The president judge fills dual roles in the county judicial system -- one as a decision maker, the other as principal policy maker for the local court. As a decider of cases, the judge acts as an arbiter of disputes between conflicting interests. Sometimes it may be the state charging an individual with a crime; sometimes it may be an individual claiming money damages against a big corporation for a negligently manufactured product; sometimes the court must say "yes" or "no" to government action. No matter what the dispute the judge presides referee like over the disputants or makes the ruling which brings the matter to judgment. In all cases, the judge must apply the law as declared in the decisions of the Appellate Courts, pay deference to the legislative process and refrain from trying to provide a remedy for every social or political ailment.

As policy maker, the president judge is responsible for overseeing and managing every aspect of the administration of justice -- assigning and moving the caseload, obtaining the funding necessary to operate the court system and seeing that it is spent wisely and efficiently. Currently, the president judge directs the following court departments: adult probation and parole, juvenile court, domestic relations, bureau of collections, jury selection and court administration. These departments employ a total of thirty-five employees.

The court over which the president judge presides is a trial court called the Court of Common Pleas. It sits at the base of the pyramidal Pennsylvania court system with the Supreme Court of Pennsylvania at the peak of the pyramid. Between the Common Pleas Court and the Supreme Court are two Appellate Courts -- the Commonwealth Court and the Superior Court. They review cases appealed to them from the sixty common pleas courts which serve the sixty-seven counties of Pennsylvania. Essentially, the Appellate Courts are courts of error. They decide if the trial court committed some kind of legal mistake, for example, in admitting evidence which the law does not permit or in erroneously applying the law in deciding a case.

Under the 1968 Constitution, the courts of common pleas have "unlimited original jurisdiction in all cases except as may otherwise be provided by law." The judge, therefore, presides over all criminal cases, family matters which include custody, divorce, adoption, non-support, estate matters and a host of miscellaneous cases including protection from abuse, injunctions, tax assessment appeals and termination of parental rights and every type of civil action. Appellate Court jurisdiction of the common pleas courts extends to appeals from final orders of the minor judiciary and appeals from certain state and most local government agencies.

Despite recent media campaigns and reformers' calls to have judges put on the bench by a so-called merit selection process, all major court judges are elected by the voters in Pennsylvania for ten-year terms. Vacancies are filled by gubernatorial appointment, subject to senate confirmation; such appointees are required to run for election in the first municipal election more than ten months after their appointment. A "merit retention" provision allows judges to run for re-election on a "Yes"-"No" vote without ballot reference to political affiliation. The idea behind this provision was to remove judges from the pressures of the political arena once they serve their first term in office. Mandatory retirement age for all judges is seventy although retired judges may continue to serve by appointment of the Supreme Court in order to ease court backlogs.

Henry J. Abraham, the distinguished James Hart professor of Government and Foreign Affairs at the University of Virginia has suggested as de minimis qualification guidelines for judges:

> *One, demonstrated judicial temperament. Two, professional expertise and competence. Three, absolute personal as well as professional integrity. Four, an able, agile, lucid mind. Five, appropriate professional educational background or training. Six, the ability to communicate clearly, both orally and in writing, especially the latter.*[52]

The following profiles of the estimable past president judges of Carbon County reveal that each judge brought to the bench, in varying degrees, these qualifications.

[52]Seventh Annual Address to the Supreme Court Historical Society (1982).

STATISTICAL DATA ON JUDGES OF CARBON COUNTY

JUDGE	VITAL DATES	COMMUNITY FROM WHICH ELECTED	POLITICAL AFFILIATION	DATES OF SERVICE	JUDICIAL DISTRICT
1. Nathaniel B. Eldred	b. January 12, 1795 d. January 27, 1867	Bethany, Wayne County	Democrat	1843-1844 1849-1853	Twelfth; Twenty-Second
2. Luther Kidder	b. November 19, 1808 d. September 30, 1854	Wilkes-Barre, Luzerne County	Democrat	1844-1849	Twenty-First
3. James M. Porter	b. January 6, 1793 d. December 12, 1862	Easton, Northampton County	Independent	1854-1855	Twenty-Second
4. Thomas S. Bell	b. October 22, 1800 d. June 6, 1861	West Chester, Chester County	Know-Nothing	1855 (8 months)	Twenty-Second
5. George R. Barrett	b. March 31, 1815 d. 1884	Curwensville, Clearfield County	Democrat	1853-1854 1855-1870	Twenty-Second
6. Samuel S. Dreher	b. April 10, 1824 d. June 28, 1893	Stroudsburg, Monroe County	Democrat	1870-1893	Twenty-Second; Forty-Third
7. John B. Storm	b. 1838 d. August 15, 1901	Stroudsburg, Monroe County	Democrat	1893 (6 months)	Forty-Third
8. Allen W. Craig	b. December 25, 1835 d. December 31, 1902	Little Gap	Democrat	1894-1901	Forty-Third
9. Horace D. Heydt	b. February 12, 1856 d. November 17, 1934	Lehighton	Republican	1901-1913	Fifty-Sixth
10. Laird H. Barber	b. October 25, 1848 d. February 16, 1928	Mauch Chunk	Democrat	1914-1928	Fifty-Sixth
11. William G. Thomas	b. November 27, 1871 d. August 11, 1947	Lansford	Republican	1928-1939	Fifty-Sixth
12. James C. McCready	b. February 13, 1889 d. January 16, 1967	Summit Hill	Republican	1940-1960	Fifty-Sixth
13. Albert H. Heimbach	b. September 18, 1907 d. July 28, 1993	Palmerton	Republican	1960-1978	Fifty-Sixth
14. John P. Lavelle	b. February 18, 1931	Lehighton	Democrat	1978-	Fifty-Sixth
15. Richard W. Webb	b. April 29, 1944	Palmerton	Democrat	1992-	Fifty-Sixth

Judge Nathaniel B. Eldred

VICTORIAN ERA BENCH
JUDGES OF THE TWELFTH, TWENTY-FIRST, TWENTY-SECOND AND FORTY-THIRD JUDICIAL DISTRICTS

Nathaniel B. Eldred
President Judge (1843-1844; 1849-1853)

Nathaniel Bailey Eldred was a plain speaking, common man whose love of people led him to an uncommon life of public service. He enjoyed productive careers as a lawyer and legislator before he became a judge. Twice he declined prestigious government positions to spend more time with his family. During his time on the bench, he came to be viewed as a model for the best in Pennsylvania judges -- intelligent, decent, and fair. These qualities marked his five years as Carbon County's first president judge.

The son of Elisha and Mary Eldred of Dolsontown, Orange County, New York, Eldred was born on January 12, 1795. He received a rudimentary education in the schools near his family's residence and educated himself by reading every book he could get his hands on. At the age of sixteen, he went to Milford in Pike County where he set his sights on becoming a lawyer. In 1811, he began to "read law" in the office of Daniel Dimmick, a leading lawyer in Milford, and completed his legal apprenticeship under Edward Mott, a deputy attorney general (prosecuting attorney) for the county. On January 27, 1817 on motion of Mott, Eldred was admitted to the Wayne County Bar. He immediately took up residence and began a private law practice in Bethany, Wayne County in April of 1818.

Honest, likeable and compassionate, he had the qualities people wanted when they had a legal problem. As his law practice grew, his reputation as a good advocate reached the Wayne County politicians who enthusiastically launched him into a political career.

In his first bid for public office, Eldred ran successfully for a seat in the General Assembly in 1822, and was then elected to four successive one-year terms. His homespun humor and industry won him many friends in the Legislature and he would have been elected speaker of the house, had he not asked to withdraw his name for the position. He was appointed state canal commissioner in 1825 by Governor John Andrew Schulze and elected by the Legislature to the board of commissioners that managed the Delaware River.

It was his life as a judge, however, that enabled him to use all his talents and make his enduring mark in judicial history. For nearly twenty years, Eldred held a seat on the bench. From 1835 to 1842 he presided over various judicial districts in the western part of Pennsylvania. He became Carbon County's first president judge in 1843 when Governor David Porter appointed him to preside over the Twelfth Judicial District. His first term presiding over Carbon County lasted only a year. In April of 1844 Carbon with Schuylkill and Monroe was moved to the new Twenty-First Judicial District, where Senator Luther Kidder was appointed president judge. It is interesting to note that Luther Kidder introduced and guided the bill for this move through the Legislature and became its chief beneficiary.

In 1849, the Legislature transferred Carbon to a newly created Twenty-Second Judicial District with Monroe, Wayne and Pike counties. Governor William F. Johnston granted Eldred's wish to return with his family to his old home in Bethany, and appointed him to the Twenty-Second District's president judgeship. Judge Eldred then began his second term on the Carbon County Bench. In 1851, a constitutional amendment empowered voters to elect judges. Judge Eldred, a Democrat, received the support of both Whigs and Democrats and was elected president judge of the Twenty-Second Judicial District. Political supporters across the state wanted to place his name on the ballot for the Supreme Court of Pennsylvania but he declined to remain near his family.

Eldred liked to tell his friends that there were other judges who knew more about the law but he knew more about the consequences of the law and its effects on ordinary citizens. This shirt-sleeve, common sense approach to the law would often find expression in his charges to the jury. An illustration of this appears in Alfred Mathews' *History of Wayne, Pike and Monroe counties, Pennsylvania (1886)*:

> *While he was on the Dauphin County bench a case of assault and battery was tried before him. The evidence showed that while the defendant and his wife were walking on the streets in Harrisburg, a rowdy used some grossly insulting language toward the wife, whereupon the husband knocked him down. Judge Eldred's charge to the jury was substantially in the following terms: "Gentlemen of the jury, the defendant is indicted for an assault and battery on the prosecutor. You have learned from the evidence the character of the offence. In law, any rude, angry or violent touching of the person of another is an assault and battery, and is not justified by any provocation in words only. But if I was walking with my wife and a rowdy insulted her, I'd knock him down if I was big enough. Swear a constable." The verdict may be readily conjectured.*

The *Monthly Law Magazine*, a prominent legal journal of the time, gave high marks to Eldred upon his installation for a second term in 1852:

> *Judge Eldred's personal, political and judicial career has always been characterized by great consistency, independence, and integrity. He is a very*

> *straight forward man. Nature furnished him with good, sound, practical common sense, and more than an ordinary share of talents. These he has improved, in a long course of professional and public life, in which he has enjoyed the unlimited confidence of every one who knew him. He has now served on the bench longer than any judge in Pennsylvania, except Judge Gibson of the Supreme Court, and is esteemed by all who have practiced before him, as one of the ablest judges in the state.*
>
> *In his charges he is always desirous to reach the justice of the case, and puts the law and facts in so close and perspicuous a light to the jury, as to leave little room for mistake or misapprehension.*

Court minutes during his term of office show that Judge Eldred came to Carbon County for about a week, four times a year. To handle the trials and various motions and petitions, it was not unusual for him to conduct evening sessions. The *Carbon Gazette* of June 12, 1851 was impressed by his judicial performance:

> *Judge Eldred deserves the highest praise for the promptness, industry and impartiality with which the duties of the office are discharged. This we believe is an expression of the views of the entire community.*

A call to a position in the Electoral College for the 1852 Presidential Election interrupted Eldred's judicial duties. Then, in April of 1853, he decided to accept an appointment by President Franklin Pierce to head the Port of Philadelphia. He resigned the judgeship and closed his legal career.

Returning to his home in Bethany, he devoted himself to working on his farm and enjoying his grandchildren. Judge Eldred married twice. His first wife, Lucinda Jane Dimmick, the daughter of Daniel Dimmick, his preceptor, died in 1824. He and his second wife, Sarah M. Dimmick of Sullivan County whom he married on November 15, 1827, had three daughters and a son. Charles F. Eldred who followed in his father's footsteps was admitted to the Bar of Wayne County in 1861. Judge Eldred died on January 27, 1867 at the age of seventy-two survived by his wife Sarah, his son Charles Franklin and his three daughters, Mary Asenath Eldred, Lucinda Jane Eldred and Caroline Westcote Eldred.

Judge Luther Kidder

Luther Kidder
President Judge (1844-1849)

The son of Luther and Phoebe Kidder, Luther Kidder was a direct descendant of James Kidder of Sussex, England who came to New England in the 1640s. Born in Waterford, Vermont on November 19, 1808, he received his education and practiced law there until he and his parents moved to the Wyoming Valley in Luzerne County, Pennsylvania.

Kidder, an active Democrat, became part-owner of the *Susquehanna Democrat* in 1831. This paper specialized in scathing reviews and satirical comments about members of the Federalist Party, particularly during political elections.

Kidder was admitted to the Luzerne County Bar in 1833 and to the Monroe County Bar in 1837. From 1841 until 1844 he served in the Pennsylvania State Senate. In April of 1844 he introduced and shepherded through the Legislature the bill which put Carbon, Monroe and Schuylkill counties into the Twenty-First Judicial District. On October 23, 1844 Governor David Rittenhouse Porter appointed Luther Kidder president judge of the district which he was the prime mover to create.

Kidder Township in Carbon County was established in 1849. To honor Judge Kidder who presided on the Carbon Bench then, the township was named after him.

While Kidder was on the bench, the district's court activity grew geometrically. The caseload, coupled with a surge in the population of Schuylkill County convinced the Legislature to make Schuylkill County a separate judicial district. The Act of April 5, 1849 officially detached Carbon and Monroe counties from the Twenty-First Judicial District and transferred them to the Twenty-Second Judicial District. With that severance, Judge Kidder's service to Carbon and Monroe counties ended. He remained on the bench in Schuylkill County until 1851, when the Act of April 15, 1851, P.L. 648 made the office of president judge elective and the term of office ten years. In the first election under this act, Charles W. Hegins was elected president judge of Schuylkill County.

Luther Kidder married Martha Ann Scott, the daughter of Judge David Scott of Wilkes-Barre on October 13, 1835. He died on September 30, 1854 in Wilkes-Barre at the age of forty-six and was survived by his wife and son, Rev. Charles Holland Kidder.

Judge James M. Porter

James M. Porter
President Judge (1854-1855)

A towering political figure, a brilliant lawyer whose knowledge of the law was encyclopedic, and a dedicated and committed educator in the early nineteenth century, James Madison Porter served only a short time as Carbon County's third president judge. He is better known as the founder of Lafayette College in Easton and the best and brightest member of Pennsylvania's distinguished Porter family.

Porter was born on January 6, 1793 at "Selma," his father's farm near Norristown, Montgomery County, Pennsylvania. His father, General Andrew Porter, served in the Army during the Revolution, and at the end of the war, he was the colonel of the Pennsylvania Regiment of Artillery. He was renowned in the scientific world as a mathematician and astronomer. His mother, Elizabeth Parker Porter, was a remarkable woman who was self-educated and of exceptional intellect. Porter attributed his success as a scholar, writer and speaker to her influence and educational guidance. His siblings included Robert Porter, who was president judge of the Third Judicial District, David Rittenhouse Porter, who was Governor of Pennsylvania from 1839 through 1845, and George Bryan Porter, who served as Governor of the Michigan territory from 1832 to 1834.

The Porter boys received their rudimentary education at home from their father and mother. When he was nine, Judge Porter, with his brothers David and George, was placed in the charge of a private tutor in his parents' home which had an excellent library. After a year of tutoring, the boys became students in the Norristown Academy, but never went to college. In 1809, Porter's father was appointed surveyor general of Pennsylvania and, requiring help in the land office, put his son, James, to work as a clerk without compensation.

In December 1809, James entered the office of John Passmore, an attorney, and then prothonotary and clerk of the court of Lancaster County. Fascinated by the law, he left Passmore in January 1812 and moved to Reading to continue the study of law with his eldest brother Robert Porter, then president judge of the Third Judicial District. He did not remain long with his brother. In August of that same year, he was persuaded to assume the office of clerk of the district court of the city and county of Philadelphia, but continued studying law under the direction of Judge William Delaney. On April 24, 1813, he was admitted into practice in Philadelphia.

He immediately opened a law office in Philadelphia and developed a successful and lucrative law practice which extended into Chester, Montgomery, Delaware and Bucks counties.

He remained in Philadelphia until 1818, during which time he served in the Pennsylvania Militia. Then, Amos Ellmaker, attorney general of Pennsylvania, appointed him deputy attorney general (prosecuting attorney) of Northampton County, and Porter moved to Easton in April of that year, and there he resided for the rest of his life. He married Eliza Michler of Easton and together they had seven children.

In June of 1839, upon the resignation of Judge Calvin Blythe, Governor David R. Porter appointed James Madison Porter to be the president judge of the Twelfth Judicial District of Pennsylvania, composed of the counties of Dauphin, Schuylkill and Lebanon. Judge Porter remained on that bench only a short time, resigning in July of 1840 and returning to Easton to take up his law practice.

Early in March of 1843, he was invited by President John Tyler to take charge of the office of Secretary of War, but because of political opposition, he was not confirmed by the Senate and he returned to Easton. In 1844, he was defense counsel for William McKay in the first murder trial held in Carbon County and saved his client from the death penalty by winning a second degree murder conviction (See **First Murder Trial**, page 21).

Mathew S. Henry,[53] a contemporary biographer from the Lehigh Valley, after extolling his talents and accomplishments, recounted Porter's own rationale for his success:

> *In the year 1843 he received from Marshall College, as the free will offering of that institution, the degree of Doctor of Laws, which, he remarked, was the only college degree he had ever taken. He is a fine classical scholar, with an immense stock of general information, and his general reading is perhaps equal to that of most men in the country.*
>
> *How he has found time to acquire the minute knowledge which he seems to possess on almost every subject, is a marvel to all, and when some person spoke to him, not long since, in relation to his extensive attainments and general literature, he remarked, "that nature had blessed him with a very retentive memory, that his father was a man of science and general reading, and had given him a good education, and that his mother was a most remarkable woman for her general attainments, especially in classical literature, and had done everything to give him a taste for the English classics, and created in him an ambition, if possible, to equal her. That he had mixed much with the world and his professional brethren, and, therefore, little credit was due him personally, if he had reached mediocrity in his attainments, for he had been but the creature of the circumstances in which he had been placed.*

---

[53]Henry, Mathew Schropp. Historyof the Lehigh Valley. Easton, PA: Bixler & Corwin, 1860, p.423.

Judge Porter founded Lafayette College in 1826. He was the first president of its board of trustees, and for a quarter of a century, without compensation, lent his boundless energies and enormous talents to Lafayette as a trustee and a professor of Jurisprudence and Political Economy. He served several years as president of the Belvidere Delaware Railroad Company. From 1853 to 1856, while Asa Packer's work crews cut through the rough terrain and built the railroad bed between Mauch Chunk and Easton, Porter was the president of the Lehigh Valley Railroad Company.

In 1853, when Judge George R. Barrett declined to be a candidate for election, Porter, as an independent candidate, was elected to the office of president judge of the Twenty-Second Judicial District (Wayne, Pike, Monroe and Carbon counties) over Democratic Congressman Milo M. Dimmick of Stroudsburg. He served in the district from December 1, 1853 until March of 1855, when he resigned because of paralysis. Albeit briefly, he brought to the Carbon Bench a bright intellect, a compassionate heart, an even temperament and a wealth of experience. Porter returned to his law practice in Easton, but only in a limited way until his death on December 12, 1862 at the age of sixty-nine.

Judge Thomas S. Bell

Thomas S. Bell
President Judge (1855)

He served with distinction both as a Delaware County trial judge and Supreme Court Justice. But Thomas S. Bell was president judge in Carbon County for just eight months. His glittering judicial record and the advantage of incumbency could not overcome his identification with the hate-mongering political party called the "Know-Nothings." This party drew the ire of many voters, especially Irish Americans, because it advocated the election of only white-Protestant-Native- Americans and had fomented race riots in Philadelphia from 1836 to 1846. The district electorate voted Bell out of office the first time he appeared on the ballot.

Born in Philadelphia on October 22, 1800, Bell studied law in Easton under James Madison Porter and was admitted to the Chester County Bar six months before he was twenty-one and to the Philadelphia bar on April 14, 1821. Public service appealed to Bell and he served as prosecuting attorney from 1823 until 1828 and was a State Senator from Chester County in 1837 and 1838. On May 16, 1839, at the age of thirty-nine, the Governor appointed Bell president judge of the Fifteenth Judicial District comprising the counties of Delaware and Chester. Henry Ashmead in his *History of Delaware County* said "Bell adorned the Delaware County Bench by his learning and his courteous bearing to the Bar and public alike." He earned this posthumous encomium despite an occasional lapse into erratic decision making. On one occasion, he stirred up a storm of controversy by sentencing a ten-year-old Delaware County boy to a long term of imprisonment for stealing a small sum of money.

On November 18, 1846, Governor Francis R. Shunk appointed him an associate justice of the Pennsylvania Supreme Court. where he served under the stewardship of Chief Justice John Bannister Gibson. His opinions on the high court, addressing for the most part cases of debt and breach of contract, reflect his common sense approach to legal issues and a determination to move away from the common law stricture of form over substance. His tenure was brief, lasting only until December 1, 1851 when the office became elective. Bell then returned to private practice in West Chester.

Judge James M. Porter resigned his judgeship because of paralysis early in March of 1855, leaving a vacancy on the Carbon Bench. On the strong recommendation of Judge Porter, Bell's friend and mentor, Governor James Pollock, made an interim appointment of Bell as president judge on March 23, 1855. The 1855 judicial election was an unusual one. Despite the endorsement of Bell by both Judge Nathaniel B. Eldred and the lawyers of the district, the voters chose Democratic nominee George R. Barrett, who never made an appearance in the district and refused to campaign. With his defeat, Bell left public life and retired.Judge Bell married twice and died in Philadelphia on June 6, 1861.

Judge George R. Barrett

George R. Barrett
President Judge (1853-1854; 1855-1870)

Rejected for the judgeship by Democratic political leaders as an "outsider" in 1853, George Rodden Barrett reciprocated by totally ignoring them after they nominated him for president judge in 1855 and rode to victory on strong newspaper support.

Barrett was born in Curwensville, Clearfield County, Pennsylvania on March 31, 1815. After attending private school, he was apprenticed at the age of fifteen to learn the printing trade to William Bigler, the future Governor of the Commonwealth. Two years later he moved to Brookeville, Jefferson County, where he edited and published a newspaper called the *Jeffersonian*. In 1834 Barrett married Sarah Steadman of Lewisburg, Union County, a union which was both happy and prolific producing along the way ten children. In 1835, he began to study law under James F. Linn, Esq. in Lewisburg and at the same time edited the *Lewisburg Democrat*. After he was admitted to the Clearfield County Bar in 1836, he moved his family there to establish a law practice.

In 1837, he was appointed a deputy attorney general (prosecuting attorney) for Clearfield and Jefferson counties and in 1840 was elected to the first of his two terms in the State Legislature, where he served on the judiciary committee. While in the Legislature, he was a leading advocate for the law abolishing imprisonment for debt and was widely recognized as the man who won its adoption. After his second term, he returned to Clearfield County determined to abandon politics and practice law. His friend and neighbor, William Bigler, however, decided to run for Governor and Barrett took to the stump to support him in conventions, caucuses and before the electorate. Bigler's election as Governor brought Barrett back to public service. After the resignation of Judge Nathaniel B. Eldred in 1853, Governor Bigler appointed Barrett to fill the vacancy and at the age of thirty-eight he became president judge of the Twenty-Second Judicial District on April 29, 1853. But Barrett had to go to the electorate to keep the office. In 1851, the Legislature, for the first time, gave the people the power to elect judges in the Commonwealth.

Barrett's selection as judge by the Governor did not sit well with the district's politicians. Because Barrett resided in Clearfield County, the Democratic leaders of Carbon, Monroe, Pike and Wayne counties, which made up the Twenty-Second Judicial District, considered him a "carpetbagger" who was depriving a "home boy" from being judge. Foreshadowing judicial elections to come, politicians quickly tried to take control of who was to be elected. As election time approached, they began to promote popular Stroudsburg Congressman Milo Dimmick for the office and launched negative and nasty attacks on Barrett. Their angry antagonism intimidated Barrett and he decided not to be a candidate for judge in the election of 1853. But James Madison Porter, a prominent trial lawyer and law professor from Easton, upset the Democratic strategy by entering the judgeship race as an independent candidate. In a campaign that was more of a "mud bath" than a model of political discourse, Porter soundly beat Milo Dimmick and the district political leaders.

Embittered by this experience, Barrett again vowed to leave the political arena and never return. But after Porter resigned in 1855 because of paralysis and Thomas S. Bell was appointed as an interim judge, the Democrats, in a surprising about face, nominated Barrett as their candidate for president judge. A secret oath-bound organization known as the "Know-Nothings" nominated Bell. Barrett refused to campaign, saying that if the people wanted him for judge, he would serve. Barrett neither visited the district nor wrote a single letter asking voters to support his candidacy. The press loved his independence and his aloofness from partisan politics. In edition after edition, district newspapers urged voters to support him. Barrett won the election by over 3000 votes.

In 1865 he was nominated by both political parties and easily re-elected to a second term. Judge Barrett took great pride in the fact that, although his decisions were reviewed often, he was reversed by the Appellate Courts only thirteen times during his sixteen years on the bench. He attempted to resign as judge in 1869. Since Governor John White Geary had difficulty in finding a replacement, he asked Barrett to remain in office for a year. Judge Barrett retired permanently in January of 1871. He returned to private practice in Clearfield County with his son Walter and remained there until his death in 1884 at the age of sixty-nine.

A Clearfield County biographer summarized Judge Barrett's demeanor and legal ability:

> *Self-possessed, dignified, courteous, easy and graceful in his bearing, firm in his rulings, logical in his reasoning, kind and forbearing toward the profession generally, and the younger lawyers in particular, Mr. Barrett, during his presidency, acquired the deserved honor of being one of the ablest and most popular judges upon the bench.*

In the grandiose prose of an era known for its extravagance, a Carbon County grand jury filed the following tribute to Judge Barrett on October 4, 1870:

MEMORIAL OF THE GRAND JURY OF CARBON COUNTY TO THE HONORABLE GEORGE R. BARRETT ON THE OCCASION OF HIS RETIREMENT FROM THE BENCH

> *As the last grand inquest that will be convened to represent the County of Carbon and the earnest sentiments of her people in her courts of Justice during the term of her present Presiding Judge, the Honorable George R.*

Barrett, and in view of his resignation so soon to take effect, we cannot refrain from giving expression to our sentiments as a jury, and as we believe those of the mass of the people of Carbon County, marking that event. Seldom in the history of any Court of justice in the Commonwealth of Pennsylvania, or in the Government of the United States, has a presiding judge so uninterruptedly maintained the respect and confidence of a judicial constituency, so impressed a people with his personal worth and integrity of purpose under all circumstances and at all times as a man, or so continually exhibited in his official career all the excellencies of human character so essential in a judge and so important to the dignity of the law and to the safety of the citizen as is instanced in the honored person to whom this testimonial is inscribed. . . . May his life be prolonged to the extreme of years and the perfection of enjoyment amid the genial surroundings of private life. Thanking him personally for unbroken kindness and courtesy to this and former grand juries of the county, we request that this brief memorial may become part of the records of the county, and be handed down to other generations as the honest sentiment of this [Grand Jury]

Signed *W. L. Stiles*
Foreman.

Judge Samuel S. Dreher

Samuel S. Dreher
President Judge (1870-1893)

During his time on the bench, Samuel Stokes Dreher was one of the most widely known judges in the Commonwealth of Pennsylvania. The extensive press coverage of the "Mollie Maguire" trials over which he presided in Carbon County in 1876 and 1877 made his name a household word in Northeast Pennsylvania. His twenty-three years of continuous service on the bench has been the longest of all Carbon County judges and represented two decades of deep commitment to the legal system and unwavering devotion to the public weal.

He was born in Stroudsburg, Monroe County, Pennsylvania on April 10, 1824, the eldest of nine children of Michael H. Dreher, a tailor, and Elizabeth Dreher. His ancestors on both sides came from Germany. Judge Dreher's father imbued him with the idea of public service while serving several terms as Monroe County prothonotary, register and recorder, associate judge and commissioner's clerk. Dreher received his early education in the Stroudsburg public schools and in the old Stroudsburg Academy. At nineteen years of age, he became an apprentice in the law office of Milo M. Dimmick, a prominent Monroe County lawyer and political figure in Stroudsburg. During this apprenticeship, he clerked in the row offices of Monroe County, gaining valuable experience in the byzantine legal procedures of the time. On December 21, 1844, he married Miss Sally Phillips and they became the parents of six children.

Dreher was admitted to the Monroe County Bar in May of 1846. He then entered a partnership with his former preceptor under the firm name of Dimmick & Dreher, which lasted until Dimmick moved to Mauch Chunk in 1854. Dreher, a Democrat, took an active role in party politics and became a very popular speaker at political gatherings. Besides managing a busy and successful law practice in Monroe, Carbon and Pike counties, he displayed extraordinary versatility as president of the Stroudsburg National Bank, a trustee in the Methodist Church and leader in the local Masonic Order.

Dreher served two terms as district attorney of Monroe County from 1850 to 1856. After the dissolution of the law firm of Dimmick & Dreher in 1853 when Dimmick moved to Mauch Chunk, Dreher continued to practice in Stroudsburg. Judge Barrett's resignation from the Carbon Bench in 1869 created a vacancy and Dreher decided to seek the judgeship. The highly political *Mauch Chunk Democrat*, in its September 17, 1870 edition, boosted its reluctant, non-political candidate with a flattering editorial under the rubric "The Judgeship":

> *We congratulate the 22nd Judicial District on the nomination for President Judge of Hon. Samuel S. Dreher of Monroe County, by the Conference which met at Milford on Tuesday. This nomination is a deserved compliment to one of the most upright men of the district, one of the most learned and successful lawyers and one of the most worthy citizens. Mr. Dreher is yet a young man, being about forty years of age. He is a native of Monroe and always has been a resident of that county, where he has practiced at the bar for fifteen years with eminent success. The nomination to the Judgeship was unsought by him, and was once positively declined, when his honor, Judge Barrett, was re-elected. Mr. Dreher is of that strange composition of men in these days that do the duty of citizens, and do it well, without asking the people to keep them in line by compensating them periodically with official position. . . . It is a proud day for the old 10th Legion when, without going hundreds of miles into the wilderness of the Alleghenies, we have a candidate for President Judge who is native to our own soil, has his home among the people, yet so constituted as to be unbent by local influences and acceptable to good men everywhere.*

His wide recognition and popularity carried Dreher to an easy victory. In January of 1870, he took his oath of office in the Monroe County Courthouse as the president judge of the Twenty-Second Judicial District composed of Wayne, Pike, Monroe and Carbon counties. He was the first native son of Monroe County to serve as its president judge.

In April 1874, the old Twenty-Second Judicial District was divided and the counties of Monroe and Carbon formed the new Forty-Third Judicial District. Dreher remained with the new district. In the fall of 1880, at the expiration of the Judge Dreher's first term of ten years, he was re-elected, without opposition. In 1890, at the age of sixty-six, he was retained for a third term.

Dreher was known as the "Hanging Judge of Carbon County" because he pronounced the death sentence on more defendants than any other judge in Pennsylvania. He was an intimidating presence on the bench looking down through flinty blue eyes from a grim stoical face. He ran the courtroom like a Prussian general, insisted on starting and ending proceedings precisely on time, and once he made up his mind on a legal point was absolutely inflexible.

Members of the bar who practiced before Judge Dreher found him to be affable and considerate. He would go out of his way to help young lawyers on the intricacies of court procedures. His reputation as a chronic procrastinator in making decisions was regarded by some lawyers as undeserved. They pointed out that although he was slow to decide, it was because he pondered all issues carefully. Both his mettle as a judge and his equanimity were severely tested during the "Mollie Maguire" trials of 1876 and 1877. Never before in the history of the court were cases more hotly contested, issues more complex and stakes higher. Judge Dreher acquitted himself well. The hordes of reporters who covered the trials found him "fair and equitable."

On June 28, 1893, Judge Dreher died unexpectedly at the age of sixty-nine at his home in Stroudsburg. He was survived by his wife and five of his children -- Oscar of Stroudsburg; Howard of Kansas; Anna, wife of Joseph Matlack of Philadelphia; Ada, wife of Dr. J. P. Mutschler, a leading physician of Stroudsburg; and Lizzie, wife of A. A. Dinemore.

At the time of his death, the Carbon County Bar had sixteen members. All of the lawyers, except Allen Craig, had been admitted to practice by Judge Dreher. The bar arranged for a special car on the Central Railroad to transport the members to Stroudsburg for his funeral services.

The *Mauch Chunk Coal Gazette*, which rarely had anything good to say about Democrats, in its July 3, 1893 obituary presented this assessment of Dreher's judgeship:

> *Taken all in all, he was above the average judge in ability, legal learning, discretion and judgment. To the law he was entirely and absolutely devoted -- all his time and thought seemed to be connected with the questions that were before him and his profession. While a steadfast Democrat, he was always careful and reticent in expressing political opinions, as well as opinions on other questions not connected with his particular business. But with all this apparent hesitancy, he was firm and decided, and stood by his views whenever called upon in a proper manner to express them. This was especially true in his judicial opinions, and his decisions from the Bench. His Courts were always a model of gentility and propriety. Lawyers felt the silent influence of the Judge, and it was a rare thing to see any collision between counsel and court, or even between counsel themselves in court when Judge Dreher was presiding. His presence and character seemed to impress all connected with the Court with the same equanimity which characterized him and his acts.*

Robert Brown Keller, a Monroe County biographer, said of Dreher:

> *Whether as a lawyer or a judge, his name has ever been a synonym for unspotted integrity and probity of character, coupled with great legal acumen and an habitual courtesy and kindliness of heart and disposition inseparable from the man's nature, which made him the friend of all, high and low rich and poor alike.*

Judge John B. Storm

John B. Storm
President Judge (1893)

The tenure of John Brotzman Storm on the Carbon Bench was filled with "Drang und Sturm." It was tumultuous and brief. His tenure in the office was but six months, the shortest of all judges in Carbon history.

John B. Storm was born in Hamilton Township, Monroe County in 1838 to Jacob Storm and Maria (Brotzman) Storm and was reared on a farm. He was a fifth generation descendant of John Storm who came from Germany about 1750 and located near South Stroudsburg. By dint of hard work and close economy, he managed to make his way through Dickinson College and graduated in 1861. After graduation, Storm apprenticed in the Stroudsburg law office of Samuel S. Dreher, who was later to become president judge of Carbon County. He was admitted to the Carbon County Bar and to the Monroe County Bar in 1863.

As Monroe County superintendent of schools, his administrative skills, tact and erudition won him the respect of the voters and they elected him twice in 1863 and in 1866. In 1870 and 1872 the voters sent him to Washington as their representative on the Democratic ticket. After four years of congressional service, he returned to the practice of law in Stroudsburg. An effective public speaker, he became a superb trial lawyer and appellate advocate. In 1882 he was nominated again by the Democratic Party as a candidate to Congress and served two more terms. Storm was a delegate to many state conventions of the Democratic Party and in 1888 was a delegate to the Democratic National Convention.

In 1893, Governor Robert Pattison appointed Storm president judge to succeed Judge Samuel Dreher, who had died in June of 1893.

Judge Storm wished to retain the Forty-Third District judgeship (Monroe-Carbon) and ran for a full ten-year term in the fall election of 1893. The Democratic leaders in Carbon, however, felt it was now time to have a Carbon resident on the bench. Carbon County's Democratic Party nominated Allen W. Craig of Lehigh Gap. Monroe County Democrats nominated Storm. At Storm's request, the Governor had the Secretary of the Commonwealth certify him on the Democratic ticket instead of Craig. This scenario infuriated the citizens of Carbon County, and a vigorous assault on him by the press followed.

Typical of the press slashing is the following column from the *Mauch Chunk Coal Gazette* in November of 1893:

Among other subjects of discussion in one of our cigar stores the other evening was the Carbon-Monroe judicial contest, and there was an outspoken expression of strong opinion on the fitness of John B. Storm for the bench since he had played such a mean political trick on Senator Craig, with the assistance of Harrity (Secretary of the Commonwealth).

The Philadelphia Press paid its respects to Mr. Storm in an editorial that was most vigorous in its declaration of his utter unfitness for the office. It is bad to have a politician on the bench at any time, but it would be absolutely shocking if such a politician as Storm should be elevated to the office of Judge. A man whose notions of honor and sense of decency permit him to profit by such a cowardly and sneaking political trick as that which put Storm on a Democratic ticket is not the man to administer justice. He knows that he is not entitled to the party nomination, and he is a party to a disreputable scheme by means of which it was filched from his upright and honorable opponent. I shall wait with some curiosity to see what honest and intelligent voters will say about it at the polls.

Craig won the election easily. This defeat ended Judge Storm's political career and removed him from public life.

Storm served as a trustee of Dickinson College for twenty years, and after he left the bench, became president of the board of trustees of the State Normal School at East Stroudsburg.

John Storm married Harriet Brown of East Stroudsburg on October 24, 1865. They were the parents of four children: Nellie K., John A., Arthur Leigh and Robert Frederick

He died in Stroudsburg on August 15, 1901.

ELDRED

BARRETT

CRAIG

HEYDT

STORM

DREHER

ARTISTS CAPTURED EARLY CARBON PRESIDENT JUDGES IN THEIR ELECTION CAMPAIGNS

Judge Allen W. Craig

Allen W. Craig
President Judge (1894-1901)

An impressive and stately figure, Allen Craig was superbly qualified to serve at the helm of the court he knew so well. He brought to the bench a bright intellect, excellent education and many years of experience as a prosecutor, legislator, political activist and an able and strong civil advocate. He was the first native of Carbon County to be elected president judge.

Born on Christmas Day 1835 in Lehigh Gap he came from an old, influential and wealthy family. The Craigs had been among the earliest settlers of Pennsylvania. Allen Craig's grandfather, Thomas Craig with many other Scotch-Irish Protestants emigrated from Northern Ireland in 1728 and settled in Northampton County. Thomas Craig then purchased a large tract of land, which he called "Craig's Settlement" in what is now Allen Township in Lehigh County, and subdivided it among his family members. Thomas Craig served as one of Benedict Arnold's generals in the French and Indian War and as a colonel in the Third Pennsylvania Regiment, took part in several battles in the Revolutionary War. His father, Colonel John Craig, operated the Old Stone Hotel at Lehigh Gap and conducted a very successful stage line which ran from Easton to Mauch Chunk. Colonel Craig was one of Carbon County's most distinguished native sons, represented his district in the State Legislature, was a school director, a postmaster and took an active interest in the civil and political affairs of the county. His military title was earned as a calvary commander in the Pennsylvania Militia.

After attending the old Vanderveer School in Easton, Allen Craig received a classical education at Lafayette College and graduated with honors in 1855. Shortly after college, he registered as a law student in the law offices of Milo M. Dimmick in Mauch Chunk and was admitted to the Carbon Bar on June 4, 1858. He spoke both English and German fluently. Allen Craig, Esq. married Belle Douglas in 1866. They had two sons and two daughters, Douglas, Henry D., Harriet and Gay Gordon Craig.

In his early years at the bar, he was doubly blessed. He practiced law with both Samuel Dreher in Stroudsburg and Milo Dimmick in Mauch Chunk giving the young barrister the benefit of honing his legal skills with two of the best lawyers in the judicial district. Elected district attorney of Carbon County on the Democratic ticket in 1859, Craig served for three years in that office. With the onset of the Civil War, Craig turned from fighting crime to serving his country as a member of the 19th Pennsylvania Infantry in 1862. After the Civil War, he ran for the State House of Representatives for Carbon and Monroe counties and was elected in 1865 for three one-year terms. Beginning in 1878, he served the districts comprising Carbon, Monroe, and Pike counties as State Senator for a four-year term.

In 1879, Craig formed a law partnership with James S. Loose of Mauch Chunk, and the law firm became one of the most prosperous and the best known in the Lehigh Valley. Scholarly, well read, and deeply involved in the political and civic affairs of Carbon County, Craig practiced law in Mauch Chunk for some thirty-five years as a corporation lawyer and litigator. In 1876 during the volatile and sensational "Mollie" trials, he participated in the prosecution of Michael Doyle, Alexander Campbell, John Donahue, Thomas Fisher, Patrick McKenna and Patrick O'Donnell and is credited with developing the legal theories for the prosecution team. A confidante and personal counsel to Asa Packer, he also represented Packer's Lehigh Valley Railroad and other large corporations in Mauch Chunk.

Judge Dreher appointed Craig as one of the first trustees of the Dimmick Memorial Library, whose construction he superintended. He served for many years as a director of the First National Bank of Mauch Chunk and several gas and water companies in the borough. His brother, Thomas B. Craig, served as a Carbon County commissioner from 1911 to 1914. One of Judge Craig's lasting contributions to Carbon County was the Civil War monument in Mauch Chunk. He was its prime mover and chaired the committee which supervised its construction. This lone Confederate soldier, erected September 28, 1886, stands watch over the courthouse at the head of Hazard Square to this day.

He had the pleasure of moving for the admission of his son, Douglas, to the Carbon Bar on April 8, 1893.

Craig had yearned to be judge for many years. When Judge Dreher died, Craig thought the Governor would appoint him to the vacancy. Governor Pattison, however, completely ignored Carbon County's preeminent lawyer and appointed John Storm of Stroudsburg. Having prepared for the office his entire life, Craig decided to use his wealth and popularity to fight Storm for the judgeship. In 1893, the general election was a heated, no-holds-barred battle. Anxious to have one of their own elected judge, Carbon County Democrats nominated Craig as their candidate. Monroe County Democrats nominated the incumbent, Judge John Storm. At the direction of the Governor, the Secretary of the Commonwealth certified Storm as the official Democratic candidate. Infuriated, the Carbon newspapers went after Judge Storm like piranhas in a feeding frenzy. On election day, the aroused electorate of Carbon County poured out to cast their ballots. (At the time Carbon had a population of 38,624 and Monroe a population of 20,111). Storm was only able to obtain 1000 votes in Carbon County. Allen Craig garnered 2987 Carbon votes and that was sufficient to elect him as the eighth president judge of Carbon County. Horace Heydt was the Republican candidate for judge in this election, and his supporters gave him a surprising 2563 votes.

During his early years on the bench, Judge Craig had to recuse himself in most of the cases coming into the Carbon County Court because he had been previously involved in them in his active litigation practice. Lawyers who appeared before him found him knowledgeable in the law, fair and generously endowed with common sense. He was rarely reversed by the Appellate Courts.

In 1901, when the Legislature made Carbon County a separate judicial district, the Republican Governor appointed Republican Horace Heydt as president judge. Judge Craig was transferred to the judicial district made up of Monroe and Pike counties. This was a bitter pill for Craig to swallow. It marked the second time that his talents and abilities were ignored by the Governor for political reasons. He felt as if he were being placed in exile. When his first term was ending in 1902, Craig decided to run for the judgeship in his home judicial district. It was his last political battle. Ailing and aging, he was no match for his youthful and vigorous opponent. Horace Heydt defeated Craig by over 300 votes. Within a month Craig died at the age of sixty-seven on December 31, 1902.

Civil War Monument, Hazard Square, circa 1920s

Judge Horace D. Heydt

TWENTIETH CENTURY BENCH
FIFTY-SIXTH JUDICIAL DISTRICT

Horace D. Heydt
President Judge (1901-1913)

Horace Heydt was born on February 12, 1856 of Pennsylvania German ancestry in Montgomery County, Pennsylvania. At the age of three, his family moved to Berks County. He received a public school education before he entered the Kutztown State Normal School. After teaching school for three years, he entered Lafayette College where he earned a Bachelor of Arts degree in 1884. During his senior year at Lafayette, Heydt began a legal apprenticeship under William G. Freyman, Esquire of Mauch Chunk. After admission to the bar in 1885, he practiced law with the firm of Freyman Heydt & Nothstein, a leading law firm in the county. He was prominent in the Lehighton Masonic Lodge serving as its first exalted ruler and in the Trinity Lutheran Church. An active Republican, Heydt served as secretary of the County Republican Committee.

On January 1, 1880 he married Ellen J. Heilman and they had four children, Gertrude, Helen, Anne and George.

In 1901 Carbon County was separated judicially from Monroe and Pike counties and became the Fifty-Sixth Judicial District. It was not surprising that the Republican Governor William Alexis Stone appointed Carbon's most prominent Republican lawyer, Horace Heydt, as the president judge of the newly created judicial district. Allen Craig was left in the Monroe-Pike judicial district. In 1902, the Democrats narrowly nominated Allen Craig over Laird Barber as their candidate for president judge; the Republicans unanimously chose Horace Heydt as their candidate. The election contest was bitterly fought. Craig's campaign was hurt by two unexpected events: (1) Craig became seriously ill. He was physically unable to sit on the bench in the Monroe-Pike district nor was he able to campaign and (2) the Socialist Party, which had a good following in Carbon, put up a candidate for judge. The Republicans took advantage of both events by promoting Heydt as the healthy candidate and the only one who would complete the ten-year term. They also attacked Craig for wasting taxpayer money because he sat on the bench infrequently and disposed of court matters very slowly.

With strong and surprising support from the voters in Lehighton, Lansford, Nesquehoning and Summit Hill, traditional Democratic towns, Heydt defeated Craig by over 300 votes. The Socialist Party candidate garnering 1610 votes, most of them from Democratic areas proved to be Craig's undoing. On November 3, 1902, Lehighton celebrated Heydt's victory with what the ***Lehighton Press*** called a "Monster Demonstration." An estimated crowd of 3000 people paraded down First Street led by the Arion and Liberty

Bands of Lehighton and the Parryville Band and cheered and shouted "Hurrah for the Dutch!" until they were hoarse.

While he was president judge, Heydt resided in the elaborate Victorian home at 301 North Third Street in Lehighton and served as both school director and president of the Lehighton School Board. Magisterial in demeanor, he liked to appear on the bench in a proper black cutaway coat and Piccadilly collar. Heydt was soft spoken and retiring in disposition and was much more impressive in his writing than in his speech.

Fred Brenckman, a contemporary historian, profiled Judge Heydt in his *History of Carbon County, Pennsylvania* and found in him the characteristics of a good judge:

> *The Judge is of a studious disposition, and the attorneys who practice before him always find him well posted in the law, and entirely up-to-date on the decisions of the higher courts. He gives his rulings firmly and without hesitation. He is particularly adept in charging a jury, no juryman with the slightest claim to intelligence and common sense having any occasion to retire from the court room for deliberation without knowing the law in the case to be decided, or without carrying in his mind a clear summing up of the evidence adduced at the trial.*
>
> *Judge Heydt has decided numerous important cases during his tenure of office, while he has often been called to preside in the courts of Luzerne, Lackawanna, Lehigh and other neighboring counties, where he has always made a favorable impression.*

1913 was a judicial election year and Heydt announced that he was seeking another term. The *Allentown Leader* prematurely and erroneously predicted in January that Heydt would retain the judgeship:

> *As Judge of Carbon he has made a splendid record and there is every indication that at this year's election he will be called to continue on the Bench, with practical unanimity.*

Laird H. Barber, Frank P. Sharkey, Jacob C. Loose, Daniel W. Sitler, Leighton C. Scott, and George E. Gray publicly disagreed with the *Leader's* assessment and announced their candidacy for the judgeship. Thirteen of the twenty-four members of the Carbon Bar signed Heydt's nominating petition. Heydt and Laird Barber went head to head on the November election ballots as the two highest vote-getters in the September primary. One of the issues raised against Heydt in the election campaign was his controversial decision in overturning a $6000 jury verdict obtained by Nesquehoning widow Emma

Watkins against the LC&N Company[54] for the gas explosion death of her husband in shaft No. 5. The LC&N Company admitted at trial that its mine foreman was not legally qualified to perform his duties and that he was negligent in failing to inspect the mine shaft for gases which exploded and killed Watkins. Applying the law which at that time insulated coal companies from almost all liabilities, Heydt threw out the jury verdict finding that there was no evidence that the LC&N Company's superintendent, Thomas J. Jenkins, knew about or sanctioned the appointment of the negligent mine foreman. Heydt's decision was upheld by the Supreme Court of Pennsylvania,[55] but it infuriated the mining communities of the county. During his campaign, Barber told the voters that were he judge he would have decided the case differently.

In August of 1913, Governor John Kinley Tener signed a bill which was supposed to take the judgeship out of partisan politics. It provided that all judges in Pennsylvania be nominated by a non-partisan ballot process in which the candidate for judge would carry no political affiliation in his nominating petitions or on the ballot.

Despite this new non-partisan election law, the voters came out on election day and voted their party's candidate. The Democratic Party swept every office on the ballot including the judgeship. Barber outpolled Heydt by over 1300 votes which, at that time, was a huge majority. It was not long after these election results were reported that the Legislature repealed the illusory "non-partisan" election law for judges.

After leaving the bench, Heydt became a senior partner in the law firm of Heydt Balliet & Seidle in Lehighton and then formed a partnership with Congressman Arthur DeWalt in Allentown. When DeWalt died in 1932, Heydt returned to his old firm in Lehighton where he practiced law actively up to the time of his death.

He died at the age of seventy-eight on November 17, 1934 at his home survived by his daughters Gertrude H. Freeman, Helen Heydt, Anne Heydt and a son, George Heydt.

---

[54] *Emma Watkins v. The Lehigh Coal and Navigation Company*, 14 October Term 1912.

[55] *Emma Watkins v. The Lehigh Coal and Navigation Company*, 240 Pa. 419 (1913).

Judge Laird H. Barber

Laird H. Barber
President Judge (1914-1928)

Judge Laird H. Barber was born on a farm near Mifflinburg, Union County, Pennsylvania on October 25, 1848. He prepared for college at the old Mifflinburg Academy, entered Lafayette College in 1867 and graduated in 1871. He taught school at Mount Carmel in 1871, moved to Mauch Chunk (now Jim Thorpe) in 1875 and taught school in the Second Ward of Mauch Chunk and in the First Ward from 1875 to 1880.

During this time, he studied law in the office of Frederick Bertolette, Esquire, and was admitted to the bar of Carbon County on June 20, 1881. Later he was admitted to the Pennsylvania Supreme Court and engaged in a general law practice with Frederick Bertolette under the firm name, Bertolette & Barber, in Mauch Chunk. Barber and his fiance, Elizabeth Butler, had the distinction of securing the first marriage license issued in Carbon County after the adoption of the Marriage License Law, which went into effect on October 1, 1885. They were married by Reverend Marcus A. Tolman, rector of St. Mark's Church.

Barber's industry, integrity, and patrician good looks quickly attracted many clients, and it was not long before Democratic party leaders were urging him to get involved in politics. At the age of thirty-four, he plunged into the raucous and rowdy world of county politics by running against the popular incumbent district attorney Edward M. Mulhearn in 1882 and lost. He ran for Congress in 1886, and lost again. Undismayed and undaunted by these defeats, Barber decided to start over at the bottom of the political ladder. As Democratic candidate for school director of the Mauch Chunk School District in 1890, he finally won an election. Mauch Chunk Borough council appointed him borough secretary in 1892 and he literally ran the Borough for seven years. After paying his political dues in municipal offices, Barber began to pursue loftier positions. In 1898, he was elected to the Fifty-Sixth Congress from what was then the Eighth Congressional District and went to Washington for one term. In 1902 his bid for the Democratic nomination for judge was narrowly defeated when the Democratic convention gave Allen Craig forty-seven votes and Laird Barber thirty-seven votes. But he continued his pursuit of the office during the term of Horace Heydt by combining his law practice with stumping for political candidates and party fund raising.

By 1913, Barber had become a seasoned campaigner and a distinct presence in Carbon County politics and civic affairs. A sine qua non for Carbon political office in the early 1900s was membership in the Masons. Barber was not only a member he was the leader of the Mauch Chunk Masonic Lodge. His non-stop electioneering had expanded his personal relationships beyond Carbon County into national Democratic politics and attracted many new and influential friends. At the age of sixty-five, he decided to draw on this political capital and top off his legal career with the Carbon judgeship-- a position which he felt he had richly deserved and been deprived of ten years before. A growing disenchantment with Judge Heydt sparked a large contending field of lawyers for the September primary. Barber joined the battle to unseat Heydt and he emerged as the second highest vote getter in the field of six lawyer candidates.

In a Democratic sweep of all offices on the ballot, Barber defeated incumbent Judge Horace Heydt of Lehighton in November of 1913. He took command of the court as president judge of the Fifty-Sixth Judicial District on January 2, 1914. When Barber took office, violations of the state liquor laws had reached epidemic proportions. The court of quarter sessions had the power to license the sale of liquor and revoke licenses for violations. At a time when alcohol sales produced huge incomes and liquor licenses had to be renewed by the court each year, the court wielded an awesome power. An unabashed prohibitionist and outspoken in his conviction that liquor spawned most of the evil afoot in the county, Judge Barber's election sent tremors through the county's hotel and tavern owners . No sooner did he take his oath of office, he warned that he would revoke any licensee who sold liquor on Sundays or after hours. He also refused to grant all applications for new liquor licenses, a practice he followed frequently during his time as judge. Even if there were no formal objections raised to renewing a license, Judge Barber wanted to hear all about the licensee. When George H. Dries appeared before Barber on January 8, 1915 to renew his license, he said:

> *I feel myself responsible for every license granted by this court and am entitled to know all about the applicant. If that allegation is true (about prostitutes being on the premises) and I were to grant a license without learning whether it is true or false, I would consider myself unfit to hold the position I am filling.*

A silver-maned eminence on the bench and always elegantly dressed, Judge Barber insisted on professional decorum in dress and behavior in court and strict adherence to the "Rules of Court" which he promulgated on April 10, 1922. He frowned on any lawyer's attempts at levity and brooked no behavioral dissent in his courtroom. He was a man of great natural dignity and the soul of courtliness which gave no hint of his professional lifetime in the rough-and-tumble world of local and national politics.

He presided over the highly charged first degree murder case of eighteen-year-old Francis Thomas in 1916 and when the spectators in the balcony burst in joyous shouts at the "Not Guilty" verdict, he held the entire gallery in contempt of court for refusing to stop their demonstration (See *Commonwealth v. Francis Thomas*, page 39). He was the last judge in Carbon County to impose the death sentence when in April of 1924 he sent both Martin Matalovack and Walter Grymkowski, neither of whom spoke or understood English, to the electric chair for the murder of Constable Elmer P. Anthony of Palmerton (See **Last Death Sentence**, page 41).

Mary Packer Cummings, the daughter of Asa Packer. appointed Barber as one of the Executors of her estate. When she died on October 29, 1912, her estate included both the Asa Packer and the Harry Packer mansions and was conservatively valued at close to two million dollars. Her chief beneficiaries were the Borough of Mauch Chunk and St. Mark's Church. Barber, who was a close friend, saw to it that the provisions of her will were carried out to the letter. With Allen W. Craig, he was a member of the committee responsible for erecting the Civil War Soldiers Monument that stands at the end of Hazard Square to this day.

In 1923, at the age of seventy-five, he was re-elected for a second ten-year term, defeating George E. Gray of Lehighton. This election marked the first time women were empowered to vote.

Judge Barber loved books and was an eclectic reader. His tastes ran from the esoteric legal treatises by *Kent* to the literary *Harper's* weekly magazine. He took great pleasure in recommending to his friends or members of the bar a book he liked or discussing it at length with fellow bibliophile and close friend, Frederick Bertolette. Over his lifetime, Judge Barber collected one of the finest law libraries in the area and upon his death, he bequeathed it to the Carbon County Bar Association. He also enjoyed travel and spent his summer vacations in St. Augustine, Florida or Martha's Vineyard in Massachusetts.

In his eightieth year, he was afflicted with Bright's Disease and passed away on February 16, 1928 in his home in East Mauch Chunk. He was survived by his wife, Elizabeth and his children Fannie Skeer, Mary Foster, Elizabeth H., and Laird H., Jr.

Judge Barber's death left the Carbon justice system in a quandry with lawyers and litigants, politicians and constituents wondering who was going to preside over their cases and who had the authority to fill the judicial vacancy. Judge Claude T. Reno, President Judge of Lehigh County, wisely stepped in and petitioned the Pennsylvania Supreme Court to address the questions. Citing the old Provincial Act of 1722 which gave them the same plenary powers as justices of the king's bench at Westminster, the high court designated Judge Reno to perform all duties of the President Judge of Carbon County until a new judge was elected. *In Re Carbon County Judicial Vacancy*, 141 A.249 (1928).

Judge William G. Thomas

William G. Thomas
President Judge (1928-1939)

William Gladstone Thomas was born in Drifton, Luzerne County, on November 27, 1871. His parents, Jeremiah and Jane Thomas, were both natives of Wales who immigrated to the United States in 1869. When his father moved to Lansford in 1884 to work in the mines of the Lehigh Coal and Navigation Company, young Thomas entered the public schools there. Because of a prolonged miners strike at Lansford, Jeremiah Thomas and his son traveled to the then territory of Washington and secured employment in the mines for eight months. The judge liked to recount his trip west. It was made in a converted freight car which was occupied by many people, including a number of families, and the only privacy was furnished by blankets suspended on wires.

When the Lansford mine strike ended in 1887, father and son returned to their home. Thomas then resumed his education in the Lansford public schools and graduated with the first graduating class of Lansford High School, the Class of 1890. He then entered Keystone State Normal School at Kutztown, graduating and becoming certified as a school teacher in 1891. Thomas began teaching in the Lansford High School, but spent his summers working in a stoneyard in Philadelphia to raise funds to attend college. Although he entered Dickinson College at Carlisle in 1893, lack of funds compelled him to discontinue his studies there. In 1895 he registered with Freyman Heydt & Nothstein as a law clerk and student supporting himself by teaching night school. At the same time, he took a short course in stenography at Banks Business College in Philadelphia. He successfully passed his law examinations and was admitted to the Carbon Bar on April 19, 1897.

On October 5, 1895 he married Elizabeth D. Thomas. They had two sons, Robert and William, and two daughters, Mildred and Helen.

Up to the time of his marriage, he had always borne the name given him at birth, William J. Thomas. Because other persons of the same name lived in his neighborhood, he renamed himself William Gladstone Thomas because of his intense admiration for British statesman William Ewart Gladstone,[56] the "Grand Old Man" who was Prime Minister four times during Queen Victoria's reign.

Following his admission to the bar, Thomas opened offices in Lansford and in Mauch Chunk. He became active in the Republican Party , membership in which was practically mandatory for miners who worked for the coal company. When the United

[56]An eloquent spokesman for the Liberal Party, Gladstone opposed imperialism abroad and at home, tried to liberate Ireland from English rule and advocated the need for education and religious toleration. He was a polished gentleman, scholar, an orator of the old school and a leader who looked every bit the part.

States Bankruptcy Act was passed in 1898, he was appointed the first bankruptcy referee in this region. Eventually, he was admitted to the highest courts of the state and nation. He attended every court term to observe and learn how to try cases. Frequently, the court turned to him to represent indigents in criminal cases and he began to develop the skills and confidence which made him an effective trial lawyer. The senior members of the bar noted that he was a born actor and particularly adept at captivating juries. Frank Sharkey and James Breslin asked Thomas to assist them in their defense of criminal cases and his reputation as one of the best pure trial lawyers in the county grew.

Like many of the trial lawyers of his day, Thomas often used histrionics to sway the jury and sometimes it touched off dramatic fireworks in the courtroom. In October of 1908, as court appointed counsel for two young men charged with pilfering shoes from a Lehigh Valley box car, he ended his closing speech by calling the jury's attention to their weeping mother sitting in the front row of the courtroom and then throwing his arms skyward entreated the jury "in the name of God and all that is holy to return the boys to their sorrowing mother." When District Attorney George Gray began a vigorous plea for conviction the mother, apparently inspired by Thomas, fell to her knees before the jury box, extended her arms heavenward and cried out "Oh please, don't say that about my boys!" As Thomas helped the woman back to her seat, the jury was in tears. No one was surprised when they brought back a verdict of "Not Guilty" within minutes of getting the case.

On June 1, 1912 he was asked to join the law partnership of Freyman & Branch, the preeminent law firm in the county. As a member of this firm, Thomas gradually drifted away from criminal cases and began to represent many important business and industrial enterprises in Carbon County including the Lehigh Coal and Navigation Company, Lehigh and New England Railroad Company, New Jersey Zinc Company and Pennsylvania Power and Light Company. He also defended numerous civil cases as counsel for various liability insurance carriers. Feeling the need to broaden his interests and the firm name, he participated in a wide variety of civic and fraternal activities. He served long and faithfully as a member of the Lansford School Board, most of the time as the board's president. During World War I, he was chairman of Carbon County's "Four Minute Men." He was director of several banks and a charter member and past exalted ruler of the Tamaqua Lodge of Elks.

When Judge Barber died in February of 1928, David Davis, the incumbent district attorney, and Ben Branch were the only applicants to fill the vacancy. Branch unexpectedly withdrew his name. Republican Governor John S. Fisher surprised everyone by appointing the fifty-three-year-old Thomas who never publicly sought the appointment. The Governor's choice was well received by the bar and the public. His colleagues considered Thomas splendidly qualified for the office. His legal career had been marked by demonstrated professional skill in the courtroom, an even temperament and exemplary character. It did not hurt that he was also an ardent Republican. Thomas was installed as president judge in May of 1928. In the primary election, leaders of both the Republican and Democratic parties endorsed Thomas, and he was elected in November of 1929 to a full ten-year term.

From his first days in office, Thomas felt completely comfortable in being a judge. Actually, he had acquired a considerable amount of experience in judging during his ten years as a part-time referee in bankruptcy. Judge Thomas ran a tight courtroom insisting on strict decorum. He was particularly harsh on young lawyers, and did not hesitate to publicly point out the errors in their pleadings and arguments. Lawyers who appeared before him remember Thomas as elegant, attentive and aloof. The long black frock coat and striped pants he preferred while on the bench heightened the aura of cool eminence he nurtured during his judgeship. A review of his written decisions reveals an autocratic, pro-coal company bent. Reflecting the English common law's obsession with matters of form, Judge Thomas decided many cases based on defects in the legal pleadings or procedures. When the Great Depression spurred many tax assessment appeals, especially by LC&N Company, he invariably reduced the assessments. In the controversial case of *Mc Laughlin vs Lansford Borough School District*, he completely rewrote a challenged school district budget, changed salaries of teachers and school administrators and increased the tax millage.

Judge Thomas established Carbon County's first probation department in 1930. He charged the office with responsibility for handling juvenile delinquents, supervising adult criminals who were placed on probation or parole, and collecting court ordered fines, costs and restitution and non-support orders. Thomas brought Blanton J. Brown, an outstanding Philadelphia parole officer, to Carbon County to head the office in February of 1930. Brown left after six months, and Judge Thomas appointed Chesley A. Gaul,[57] also from Philadelphia, to take his place.

It was his Welsh ancestry which gave Thomas his keenest enjoyment in life. No Pennsylvania Eisteddfod (a Welsh competitive festival of the arts, especially singing) was held without his active participation. He retired at the end of his ten-year elected term in January of 1940. On April 12, 1947, he was honored by the County Bar Association on the fiftieth anniversary of his admission to the bar. After leaving the bench, he enrolled at Columbia University as a student of literature and philosophy, an experience that gave him great enjoyment, but failing health prevented him from completing his courses. He died August 11, 1947 at the age of seventy-five at the University of Pennsylvania Hospital in Philadelphia. Surviving him were his widow Elizabeth, daughter Mildred Moore, and son Robert.

---

[57]In his first annual report, Gaul reported that he supervised nine probationers and four parolees and that he collected a total of $277.26 in fines, costs and restitution.

Judge James C. McCready

James C. McCready
President Judge (1940-1960)

James Campbell McCready called himself the "people's judge" and rejected efforts of the bar to have him don the black robe. He was born on February 13, 1889 in Summit Hill to Thomas and Rebecca (Campbell) McCready. His father, a native of Summit Hill and a prosperous clothing merchant, and his mother, a native of Scotland, imbued in the future jurist from an early age the value of hard work. While going to Summit Hill High School, he worked as a water boy, a slate picker, a clerk and gang foreman at No. 8 colliery of the LC&N Company. His parents, however, recognized that he had a bright and analytical mind and encouraged him to get an education.

They sent him to the Conway Hall Preparatory School and then to Dickinson College, where he received both Bachelor of Arts and Master of Arts degrees in 1917. While an undergraduate, he excelled in track and cross-country running.

Immediately after graduating, he enlisted in the Army. During World War I, from 1917 to 1919, he served with the American Expeditionary Force in France where he rose to the rank of a staff sergeant. Upon discharge from the Army, he entered the Dickinson School of Law and earned his law degree (LL.B.) in 1921, a year in which he was elected president of his class. He maintained his interest in the law school throughout his life and was elected to its board of trustees in 1951.

McCready was admitted to the Carbon County Bar on September 11, 1922. After that, he maintained an active law practice at 107 Patterson Street in Lansford as a sole practitioner handling both criminal and civil cases. Like every young lawyer, McCready undoubtedly dreamed of ascending to fame overnight through victory in one sensational, supposedly indefensible case. Judge Thomas handed him that case in April of 1931 when he appointed McCready to defend Michael Vladyka, a nineteen-year-old unemployed miner from McAdoo, who was charged with first degree murder in the shooting death of Thomas Gibbons in the Weatherly area. Vladyka and his girlfriend Anna Ignatovitch had attempted to rob the White Haven Bank on March 17, 1931 and during their getaway were given a lift by Gibbons and his brother who were driving to a church social. Vladyka shot Thomas Gibbons in the head when he refused to obey his directions and put five bullets into his brother James Gibbons. Local police and a group of citizens took Vladyka and his girlfriend into custody in Weatherly where he gave a full confession of the attempted robbery and shootings. On April 10, Judge Thomas appointed McCready to represent Vladyka and George Shutack to represent Anna Ignatovitch. With incredible swiftness[58] ***Commonwealth***

[58] *Commonwealth v. Michael Vladyka, 36 April Sessions 1931.*

v. Vladyka began on April 17 before a packed courtroom with many people standing in the corridors and a substantial press corps in attendance. District Attorney David Davis, at his strident best, presented a strong case for the prosecution which included Vladyka's confession. When Vladyka took the witness stand, he admitted the shootings but said there was a struggle with James Gibbons before his guns went off. McCready took him through his whole life from the time he left Russia, his work in the mines, through his military service in the U.S. Army in World War I and his futile struggle to find work after he returned from the war. He and Shutack never asked the jury to find him not guilty, but stressing his youth and military service asked the jury to spare his life. The strategy was successful. The jury returned a verdict of "Guilty of first degree murder and life imprisonment."[59] It was met by loud hisses and boos from the spectators and sheriff's deputies had to restore order before Judge Thomas could pronounce sentence. The *Lehighton Press* edition of April 24, 1931 called the verdict "the most unpopular ever returned by a Carbon County jury" and pronounced it "a crime upon a crime."

The *Vladyka* case, despite its unpopular outcome, raised McCready's stature as a lawyer immeasurably and clients poured into his office. He plunged into public service activities and became a major player in the banking community. He was solicitor for the Borough of Summit Hill, the Summit Hill School District and the County of Carbon. He was the solicitor and a director of the Workingmen's Building and Loan Association and the Citizens National Bank of Lansford and served as president of the Citizens Bank for many years. He served as a Summit Hill school director and president of the school board from 1928 to 1936. He also was a member and president of the board of trustees of the Coaldale State General Hospital (now Miners Memorial Medical Center).

After seventeen years as a practicing attorney and with his legal career in full flower at the age of fifty, McCready decided to seek the judgeship. Undoubtedly wanting to define the judgeship differently than the unapproachable Judge Thomas, he campaigned on the theme that he would be a "judge of the people" and that his chambers would be "open to all." To support his populist rhetoric he volunteered his legal services to the Stevens' family whose daughter was shot and killed by Pennsylvania State Trooper Ben Franklin in June of 1939. Although he was a registered Republican, he ran on both tickets as permitted by law and won the Democratic primary. He then defeated the Republican candidate George Gray in the election of 1939 winning his first ten-year term on the bench.

True to his campaign promises, McCready opened his chamber doors wide. Personable and friendly, he encouraged lawyers to come to see him about any procedural problem they might have. His lack of pretense and occasional lapses into the unpolished

[59]In 1925, the Legislature changed the long standing law of Pennsylvania by permitting a jury to give either a death sentence or life imprisonment with a first degree murder conviction.

language of the coal miner were seen as refreshing proof of his coal region roots and stood in stark contrast to the studied elegance of his predecessors.

With the changing of the guard, a conservative judicial ideology which began at the turn of the century went with it. Judge McCready seemed determined to extend power to the people, especially in their legal battles with governmental bodies and big corporations. In one of his first cases, *Mauch Chunk Township Taxpayers Ass'n vs.Kern et al.*, 14 A.2d 329 (1940), he granted an injunction to a local taxpayer group to restrain the County Commissioners from collecting taxes on properties which were allegedly improperly assessed. He reversed the Liquor Control Board and granted resort liquor licenses to local businessmen after the Board refused to grant them. In a taxpayers suit, he removed three Mauch Chunk Township school directors from office because they did not sue the local tax collector to recover money he had stolen. In *Fountain Hill Underwear Mill vs. Amalgamated Clothing Union*, 143 A.2d 354 (1958), he threw out of court, without a hearing, a manufacturer's injunction action to stop picketing and violence by union members around its Lansford plant. Local residents hailed these victories for the " working man" but their elation was short-lived. All of these decisions were reversed on appeal by the Supreme or Superior Court.

In 1949, the popular McCready easily won re-election for a second term. Taking on District Attorney Carl A. Niehoff, he captured both the Republican and Democratic nominations and had no opposition in the November election.

McCready's ability to make important things happen was his chief public asset. He used the judgeship as a bully pulpit to encourage a better way of life in the local communities delivering over 1000 speeches during his twenty years on the bench. In a visionary move, he formed and led the First Citizens Committee, made up of the top officials of each municipality in the county. This group met regularly to discuss local and county issues and the committee sparked a number of innovative programs. His involvement in local civic, fraternal and church organizations was deep and extensive and earned him innumerable awards and citations of merit. He was a member of the Methodist Church of Summit Hill and was affiliated with the First Baptist Church of Lansford. He was active in the Boy Scouts of America, the Lansford Rotary Club, the Red Cross, the Carbon County Council of Civil Defense and the Carbon County Historical Society and held memberships in many local veteran and masonic organizations.

On November 14, 1928, McCready married Margaret Thomas Smith, a union which produced one son, Thomas S. McCready, a member of the Carbon County Bar, and four grandchildren, Susann McCready Laverty, Amy Reed McCready, Elizabeth Smith McCready and James Thomas Paul McCready. Judge McCready died on January 16, 1967 at the age of seventy-seven, having resided in Summit Hill all his life.

Judge Albert H. Heimbach

Albert H. Heimbach
President Judge (1960-1978)

Albert H. Heimbach followed the traditional route through the office of district attorney to the Carbon Bench. Born in Palmerton on September 18, 1907 to Oscar H. and Edna (Stone) Heimbach, he developed a strong sense of duty and a solid work ethic early in life. His mother died in 1919 when he was twelve years old. His father, who was of Pennsylvania German extraction, operated a livery stable and later a garage in Palmerton. With his sister Irene, and brother Raymond, Heimbach worked in his father's business during his teenage years.

Heimbach began his formal education in the Palmerton public schools. Upon graduation in 1925, he joined the Merchant Marines for about a year where he first experienced the joys of going to sea. He attended the University of Vermont from 1926 to 1928 and then transferred to Penn State University where he earned his A.B. degree in 1930. While at Penn State, he decided to pursue a career in the law and he applied and was accepted at Yale Law School. His father's illness interrupted his plans, however, and he returned to Palmerton to take over management of his father's garage until his father recuperated. In September of 1931 he entered the University of Pennsylvania Law School where he was awarded a law degree in 1934.

He was admitted to the Carbon County Bar on April 1, 1935 and to the Northampton County Bar on June 17, 1935. After opening a law office in Northampton in May of 1935, he decided to return to Carbon County to run for district attorney.

In the general election of 1935, as the Republican candidate, Heimbach was elected district attorney over Democrat George A. Shutack. At the age of twenty-eight, he was the youngest person ever elected to that office in Pennsylvania. In 1939, he retained the office against the same Democratic challenger, George A. Shutack. As chief county prosecutor, he tried Corporal Ben Franklin of the Pennsylvania State Police in January of 1940 for first degree murder in the *Toy Gun Murder* case (See pages 43-46), the most highly publicized case in Carbon County since the "Mollie" trials. In the 1943 general election, despite a Republican sweep of all county offices, Carl A. Niehoff, a Lehighton Democrat, beat back Heimbach's bid for a third term.

Not surprisingly, the new commissioners appointed him Carbon County Solicitor, and he served in that office from 1944 until 1948. Heimbach successfully engaged in the general practice of law in Jim Thorpe from 1944 until he went on the bench. He had the kind of "generalist" practice which was common among rural county lawyers -- some litigating, a great deal of corporate and family counseling, and always governmental and political advising. In 1957, he formed an association with fellow Palmerton lawyer, Roger N. Nanovic.

In 1959, after Judge James C. McCready announced his intent to retire, Heimbach, at the age of forty-eight, decided to seek the judgeship. It was an uphill battle all the way. Joseph Greco and George Shutack vied with him for the nomination in the primary election, but he emerged as the Republican nominee. District Attorney Carl A. Niehoff of Lehighton won the Democratic Primary. Niehoff had been district attorney for sixteen years and local political insiders considered him a certain victor. To focus attention on his "law and order" campaign, Niehoff convened a grand jury in May of 1959 to investigate voting irregularities. He subpoenaed various Democratic Party officials to appear, including the powerful Tresckow political leader Nick Petrole. Nothing ever came of the investigation and party leaders became not only disenchanted they were downright hostile to Niehoff. Three days before the election he inexplicably ordered and led a county-wide raid on several non-profit organizations and confiscated their illegal slot machines. On election day, Heimbach, the underdog, emerged victorious.

Upon his installation on January 7, 1960, the Carbon County Bar Association presented to him a judicial robe, and he became the first Carbon judge ever to wear the black robe while presiding over his court. Judge Heimbach suffered a heart attack shortly after going on the bench and was unable to assume a full judicial caseload until the middle of 1961. While he recuperated, Judges Paul R. Selecky of Luzerne County, Paul R. Campbell of Centre County and Edward Little of Susquehanna County presided.

A soft-spoken, gentle man, Heimbach conducted court business and trials in an unhurried, low keyed atmosphere. During oral argument, he was an attentive listener; at trials, he let the lawyers try their cases. Cautious and conservative by inclination and commitment, his written decisions and rulings, set forth in Volumes One through Six of the *Carbon County Law Journal*, reveal that he usually upheld police action and local government authority, but often overturned decisions of the Liquor Control Board and Department of Transportation in license cases. Motions to suppress evidence based on illegal searches and seizures were rarely successful before him. In five different mandamus actions from 1970 through 1974, he ordered the county controller, Allen D. Kistler, to pay bills and salaries of government officials (approved by the county commissioners) when Kistler refused to sign their checks. In *Holpoco Civic Association v. Jarell et ux*, 3 *Carbon Law Journal* 378 (1971), he refused to allow a property owners' association to collect dues and assessments for road maintenance and recreation facilities by narrowly construing deed covenants and by-laws.

During his early years on the bench, Heimbach presided over a number of controversial cases. In May of 1961, the board of trustees of the new Gnaden Huetten Memorial Hospital in Lehighton removed three doctors from the medical staff and demoted three others. Their action triggered a firestorm of angry debate over hospital control which sharply divided the community. Thirteen doctors sued the hospital board claiming they were denied due process. Judge Heimbach, after long and acrimonious hearings during the summer of 1961, ordered the doctors to be reinstated. In September of 1962, his courtroom was the battleground for the first and last criminal libel case in county history -- a case in which Lehighton Evening Leader publisher Marion A. Morthimer and her editor Will J. Smith were acquitted by a jury.

Judge Heimbach was not a judicial activist and strongly believed that it was the lawyer's and not the Court's responsibility to settle litigation and to move cases through the system. Although his stewardship as president judge may very well be remembered overridingly for preserving the traditions and procedures of the past, he introduced several progressive innovations in court administration: the selection of juries for all cases on the trial list on the first day of the trial terms; encouraging the appointment of a public defender for indigent defendants before state law required the establishment of such an office; the use of pre-trial conferences in civil cases to refine the issues and discuss anticipated evidentiary rulings; and the revision and adoption of new local civil rules.

In 1969 he was retained by the electorate for a second ten-year term on the new "Yes"-"No" Retention of Judges law which was adopted in 1965. Heimbach frequently took assignments from the Supreme Court to sit in Philadelphia, Northampton and other neighboring counties. In the mid 1960s, when the community of Palmerton was taking over the responsibility for the Palmerton Hospital from the New Jersey Zinc Company, Judge Heimbach became a valuable addition to the hospital's board of trustees and lent his wise counsel to many committees during the modernization of that hospital.

An avid hunter, he kept his hunting gear in his car for quick retrieval should he spot some game running. He regularly went with close friends to a blind on the coast of Maryland to shoot ducks and in his leisure hours he indulged his passion for woodworking. Heimbach and his wife Evelyn were inveterate travelers and every year their love of the sea would take them on long freighter trips to the far corners of the globe.

Judge Heimbach retired on September 18, 1978 at the age of seventy as mandated by state law, but continued serving the county as a senior judge by appointment of the Supreme Court until 1983.

Albert H. Heimbach married his high school classmate, the former Evelyn Tucker, a registered nurse, on September 1, 1934 and lived in Residence Park in Palmerton. Their union produced two daughters Sara Ann (Sally) Determan of Falls Church, Virginia, an attorney practicing in Washington, D.C. and Judith T. Heimbach, a teacher of Rockaway, New Jersey. Judge Heimbach died on July 28, 1993 at the age of eighty-five while living in retirement at Foxdale Village in State College, Pennsylvania. He is survived by his wife Evelyn and daughters Judith and Sally.

Judge John P. Lavelle

CHAPTER IX

THE BENCH IN 1993

John P. Lavelle
President Judge (1978-)

[At this point, Judge Lavelle leaves his word processor and defers to Dr. T. Robert Milligan, Associate Professor Emeritus and former Chairman of the Modern Foreign Languages Department at Manhattan College in New York City.]

John Patrick Lavelle is the current president judge of the Carbon County Courts, and the fourteenth in the succession of judges to hold that position since 1843. He also became, in effect, the last of the single judges of the Fifty-Sixth Judicial District when in 1992, the Legislature created a second judgeship in Carbon County.

In the panoply of traits that John Lavelle has brought to the bench, certain to be counted among them is his independence and his willingness to fight for what he believes is right, traditionally ascribed to those of Irish origin. In any case, he comes by them naturally. His father, John P. Lavelle, was a native of County Mayo in Ireland, and his mother, Sarah McBride Lavelle, also from Ireland, was born in County Donegal. A sad note here is the death of his mother when he was but sixteen months-old. Subsequent to her passing, he was raised in Philadelphia by his aunt, Mary Coll (nee McFadden) with her family of twelve children.

Lavelle's career was built on the solid foundation of a good education. He earned his Bachelor of Arts degree in 1953 at Niagara University in New York, and went on to get his law degree in 1958 from Villanova University School of Law. He has the distinction, along with his classmates, of having been a member of the first class held at the Villanova School of Law in 1953. During that time his studies were interrupted for two years by military service in the United States Army, with duty in Italy and Austria. In 1958 he married Marianne Shutack of Nesquehoning, who supplied her own distinguished "first" by becoming the first woman admitted to the Carbon County Bar.

Lavelle's professional life was fairly launched in Center City Philadelphia in the law offices of Morton Witkin, a renowned criminal lawyer. Witkin became his mentor and his role model. He taught the neophyte lawyer the value of intensive case preparation and the art of advocacy in the courtroom. After carrying Witkin's briefcase for a year, he moved on to work briefly for the negligence firm of Bennett & Bricklin where he honed his legal skills in trying and settling lawsuits. During this period, he indulged his love of classical language by teaching Latin as a part-time professor at Villanova University.

The year 1959 proved to be an important one for John Lavelle. For in that year he moved to Carbon County and began an active general law practice with his father-in-law and wife in Lehighton under the firm name of Shutack Lavelle & Lavelle. Just as important were two other events: he was admitted to the Pennsylvania Supreme Court in May of 1959, and to the Carbon County Bar on March 24, 1960. His father-in-law, George A. Shutack, Esquire, moved for his admission in both instances.

During those early years, Lavelle began building a broad civil and criminal practice. He gradually developed a reputation as an advocate of heart and spirit, and a counselor of character and wisdom. He tried civil and criminal cases in both the county and the Federal Courts in Scranton and Philadelphia, representing primarily the working man and woman. Some of his cases took him to the Appellate Courts of Pennsylvania and before administrative agencies in Harrisburg and Washington. His roots and upbringing gave him a natural empathy for the underdog and many of his legal battles were fought for little people overwhelmed by big business or big government. Inspired by President John F. Kennedy, whom he deeply admired, he became active in Democratic politics and was a speaker, speech writer, adviser and strategist in many state and local elections during the '60s and the '70s.

In 1965, Lavelle and his wife built a home in Lehighton and have resided in that community ever since. Whenever he saw an opportunity to improve his adopted community, he assumed a leadership role. Examples of this are legion. He obtained the federal and county funding and spearheaded the building of the Carbon County Airport in 1961. He was the first solicitor of the Carbon County Airport Authority and served in that capacity for ten years. He was a charter member of the Carbon County Planning Commission. He arranged for the financing and construction of the first Professional Building in Lehighton, as well as Park View House, the first modern apartment commercial building in the town. In 1966 he organized and obtained the charter for the First Federal Savings and Loan Association of Carbon County and, in so doing, brought to the county its first federally insured savings and loan association. In 1971 he was appointed county solicitor, and he was legal advisor and counsel to majority Commissioners Charles E. Wildoner and Albert "Brady" Koch for seven years until 1978.

By the age of forty-six, Lavelle had become a seasoned lawyer. Tested in numerous courtroom contests, tempered by many state and local political battles and professionally matured by a broad-based law practice and community involvement, he felt ready to lead the court system -- and the opportunity was there.

In September of 1977, Judge Heimbach reached mandatory retirement age. Lavelle and several other lawyers sought gubernatorial appointment to the judicial vacancy. Lavelle obtained the recommendation of the Judicial Nominating Committee and Governor Milton Shapp sent his name to the State Senate for confirmation on October 1, 1977.

Before any Senate action, however, the Pennsylvania Supreme Court on October 15, 1977 ruled that the Governor did not have the right to appoint the judge in Carbon County because the State Election Board should have known early in 1977 that Judge Heimbach had to retire on his seventieth birthday and should have placed the Carbon judgeship on the ballot. The high court directed the Carbon County Election Bureau to allow the voters to elect a judge on November 8. It was a confusing time for election officials. No one was quite sure just how the nomination of candidates was to proceed. It was decided to let both political parties call conventions and have committee people elect their candidates. The Democrats nominated Lavelle and the Republicans named William H. Bayer as their candidate. In the shortest election campaign in Pennsylvania history, Lavelle won the judgeship over Bayer and John Deutsch, an Independent candidate.

On January 2, 1978, Lavelle took the oath of office administered by Judge Heimbach, and became president judge. From the moment he took the constitutional oath, Lavelle seemed to understand his role, had a clear vision of where he wanted the court to go, and devoted himself to it with uncommon zeal. He recognized that a judge, first and foremost, must make decisions and unlike Hamlet, he liked to make decisions. He strongly believed that the president judge should be the leader of the justice system and that it exists to serve the citizens not the lawyers.

The newly minted jurist assumed his judicial duties with typical energy and enthusiasm. After a year of study and evaluation, he abandoned centuries-old tradition and practices, and started the process of bringing the court system into the computer age. He modernized and streamlined the office procedures in all court offices and adopted new Rules of Court to govern the processing and flow of cases. He hired David R. Fink of Tridata Corporation of Allentown, a brilliant computer programmer, and together they invented the court computer system. He installed high tech computers, and designed computer programs to automate the antiquated manual record-keeping in all court and court-related offices with data bases that could be accessed with the speed of light. He wrote training manuals and personally trained personnel in the court and court related offices to operate the computer programs.

Significant additional changes were effected during Lavelle's first term on the bench. In 1979, he initiated the one-day, one-trial jury system and automated the selection of jurors. He developed and produced a unique audio-visual jury orientation program that was shown to all jurors beginning in 1979 and continues in use today.

He restructured and reorganized all court offices. He created a domestic relations department, separate juvenile and adult probation departments, and court administration department, making them all separate units of the court system, each with its own director, office space and support personnel. He brought in the first court administrator to oversee the court system and in what became one of the benchmarks of

Lavelle's administration, he appointed women to key positions of the court system.

In 1980, Lavelle planned and obtained federal funding to defray one-half of the cost of converting the old arbitration room on the third floor of the courthouse into a modern wood panelled courtroom.

From the outset Judge Lavelle exercised the power and authority of the office with ease and grace. His caseload grew each year, and the demands on his time and energies escalated proportionally, but he always seemed to bring to his work a reserve of strength to meet the challenge. He also brought something else. He loved his work and his ardor never cooled.

Also, during that very busy first term, Judge Lavelle's courtroom became the focal point for several widely publicized cases. In November 1979, he made the unprecedented decision to call off and nullify the county general election when the election machines used throughout the county would not permit cross voting. He ordered all voting machines closed down and then directed that a new election be held two weeks later. In January of 1982, he presided over the murder trial of "Mudman" Simon,[60] a member of the notorious Warlock Motorcycle gang, who was convicted of killing an eighteen-year-old girl whose body had been found in a mine pool seven years after her death. Also of importance was the Bonnie Leskin murder trial held in 1985,[61] when the battered wife syndrome defense was used for the first time, and resulted in a jury acquittal of the defendant in the shooting death of her husband.

In November of 1987, the electorate retained Lavelle for an additional ten year term by a large plurality of "yes" votes. On January 2, 1988 Judge Peter Paul Olszewski of the Pennsylvania Superior Court administered the oath of office to formally begin Lavelle's second term as president judge. Not surprisingly, he threw himself into his second term with characteristic vigor and enthusiasm.

By appointment of the Supreme Court of Pennsylvania, he specially presided over the two long and complex civil libel trials of Supreme Court Justice James T. McDermott against the *Philadelphia Inquirer*[62] during the fall of 1991. After a seven and a half week trial in Philadelphia, he received a split jury verdict of $6 million in one case and no damages in the other. On February 13, 1993, Judge Lavelle struck down both verdicts

---

[60]*Commonwealth v. Robert Ronald Simon*, 202 CR 1981.

[61]*Commonwealth v. Bonnie Leskin*, 371 CR 1985.

[62]*Honorable James T. McDermott v. Daniel R. Biddle, Philadelphia Inquirer et al*, 262-June-1983; 3693-March-84, Philadelphia County.

because they were inconsistent and granted new trials.

In 1989, when County Commissioners Albert Koch, Luther Getz and Dean DeLong removed funds from the court budget and refused increases for court employees, Lavelle filed a lawsuit against the commissioners to compel the funding (See **Chapter X**, page 170).

In 1990, Judge Lavelle went to the Legislature for help in handling a caseload which had become unworkably heavy for one judge and successfully lobbied for the creation of a second judgeship for Carbon County. In 1991, he completely revised and adopted new rules of civil procedure, and in 1992 and 1993 he launched new case management systems for both criminal and civil cases which require cases to be disposed within time standards adopted by the court.

Known as a tough sentencer who does not blink when sending drug pushers to jail for lengthy terms, he does not hesitate to throw out cases where he finds defendants' rights are violated. His court orders, on occasion, have been unusual and creative. When a delinquent father refused to support his children and used overweight as an excuse not to work, he directed the father to lose fifty pounds or go to jail. He sentenced a woman with a long record of calling in false alarms to the Lehighton Fire Company to clean the fire trucks for six months. He was one of the first trial judges in Pennsylvania to order striking teachers and a school board to negotiate daily in order to break a contract impasse which had closed down schools in the Panther Valley School District for over thirty-seven days in October of 1984. He has shown patience and compassion when dealing with children's cases and considers them the most important and difficult cases he handles as a judge.

Judge Lavelle has, to date, authored over 800 written legal opinions covering a wide spectrum of Pennsylvania law. His prolific output comes from his conviction that written opinions from the county bench have great value, because they not only explain the legal basis for the court's decision to the parties and the community, but they also provide written precedents to guide the local bar in its practice of law.

Judge Lavelle and his wife Marianne have been married for thirty-five years, a marriage that has been graced with four children: Marianne Lavelle, who is a staff reporter in the Washington, D.C. offices of the *National Law Journal*; John P. Lavelle, Jr., an attorney with the Philadelphia law firm of Hangley, Connolly; Jacqueline H. N. Lavelle, a park supervisor with the National Park Service; and James M. Lavelle, a graduate student at New York University. They have one grandchild, Moira Sarah Coonelly-Lavelle, born on September 4, 1993.

Judge Richard W. Webb

Richard W. Webb
Judge (1992-)

On his father's side, Richard William Webb is the grandson of Algernon Vincent (Dick) Webb, an immigrant from Pewsey, England and a Welsh girl from Eckley, Pennsylvania; on his mother 's side, he is a descendant of Welsh and German grandparents. Most of Webb's defining characteristics -- his deep-throated, booming voice, and gregarious personality -- come from his father, Sidney R. Webb, an ebullient Palmerton lawyer. His inexhaustible curiosity about how the world really works and his lifelong fascination with the German language and love of reading come from his mother, Ellen Williams Webb.

Born in Palmerton on April 29, 1944, Webb received his early education in the Zinc town's public schools where he played varsity football and baseball. He attended Penn State University at the main campus in Centre County and earned a degree in Political Science (B.S.) in 1966. Following in his father's footsteps, the future jurist moved on to the University of Pittsburgh School of Law and was awarded a law degree (J.D.) in 1969. He was admitted to the Pennsylvania Supreme Court on November 17, 1970 and the Carbon Bar on April 20, 1970. Webb worked briefly in Pittsburgh as a tax specialist at Arthur Anderson Company. He then returned to Palmerton and joined his father Sidney R. Webb in the practice of law.

In 1973, the county commissioners appointed Webb to bolster the undermanned public defender's office which up to that time was Thomas S. McCready. Over the next three years, he defended hundreds of indigents in every type of criminal case. In 1973, he represented Robert W. Snyder of Palmerton in an unusual homicide case in which Snyder shot and killed his wife after she "dared" him to shoot her when he caught her in a compromising position with another man. Webb argued for and won a second degree murder conviction from Judge Heimbach.[63]

At the age of thirty-two, the youthful public defender decided to move his legal talents to the prosecutor's side of the docket. He won the Democratic nomination for district attorney in the spring of 1976, and in the fall general election, he stunned Carbon political pundits by unseating the long time incumbent district attorney, John Deutsch. For sixteen years - from 1976 to 1991 - Webb built a solid, county-wide reputation as a hard-hitting, law-and-order district attorney. Many chief prosecutors avoid the stressful work of trials and opt to administrate the office. Webb, however, eagerly assumed the prosecutor's role and personally tried all the major cases during his tenure. His love of the courtroom was palpable and infectious. Endowed with his father's gift of storytelling and strengthened by the mysteries and thrillers he likes to read, Webb's dramatic instincts allowed him to

---

[63]*Commonwealth v. Robert W. Snyder*, 26 June Term 1973.

touch juries in a way that captured their hearts as well as their minds. He took on the tough cases and he regularly won them.

The "Mudman" Simon murder case[64] in January of 1982 was a prosecutor's nightmare. The mummified body of Beth Ann Dusenberg Smith, a nineteen-year-old girl from Philadelphia, was found in a waterfilled strip mine in the Hazleton area seven years after her disappearance. State police were led to the strip mine by Leslie Hale "Scraggs" Smith, a convicted felon, who told police that Smith had been shot to death by "Mudman" Simon in a Jim Thorpe home in January of 1974. Simon and Smith were both members of a notorious gang of bikers known as the "Warlocks" who sold drugs and prowled the roads of Southeast Pennsylvania during the late 1960s and 1970s. The motive for the killing, according to "Scraggs," was because she refused to have sex with gang members.

This toxic stew of violence, sex and cycle gangs attracted wide press and television coverage for the trial and the case proceeded under heavy court security. John McDougall, a veteran criminal lawyer from Delaware County, represented "Mudman". Webb had the difficult task of making his case on the testimony of four "Warlocks." In a tour-de-force performance, he masterfully presented the chilling eyewitness testimony of the killing from Mudman's former gang members in such a compelling and credible way that the jury, after only four hours, returned a verdict of guilty of second degree murder.

During the last decades of the eighties, his prosecutorial skills were tested in the murder trials of Bonnie Leskin[65], Edward Lusch[66] and Wilbur Moyer.[67] As district attorney he tried more murder cases than any other prosecutor in Carbon County history. When the opportunity for higher office came in 1991 with the creation of a second judgeship in Carbon County, he promptly announced his candidacy. Running on the Democratic ticket, Webb defeated his Republican opponent William G. Schwab. Judge Albert H. Heimbach, a personal friend of the Webb family, swore Carbon's fifteenth judge into office on January 6, 1992.

On January 14,1966, Judge Webb married his wife Janet, a registered nurse from Pittsburgh and they have two sons, Thomas, now serving with the United States Army in Germany and Richard, Jr.,a recent graduate of Penn State University.

---

[64] *Commonwealth v. Robert Ronald Simon*, 202 CR 1981

[65] *Commonwealth v. Bonnie Leskin*, 371 CR 1985.

[66] *Commonwealth v. Edward Lusch*, 111 CR 1987.

[67] *Commonwealth v. Wilbur Guy Moyer*, 112 CR 1987 continued to 402 CR 1988.

CHAPTER X

COURT ADMINISTRATION AND CASE MANAGEMENT

If a nineteenth century Carbon lawyer walked through the courthouse in 1978, he would find very little had changed in the way the court and court-related offices looked and operated in Carbon County. Business in the row offices was carried on just as it was at the turn of the century. Court filings were stored in steel boxes which were placed in cubbyholes along the walls of vaults. Clerks manually entered court minutes and case histories in huge docket books. Case flow was strictly lawyer driven. Civil cases moved through the system only when one of the lawyers involved in the case chose to accelerate it or the client prodded the lawyer to activate it. The district attorney decided when a criminal case was to be tried.

From 1894 to 1979 legal pleadings and documents were four folded and stored in these steel boxes known as "pigeonholes."

Procedural Changes

In 1980, Judge Lavelle began a sweeping transformation of the management and operations of the Carbon Court system.

The four terms of court, relics of the past, were eliminated. Juries were brought in for one week or more every month for civil and criminal trials. All court proceedings were scheduled by court order. Computer generated notices of trials, hearings and arguments were sent to the attorneys and parties by the court scheduling officer.

Continuances, the bane of case dispositions, were required to be in writing and presented to the judge in motion court. A strong policy of refusing continuances except for compelling reasons was adopted. The time consuming call of the civil trial list was ended. Replacing it was a judge-driven pretrial conference system which featured realistic case analysis, aggressive settlement discussions, and a firm trial date. The long wait to argue pre-trial and post-trial motions was replaced with a regular monthly argument list and prompt dispositions. The practice of lawyers sauntering into the judge's chambers at any time with a motion or petition and a little chat while they tried to obtain some judicial advice on a "procedural problem" also ended. A motion court convened on Monday and Thursday of each week at 9:30 A.M. for the immediate consideration and disposition of most civil and criminal motions and petitions.

No longer would the judge walk into the courtroom on the first day of criminal jury trials with a courtroom full of jurors and hear the district attorney announce that there were no cases to be tried. A criminal pretrial system was introduced where every misdemeanor and felony case was scheduled for a conference three weeks before a jury panel was called in; at the conference, plea bargains were struck and a firm list of cases for trial was forwarded to the court. A deputy court administrator began scheduling cases for trial -- something virtually unheard of in Pennsylvania courts where tradition kept that function in the office of the district attorney.

Simultaneously, the arbitration system underwent major changes. Before that time, the prothonotary had the responsibility of manually selecting the panels, assigning cases to panels, and notifying the parties and counsel. It was a long, time consuming process with no monitoring of the panels. The new system, with the aid of a sophisticated computer program, assigned all arbitration cases to panels for hearing, selected the arbitration panels after reviewing them for conflicts, and assigned hearing days immediately upon the filing of a certificate of readiness. The computer produced arbitration hearing notices. The scheduling office notified attorneys and unrepresented parties of the dates and times for hearing and made sure the cases were heard. By using this management technique on the arbitration calendar, the time from certification to the actual hearing date has been less than two months since 1986 and all cases are closely monitored from scheduling to disposition. Beginning in 1992, the jurisdictional limits for compulsory arbitration were increased to $25,000 and this has helped to relieve some pressure on the workload of the court.

New Positions and Departments

On January 1, 1981, Judge Lavelle created the position of deputy district court administrator to oversee, manage, and monitor all civil, criminal, juvenile, and orphans' court matters which were brought before the court for hearing and dispositions. This position was responsible for processing and scheduling all matters to be heard by the court and court hearing officers and notifying the parties and lawyers to appear. The position of special court administrator was also put into place to coordinate the operations of the four district justice offices, to monitor all warrants issued by the district justices and to process all applications for public defenders. Betty Ann Rader was appointed as the deputy district court administrator and Alberta Boyle as special court administrator.

The ever increasing volume of cases eventually required the creation of a full-time scheduling officer and, in 1987, Linda McDonald was appointed to this important position. As the court system grew in numbers and complexity during the 1980s, it became apparent that a separate department headed by a professional administrator was needed to oversee and manage its internal operations, personnel and budget. On October 1, 1992, Richard P. Abbott, a lawyer with a Master's degree in Business Administration from the University of Pittsburgh, was appointed district court administrator and charged with these responsibilities.

Five new departments were created in the court system, each focusing on a specific area of court responsibility: (1) domestic relations, (2) juvenile court office, (3) adult probation department, (4) jury commission office and (5) bureau of collections.

Domestic Relations Department

On January 1, 1980, the domestic relations office became a separate division of the Court of Common Pleas. New procedures were put in place and its staff of five was restructured. To accommodate the growing caseload, major renovations of space on the third floor of the courthouse formerly occupied by the district attorney and civil defense began in 1979 and were completed in 1980. Most of the funding for these improvements came from the Title IV-D Cooperative Agreement between the County of Carbon and the Pennsylvania Department of Public Welfare. Judge Lavelle directed that the filing and docketing of new non-support complaints and modifications of support orders take place in the domestic relations office instead of the clerk of courts office. With this change, non-support cases which had been criminal in nature and filed in the clerk's office since 1843 began to be processed like other family law civil matters. A Datapoint computer system was installed in 1981 to capture information on non-support cases and drive the processing, monitoring, and enforcement of support orders. The system of child support claims moved from the paper age to the electronic superhighway of interstate child support automation which included routine wage withholding. Charles W. Ripkey was appointed director of the domestic relations office and Judith Fatzinger, assistant director. When Ripkey left in 1984, Judge Lavelle appointed Judith Fatzinger to succeed him as the director. Daniel F. Zeigler, Esquire was appointed as hearing officer and Robert Reese was named chief enforcement officer. Deborah Tout was installed as bookkeeper and Kathy Miller as intake officer. In its first year of operation under the new system, the department had an active caseload of 948 cases and collected and disbursed $1,081,733 to mothers and children.

By 1990, non-support cases and the pursuit of delinquent parents by contempt proceedings had exploded to a caseload of 2418. In December 1991, the domestic relations office moved to the first floor of the courthouse to the space occupied for many years by the county commissioners and the election bureau to make room for the second judge and court judge and court administrative offices. The department's facilities were renovated and in 1993, its computer system was upgraded to a state of the art Unix driven system. In 1992, domestic relations handled a total active caseload of 2708 cases and collected and distributed $4,076,258. Currently, the office consists of Judith M. Fatzinger, domestic relations director, Robert Reese, chief domestic relations officer, Mary Kunkle, deputy chief domestic relations officer, Susan Snyder, domestic relations officer, Michael Hydock, domestic relations fiscal officer, Deborah Tout, domestic relations bookkeeper, and Mary Ann Balogach, domestic relations technician. Domestic relations intake officers are Stacy Kattner and Fay Schlenner. Daniel F. Zeigler and Carole J. Walbert are the domestic relations hearing officers.

Juvenile Court Department

A separate juvenile court office for delinquency cases was also created in 1980. It opened offices at 5 Broadway in Jim Thorpe with a court directive to work closely with the office of children and youth. Juvenile delinquent cases had since the 1930s been processed by the adult probation office along with nonsupport cases. New rules of procedure for the handling of cases in the juvenile court system were adopted. Gary Dobias, an assistant district attorney, was assigned by the district attorney to prosecute all juvenile delinquency cases. A policy of allowing press coverage of juvenile cases was adopted by the court for the first time. The court appointed Joseph J. Hornick, Jr. as the chief juvenile court officer and instituted a student court visitation program where local high schools came to juvenile court to see and hear actual cases. James E. Dodson now heads the juvenile court office. Kimmy L. Redline and Paul R. Zona round out the professional staff. In 1992, the juvenile office processed 208 delinquency cases and supervised 129 juveniles.

Jury Commission

Judge Lavelle began a complete revision of the jury selection system in July of 1978 as Carbon became one of the first counties in Pennsylvania to take advantage of new jury management legislation. Until that time, the jury commissioners would solicit names of jurors from the committeemen and committeewomen of their respective political parties. The jury commissioners and a secretary would then spend two or three days writing these names on two by four inch slips of paper and placing them into the "jury wheel" to be drawn four times a year for the civil, criminal and grand juries for the terms of court. The county jury pool was probably illegally constituted because it was dominated by pre-selected retired citizens, did not have proportionate representation of the county municipalities and deliberately excluded young people.

In 1972, the Legislature allowed the use of computers to select the names of prospective jurors and in 1980, the Jury and Compensation Act enabled courts of common pleas to use the one-day, one-trial system of jury management. Taking advantage of this legislation, Judge Lavelle applied computer technology to the jury system and designed a selection process which would have no discrimination potential. The computer was programmed to randomly select each month a jury pool by obtaining from each municipality a number of jurors proportionate to its percentage of the total county population and produce a summons for each juror selected. He initiated the one-day, one-trial jury system in Carbon County where a citizen summoned for jury service is either selected for one trial on the day he or she reports or is released from service at the end of the jury selection process. A database of some 40,000 Carbon County citizens consisting of a combination of registered voters, tax payers, motor vehicle licensees, and recent high school graduates was carefully and painstakingly entered into the computer system. In 1983, the system was further refined to choose individual jury panels and produce printouts of background data on each juror which can be used by the attorneys during jury selection. As a convenience for jurors, panels were divided into active and stand-by jurors. The stand-by juror was required to phone into the jury commissioner's office during the weekend before trial began and was told by a recorded message whether he or she had to report for active duty. Active jurors were only called in when cases were reasonably expected to be tried. One of the unique features of the system was that upon completion of jury service, each juror was immediately paid by check and reimbursed for mileage expenses. The jury selection process has been under the able supervision of Mary Alice Herman, director of the jury commission office since 1984. Willard Hill and Russell Zellner are the current jury commissioners.

On June 15, 1979, a new jury orientation program using color slides and tape recordings was unveiled. Developed and written by Judge Lavelle, it informed jurors about the trial process and instructed them on how to perform their duties as jurors. It continues to be shown to all jury panels in the main courtroom to this time.

Adult Probation and Parole

In 1980, the adult probation and parole office was set up as a separate court department and given responsibility for the community behavior of all adults who were placed on ARD, probation, or parole, and to collect fines, costs and restitution. For the first time, this office prepared for the court pre-sentence investigations and sentencing recommendations. Anthony C. Harvilla was appointed the chief adult probation and parole officer with a staff of two officers, Marvin Corra and Jeanne McArdle. In 1980, the office monitored a total of 138 probationers and parolees and prepared twenty-eight pre-sentence reports.

By 1992, the office had outgrown its quarters in the courthouse annex. It had expanded to a chief and five field probation specialists with a mean average caseload of 539 defendants. It was producing eighty-three pre-sentence reports a year. The probation offices were moved to the first floor of the courthouse into renovated office space which had been vacated by the recorder of deeds. The current chief probation officer is Ronald S.

Kokinda and his staff of five consists of Jeanne B. McArdle, Joseph J. Burke, Michael T. Degilio, Patrick T. Henry, and Elizabeth Amy Ritz.

Bureau of Collections

The Carbon County bureau of collections was established in May of 1983 and charged with the collection and monitoring of all costs, fines, and restitutions imposed by a court order of the Common Pleas Court. Judge Lavelle designed a computer program which interfaced with the clerk of courts computer system to monitor all payments by defendants and to enter all monies collected and disburse it to the appropriate payee. The court appointed William C. McGinley as the first director of the bureau and with collection officer Dolores Scaran, this small staff operated the entire system. Within a year of its operation, delinquent accounts declined from about sixty percent (based on preautomation sampling) to twenty-two percent and the rate of collection increased from twenty percent to eighty percent. In the first seven months of operation, the bureau increased collections of costs, fines, and restitution by $55,000 over 1982. The effectiveness of the bureau has been clearly proved by the steady increase in collections over the past decade. In 1983, the bureau effected a total collection of $111,893; in 1992, the bureau collected a total of $399,493 from a total caseload of 1558 defendants. Its impressive record is largely the result of the leadership of Dolores Scaran who became the director of the bureau in 1985 and her dedicated staff of Madeline T. Ligenza, Heather Frantz and Lori Haydt.

Law Clerks

One of his most important contributions to court administration was Judge Lavelle's successful lobbying for a law clerk. Because so much of the judge's day was being spent on the bench presiding over trials and hearings, there was little time for doing legal research, the endless reading and analysis of cases, statutes and legal briefs which constitute the grist for grinding out judicial decisions. In addition he recognized the need for the judge in a busy court to have a sounding board on how cases should be decided and how the decisions should be reached. The creation of the law clerk position in 1978 was designed to address these needs and the law clerks have collaborated with the judge in producing the required writings for the Appellate Courts and written opinions on the major issues which come before the court.

The following have served as Judge Lavelle's law clerks: Stephen J. Hartz (1978); George T. Dydynsky (1981-1982); Susan Rooney (1983-1984); Paul Curran (1984); Carole J. Wildoner (1985-1986); David Addy (1986-1988); Kerry S. Freidl (1988-1989); Gregory L. Mousseau (1989-1991); Edmund J. Healy (1991-1993) was appointed by Judge Lavelle in 1991 and became Judge Webb's law clerk in January of 1992; George C. Parrish (1991-1993); L. Kimberly Law (1993-). Lance Gordon (1993-) presently serves as law clerk to Judge Webb.

Court Automation

Computer technology in the 1970s created new ways of doing business in the courts. Overwhelmed by the burgeoning case load, mandated new programs, and the problems of managing the overburdened court system, the court became one of the first in Pennsylvania that looked to computers for the solution. In 1981, Judge Lavelle persuaded the county commissioners to purchase for the court a Datapoint Computer hardware system, first for the domestic relations office, and then other court offices. Starting from ground zero, he designed and with David R. Fink of Tridata Corporation of Allentown developed a fully integrated computer system for every court-related office in the county -- a process which went on for seven years. The evolution of the Carbon County Court computer system and how automation is used in the operation of the court and court-related offices are detailed in **Chapter XI** of this book. In 1992, a Unix operating system replaced the old Datapoint Resource Management system and today forty terminals enter and share data from all court-related offices. A state of the art PC network featuring WordPerfect 5.2 and electronic mail for the judges and court administration personnel has also been installed. Roberta Brewster has assumed the difficult and complex responsibility for managing the court computer operations as well as handling all trouble shooting calls for the system.

District Justices

Before 1970, there were four elected justices of the peace in Carbon County. Lawyers were only speaking half in jest when they said a justice of the peace or J.P. meant one of two things: judgment for plaintiff or judgment for prosecutor. Their civil jurisdiction was limited to landlord-tenant cases and trespass/assumpsit cases involving amounts up to $300. Traffic violations were required to be taken to the "nearest available magistrate" so speed traps were placed by the police near a J.P. to be favored. (All fees were paid to the personal use of the J.P.) While the J.P. then as now acted as the issuing authority in all criminal processes, venue was countywide and police could take their cases wherever they chose.

In 1968, the Pennsylvania electorate changed the Judiciary Article of the Constitution and among other things, abolished the J.P. fee system. It was replaced by a system of elected district justices who were to be salaried judicial officers of the Commonwealth no longer dependent upon fees for their livelihood. Their jurisdiction was not to extend beyond the boundaries of their magisterial district except upon order of the president judge of the Court of Common Pleas of the county having jurisdiction over them. All fees are paid over into the general fund of the county which has the duty of insuring that each district justice has a court facility with a courtroom and such office or offices as might be necessary so that the business of the court could be conducted "with dignity, decorum and dispatch."

The Supreme Court of Pennsylvania in 1969 approved the establishment of five magisterial districts for Carbon County conforming to district boundaries drawn by President Judge Albert H. Heimbach. Judge Heimbach later reduced the number to four districts: District 1 in Jim Thorpe under District Justice Harry Heydt; District 2 in Palmerton under District Justice Willard Steigerwalt; District 3 in Lansford under District Justice Joseph Svercheck; District 4 in Beaver Meadows under District Justice Andrew Moisey.

District Justices in 1986: Andrew Moisey and Joseph Svercheck, President Judge John P. Lavelle, District Justices Paul Hadzick, Harry Heydt and Willard Steigerwalt

With the establishment of the new districts, a new system of processing summary violations of the law, particularly the traffic laws, was begun. The citation replaced the information/complaint for these cases. Processing time was cut in half. The constitutional changes also required that if a district justice was not trained in the law, he or she must successfully complete a course of training established and administered by the Minor Judiciary Education Board of Pennsylvania before taking office. Every district justice is now required to attend education courses each year. Alberta Boyle who was appointed by Judge Lavelle in 1982 as the first special court administrator, attended to the logistical

CARBON COUNTY MAGISTERIAL DISTRICTS

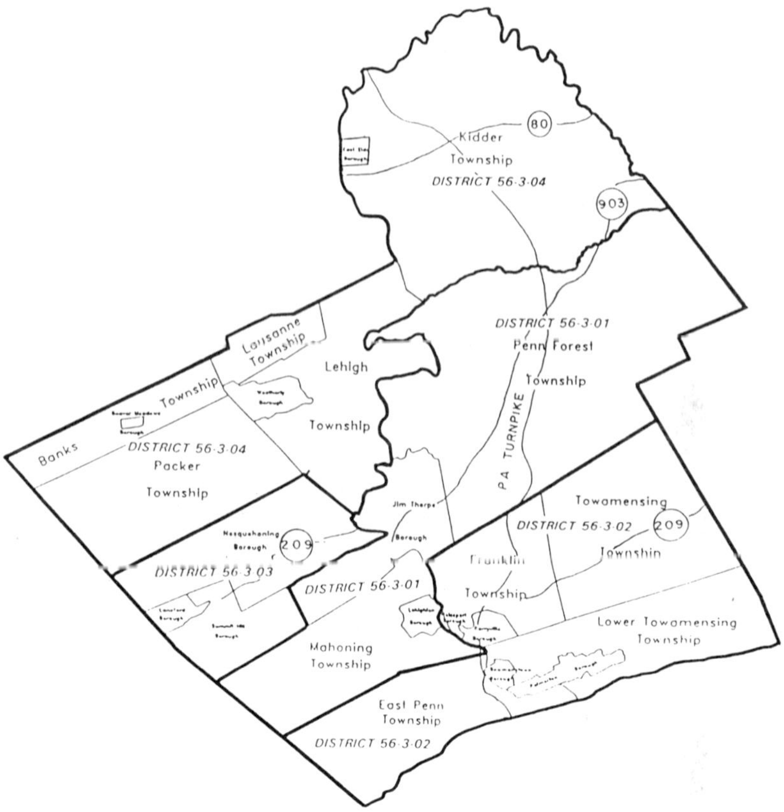

Magisterial Districts established in 1993

and personnel needs of the four district justice offices, conducted training seminars for the clerical staff, and processed all applications for the appointment of public defenders. When Mrs. Boyle passed away unexpectedly, Aileen Cassidy, who had many years of experience as a clerical officer in District Justice Harry Heydt's office, was appointed special court administrator for the district justices. During Aileen Cassidy's tenure as administrator, all four district justice offices were computerized, placed on-line with the main court computer and trained by the president judge in how to enter all criminal and traffic case data into the court computer system. This allowed the court to immediately access data and monitor the district justice caseload.

District justices of the peace are now state judicial officers and therefore are salaried employees of the Commonwealth. Since 1970, they are required to file with the AOPC office and the president judge monthly reports on their case activities, new filings and dispositions by type of case and type of disposition, and to report the age of pending cases. Part of the responsibility of the office of the court administrator is to monitor these reports and see that the district justice calendars are kept current.

In 1992, under the leadership of Supreme Court Justice Stephen Zapalla the Administrative Office of the Pennsylvania Courts completed a computerization of all district justice courts in the Commonwealth. Now all financial and case activity transactions are entered directly into a state computer database located near Harrisburg. Numerous reports are produced in a variety of formats, although little is reported or is reportable that is yet of any use to the president judge or court administrators at the county level. The arrival of this system resulted in the termination of the district justice's on-line system with the Carbon County Court computer system.

District Justices of Carbon County. Clockwise: Paul Hadzick, Bruce Appleton, Irene Hudasky, and Edward Lewis.

During the period from 1990 to 1992, the county provided new and well appointed office facilities for each of the district justices. District Justice Hadzick's office in Weatherly is the only magisterial office in Pennsylvania with a drive-in window. In 1993, the four district justices of Carbon County are: Edward Lewis of Jim Thorpe who presides over District 1, Irene Hudasky of Lansford who presides over District II, Paul Hadzick of Weatherly who presides over District IV, and Bruce Appleton of Palmerton who presides over District III.

The Court and the County

Over the years, mirroring a condition common throughout Pennsylvania, the relationship between the court and county government has been variously harmonious, contentious, and litigious. During the latter part of the 1980s, as the loss of federal revenue sharing funds began to affect county budgets, the differences of opinions widened dramatically over what the court felt was necessary to run an efficient judicial system and what the county commissioners felt was needed. The issues of separation of powers, management of court employees, control of court funds and the amount of funding needed by the court became the subjects of heated discussions and eventually a court case.

In 1989, in the case of *Lavelle v. Koch et al*,[68] the issue of who determines what is reasonable and necessary compensation for court employees, and what the burden of proof is in such a case, was the subject of litigation which lasted over two years. Judge Lavelle, as president judge of the Court of Common Pleas brought a mandamus action against County Commissioners Albert Koch, Luther Getz, and Dean DeLong because of their unilateral removal of funds from the court budget and refusal to approve (for court

[68] *617 A.2d 319 (Pa. 1992).*

employees) proposed salary increases which had been established in a court designed pay scale. The commissioners hired former county solicitor Roger Nanovic to represent their interests in the lawsuit. Acting on behalf of the court, John M. Elliott, a bright, talented and resourceful Philadelphia lawyer with roots in the hard coal regions, petitioned the Supreme Court to assume plenary jurisdiction. The Supreme Court agreed to accept jurisdiction and promptly ordered the county commissioners to return the funds they had removed from the court budget. It then assigned the case to the Commonwealth Court for hearings on the salary issues. After two days of hearings in April of 1990, Judge Silvestri Silvestri of Allegheny County, who was appointed as a Special Master, filed an eighty-four-page report ruling that the president judge had to show that the court "ship" is sinking in a backlog of cases and court employees are abandoning ship before being entitled to relief in mandamus. He recommended dismissal of the lawsuit. Argument on exceptions to Silvestri's report followed. The Supreme Court of Pennsylvania rejected the "sinking ship" standard proposed by Judge Silvestri. It ruled that Judge Lavelle had not met his burden of proving that the proposed increased compensation for the court employees was reasonable and necessary based on two findings:

> (1) despite his use of various labor market studies and wage rate comparisons to establish job salary scales and grading "Judge Lavelle has not offered any evidence showing how his proposed salaries compared with those offered by any other employers."
>
> (2) Judge Lavelle did not provide information to satisfy the Supreme Court "that his ability to attract and retain qualified employees was impaired."

Although the ruling was not favorable to the local court and dismissed Judge Lavelle's complaint, the case established an important precedent. The Supreme Court, for the first time, spelled out the type of evidence Common Pleas Courts of Pennsylvania must present in court to meet their burden of proof to obtain relief when county governments refuse to meet the reasonable and necessary needs of the judicial branch of government. The Supreme Court also ruled for the first time that the AOPC Office is to provide legal counsel to the local courts in court funding disputes.

More importantly, the lawsuit had a salutary effect on the way county officials established salaries for county non-union employees. It provided the impetus for the progressive Russell Salary Study of 1991 which graded county jobs and established salaries for them comparable to the Carbon County business market area. In 1992 when the salary board used the Russell Study to set salaries for county employees and the salary scales prepared by Judge Lavelle for court employees, it marked the first time in county history that county salaries were based on market studies of comparable jobs rather than political and personal considerations.

Time Standards

In the court's continuing effort to seek innovative and effective ways to improve the flow of criminal cases, Judge Lavelle with the cooperation of District Attorney Gary Dobias and Public Defenders Stephen Vlossak and Robert Yurchak, and the four district justices, introduced a new criminal case management program on May 6, 1992. Based on recommendations of the American Bar Association and the National Center for State Courts, time standards between various events in the criminal system were developed and put into effect. Criminal cases are now being processed through the court system in accordance with these time standards. The goal of the program was to adjudicate 90% of all criminal cases within 150 days of filing a criminal complaint and 98% within 180 days. The key feature of the program is that the district attorney's office and defense counsel share information, address case issues and strike plea agreements at the preliminary hearing instead of at the latter stages of the criminal proceedings. In its first year of operation under the time standards, a study of 392 cases processed in 1993 showed that the average time between bind over and adjudication was decreased from 162 days to 96 days -- an overall reduction of 66 days. The following graphic reflects the current time standards:

CRIMINAL CASEFLOW MANAGEMENT SYSTEM
(EFFECTIVE MAY 6, 1992)
CARBON COUNTY CRIMINAL CASE FLOW CHART*

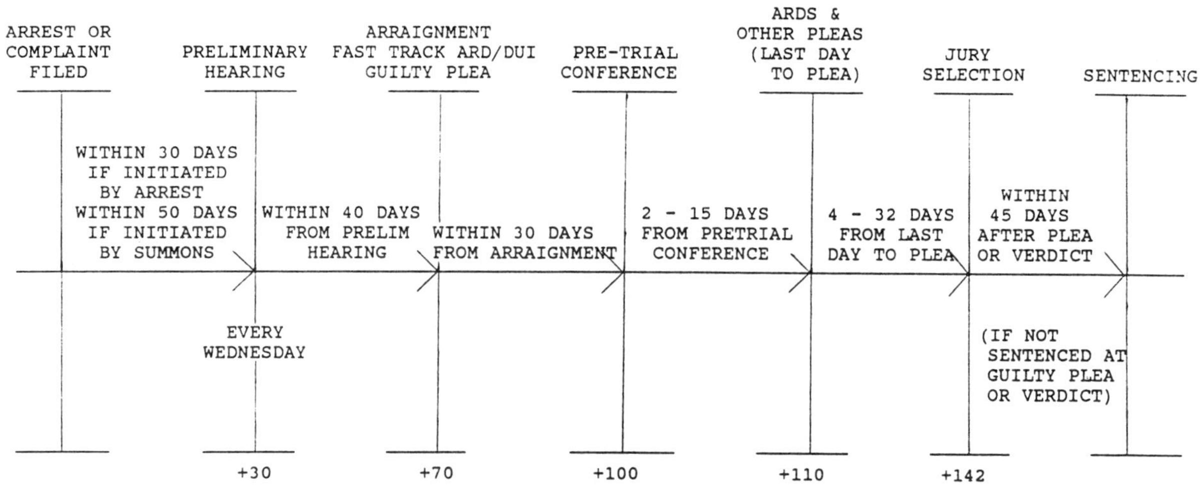

*The County will be divided into a Northern Division and Southern Division for Preliminary Hearings in Misdemeanor and Felony Cases. Four District Justices will conduct Preliminary Hearings in clusters every Wednesday. Two District Justices in each division will conduct their Preliminary Hearings commencing at 9:00 A.M. and two District Justices in each Division will conduct their Preliminary Hearings commencing at 1:00 P.M.

N.B. DELIVERY OF DISCOVERABLE INFORMATION - AS RECEIVED

In 1992, the court began a proactive rather than the traditional reactive approach to the civil caseflow. Over a year in preparation, a completely new set of civil court rules were adopted in July of 1993 streamlining the motion practice and laying the groundwork to move cases expeditiously through the system. The number of jurors in civil cases was reduced from twelve to eight. Arbitration limits were raised to $25,000. Processing of custody cases was refined to allow earlier and more expeditious dispositions. These rules were made available to lawyers not only in printed form but also in the public access data base of the court computer system. With the new rules as the foundation, a new civil case management system began. The court assumed control of all civil cases from the time of filing. Within ninety days of filing, all potential court cases are sorted by computer, picked up by the court scheduling office and earmarked as Fast Track, Standard or Complex cases. Disposition of these cases are to take place within definite time standards established by the court for each category. At the earliest stages of the litigation a judge will be involved in the case through telephonic management conferences and will set dates for completion of discovery, pretrial motions and trials. The goal of the system is to dispose of all cases within two years of filing.

As the court moves into the twenty-first century, current technology and national trends indicate that television cameras will capture court proceedings and video taping will replace the court stenographer. Personal computers will be in front of the judge, lawyers, jurors and witnesses. These screens will be able to show computer-animated graphics, documentary evidence and instant replays of the proceedings. Pleadings will be filed by FAX. WestLaw and Lexis with their CD-ROMs will put a law library on every lawyer's desktop. Much of the communication between lawyers will be through computers and not U.S. mail. If Carbon County's Court of Common Pleas is to continue to serve the legal needs of the county promptly and efficiently, it will have to keep pace with these high tech developments. Only then will the court be able to carry out the mandate of William Penn that "justice shall neither be denied or delayed."

CHAPTER XI

HIGH TECH COURT SYSTEM

[On March 21, 1990, President Judge John P. Lavelle gave the following talk to members of the Northampton County Bar at a meeting of the Northampton County Bar Association at the Holiday Inn in Bethlehem. His remarks contain a complete history of the development of the Carbon County Court computer system, and are, therefore, printed in their entirety.]

In many respects it may seem peculiar, indeed, even presumptuous, for a Common Pleas Court Judge to address a group of lawyers to talk about Court computerization. Many learned commentators have said that our nation's court systems are the last frontier in the computer age. One critic has caustically observed: Courts would still be using quill pens if there were enough people raising geese.

This is pure hyperbole, of course, but I do think it is a fair criticism to say that judges and court systems generally are lagging behind you in the world of computers.

The very nature of the law's reliance on precedent -- a reluctance to change what is known and familiar -- leaves us behind the lawyers, not only in the use of computerized legal research, but also with many other basic technological tools most lawyers take for granted -- such as word processing, electronic transcription of court reporters' keystrokes and case management systems. There are, of course, other reasons why so many Courts lag behind other government agencies and law firms in the use of computers. One is the complex organizational structure of the courts themselves. Many states, like Pennsylvania, have what could aptly be described as a maze of jurisdictions. These mazes create inevitable turf battles and complicate ordinary decision-making.

Another is the lack of adequate budgets for the court systems. Courts typically receive between one percent and two percent of the local tax dollar. Many jurisdictions have found it expensive to design computer systems for a dynamic body of information that changes constantly and requires a high degree of reliability and accessibility.

After some eight years' experience in designing and operating a computerized court management system in my own County of Carbon, I have faced these obstacles and I would like, tonight, to bring you a message of hope for the judges and the courts. I will tell you what a small court system has been able to accomplish with a modest budget and monumental amount of hard work.

In January of 1978, as a newly elected president judge, I confronted a slow moving, antediluvian court system, ill-equipped not only to handle the current caseload, but totally unprepared to face any increase in the business of the Courts. Carbon's legal system could best be described as a stumbling dinosaur: overweight with paper, hobbling along with a centuries-old tradition of customs and practices.

Civil and Criminal Court clerks laboriously made manual entries in huge docket books recording the sequential case history and manually issuing receipts. Pleadings and legal documents were stamped and folded, not once but twice, and placed in small pigeon hole files after being bound with string or a rubber band. Pleadings were not docketed for weeks, sometimes months.

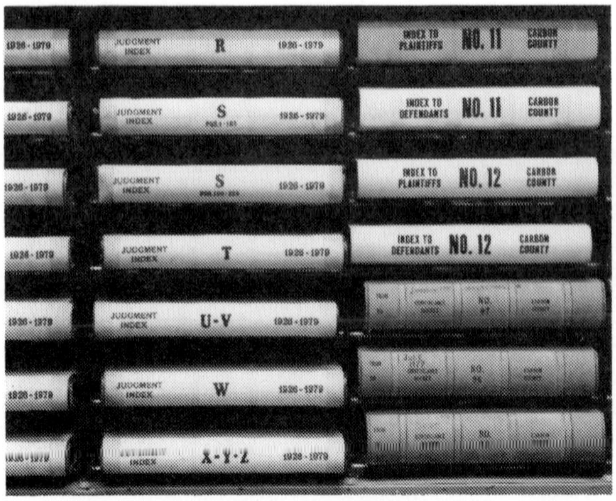

Case docket books and indices.

The system truly was grinding to a halt. Reform became a practical necessity. I began to look around for some solutions. By coincidence the world of computers was in the late '60s and early '70s leaving the exclusive domain of the world of science, and the business and banking worlds were rapidly making and proudly announcing remarkable advances through their use of computers. Many urban law firms were producing pleadings and briefs on word processors and their files and clients were being managed by computerized systems.

I studied computer systems which were already in existence in Philadelphia, Montgomery and Delaware counties. The most important lesson I learned from studying the other systems was "you cannot solve a problem by computerizing a process that does not work manually": you just get a system that makes mistakes at a higher speed -- at the speed of light. Before any court office could be successfully computerized, that office's procedures had to be modified and modernized to make it more efficient regardless of whether the procedures became automated or were left as manual ones. Parenthetically, I believe the authority to require the modification and modernization of procedures is critical to the success of any court computerization process.

So the first thing I did in the automation process was to amend the local rules and modify the office procedures in the court related offices to create an efficient and productive manual system of procedures. In 1982, I made the most critical decision in the computerization of the court system. I hired, on a part-time basis, David R. Fink, a brilliant computer programmer with Allentown's Tridata Corporation. He brought to the court a bright, quick mind and a talent for creating user friendly programming. Together we set out on the long and arduous road to computerizing the Carbon County Court system.

In automating we had a self-imposed restraint: each design of a computerized system had to have at least a ten-year design life. In other words, whatever we came up with had to be expected to work efficiently for at least ten years.

We also insisted that each court-related office's data system be integrated with the others -- meaning that the different offices had to use computers with similar operating systems, and that all programming had to use similar computer language; but both the hardware and the software had to be compatible for use on IBM or IBM-compatible hardware.

In 1981, computers replaced the docket books and provided instant retrieval of case information.

The offices that were automated first were those that would result in the greatest improvement or needed help the most. The jury system was one of the first to be automated because it was the most unpopular link between the public and the court system.

We then moved to the court-related offices which pipelined cases into the Common Pleas Court system. First the Office of the Prothonotary, then the Clerk of Courts and the District Attorney, then the Office of the Register of Wills and Orphans' Court, and finally the four District Justice offices. The collection of fines, costs and restitution in criminal cases had been notoriously inefficient for years. I established, as an arm of the Court, a separate Bureau of Collections to oversee this badly neglected area of the court system and provided it with a highly sophisticated computer application. Having computerized these filing offices, we then went on to automate a case-management and scheduling system for court administration.

In 1988, we added the Recorder of Deeds Office to the database. At the time there was an eight-month backlog in indexing deeds and mortgages in the county. Our goal was to replace the manual indexing in docket books with an automated system of indexing which would include bookkeeping and receipt-issuing functions. I designed a program which required each land document to carry same parcel number used in the tax assessment office to identify each tract of land and when entered in the database would allow a title search by computer rather than by docket books. Within two months after the system was installed, the backlog was cleared and the system has operated smoothly and efficiently.

Our overall objective was to design a computer system that would allow the Judge and court officials to have immediate access to all information in the court system, to schedule trials and hearings which were conflict-free, and most important, to permit lawyers to perform many of their functions including title searches in their offices instead of in the courthouse.

After seven years (and you must remember I only had my one programmer about twice a month), we completed the process.

What can we now do with the Carbon Court computer system?

Let me relate just a few of the benefits.

All active civil, criminal and juvenile cases have been indexed and docketed, and court papers are entered into the database of the system within fifteen minutes after filing.

The computer prepares argument lists, civil and criminal trial lists, miscellaneous hearing lists, arbitration lists and pre-trial conference lists. The system checks for conflicts in lawyer's schedules. When a case is scheduled for trial by the computer, the computer automatically checks the chosen dates with the attorney's other cases to be sure there are no conflicts. This has been uniquely successful and has dramatically cut down the number of continuances (continuances due to conflicts are the single most common cause of continuances in most courts in the country.)

Besides computerizing the Clerk of Courts Office and the District Attorney's Office, the system has been applied to the back half of the criminal justice structure -- that part concerning fines, costs and restitution assessed on defendants. When computers were first introduced in this area six years ago, the initial statistics were startling. Sixty-five percent of defendants had never paid anything and all but six percent of the rest were delinquent in their court-ordered payments.

Now the computer system sends each defendant a letter within a week of sentencing setting forth the amount owed, the payment schedule and the instructions for payment. It keeps track of payments and issues a notice if the person falls behind. If two notices go by without response, the computer produces a contempt petition. Delinquencies have dropped substantially and between 1983 and 1989 there has been a 265 percent increase in the collection of costs, fines and restitution. The lesson we can all learn from this fine-collecting activity, I believe, is that if the Courts handle any function that is essentially financial, computers can really perform that function very well. Our Domestic Relations Office is also computerized on a stand-alone system and its collection efficiency on support orders has also been dramatically improved.

Carbon County went to a one-day, one-trial system for jurors in 1982. The computer system automatically selects candidates to receive juror questionnaires, automatically prints and mails the questionnaires, issues summonses, produces voir dire information on each juror, recycles unused jurors, computes pay and mileage, issues checks, keeps track of juror utilization and provides ongoing statistics. We have not only eliminated jurors hanging around the Courts with nothing to do, but we have also cut the cost of using jurors and the amount of time to select a jury.

Remote access is undoubtedly the most popular feature of our computer system. All courthouse information which is public is accessible to the public through computer modems, and access is presently free of charge. If a lawyer wants case information, if he wants to check the judgment or miscellaneous index, if he wants to check his own inventory of active cases in the court system or the court's calendar or his own Court appearances, Recorder of Deeds indexes -- all of that information is available to him or her twenty-four hours a day, seven days a week through the telephone and the caller's computer. It is also available during business hours at public terminals in the courthouse.

What has been the cost of this system?

It may surprise you to learn that the cost of our hardware was $190,000 and the software was $172,000 for a total cost of three hundred sixty thousand dollars paid out over a period of seven years. The total cost for the computerization of the Recorder of Deeds office including training was a mere $10,000. The computer investment for the county amounted to a little over $50,000 per year.

Whether offsite public access to the computer system should be free or paid for like WestLaw and Lexis or some other fee system, is being debated in many quarters. I strongly believe that the cost of computerizing the courts, including the public access, should be paid by the front end users of the system, i.e. the litigants in civil cases, and in criminal cases the defendants. To recover the costs of the hardware and software in Carbon County, we added a *data processing fee* in all of the court-related offices within the structures of the state statutory fee limits. This fee is paid at the time of the first filing in civil cases and is added to defendant costs in criminal cases.

Presently we have an electronic bulletin board for the members of the bar that includes information on how the various public access programs work, a quick reference to every written court opinion and jury verdict of the Court of Common Pleas of Carbon County since 1978. We are presently adding the Local Rules of Court we have recently recompiled, and plan to develop an electronic mail system so that attorneys can send messages to other attorneys by computer.

Automation produces a galaxy of benefits. Most departments in the court system will show an increase in productivity and efficiency. The collection of monies by the Bureau of Collections will double, even triple. Other departments will noticeably improve the quality of service to the public. The most pervasive benefit, which applies to all automated departments, is the regaining of control. The court system is now in the driver's seat instead of being driven by its users. As lawyers, you should have a vital interest in this new frontier for the courts. If the court systems are truly going to do the work of serving your clients and giving them their "day in court," you must help your judges get the financial support from county executives to complete the automation of your court system.

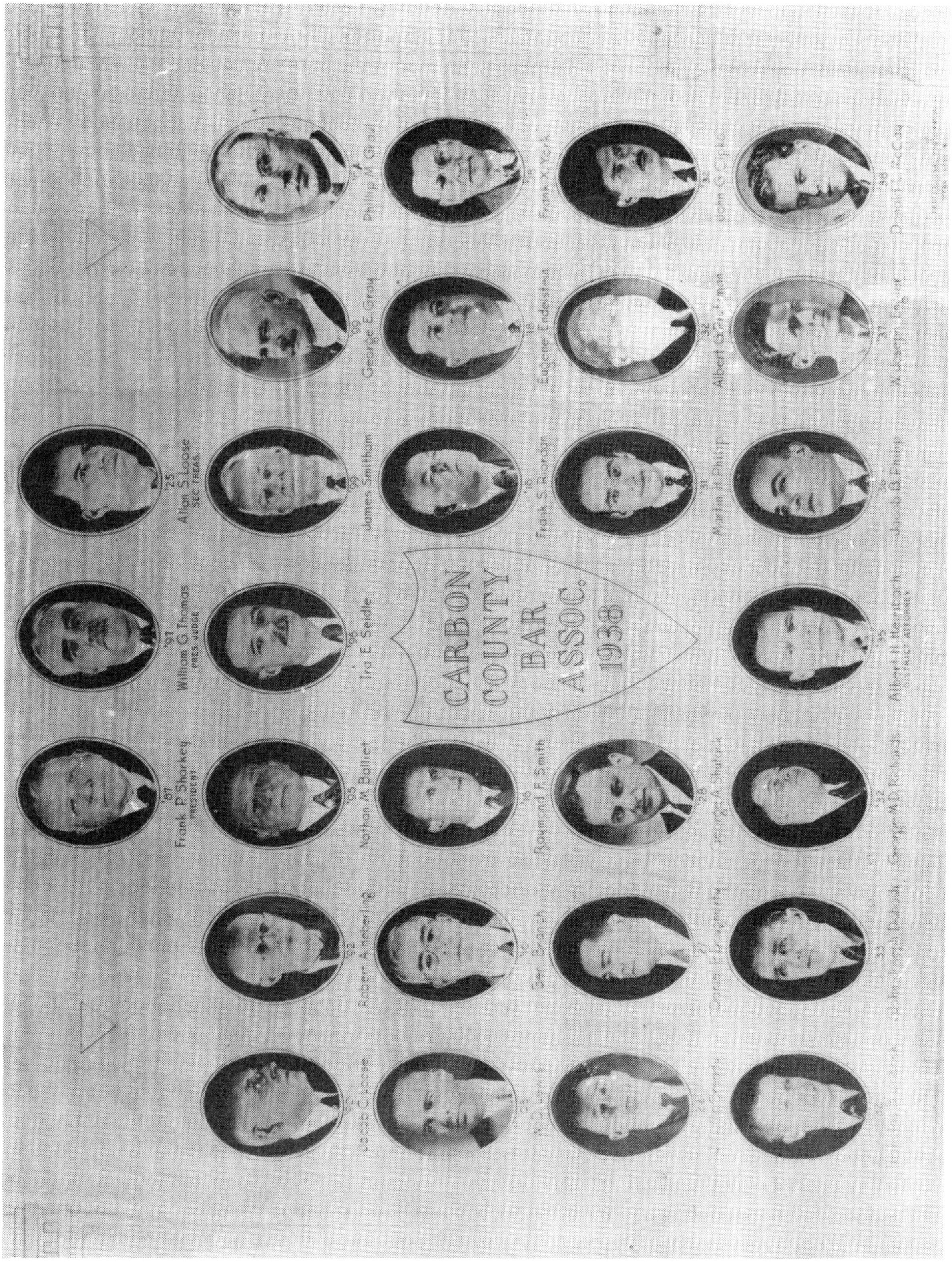

1938 Carbon Bar

CHAPTER XII

CARBON COUNTY BAR ASSOCIATION

The early Carbon County Bar Association was a loosely knit organization made up of lawyers admitted to the Carbon County Bar and judges, both president judges and associate judges. It had a president and a secretary, but little other structure and no regular meetings. Although court records and dockets provide information on individual members admitted to the bar and reveal many bar resolutions, no minutes of meetings, if they were ever kept, have been preserved. Court orders generated all activities of the bar. The court directed various members of the bar to draft memorial resolutions, serve on various committees, audit accounts and investigate problems in the row offices.

Admissions to the Bar

The most prestigious and powerful committee appointed by the court was the Board of Law Examiners. In the early years of the bar when most aspiring lawyers "read law" in a local law office, this committee and the president judge administered the law examination tests and decided whether the applicant was qualified to practice law. In the 1950s the Supreme Court took over the supervision of qualifications to practice law and bar examinations. The Carbon Board of Law Examiners was then charged with examining moral qualifications. If this committee decided against the applicant, he or she could not be admitted to local practice. If the committee approved, it would then present a petition to the court recommending the admission of the applicant to the bar. Admissions to the bar were held formally before the president judge with the neophyte lawyers' family, friends and bar members in attendance. After welcoming remarks by the judge and president of the bar, the bar extended congratulations and the judge would, as soon as possible, give the new member his first legal work by appointing him a master in divorce, a guardian ad litem or auditor in a contested orphans' court proceeding.

The most unusual bar admission occurred on May 15, 1942. World War II was raging. George Brinley Richards had, almost simultaneously, passed his state bar exam and been called into the United States Army. To assure his admission to the bar before he went off to war, Judge McCready called a special session of court at 7:00 in the evening. Attired in his new military uniform, Richards, in the presence of his proud parents and members of his family, became a member of the Carbon Bar and then returned to New Cumberland for basic training. The motion for his admission was made by his preceptor and namesake George M. D. Richards of Lansford.

Chancellors of the Bar

From the beginning, the oldest member of the bar was elected chancellor or president and he retained the office until his death. This tradition could be viewed as the bar's way of showing respect for its most senior member. Given the reluctance of most lawyers to make changes, this custom persisted, no doubt, because of their desire to preserve the status quo. After the bar association incorporated in 1957 and younger lawyers began to dominate its membership, there was agitation to rotate the chancellorship each year starting with the member who was longest in years of admission to the bar being succeeded by the member who was the next senior in admission. It was felt that every member would then have the honor of being chancellor. This tenure rule was adopted in an amendment to the by-laws in 1962 and was followed until 1983. At that time, most of the bar felt that the chancellor needed at least two years to initiate and follow through on bar association programs. The term of the chancellor was changed to two years. At the August 1993 annual meeting held at Sciota the association decided to return the chancellor's term to one year. A listing of the chancellors of the Carbon Bar and their terms appears in **Appendix C**, page 407.

Bar Chancellor Nathan M. Balliet welcomes new lawyer John Deutsch to the Carbon Bar in 1948.

The major interests of the bar in the late 1800s and early 1900s was to formulate and enforce a minimum fee bill, commemorate deceased members, organize and maintain a law library for the use of its members and attend the annual lawyers picnic and outing at Linden Court in Sciota.

Minimum Fee Bill

Without question, the minimum fee bill was the major topic on early bar associations' agendas. Bar members argued that such a bill would assure high quality legal services. It cannot be disputed, however, that the principle purpose of the bill was to prevent lawyers from depriving other lawyers of business by cutting their fees. The first minimum fee bill appeared in pamphlet form in 1922 and was distributed among the members of the bar. The minimum fee bill specified the minimum charges which lawyers should make for different types of legal services.

In 1947, a revised version was put together by a bar committee of George A. Shutack and Ben Branch and contained the following preamble:

> *This is a minimum fee bill and the fees established are exclusive of costs and expenses. It is not intended as a criterion for the fee to be charged for a particular service, but on the contrary, establishes the fee which that client the least able to pay shall be charged for that service. However, nothing herein shall prohibit an attorney from rendering professional services absolutely gratis.*
>
> *No contract shall be made by any attorney for the division of sharing with any person of any fee as a reward or compensation for the procuring of business, except, however, that where business is forwarded local attorneys may divide the fee with the forwarding attorney. Nothing herein shall preclude an attorney from handling a case on a contingent fee basis.*

Excerpts from 1947 Minimum Fee Bill

APPEALS FROM JUSTICES OF THE PEACE:

Preparing and filing complaint or answer	*$ 10.00*

ASSUMPSIT AND TRESPASS:

Entry of appearance where other papers are to be filed	*$ 5.00*
Entry of appearance when no papers are to be filed	*$ 15.00*
Preparing and filing praecipe and statement of claim or complaint	*$ 25.00*
Preparing and filing affidavit of defense or answer	*$ 25.00*

Taking judgment by default . . . . $ 5.00
Preparing and filing motion for judgment for want of a sufficient affidavit of defense or answer . . . . $ 15.00
Rules . . . . $ 10.00
Bringing in additional defendant . . . . $ 25.00

ATTACHMENTS:

Praecipe, affidavit, bond and directions to Sheriff . . . . $ 25.00
Motion to quash, dissolve or show cause of action . . . . $ 25.00
Preparing interrogatories . . . . $ 15.00
Answer to interrogatories . . . . $ 15.00
Subsequent proceedings same as in Assumpsit.

COLLECTIONS:

For the collection of uncontested claims, the minimum charges should be as follows:
On the first $500 . . . . 20%
On the excess over $500 . . . . 10%
Minimum fee for any collection . . . . $ 7.50
On items of $15 or less 50%

For suit: a suit fee, of not less than $7.50 to be added to commissions, the whole not to exceed 50% of the amount of the claim. Suit fees are not contingent.

(NOTE: The above rates concerning collection items are subject to change if a new set of rates is promulgated by the Pennsylvania Bar Association and if such rates shall be higher than the above rates.)

Requests for financial report $1.00

DECLARATORY JUDGEMENT:

Preparing petition and argument . . . . $ 50.00

DEEDS:

Preparing and filing papers in proceedings to supply lost deed . . . . $ 50.00

DEPOSITIONS:

Rule to take, notice of and taking depositions in County . . . . *$ 15.00*
Same, out of County . . . . *$ 25.00*

DIVORCE:

Representing Libellant in uncontested divorce proceedings minimum charge for uncontested divorce proceedings *$350.00*

(NOTE: This includes Master's fee, Stenographer's charges and Prothonotary's costs. Additional charge shall be made for obtaining service on non-resident respondent.)

EQUITY:

Drawing bill . . . . *$ 50.00*
Drawing answer . . . . *$ 50.00*
Preparing and filing preliminary objections to bill . . . . *$ 50.00*
Formal decree . . . . *$ 25.00*

TRANSFER OF ANY LICENSE:

All proceedings, including appeal to court from refusal of Liquor Control Board to grant restaurant liquor license for a previously licensed premises *$300.00*
Transfer of any license under Liquor Control Board jurisdiction shall be 2% of consideration involved but in no event shall be less than *$75.00*

ORPHANS COURT MATTERS:

ACCOUNTS:

Petition for citation, to file and presenting same to court *$20.00*
Preparing and filing exceptions -- not including appearance in court *$20.00*
Argument on exceptions, either side *$25.00*

AUDITS:

Representing creditor or heir before auditor *$25.00*
Motion for appointment of auditor *$15.00*
Preparing and filing exceptions to auditor's report *$25.00*

Over the years, complaints about violations of the minimum fee bill and investigation of alleged violations consumed a considerable amount of bar association energy. The bar association minutes do not reveal what sanctions, if any, were imposed. The association frequently appointed committees to revise the minimum fee bill although fees were not increased appreciably. The United States Supreme Court in 1975 declared that a minimum fee bill was a violation of the anti-trust laws. With this decision, its use in Carbon County and other counties across the Commonwealth ended. What for many years was an overriding priority of the bar association is now an historical curiosity.

Memorial Resolutions

From the beginning, because it had a family-like size and closeness, the bar customarily assembled and eulogized a deceased member. A close colleague was asked to compose a memorial resolution. These resolutions did not contain much biographical material and consisted primarily of florid comments on the character of the deceased. When a lawyer died, the members of the bar would gather at a special meeting, usually in the prothonotary's office, adopt the memorial resolution and then attend the funeral as a body. These resolutions were filed of record in the prothonotary's office and sent to the deceased's relatives. Typical was the memorial resolutions adopted by the bar upon the death of Milo M. Dimmick in 1872:

To the Memory of Milo M. Dimmick.

Assembled for the first time in the recollection of living members of the Bar of Carbon County to commemorate the death of an associate, it is proper, and our hearts prompt us, to give, and perpetuate, an earnest testimonial to the character and worth of the oldest practitioner of the law in our county, Hon. M. M. Dimmick, whose death occurred yesterday.

With sad appreciation of the loss which the courts of our County have sustained in his death, and a desire to place upon the records of the County a suitable expression of our regard for the deceased and respect for the purity of his personal character,

Resolved, That we, the members of the Bar of Carbon County, bear united testimony of sorrow at the stroke of Providence that has created a vacancy in our roll and at the gatherings of our association.

Resolved, That in the character of the late Hon. M. M. Dimmick we recognize the model lawyer and the highest type of the good citizen.

Resolved, That this association, appreciating the unfailing courtesy that marked his associations with us in life, and his general, eventempered, and ever-courted companionship, will hold him in Kindly and lasting remembrance.

Resolved, That we tender our heartfelt sympathy to his bereaved family, and, as a mark of respect, the Judges of the Courts, Members of the Bar, and officers of the county will attend his obsequies in a body.

Resolved, That a copy of these Resolutions be respectfully presented to the family of the deceased as a token of the high esteem entertained for him by the members of the Bar of this County, and that these Resolutions be published in the newspapers of the County.

James Houston
Chairman
November 15, 1872 *F. A. Doney*
Secty.

Law Library

Lobbied by members of the Carbon County Bar, the State Legislature, on April 9, 1868 passed an act for the establishment of a law library in the County of Carbon. The act provided that all fines and penalties imposed by the court and all forfeited bonds not payable to the Commonwealth be used to establish and maintain a law library to be set up in the courthouse for the use of the court and the bar. The act also provided that the court would appoint three resident members of the bar to serve on the law library committee for a period of one year and directed the county commissioners to designate a room in the courthouse for the library. Pursuant to said act, Judge George R. Barrett on January 9, 1869 appointed Allen Craig, M. M. Dimmick, and N. F. Handy as the first law library committee.

The Law Library Committee decided what books were to be purchased and each year the committee filed with the court an accounting of the funds which they had received from the fines and forfeitures.

On March 17, 1915 M. Louise Bertolette, Helen A. Dieffenbach and Florence Chapin, the widow and two daughters of Frederick Bertolette, at his expressed request, donated to the County of Carbon the extensive law library which he put together in his offices in the Navigation Building. The deed of gift provided that the books were for the use of the court and "present and future resident members of the Carbon Bar." At a meeting of the bar on March 20, 1915, the gift was accepted. Bar Secretary Frank P. Sharkey was directed to place the books in a special room to be marked "Frederick Bertolette Memorial Law Library" and a portrait of Mr. Bertolette be procured and placed in the room. The Bertolette Library was placed in the second floor of the new wing of the courthouse which was built in 1937 and his portrait hangs there today.

The law today requires the library to be a public facility and the county currently provides funding through the court budget. Its daily operation and maintenance is by law overseen by the president judge and court personnel. The Judicial Code repealed the old 1868 law allowing county fines to be used for the law library and the authority for a law library committee. Judge Heimbach appointed the last law library committee consisting of George A. Shutack, Roger N. Nanovic, Thomas W. Durnin and John G. Cipko. They decided what books and law reporters were to be purchased from 1960 to 1977.

The advent of WestLaw and Lexis in the early 1980s revolutionized legal research by providing swift computerized access to state and federal court opinions found previously only in the law reporters. Judge Lavelle installed computers in the law library in 1986 to take advantage of WestLaw's database and began a program of downsizing the out of state inventory of case reports.

Fifty Year Members

Bar members enjoyed honoring the longevity of their colleagues. It has been traditional to hold testimonial dinners to honor lawyers who practiced at the bar for fifty years. In the early years of the bar, there was virtually no one who reached that lofty plateau. It was not until the late 1920s that the first golden anniversary of a bar member was celebrated. On June 20, 1923, the bar association paid tribute to Edward M. Mulhearn on the fiftieth anniversary of his admission to the bar and presented him with a gold watch. Mulhearn died less than five months after the testimonial dinner.

Carbon Bar members of the twentieth century, exposed less to smoke filled rooms and fortified by better diet and exercise, fared much better in reaching their golden anniversaries than their predecessors. The following were, with appropriate remarks and testimonial dinners, inaugurated into the Half-Century Club of the Carbon Bar during this period:

Frank P. Sharkey	*1937*
Jacob C. Loose	*1940*
Nathan M. Balliet	*1945*
Judge William G. Thomas	*1947*
Leighton C. Scott	*1948*
Eugene Edelstein	*1968*
George A. Shutack	*1978*
Martin H. Philip	*1981*
John G. Cipko	*1982*
George M. D. Richards	*1983*
Albert H. Heimbach	*1985*
Jacob Philip	*1986*
W. Joseph Engler	*1987*
George Brinley Richards	*1992*

From the early part of the 1900s through the 1950s, the bar association railed against the unauthorized practice of law by district justices and lay persons, lobbied the court for comprehensive rules of court and urged the court to protect its turf by requiring that all lawyers desiring to practice law in the courts of Carbon County maintain an office in the county. It also monitored and tried to control unethical advertising by members of the bar.

Unauthorized Practice of Law

From colonial times there was always someone who was willing to draft a deed, prepare a will, or administer an estate "cheaper than a lawyer." These lay activities invariably produced legal problems which lawyers and the court had to unravel and some times produced long and expensive litigation. Individual members of the bar constantly warned their clients about this practice but it grew during and after the Depression. In 1936 the bar took their case to the Carbon County grand jury which issued the following report:

> *We, also, recommend a complaint brought to our attention by a prominent member of the Carbon County board of law examiners. We find that the unauthorized practice of law is prevalent in Carbon county, being pursued by Justices of the Peace, conveyancers, notaries public, and others of similar business activities. We understand that only those duly admitted to the bar may practice law as a profession and that for others to prepare legal instruments and give advice on legal matters is by statute made a misdemeanor and punishable by fine and imprisonment. The lawyer who misbehaves is subject to the discipline of the courts, in addition to his civil and criminal responsibility, but the same is not true of those who practice law without being members of the bar. The clients (?) of such unauthorized practitioners of the law easily may be victimized and be able to obtain no practical redress from the duly constituted judicial authorities. It is to be hoped that these remarks of the Grand Jury will serve as a warning and to deter such unauthorized activities. If this warning is not sufficient, no doubt, the Bar Association of Carbon County and the Court will find means to put a stop to the practice.*

Realtors and insurance brokers responded by saying as long as lawyers were selling real estate and insurance, they were going to make deeds and wills. The minutes of the meetings of the bar association during the late 1950s and through the 1960s were filled with complaints and concerns about the practice of law by non-lawyers. The area of wills and estates seemed especially vulnerable to unauthorized practice of law. In 1959, in order to stop lay invasion into estate practice, the association printed its own petitions for letters testamentary and administration and limited their distribution to bar members. A motion

*Members of the Carbon Bar joined picnic outing of County Republican leaders in 1939 at Mahoning Valley Country Club. Standing: **Dist. Atty. Albert Heimbach**, CNJ executive James Rementer, Deputy Sheriff Steve Angelovic, County Commissioner James Bradley, Court Stenograher Roy Mohrbach, Ted Dermott, Sheriff William "Butch" Hatrick, **Alan Loose**, Esq., **Daniel Dougherty**, Esq., businessman B. W. Freed. Seated: Charles Sharkey, **Frank Sharkey**, Esq., **Fred Lewis**, Esq., **George Gray**, Esq., **Judge William Thomas**, Dr. Numa Heaten, D.D.S., unknown.*

was passed requiring each member to withhold the use of these forms to non-resident lawyers or laymen. This system worked well for about ten years but was discontinued in the early 1970s when the register of wills took the position that anyone should be entitled to use his office's forms and began issuing his own forms.

Statewide Practice

From the beginning, Carbon, like most of the smaller counties, had a closed shop when it came to practicing before the court. The county court historically controlled who was admitted to the bar and permitted only a lawyer whose principle office was in Carbon County to handle cases before the courts. In August of 1936, Judge Thomas crystallized this long-standing policy in Local Rule No. 9:

> *Attorneys not maintaining an office within the county of Carbon, shall not be permitted to enter an appearance, nor begin any action nor issue process in any case, except as an associate of local counsel.*

This rule meant that an out-of-county lawyer could work here only by establishing a relationship with a Carbon County lawyer who would then get a portion of his fee. After World War II there was a movement, primarily from the Philadelphia area, to allow lawyers who were admitted to the Supreme Court to practice in any county of the Commonwealth. Perceiving this statewide practice movement as a threat to the livelihood of its members, many rural and suburban bar associations fought against this proposal. The Carbon County Bar Association passed a resolution in 1965 stating its opposition to statewide practice. The bar association position reflected the fear that Philadelphia lawyers would come in and take away local legal business from Carbon County attorneys.

Statewide practice permitting lawyers admitted to the high court to practice anywhere in the state was adopted by the Supreme Court of Pennsylvania in 1966. Out of county law firms did not, in fact, take away substantial portions of the law business as was originally feared. There is no question, however, that most civil trial work and large fee criminal defenses were, and continue to be, taken over by out of county law firms.

Bar Involvement in Court Rules and Improvements

In the early 1920s, Judge Barber appointed a committee of the bar made up of Jacob C. Loose, Frank P. Sharkey, and William G. Thomas to revise and compile in book form the local rules of court. On March 1, 1922, the committee delivered its completed product to the court and Judge Barber adopted the first comprehensive set rules for the regulation of practice in the Court of Common Pleas of Carbon County. The 1922 court rule book which was distributed to all the members of the Carbon County Bar included all of the rules of court for civil cases and a complete list of all the resident members of the

Carbon County Bar together with their dates of admission. The book was 117 pages long. There were twenty-seven lawyers listed in the rules book as resident members of the Carbon County Bar -- the oldest being Edward M. Mulhearn and the youngest Frank X. York and Eugene Edelstein.

During the 1930s and the 1940s the bar association worked with the judges and the county commissioners to improve the operation of the row offices. Frustrated by the filing system used in the recorder of deeds office and concerned about the lack of proper filing in the prothonotary's office, members of the bar urged Judge Thomas to endorse the adoption of the Russell system, also known as the "LMNRT system," which was used in Monroe and Lehigh counties and asked Ben Branch to have a grand jury look into the prothonotary's office. The grand jury on April 6, 1935 reported that the files in the prothonotary's office were insufficient to conduct the business of the court. Judge Thomas immediately appointed George A. Shutack, Ben Branch and Alan Loose to a committee to investigate and straighten out these offices. They were also instrumental in getting a reluctant Judge Thomas to adopt a court rule to install the Russell system in all of the row offices of Carbon County.

In 1948, a committee of the bar association made up of Albert H. Heimbach, George A. Shutack, Martin H. Philip and Frank D. Llewellyn appeared before the Board of Commissioners Ambrose O'Donnell, Nathan Drumheller and C. D. Reinhard to protest the conversion of part of the recorder of deeds office into office space for the new tax claim bureau and the controller's office. They also asked the commissioners to renovate the main courtroom. Shutack pointed out that "the courtroom is less modern than the ones in which Abraham Lincoln pleaded his court cases more than a hundred years ago." The commissioners acceded to the lawyers' request and did not use the space in the recorder's office. Several months after this meeting they bought new red carpeting for the courtroom and installed new chairs in the jury box and new leather chairs for the use of the lawyers in the courtroom.

In 1969, members of the bar, noting the departure of Dundena Groff, a part-time court stenographer due to inadequate salary, unanimously recommended that Judge Heimbach appoint a full-time stenographer. The judge responded by hiring George Repinec as a full-time stenographer and he has served the bench and bar faithfully and competently from that time.

Lawyer Advertising

In the latter part of the nineteenth century, lawyers, like the business community, promoted themselves and their services by newspaper advertising. Carbon attorneys used the front pages of the ***Mauch Chunk Gazette*** and the ***Mauch Chunk Democrat*** to extol their professional experience and let the public know where they were located. Overblown and even deceptive ads by some Pennsylvania lawyers eventually drew the ire and finally the condemnation of the Pennsylvania Bar Association. It persuaded the Supreme Court to forbid attorneys to advertise in the early 1920s. The only places a lawyer could put his name before the public was in the telephone book and at his office location. An exception to this rule was carved out to allow the lawyer to advertise when he or she was first admitted to the bar and when running for public office. The penalty for violation of this rule was either suspension from practice or disbarment. Close policing of their colleagues' attempts at publicity by members of the Carbon Bar during the 1950s and 1960s kept violations to a minimum and they were minor in nature. For example, one member was directed by the chancellor in 1962 to reduce the size of his name in the telephone book and another was asked to remove his name from the telephone poles and rocks after an election.

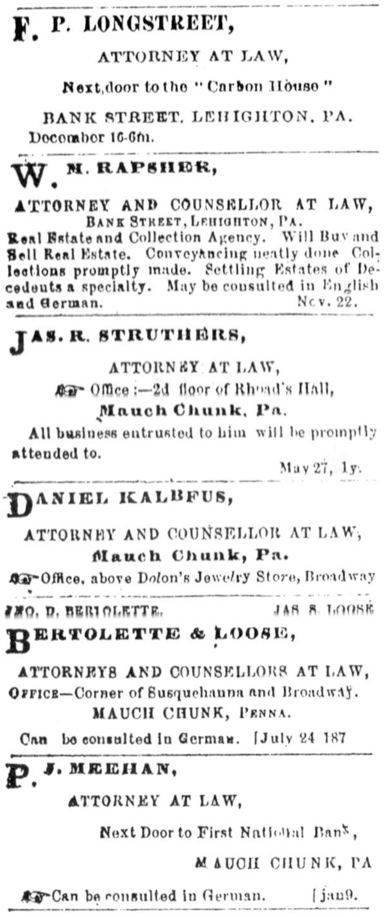

F. P. LONGSTREET,
ATTORNEY AT LAW,
Next door to the "Carbon House"
BANK STREET, LEHIGHTON, PA.
December 16-6m.

W. M. RAPSHER,
ATTORNEY AND COUNSELLOR AT LAW,
BANK STREET, LEHIGHTON, PA.
Real Estate and Collection Agency. Will Buy and Sell Real Estate. Conveyancing neatly done Collections promptly made. Settling Estates of Decedents a specialty. May be consulted in English and German. Nov. 22.

JAS. R. STRUTHERS,
ATTORNEY AT LAW,
Office :—2d floor of Rhoad's Hall,
Mauch Chunk, Pa.
All business entrusted to him will be promptly attended to.
May 27, 1y.

DANIEL KALBFUS,
ATTORNEY AND COUNSELLOR AT LAW,
Mauch Chunk, Pa.
Office, above Dolon's Jewelry Store, Broadway

JNO. D. BERTOLETTE. JAS. S. LOOSE
BERTOLETTE & LOOSE,
ATTORNEYS AND COUNSELLORS AT LAW,
OFFICE—Corner of Susquehanna and Broadway.
MAUCH CHUNK, PENNA.
Can be consulted in German. [July 24 187

P. J. MEEHAN,
ATTORNEY AT LAW,
Next Door to First National Bank,
MAUCH CHUNK, PA
Can be consulted in German. [jan9.

Lawyer advertising in the Carbon Advocate, January 6, 1877.

Judges' Portraits

The bar during the late 1930s also recognized the importance of preserving the judicial history of the Carbon County Court. The portrait gallery was conceived and organized during this time. Bar members convinced the county commissioners of the value of a portrait gallery in Courtroom I and the county agreed to pay for the photographs of all the president judges and hung them over the jury box. In the early '70s Tom McKinley proposed that the bar association commission and pay for an oil painting of the president judge for presentation to the court. This proposal, after some debate, was adopted and the impressive portraits of Judges McCready and Heimbach were painted by the distinguished portrait artist Robert Burns of Princeton, New Jersey. They now provide a touch of color and history in the main courtroom.

Incorporation of Carbon Bar Association

Late in the 1950s younger members of the bar agitated to broaden the activities of the bar and assume more responsibility for policing the legal system. It was decided to incorporate the association and take on a more formal legal structure. On October 28, 1957, George A. Shutack, Alan S. Loose, Raymond F. Smith, Sr., Albert Heimbach and Donald L. McCay petitioned the Court of Common Pleas of Carbon County to charter the Carbon County Bar Association as a non-profit corporation. After the customary hearing, Judge Ethan H. Gearhardt of Lehigh County, who specially presided, approved the issuance of a charter.

The stated purpose of the association was to promote the administration of justice, to uphold the honor and dignity of the bar, to exercise a general supervision of the conduct of the members of the bar, to cultivate social relationships among its members and perpetuate the memory of those deceased. The admission fee was set at $10 and the annual dues set at $30 except for those members who were admitted less than five years who were allowed to pay $15 annual dues. The by-laws provided for seven standing committees each consisting of three members and they were as follows: (1) legal ethics, (2) legal biographies, (3) legal aid, (4) social activities and entertainment, (5) legal education, (6) membership defense, (7) grievances. At a meeting of the bar association held on January 9, 1959, in the main courtroom of the courthouse at 4:00 P.M., Raymond F. Smith of Palmerton, who was the incumbent president of the old association, was elected the first Chancellor of the newly incorporated Carbon Bar Association. George Kerestes was elected secretary and Albert Heimbach was elected treasurer. Donald McCay, Carl A. Niehoff, Martin Philip, Joseph Engler, William Scott and Roger Nanovic were elected to the first board of directors. Twenty-six members of the bar attended this meeting:

Raymond F. Smith	*Albert Leonzi*
Raymond F. Smith, Jr.	*Thomas McCready*
Donald L. McCay	*William Quinn*
Roger Nanovic	*Joseph Greco*
Robert Lazorchick	*Daniel Dougherty*
Jacob Philip	*William Wyatt*
Thomas Durnin	*Daniel Minnick*
Carl Niehoff	*Albert Prutzman*
George McKinley	*Joseph Engler*
George Shutack	*William Bayer*
Albert Heimbach	*George Kerestes*
William Scott	*Martin Philip*
Russell Chaplinsky	*John Cipko*

10. Times-News & Record, Lehighton, Pa., Mon., Jan. 26, 1970.

CARBON LAWYERS ENTERTAINED BY THEIR WIVES

Carbon County lawyers were dinner guests of their wives at a dinner party held Saturday evening at the Mahoning Valley Country Club. The committee in charge of the affair was composed of Mrs. Raymond Smith and Mrs. Sidney Webb, both of Palmerton, and Mrs. John Cipko, Lansford , who is chairman of the Carbon County Lawyers Wives Association.

PICTURED BEFORE DINNER WAS served at the Mahoning Valley Country Club are District Attorney and Mrs. John Deutsch, and Attorney and Mrs. John P. LaVelle

DISTRICT ATTORNEY JOHN DEUTSCH, Lehighton, enjoying snacks before dinner.

JUDGE AND MRS. ALBERT H. HEIMBACH, Palmerton, arrive for the dinner meeting and enjoy the hospitality.

ENJOYING THE HOSPITALITY are Attorney and Mrs. Thomas S. McCready and Attorney Martin H. Philip.

ATTORNEY AND MRS. THOMAS DURNIN, Jim Thorpe, pictured in the living room of the Mahoning Valley Country Club.

ATTY. AND MRS. JOHN CIPKO, Lansford and Judge and Mrs. Albert H. Heimbach enjoy the hors d'oeurve at the party.

ARRIVING AT THE COUNTRY CLUB are Attorney and Mrs. Murray Mackson, Palmerton.

ATTORNEY WILLIAM H. BAYER, Lehighton, and Attorney Roger N. Nanovic, Palmerton, discuss the dinner.

ATTORNEY AND MRS. MARTIN H. PHILIP, Palmerton, with Attorney and Mrs. John Cipko.

PICTURED AT THE SNACK TABLE prior to the dinner are Mrs. Raymond Smith, Mrs. Thomas McKinley; Atty. Smith and Atty. McKinley.

Carbon Bar Association fetes wives at Mahoning Valley Country Club -- 1970

Preceptorship

From 1896 to 1968 in Pennsylvania, before entering law school, an aspiring lawyer had to find a preceptor. The preceptor was supposed to train and guide the preceptee in the practical and ethical aspects of the law office and also had to agree to employ the law student for six months at the end of law school. The state Supreme Court established the procedures for gaining admission to the legal profession and its rules were augmented by county rules. Educational qualifications were determined by state bar examinations conducted under the auspices of the Supreme Court Board of Law Examiners. To be admitted to the examinations, however, the law student needed the approval of the local board of law examiners appointed by the county court who passed on his moral character.

Argument court sessions and calls of trial lists each term of court served as a training ground for young lawyers in court procedure and decorum. Many of the lawyers who actively practiced in the courts of Carbon County would appear before the court for these sessions. The young lawyer had an opportunity to observe the veteran practitioners in action before the court and the senior members of the bar would answer the junior members' questions about procedure after the session. The judge also took pains to make sure that young attorneys knew every aspect of the motion being presented. They benefitted not only from their own exchange with the judge but also from the experience of crossing verbal swords with veteran members of the bar.

Public Defenders

Arraignments and trials which took place four times a year launched many lawyers of the Carbon County Bar into trial work. The trials usually began immediately after the arraignments. It was during the arraignments that the judge appointed young lawyers to represent indigent defendants in criminal cases. When a criminal defendant told the court he could not afford a lawyer, it was not unusual for the court to look around the courtroom and appoint the first young lawyer he saw to provide representation. The already nervous lawyer was further unnerved by the judge notifying him he would have ten minutes to confer with his client before the trial began. William Wyatt vividly recalls sitting in court as a newly minted member of the bar when Judge McCready appointed him as defense attorney in a first degree murder case. The judge allowed him a continuance to prepare his client's defense and he won an acquittal.

Although this system of selecting young lawyers for indigent criminal defendants provided many young lawyers with their first courtroom experience, it was obviously unsatisfactory and probably denied the defendants due process. In 1964 at a meeting of the bar Judge Heimbach expressed the need for a part-time public defender in criminal cases. It was his opinion that $1500 a year would be very fair compensation because the work would provide advertising and bring other work to the lawyer. He asked the bar association to work out an arrangement with the county commissioners in which the bar association would provide the lawyer, and the county would provide the funding. The bar association contracted with the county to provide Thomas McCready as a public defender and such additional lawyers as would be needed should conflicts arise. The county agreed to reimburse the association for moneys expended to pay the lawyers.

In 1967, the State Legislature, recognizing that the criminal caseload throughout the Commonwealth consisted primarily of indigents and that they needed a full-time public defender, passed an act requiring each county to create a public defender's office and provide the funding for it. Pursuant to this legislation the Carbon County commissioners created the position of public defender and funded it with $8000 per annum.

The bar association at its meeting on March 28, 1968 recommended the appointment of Thomas S. McCready as chief public defender for Carbon County. He served with distinction as chief public defender from 1968 to 1991. In 1970, Richard W. Webb joined McCready as an assistant public defender and when he resigned to run for district attorney in 1975, John F. Gibbons was appointed to take his place. Gibbons met a tragic death in an ultralight plane crash in 1981. The public defender's office was then expanded to three lawyers by the addition of Steven P. Vlossak and Robert T. Yurchak. Today the defender's office, which handles ninety percent of the criminal caseload, is staffed by Steven P. Vlossak and Robert T. Yurchak as chief defenders and Gregory Mousseau, as associate defender.

Pro Bono Work

In addition to representing the poor charged with crimes, members of the bar, beginning during the Depression years in the 1930s, voluntarily rendered free legal services in civil cases to people who were hard pressed financially. This tradition continued during the 1950s and 1960s. Any lawyer wishing to do pro bono work would advise the court. From time to time the court would appoint lawyers from this list of volunteers in custody and termination of parental rights cases.

Northeast Pennsylvania Legal Services was incorporated in 1977 and William Schwab, a bar association member, became its first full-time employee in Carbon County. Holly Heintzelman and Joseph Matika headed the office after Schwab and Paul Levy currently serves as the local director. The Office of Economic Opportunity and later the Legal Services Corporation in Washington provided funding for the staff which had offices in the Masonic Building in Lehighton.

In 1981, President Ronald Reagan, in his budget-cutting blitz, made a direct hit on the Legal Services Corporation contending that voluntary pro bono efforts should take the place of this costly federal program. This cutback in funding reduced the number and kinds of cases handled by the legal aid office. In January of 1993 Judges Lavelle and Webb asked the bar association to start a pro bono program for poor persons whose needs could not be met by Northeast Pennsylvania Legal Services.

Carbon County Law Journal

The establishment of the *Carbon County Law Journal* in 1966 was significant to the bar association history for two reasons. First, the growth and complexity of the court system demanded that lawyers have prompt access to court opinions and legal notices. The *Law Journal* provided that information on a weekly basis. Second, it greatly increased the financial resources of the bar association which began to finance its public service projects and bar association activities through funds generated by the *Law Journal.*

The recommendation that the association publish a weekly legal periodical originally came from Martin H. Philip in 1965. He felt that the fees generated by mandatory legal advertisements would be more than sufficient to support the periodical. Roger Nanovic later proposed that a bar committee study the feasibility of creating and operating a law journal and he and George McKinley were appointed to a legal periodical committee. In September of 1965, this committee recommended the establishment of a legal periodical. It also suggested that the court be asked to name the *Law Journal* the official legal publication for the county and to provide free office space in the courthouse for the publication.

In 1965 Judge Heimbach designated by rule of court the *Carbon County Law Journal* as the official legal periodical of Carbon County. George T. (Tom) McKinley became the first editor at a salary of $100 per month and Ethel Kitchen was named as secretary for the publication. An office was established in the probation office on the second floor of the courthouse and an agreement was made with the *Times News* for printing. The first issue appeared on January 8, 1965. Members of the bar association received the *Law Journal* free of charge.

By the end of 1967, two short years after its birth, the *Law Journal* showed an annual net profit of $1443. It has continued to run profitably since that time. The profits from the *Law Journal* have enabled the bar association to undertake new projects, underwrite the costs of printing rules of court and contribute to causes which benefit the members of the bar and promote the administration of justice.

As the *Law Journal* profits escalated, bar members raised concerns about the tax status of the association. During the chancellorship of Roger Nanovic in 1982, after consultations with Luther Campbell, accountant for the bar, and Peter Roper, executive director of the Pennsylvania Bar, the association unanimously resolved to apply for tax exempt status and that all funds of the *Law Journal* be managed by the board of directors of the association to be applied for purposes set forth in the by-laws.

Judicial Selection

The one issue which the bar association had avoided throughout its history was judicial selection. In 1987, the bar association conducted a plebiscite among its members on whether Judge Lavelle should be retained for an additional ten years. Thirty-six of the fifty-five members of the bar participated. The procedure used followed the recommendation for such plebiscites by the Pennsylvania Bar Association, with each attorney, by secret ballot, marking a column "should be retained, should not be retained or not voting." The association members voted 27-9 in favor of retention of Lavelle as president judge. This was the first time the Carbon Bar Association as a body became actively and publicly involved in who was qualified to serve on the bench. Interestingly, the 75% favorable retention vote mirrored Lavelle's retention vote on election day.

In 1991 in the judicial contest for the second judgeship, which had just been created by the Legislature, the bar association voted by secret ballot on the two candidates, Richard W. Webb and William G. Schwab. Two weeks before the general election, the association voted on whether the candidates were "qualified, not qualified, well qualified or exceptionally well qualified" and then published the results in the local newspapers. A total of forty-six of the fifty-nine members of the bar voted in the plebiscite as follows:

	WEBB	SCHWAB
Exceptionally well qualified	17	2
Well qualified	12	6
Qualified	16	23
Not Qualified	1	15

Bar Activities (1980-1993)

By the late 1970s the Carbon County Bar had grown to forty members. The bar association continued to maintain some of its old traditions like the annual picnic at Sciota; others like the Minimum Fee Bill faded away. On March 18, 1982, a bar committee made up of George McKinley, Chairman, John Deutsch and William Scott, Jr. presented to the association for adoption a new set of by-laws which they prepared to replace the original by-laws now obsolete and contrary to existing law. These by-laws were unanimously adopted at the meeting.

It was at this time that a movement began to make the public more aware of the good works of the legal profession. Several activities were undertaken to create goodwill and involve lawyers in the work of the community. A Law Day committee, led by Jean Engler and David Addy, undertook programs for the annual Law Day celebration on May 1 of each year. Mock trials were held; prizes were given for the best essay on the meaning of Law Day and, from time to time, lawyers set up booths in the malls throughout Carbon County to answer legal questions. The bar association sponsored an Explorer group in the Lehighton Boy Scout Troop and funded trips to historical sites and educational forays. In its most widely publicized effort, the association worked closely with Judge Lavelle in 1993 to produce the highly lauded "Mock Trial of a Mollie", a recreation of the 1876 murder trial of Alexander Campbell.

Members of The Theatre Outlet, Allentown, as witnesses, were among those with roles in the recreated trial of Alexander Campbell. Standing from left: Bernie Berg as John J. Slattery, Lee Burkett as Hugh Dugan, Neil Hever as Patrick McNealis, Mariene Johnson as Catherine Dugan, Kate Scuffle as Ellen Breslin, Steven Lally as John R. McGinley, Edwin Booth as Robert Linden, Judge John P. Lavelle, Genia Miller as Mrs. Alexander Campbell, J. Brian Campbell as Alexander Campbell, Terry Abbott as James Kerrigan and George B. Miller as James McParlan, alias James McKenna. Seated from left: Stephen P. Vlossak, Sr., Robert T. Yurchak and Gregory Lee Mousseau, lawyers from Carbon County's Public Defender's Office; Patrick Campbell, author of "A Molly Maguire Story"; Gary F. Dobias, Jean A. Engler and David W. Addy, lawyers from Carbon County's District Attorney's Office.

Gary Dobias, David Addy and Jean Engler portrayed the prosecutors; Steve Vlossak, Robert Yurchak and Gregory Mousseau took on the roles of defense counsel. Judge Richard W. Webb ascended the bench to become the presiding judge, Samuel S. Dreher.

PA Bar President-elect Paul L. Stevens (left) and PA Bar President Robert E. Fiebach (right) award Carbon Bar Chancellor Anthony Roberti (center) for the "Mock Trial of a Mollie" in 1993.

This theme of good lawyer-client relations and public image continues today. The chancellors of the '90s have urged bar members to establish a pro bono program and communicate regularly with clients. The association has sponsored at least two continuing legal education courses a year. At the annual meeting held at Linden Court in Sciota in 1993 it was reported that the bar membership had grown to seventy-nine members.

CHAPTER XIII

NOTABLE MEMBERS OF THE BAR

During the past 150 years, 190 lawyers have been admitted to the Carbon County Bar. Besides practicing law, bar members during this time have also been active in politics, business and civic affairs, many having served as elected officials and civic leaders. Forty-two lawyers have served in the military with distinction. Many others have been involved in breaking the ground or laying the foundations for programs and institutions which are an integral part of the county's life today.

A history of the bar would not be complete without, at least, a brief reference to some of these lawyers and their contributions. Although many current members of the bar deserve recognition because of what they have done and are doing for the county and its institutions, we have arbitrarily used a minimum of thirty years at the bar as the benchmark for inclusion of living members of the bar in this chapter.

James R. Struthers, Esquire (Adm. 1843) was a man of many firsts. A native of Paisley, Scotland and the recipient of a classical education in Latin and Greek, Struthers was a member of the first class to graduate from Lafayette College. He "read law" in the office of James Madison Porter, the Easton lawyer who later became the third president judge of Carbon County. After moving to Mauch Chunk in 1840, Struthers enjoyed an active career in law and politics. In the first session of the Carbon Court in 1843, he was among the first to be admitted to the Carbon Bar. Governor David Porter appointed Struthers as the first prosecuting attorney for Carbon County and he served from 1843 to 1846.

He was elected to the Legislature in 1845, and again in 1852 and 1853. In 1859, he formed one of the earliest law firms by taking in as his partner Stephen E. Sites. The early civil court dockets show frequent entries of the initials "S&S" (Struthers & Sites) as attorneys for the plaintiff.

Together with Judge Washington McCartney, president judge of Northampton County, and other prominent lawyers, Struthers was a founder of one of America's earliest law schools, the Union Law School in Easton.

In 1862, he broke up his partnership with Sites and went into the newspaper publishing business in Iowa, then tried farming for a while in Wisconsin. He retired in 1884 and resided in Wilkes-Barre to be near his sons who were in business there. Upon his death in 1885 at seventy years of age, he was buried in the Mauch Chunk Cemetery. He was survived by his second wife Margaret Van Dyke Struthers and ten children.

William H. Butler, Esquire (Adm. 1843). Noting the paucity of local lawyers in newly erected Carbon County, this Union County Pennsylvania native moved to Mauch Chunk in 1843 and opened a law office. A charter member of the Carbon Bar, he was appointed prosecuting attorney for the county in 1845. He then parlayed the trial experience and wide recognition he gained as a prosecutor into a successful law practice in Mauch Chunk until 1860. He was elected to the State Legislature for the session of 1861, but his political career was interrupted by the Civil War and he joined the City Troop of Philadelphia. In 1863, Butler decided to return to public service by becoming a member of the Surveyor General's staff in Harrisburg, but he met an untimely death in a railroad accident on the Pennsylvania Central Railroad in 1865.

Orville H. Wheeler, Esquire (Adm. 1843) was a lawyer, a business entrepreneur and one of Carbon County's first newspaper publishers. A native of Galway, New York where he was born in 1817, he studied law in Wilkes-Barre and moved to Mauch Chunk in 1843 when the county was erected. He was among the first admittees to the Carbon Bar and practiced law in an office at the west entrance of the first courthouse, sharing office space with Thomas Lansford Foster. Like many lawyers of the time, he used his law office to engage in the real estate and insurance business. With Joseph H. Siewers, he also owned and published a newspaper in Mauch Chunk called the *Carbon County Transit*. On November 30, 1848, he was sworn in as the county prosecuting attorney by Judge Kidder, replacing William H. Butler, and served in that office until 1854. In 1855, he worked closely with Milo Dimmick and A. W. Leisenring by going to Harrisburg and convincing the Legislature to charter Carbon County's first bank, the Mauch Chunk Bank. He became one of the bank's first directors. Despite his high profile in the community, his various enterprises lost money and he eventually left the county to try to make his fortune elsewhere.

Samuel McLean, Esquire (Adm. 1855) was the first Carbon County native admitted to the Carbon Bar and a man who never stayed in one place very long. Like many Carbon County lawyers after him he received his undergraduate education and degree at Lafayette College. Graduating in 1848 he read law in the offices of Andrew H. Reeder, who later became territorial governor of Kansas in 1854 by appointment of President Franklin Pierce. In 1852 he moved to California briefly, but returned to Easton to marry and then settled in Mauch Chunk to practice law. He was elected district attorney in 1856. After one term the lure of instant wealth caused by the discovery of gold at Pike's Peak enticed him to move to the West where he struck it rich. He then moved on to Montana where he became the first elected delegate to the United States Congress from that territory. When his term in Congress expired he returned to Easton seeking local investors in his McLean Silver Mining Company, Montana. After several years of residence in Montana, he purchased a plantation in Virginia where he lived in retirement with his family until his death in 1877.

Thomas Lansford Foster, Esquire (Adm. 1845) was the oldest son of the legendary Carbon pioneer Asa Lansford Foster who developed the coal collieries in Buck Mountain and the Panther Valley which now are municipalities bearing his name, Foster Township and the Borough of Lansford. Although Thomas was trained to be a lawyer and admitted to the Luzerne County and Carbon bars, he never practiced law.

Born in Bloomsburg in 1823, his family settled in Mauch Chunk in 1827. After receiving his education in Boston and reading law in Wilkes-Barre, he returned to Mauch Chunk in 1845 where he took over the *Carbon Transit* (later the *Mauch Chunk Gazette*) founded by his father. In 1857, he was elected superintendent of schools of Carbon County and served in that position until 1863. When the Second National Bank was organized in 1860 he became its first cashier and his name was inextricably linked with that institution until it dissolved in 1902. He succeeded General Albright as the president of the bank when Albright died in 1880 and established a well earned reputation for honesty, integrity and banking acumen.

His involvement in county affairs was deep and varied. He was president of the Carbon County Agricultural Society, secretary for the Middle Coal Field Poor District, vestryman of St. John's in East Mauch Chunk, and a member of East Mauch Chunk's first borough council.

Foster died at the age of eighty-four at his home in Center Street in East Mauch Chunk on April 14, 1908 and was survived by his wife Henrietta Pratt Lansford and ten children.

Joseph H. Siewers, Esquire (Adm. 1846) became a prominent member of the early Carbon Bar after a distinguished career as an educator. Born on St. John's Island, West Indies of Moravian missionaries, he was educated at Nazareth Hall, the famous Moravian boarding school for boys. After graduation in 1830, he taught at the Plymouth Academy in Wilkes-Barre and then in Lewisburg, Pennsylvania, Beverly, Massachusetts and Charleston, South Carolina. He came to Mauch Chunk in 1842 and took charge of the high school. He also took a short fling in the newspaper business with Orville H. Wheeler by purchasing Carbon's first newspaper the *Lehigh Pioneer and Mauch Chunk Courier* from its founder Asa Lansford Foster. They sold it back in 1845 to Foster. Somehow he found time to study law and passed his law examinations. After his admission to the bar, he opened his law office right across from the courthouse. He served as superintendent of the county schools from 1854 to 1857. He was a very successful trial lawyer but a hearing impairment forced him to leave the profession in 1862 and open up an insurance business. In 1863, he was elected prothonotary and was re-elected twice. A staunch Democrat, he worked diligently for his party and became involved in any movement to promote Mauch Chunk and Carbon County. His son, Edward R. Siewers, became district attorney of Carbon County in 1874. He died on November 21, 1880 at the age of sixty-eight. He left a widow and three children.

Milo Melancthon Dimmick, Esquire (Adm. 1852). The son of lawyer Daniel Dimmick of Milford, Pike County, Pennsylvania, he practiced law in Stroudsburg, Monroe County, for many years before coming to Carbon County. He was known as a tireless worker for his clients, and a thoroughly prepared advocate. Democratic politics consumed a great deal of his time and energies in his early years. A classic profile, charismatic presence and commanding voice made him a popular candidate for public office. He was elected to Congress in 1848, and re-elected in 1850 from the district then composed of Carbon, Monroe, Northampton, Pike, and Wayne counties. Dimmick was candidate for president judge in 1852, but was defeated in a hotly contested campaign by James M. Porter, an Independent candidate. Samuel Dreher, who later became president judge of Carbon County, served his legal apprenticeship in Dimmick's office and later formed a law partnership with him in Stroudsburg. In 1853, Dimmick moved to Mauch Chunk where he lived at 110 Broadway and had an active and successful law practice. He was one of the organizers and original directors of The Mauch Chunk Bank, Carbon's first bank, which opened for business on October 11, 1855 in a building on the site of the present Jim Thorpe National Bank. He served as a vestryman of St. Mark's Church and was president of the Mauch Chunk Cemetery Association. He was married to Mary Alice Cooper and had three children, Elizabeth Mattilde Baldy, John Card Dimmick and Milton M. Dimmick

Milton M. Dimmick provided the funds to Mauch Chunk Borough to build the Dimmick Memorial Library in 1889. John C. Dimmick, studied law in his father's office and after being admitted to the Carbon Bar in 1869 practiced with his father. Milo Dimmick died on November 22, 1872 at the age of sixty.

Charles Albright, Esquire (Adm. 1856). By any measure, Charles Albright led a rich and remarkable life even though he did not reach the fullness of years. He was an authentic Carbon County hero of the Civil War. He also enjoyed a number of careers in both the private and public sectors in which he won plaudits, stature and power. Flamboyant, courageous and given to high blown rhetoric, Albright dominated the news for twenty years and indelibly imprinted himself on his times in Carbon County.

Albright was born in Bucks County in 1830. He graduated from Dickinson College in 1851, read law, and was admitted to the Carbon Bar in 1856. He opened a law practice in Mauch Chunk in 1856, and was a delegate to the Republican National Convention that nominated Abraham Lincoln for President in 1860.

When war came to the Union, Albright entered the Army as major of the 132nd Regiment of Pennsylvania Volunteers on August 22, 1862. Four weeks later, at the battle of Antietam in Maryland, he displayed unflinching coolness and bravery under heavy enemy fire. Many members of the Blue Army were killed and wounded in the fields of Antietam. A young lieutenant from Boston who took two bullets in the chest and miraculously survived was Oliver Wendell Holmes who later became one of the great justices of the United States Supreme Court. Albright's courage and leadership in battle earned him the commission of a brevet general, the highest rank attained by a Carbon County soldier in the Civil War. Near the end of the war, he led a charge against the men of Rebel guerrilla fighter, Colonel John Mosby -- the legendary Gray Ghost of the Confederacy -- whose men were attempting to capture a Union wagon train. In this attack General Albright dashed into the midst of the guerilla forces firing pistols with both hands in face to face combat. Inspired by his brave example his troops routed Mosby's men, and Albright became a legendary military figure of the Civil War. He was mustered out of the service in 1865.

In addition to distinguishing himself in battle, Albright proved himself adept in raising, organizing and motivating troops. Sounding the "Union undivided" theme at local rallies to recruit new soldiers, in August of 1862, Albright predicted that the war would be ended by March 1865:

> *By then, the rebellion by the southern states would be a matter of history and the unity of our government, as handed down by our revolutionary ancestors, would be preserved and perpetrated.*
>
> *If the war had gone the way of the rebels our government would have been severed, destroyed, annihilated, and our Federal Constitution -- the noblest work of man -- would be the scorn and contempt of tyrants and crowned monarchs throughout all nations.*
>
> *Let us rally around the constitution as the greatest sun and only light of the republic. United we stand, divided we fall. All the friends of constitutional liberty must be united against any and all the powers which rise up against the standards held forth by our founding fathers through the constitution. I pray to Him that He keeps me steadfast in this, my resolution: My country first, my country last, and my country all the time, right or wrong!*

After the war, Albright returned to his law practice in Mauch Chunk taking in William G. Freyman as a partner and then in 1862 another Civil War veteran, John D. Bertolette. He also resumed his interests in iron, slate, coal and banking. Not surprisingly, the firm of Albright & Freyman soon became the busiest and most prosperous firm in the county. The firm's offices and Albright's home were located at 66 W. Broadway in one of the stately Victorian mansions on "Millionaires' Row." Here he began to fashion ambitions which would bring him to the upper echelons of power. He became counsel for one of the largest coal companies in the area, the Lehigh and Wilkes Barre Coal Company. In 1873 he decided to enter the political arena. His immense popularity and fame as a Civil War hero swept him into the U. S. House of Representatives for a term.

It was as a prosecuting attorney in the Carbon County courtroom, however, that he fought his most famous battles and reached the pinnacle of his public acclaim. In 1876, wearing his Civil War brigadier general's uniform, he acted as chief counsel for the Commonwealth in the "Mollie Maguire" trials. His fiery temper and soaring rhetoric were on display almost daily before the huge crowds and the national press which jammed into the courtroom.

When a Carbon County jury found Michael J. Doyle guilty of first degree murder in February of 1876, the *Philadelphia Times* gave high praise to the general:

> *This is the first conviction obtained for any of the numerous assassinations which have disgraced the coal regions, and the credit is, in a large degree, due to Gen. Charles Albright, who worked up the case with great energy and sagacity . . . . The array of evidence was so strong and so skillfully marshalled that the defense gave up in despair and produced no testimony at all.*

As the *Kelly* case began in April of 1876, he learned that his only child, Annie, an adopted daughter, had died in Washington, D.C. Only three months before he had led her down the aisle as the proud father of a new bride in the Episcopal Church in Mauch Chunk. Despite this devastating blow, he conducted the case for the Commonwealth against Kelly after the funeral.

Albright, not content to rest after winning first degree murder convictions in all five of the gruelling "Mollie" cases he tried, became a candidate for re-election to Congress in 1878 in the Eleventh District, but was defeated in a close and spirited campaign. In addition to his law practice, he owned and operated the Mauch Chunk Iron Works from 1855 to the time of his death. He was also one of the organizers and the president of the Second National Bank in Mauch Chunk for seventeen years. Both Presidents Grant and Cleveland visited him at his home on Broadway to pay their respects. General Albright's bright star illuminated Carbon County for twenty-four sparkling years, but it flamed out before its time. He died at the age of fifty on September 9, 1880 from what the local newspapers reported as "overexertion." He is buried in the Mauch Chunk Cemetery. A wife, but no children, grieved his death.

Daniel Kalbfus, Esquire (Adm. 1859). A native of Columbia County, Pennsylvania, he became widely known in the county for his eloquence as a speaker and one of the lead defense counsel for the "Mollies." Sadly, he also became one of the bar's most tragic figures. In his early years, Kalbfus engaged actively in Democratic politics and was a very popular speaker in every election contest. He twice stumped the whole State of Pennsylvania, and frequently campaigned for candidates in other states. It was this combination of speaking prowess and political charisma that led the Ancient Order of Hibernians to retain his services for several of the "Mollie" defendants and put his name in newspapers across the country.

During the "Mollie Maguire" trials in 1876, he represented Michael Doyle, Edward Kelly, Patrick O'Donnell and Alexander Campbell at both the trial and appellate level. Newspaper reporters covering the trials praised his courageous, against-all-odds efforts for his hopeless clients and his riveting courtroom oratory. His summations were reported in great detail and reveal that he relied on wit, sarcasm, biblical and literary references and the stormy force of his personality. But he also drew heavy criticism from the court for his vitriolic attacks on the Coal and Iron Police.

He was married to Elizabeth Barker Kalbfus of East Mauch Chunk. She died in 1875 leaving him with three children. Much to the surprise of his friends and fellow lawyers, he married again in December of 1876 to Mary E. Jones of Stevensville, Bradford County and went off on his honeymoon immediately after the second Alexander Campbell murder trial.

In 1878, he began to show signs of dementia and during court proceedings, there were maniacal outbursts. On January 22, 1879, his brother Joseph Kalbfus petitioned the court to have him adjudicated a "lunatic" and confined to a hospital for the insane. The petition alleged that Daniel Kalbfus was indigent. On March 15, 1879, a commission made up of Dr. Horace DeYoung, James R. Struthers and Edward R. Siewers found that he was insane, and Judge Dreher ordered that Kalbfus be confined to the State Hospital at Danville. He died there on February 1, 1881 at the age of forty-two. His arduous and embattled days of representing three "Mollies" who went to the gallows, undoubtedly, led to his breakdown and early death.

Wesley B. Leonard, Esquire (Adm. 1861), a native of Hancock, New York and an honors graduate of Alfred University, took a train to Mauch Chunk to spend the summer at the home of his brother, Dr. Robert Leonard, in 1859. He liked it so much he decided to stay. Opting for a career in law and politics, he studied law in the offices of Struthers & Sites. After admission to the bar in March of 1861, he formed a partnership with Horace B. Burnham, but that quickly ended when Burnham joined the Union forces to fight in the Civil War. Leonard cut a handsome figure in the courtroom and his skillful handling of trials brought him popularity and respect in Mauch Chunk. A leader in Democratic politics during the 1860s he was elected district attorney as Democratic candidate in 1862 and re-elected in 1865. He was also elected to the State Legislature to represent the counties of Carbon and Monroe in 1869 and 1870. After his service in the Legislature, he returned to the private practice of law until his untimely death on January 1, 1875 at the age of forty.

John D. Bertolette, Esquire (Adm. 1867), a native of Reading, came to Mauch Chunk and entered the law office of Charles Albright as a law student in 1860. When the Civil War erupted, he was among the first to enlist and quickly rose to adjutant of the Sixth Regiment Nine Months' Volunteers, Pennsylvania. When his term expired, he immediately re-enlisted, and served with distinction through the war under General John Hartranft, becoming an adjutant-general with the rank of colonel. He was severely wounded in the Battle of Bull Run in 1862. After the war was over, he resumed the study of law at Albright's office and was admitted to practice in 1867. He was elected district attorney in 1868 and served one term until 1871. For a short time he was a partner with General Albright's firm and then opened his own office and practiced very successfully with James S. Loose from 1875 to 1877. Bertolette was known throughout the Lehigh Valley as a very careful and artful composer of legal briefs and pleadings. When Hartranft was elected Governor of

Pennsylvania in 1875, he did not forget his civil war comrade in arms and appointed Bertolette Inspector-General of the Pennsylvania National Guard. He died of consumption on April 17, 1881 at the age of forty-two and is buried in the Lehighton Cemetery.

William M. Rapsher, Esquire (Adm. 1871) was one of Carbon County's best known citizens and most prominent politicians during the late 1800s. Born in Northampton County on April 23, 1843, he was orphaned at nine years of age and worked his way through Albion Commercial College in Michigan.

When Lincoln called for troops in July of 1861, Rapsher, at the age of eighteen, enlisted as a private and served continuously with the Union forces until August of 1865. He participated in many Civil War battles including the assault at Port Yuron. After the war, he moved into Mauch Chunk and embarked upon a teaching career, teaching four years in the public schools of Summit Hill and Lehighton and Weissport. He devoted his spare time to the study of law under the tutelage of attorneys Albright and Bertolette of Mauch Chunk. After passing his bar examination, he was admitted to the Carbon Bar in January of 1871 at the first term of court held by newly elected Judge Samuel Dreher and opened a law office in Mauch Chunk. His early days at the bar were spent in criminal court where he had singular success in winning acquittals for his clients. His moving summation and impassioned plea for the life of John "Yellow Jack" Donahue in 1876 won him plaudits from lawyers on both sides of the case. Frank W. Hughes, his opponent in the case, complimented it as a "speech of marked force and ability."

Unsuccessful campaigns for county superintendent of schools and district attorney in 1871 were followed by a successful run for the State Senate on the Republican ticket. Rapsher served in that body during the sessions of 1877 and 1878. His later law partner, Michael Cassidy, defeated him for the Senate in 1878. In 1885, as the Democratic nominee for district attorney, he defeated Republican Joseph Kalbfus. While he was district attorney he tried to convict several Lehigh Valley Railroad employees who were charged with criminal negligence at Mud Run in causing a railroad accident. Because the railroads were so powerful at the time and employed many county residents, it took a great deal of independence and courage to prosecute the cases. In 1888, Rapsher moved to Lehighton to practice law. After he left the district attorney's office, he returned to the defense side of the docket where won just about every major trial he undertook. He served as a member of borough council for nine years and one term as a school director. In 1895, while addressing the court, he suffered a stroke from which he never recovered. He died on January 26, 1897 at fifty-three years of age. He was survived by two sons, Charles and William.

Edward M. Mulhearn, Esquire (Adm. 1873) of Mauch Chunk, a twenty-seven-year-old lawyer with an indifferent past and unremarkable prospects, quite unexpectedly seized the public limelight as defense counsel for Michael Doyle, Edward Kelly, and Alexander Campbell in the highly charged "Mollie" trials in 1876 and remained center stage for most of his luminous political and legal career.

Born in Mauch Chunk on June 15, 1849, Mulhearn attended the public schools there and during his summers was employed as a slate-picker at Hacklebernie and for five seasons worked on the coal boats on the Lehigh Canal. As the son of poor Irish immigrants, he realized early in life that he was an outsider. He was also ambitious and he wanted to be part of the wealthy establishment around him. A college education would be his bridge to Mauch Chunk mainstream. Mulhearn entered Villanova College where the Augustinian fathers provided him with a solid liberal arts education. After graduating in 1871, he read law in the offices of Daniel Kalbfus, John C. Dimmick and Edward C. Dimmick and passed his law exams.

Within three years, he and his mentor Daniel Kalbfus were embroiled in the "Mollie" cases, an effort which would plummet the bedeviled Kalbfus into madness and launch Mulhearn into an incandescent political career. As the only local lawyer with Irish roots, he was trusted by his "Mollie" clients and he was given the difficult work of finding and bringing in witnesses to testify for the defense. Although the trials had devastating results for his clients, the press lauded his enormous energy and dedicated advocacy. Within three years he was elected district attorney taking office in 1880 and re-elected in 1882. During his first term Mulhearn married Mary Behrens of Mauch Chunk. In 1889 he won a seat in the State Legislature but declined a second term. Active in the Republican Party, he served as secretary and chairman of the County Republican Committee for almost ten years.

Intelligent and intuitive in his lawyering and gifted with a powerful voice, his skills in the courtroom and as public speaker were constantly in demand. By court appointment, he represented the deranged Oliver Stangley in his 1890 murder trial[69] and unsuccessfully tried to save him from the gallows with an insanity defense. In a knife-fight

[69] *Commonwealth v. Oliver Stangley*, 1 January Term 1890.

Summit Hill murder case of 1904,[70] he persuaded District Attorney Frank Sharkey and the court to accept a manslaughter plea from his client John Damasovica a miner from Summit Hill. He then moved to the prosecution side of the docket to assist George Gray in prosecuting John Brinkosh and Martin Pavlish for the murder of Simon Fuchilla in 1905.[71] In 1918, he formed a law partnership with Frank X. York who had studied for his bar exams in his office and they practiced together in the Schweiting Building until Mulhearn's death. He died on November 14, 1923 at his home on West Broadway, about five months after he celebrated the fiftieth anniversary of his admission to the Carbon Bar at the age of seventy-four. One son, John B. Mulhearn, and one daughter, Mrs. Walter Meekin, survived him.

William G. Freyman, Esquire (Adm. 1873) of Mahoning Township was the founding father of one of the oldest and preeminent law firms in Carbon County spanning both the nineteenth and twentieth centuries. His law firm produced two president judges, Horace Heydt and William G. Thomas and one district attorney, Ben Branch. At a time when pomposity and bombast were the norm at the bar, he was modest and quiet, and he stood tall with his facile, imaginative mind and quiet dignity. During the Civil War, he served as orderly sergeant of Company G, One Hundred and Seventy-sixth Regiment, Pennsylvania Volunteer Infantry. At the expiration of his term of service, he recruited a company of which he was commissioned lieutenant. Before it was mustered into service, the war closed, and he returned home.

Freyman became a civil engineer and surveyor and pursued that profession for about twelve years. He also engaged in merchandising. Carbon title searchers frequently find Freyman's name after early deed descriptions as the surveyor of record. His interest in surveying and real estate transactions eventually led him to the law.

He apprenticed in the office of General Charles Albright at Mauch Chunk from 1871 to 1873 when he was admitted to the Carbon Bar. Shortly thereafter, he became the partner of his former preceptor, and they practiced law together under the firm name of Albright & Freyman until the general died in 1880. As a member of this firm he participated in the sensational "Mollie Maguire" trials.

---

[70] *Commonwealth v. John Damasovica*, 1 October Sessions 1904.

[71] *Commonwealth v. John Brinkosh and Martin Pavlish*, 23 & 24 January Sessions 1905.

In 1881, Freyman moved into new offices at 78 Broadway which were widely regarded as the most beautifully appointed offices in the county at that time. After practicing alone for several years, Freyman formed a partnership with James Kiefer, a prominent attorney from Seattle, who had been a student in his office. Kiefer retired from the firm after five years and Freyman became associated with Horace Heydt, also a former student of his, under the name of Freyman & Heydt. Later, Eugene O. Nothstein, a nephew of Freyman, was taken into partnership, altering the firm name to Freyman Heydt & Nothstein. Freyman had been Nothstein's preceptor.

In September 1901, Heydt was elevated to the Bench of Carbon County. From this time until the spring of 1912, when Nothstein died, the practice of the firm was conducted under the name of Freyman & Nothstein. Freyman later took in William G. Thomas and Ben Branch as law partners, and this firm engaged in an active corporate and litigation practice under the firm name of Freyman Thomas & Branch. In 1903, Freyman founded the Mauch Chunk Trust Company and served as its president until his death on May 28, 1928.

His twenty-page holographic will probated on May 29, 1928 in the office of the register of wills, reveals many interesting insights into the life and loves of this very successful Victorian-era lawyer. The will indicates that he died a widower with no surviving children because his will specified gifts to St. John's Church in Mahoning Valley for the perpetual care of the graves of "my dear wife Matilda Gilbert Freyman" and "my two children who died in infancy." It also shows his belief in the future of his bank and desire to keep its stock in his family. He directed that his stock in the Mauch Chunk Trust Company not be sold for twenty years. His deep religious convictions, love of his sister and affection for General Albright also show in his bequests. He left his home and law office on the north side of Broadway and its contents to his sister Sadie L. Nothstein for life and his residue to the Mauch Chunk Trust Company in trust for the benefit of his sister and members of her family. The will makes twenty-five specific money legacies -- many to the churches of Carbon County and even a bequest to the Mauch Chunk Cemetery for the perpetual care of the grave of his friend and mentor General Charles Albright.

Edward R. Siewers, Esquire (Adm. 1873) No member of the Carbon Bar rose to prominence so early or so easily; no member fell from the pinnacle so quickly. The son of Attorney Joseph H. Siewers, a prominent, well-regarded lawyer, politician and former superintendent of schools in Carbon County, Siewers rode the fame bestowed by his last name when he made his first run for public office. His father's political clout and money did not hurt either as he was easily elected district attorney over Frederick Bertolette in 1874. He had scarcely been at the bar a year As the district attorney during the most highly publicized trials in Carbon County history, the "Mollie Maguire Trials" (See **Chapter XV**, page 267) he received a great deal of the credit for their successful prosecution. Actually, he played only a minor role allowing counsel for the leading coal and railroad companies in the county to conduct these trials. Siewers won re-election as district attorney in 1877. After he left office, he engaged in the general practice of law, and dabbled in the real estate and insurance business in Mauch Chunk.

A disastrous Mauch Chunk real estate investment caused Siewers' downfall. In 1885, he fed enormous amounts of his own and borrowed money into the Wahnetah Land and Improvement Company to build the ill-fated, four-story Wahnetah Hotel at Glen Onoko. Although it had a promising start, the hotel's lack of easy accessibility led to a lack of tourist trade. The hotel's high vacancy rate eventually had Siewers awash in debt and pursued by irate creditors. In a desperate attempt to save the hotel, he borrowed heavily from his friends and when their funds dried up, he resorted to fraud, theft and embezzlement to raise money. His forgery of his mother's name on ten Lehigh Valley Railroad bonds at the First National Bank of Mauch Chunk brought him to the brink of being arrested and charged with embezzlement in June of 1891. His mother saved him from criminal prosecution by signing a release exonerating the bank from all liability which might arise from her son's forgery. As numerous creditors and fraud charges closed in on him, he suddenly disappeared from Mauch Chunk. His remaining personal property including a substantial law library was sold at sheriff's sale for $1000.

Years later he turned up as a financial editor for the *Philadelphia Times*. In June of 1917, Siewers was found drowned in the Delaware River near the Market Street wharf, an apparent suicide. His remains were brought back to Mauch Chunk where a small group of Carbon lawyers led by Judge Barber and Judge Heydt laid him to rest in the Mauch Chunk Cemetery. He was seventy-four.

Frederick Bertolette, Esquire (Adm. 1874) Born near Pottstown, Montgomery County in 1851, he grew up in Lewisburg, Pennsylvania and had the good fortune to attend Mifflinburg Academy. One of his classmates there was Laird Barber. They formed a close relationship which later blossomed into one of Carbon's finest law partnerships. Shortly after his graduation from Bucknell University in 1872, he came to Mauch Chunk and read law in the office of his cousin, Colonel John D. Bertolette. He was admitted to the Carbon Bar in 1874 and immediately made a bid for public office by running for district attorney against Edward R. Siewers. Although he was defeated, Bertolette's commanding presence and self assured manner drew the attention of the Court and his fellow lawyers. Judge Dreher appointed the young lawyer to represent two of the "Mollies" John Donahue and John Malloy for their 1876 trials.

In 1881, Laird Barber joined him at the bar. They practiced law together under the name of Bertolette & Barber with offices in the Dolon Building and later in the Navigation Building. Barber's wide circle of political contacts and Bertolette's expertise in corporation law attracted such clients as the Lehigh Coal and Navigation Company, the New Jersey Zinc Company, the Central Railroad of New Jersey, the Mill Creek Coal Company and the Carbon County Liquor Dealers Association. During his forty-one years of practice, Bertolette was a peerless and energetic civic leader in his adopted hometown of Mauch Chunk. He was particularly active in the Marion Hose Company and took great pleasure in serving as its president. In 1914 Judge Barber appointed him chief burgess (mayor) to succeed Asa P. Blakeslee who had died in office. Bertolette was also deeply committed to the Pennsylvania Bar Association serving on various committees and rarely missed a meeting.

Over his lifetime he acquired one of the largest law libraries in the Carbon-Lehigh area. After his sudden death on March 10, 1915 at the age of sixty-four, his wife Louise and two daughters, Helen and Florence honored a request he made to them during his lifetime by donating his extensive law library to the County of Carbon for the use of the court and members of the Carbon Bar.

Joseph Kalbfus, Esquire (Adm. 1876) One of the founding fathers of the conservation movement in Pennsylvania, Dr. Kalbfus was the first full time secretary of the Pennsylvania Game Commission and Chief Game Warden. For the first time, under his leadership, game laws were enforced, hunting licenses for residents required and wildlife management regulations adopted. Many of his visionary programs endure to this day.

Born in Williamsport in 1852, he pioneered in the West during his youth, herding cattle and fighting Indians. He came to Mauch Chunk in 1874 and began the study of law in the office of his flamboyant brother, Daniel Kalbfus. His first assignment after admission to the Carbon bar was to assist Daniel in his ill-fated albeit spirited defense of several of the Molly Maguires during 1876 and 1877. He ran unsuccessfully for District Attorney in 1885 and later served as a federal revenue agent.In a mid-life change of careers, Kalbfus enrolled in the Philadelphia School of Dentistry and after graduation moved to Harrisburg where he had a very successful dental practice. From 1898 to 1919, the distinguished looking gentleman with the high starched collar and the white goatee and mustache was a familiar figure lobbying and fighting for the preservation of Pennsylvania's forests and wildlife. Kalbfus was killed in 1919 while on an inspection tour in Warren County. He was sixty-seven.

Joseph S. Fisher, Esquire (Adm. 1885). From abject poverty as a grimy unschooled slate-picker at the LC&N Company breaker in Summit Hill he rose to become a two-term district attorney and successful lawyer in Carbon County. Born April 15, 1854 in the mining shanty village of Jamestown in the Panther Creek Valley (now Summit Hill), he like all coalfield children had no adolescence. At nine years of age he was one of the two hundred boys who separated the slate and refuse from the coal in the inclined breaker chutes for forty-five cents a day. He worked ten hours a day six days a week. When he was sixteen, he moved into the deep mines where he labored for $2 a day and on his days off took courses at a normal school. By the time he was twenty-one, he had obtained a teacher's certificate and began teaching in his hometown. In 1884 he began to read law in the offices of Craig & Loose and within a year he gained admission to the bar.

Five years later he was elected to the office of district attorney where he distinguished himself as a prosecutor of courage and ability for six years. He prosecuted the last death penalty case in Carbon County when he obtained a first degree murder verdict against Oliver Stangley which sent him to the gallows in 1891. He courageously and successfully prosecuted a number of election fraud cases against members of his own party in Lansford.

In 1887 he moved to Mauch Chunk and established his law office on First Street on the East Side where he lived with his brothers and sisters. He became a director and president of the East Mauch Chunk School Board in 1896, served as borough solicitor of Mauch Chunk and Summit Hill and was attorney for the Building and Loan Associations of Summit Hill, Nesquehoning and East Mauch Chunk. At the acme of a successful and lucrative practice, his early years of exposure to coal dust extracted the inevitable penalty. He developed anthrasilicosis and died at the age of forty-four on January 15, 1899. He was survived by two brothers, Thomas and Patrick and three sisters, Mary, Margaret and Maria.

Frank P. Sharkey, Esquire (Adm. 1887). His colleagues considered him the most erudite and scholarly member of the early twentieth century Carbon Bar. His father, Patrick Sharkey, was a prominent figure in Carbon County and influential in both business and politics. A native of Mauch Chunk, he attended public schools there, attended St. Joseph's Academy in Madison, New Jersey and received his undergraduate degree at Seton Hall College. His family then sent him to Europe where he studied at Carlow University in Ireland and at the University of London.

After returning to this country, he began to study law at the offices of Allen Craig and gained admission to the bar. Sharkey was elected district attorney in 1901 and participated in the widely publicized criminal prosecution of Big Martin Leskoski of Lansford for the murder of his landlady. The case featured a first degree murder conviction, two jail breaks, a death sentence, appeals, and ultimately a governor's pardon.

Sharkey was well read and had an extensive personal library and law library replete with ancient and modern law books. He liked nothing more than inviting friends to his home and engaging them in lively debate on every topic in his wide spectrum of interests. A bachelor for most of his life, he surprised everyone by marrying his long-time girlfriend when he was eighty. In his early years, he served as court stenographer, a postmaster in Mauch Chunk during the term of President Grover Cleveland and a delegate to the national Republican convention that nominated Cleveland. He practiced at the Carbon Bar for fifty-six years right up to the time of his death and for twenty-five years was president of the bar association. He died at the age of eighty-three on June 1, 1943 at his home at 59 Broadway.

Jacob C. Loose, Esquire (Adm. 1890). In his fifty-two years of practice he answered the call of his hero, President Theodore Roosevelt, to a "life of strenuous endeavor" by an energetic and single-minded dedication to his profession, his clients, and his community. A stranger when he came to Mauch Chunk in 1890, at his death in 1942 he had become the town's most renowned citizen, and an icon to his colleagues at the Carbon County Bar.

Educated in the public schools of Palmyra, New Jersey and at Dickinson College where he earned his B.A. and M.A., he "read law" in the offices of Allen Craig and his uncle James S. Loose and then joined the firm. When Allen Craig was elected to the bench in 1894, his son Douglas S. Craig formed a new law firm with James Loose under the name Craig & Loose. Jacob Loose's legal acumen and success in handling difficult corporate matters earned him a partnership with the firm in 1898. Craig & Loose had a large and prestigious law practice in Carbon County at the turn of the century. Their clients included the Lehigh Valley Railroad, the Bethlehem Water Authority and the Mauch Chunk National Bank. After Craig died in 1923, Jacob Loose practiced alone until his son, Alan S. Loose, joined him in 1925. Their offices were located in the Navigation Building.

In his demeanor and public persona, Loose was a lawyer right out of Dickens -- reserved, scholarly, coolly efficient and thorough. During vacations, he liked to take extensive trips, travelling to South America, Europe and the western part of the United States. His legal and banking career was characterized by unremitting involvement in the improvement and promotion of Mauch Chunk. From 1919 he was a director, and from 1935 president of the Mauch Chunk National Bank (now Jim Thorpe National Bank), succeeding Ira Ross. Loose was the first librarian of the Dimmick Memorial Library and was later appointed as a trustee serving from 1901-1939. He was also secretary of the Chamber of Commerce, and junior warden and ardent supporter of St. John's Episcopal Church in East Mauch Chunk. A rock-ribbed Republican, he served four years as chairman of the County

Republican Committee, and was also solicitor for the register of wills, the county treasurer and recorder of deeds.

His deep commitment to the legal profession included regular attendance at all annual meetings of the Pennsylvania Bar Association and several years of service as chairman of its Executive Committee. The Carbon Bar honored him at the American Hotel on January 14, 1940 in recognition of his fifty years as a lawyer. His sudden death at the age of seventy-six on August 27, 1942 came as a profound shock to Mauch Chunk because of his vigorous work habits and robust constitution. Alice M. Bear, his widow, and Alan S. Loose, his only son, survived him.

Eugene O. Nothstein, Esquire (Adm. 1893). Outside, he had the body of the football player he was in his college days -- big, powerful and barrel-chested. Inside he had the soul and character of the clergyman he at one time wanted to be. Born at Pleasant Corners in Mahoning Township in 1867, he felt an early calling to the ministry and began training for the life of a clergyman at the Palitanate College Prep School at Meyerstown. He taught school briefly at the Beaver Run School and then entered Franklin and Marshall College in Lancaster where he excelled in football and graduated with honors. His uncle, William G. Freyman, who was then Dean of the Carbon Bar, persuaded Nothstein to turn his talents from saving souls to winning cases and in 1890 he began the study of law in his office. In quick succession he was admitted to practice, became a partner in the Freyman firm and in 1894 was elected district attorney for one term.

Nothstein devoted enormous energy to his cases and meticulously prepared every case, studying it from every angle so he could defend it from even the most remote attack. For almost twenty years the firm of Freyman & Nothstein rode his effervescent personality and herculean hours of work to great financial success.

In January of 1900 he bought the American Hotel and remodeled it so that it became Mauch Chunk's leading resort hotel. He was one of the first in Mauch Chunk to buy an automobile. One of his favorite and frequent pastimes was taking groups of children for rides up and down Broadway.

When the Lehighton Building and Loan Association went into the hands of a receiver in 1911, Freyman & Nothstein were engaged to assist the receiver in winding up its affairs. Nothstein was determined to get every cent possible for the individual shareholders and spent long hours, every day, preparing a case against the officers and directors for mismanagement. He developed pneumonia following complications from a tonsil operation and died unexpectedly at the age of forty-five on April 20, 1912. Undoubtedly, the stress and strain of the case caused his untimely death. He was survived by his widow Sadie Kuhns Nothstein and three children, Wilbur, Harlan and Kenneth.

Nathan M. Balliet, Esquire (Adm. 1895) of Mahoning Township was the president of the Carbon County Bar after the death of Frank Sharkey in 1943, and was Nestor of the Bar for eight years. He was one of the first lawyers in Carbon County and one of the few lawyers of his era to have a university education in law.

He acquired his early education in the public schools and at the Normal Institute, located in his native township and founded by his brother, Prof. Thomas M. Balliet. He attended Kutztown State Normal School, and later studied at Franklin and Marshall College, from which he graduated with an A.B. in 1886, and an M.A. in 1888. Balliet taught briefly in the public schools, after which he became an instructor in Greek and Latin at Palatinate College (now Albright College) for two years. Accepting a professorship at Ursinus College, he taught Latin and Roman literature there from 1890-1892, during which time he was also president of the Summer School of Languages at the same college. Forsaking a career in education, he entered New York University Law School, graduating in 1895 with a law degree. After admission to practice before the courts of the State of New York, he maintained an office in New York City for a brief period.

In October of 1895, Balliet was admitted to the Carbon County Bar and took over the practice and office of Senator William M. Rapsher in Lehighton. In 1896 he had formed a partnership with his brother-in-law, Ira E. Seidle, under the firm name of Balliet & Seidle, and for a short time Albert Prutzman joined the firm. They maintained offices in Lehighton and Palmerton. Balliet specialized in the fields of estate administration and real estate and was considered by his peers as an expert practitioner in those areas.

He was an active member of the Lehighton Masonic organization for fifty years and served as a elder and Sunday school teacher for many years in the Lehighton Reformed Church. Balliet was also a trustee of Cedar Crest College in Allentown for more than twenty years.

After the death of Ira Seidle in 1943, Balliet formed an association with George A. Shutack and they practiced together in the Masonic Building in Lehighton until Balliet's death on October 3, 1951 at the age of eighty-nine. He was survived by a daughter Katie S. Swavely and three sons, Charles N. Balliet, Paul S. Balliet, and Nevin E. Balliet.

Theodore Allen Snyder, Esquire (Adm. 1895) was a success in everything he did and he did just about everything. He was an educator, lawyer, banker, brewer, trolley line operator, farmer, socialite and churchman. What is even more remarkable, he did it all within a brief lifetime of fifty years.

Born in Stroudsburg in 1857, he was educated in its public schools and then completed a scientific course of studies at Millersville State Normal School. At sixteen he was teaching in a grammar school in Stroudsburg and he then moved to Lehighton where he taught and was a school principal for two years. He returned to Stroudsburg and read law in the office of John B. Storm until he was admitted to the bar in Monroe County in 1883 at the age of twenty-four. Following the example of his preceptor, he returned to teaching and from 1885 to 1894 was superintendent of schools in Carbon County. "T.A.", as he was best known, owned Lehighton's most beautiful home. Located on the northeast corner of 7th and Iron Streets with stately pillars, broad verandas, and balconies, it looked like it had been imported from a southern plantation. Actually, Snyder found it at an Exposition in Buffalo, bought it, dismantled and moved it by rail to Iron Street where he had it rebuilt in 1902. Tending the spacious gardens around his mansion was his chief delight and pastime. He was an avid student of horticulture, forestry and farming and spent all his spare time pursuing these interests. His home was the center of many social gatherings in Lehighton. His delightful companionship and friendly outgoing manner always attracted a large crowd.

In 1895, he opened a law office in Lehighton from which he not only practiced law but engaged in various business enterprises. He built and operated the Flagstaff Trolley Line; he helped organize and was attorney for the Lehighton Building and Loan Association; he owned and operated the Stroudsburg Brewery Company. In 1903, he formed a legal partnership with his brother in law Charles A. Hauck under the firm name of Snyder & Hauck until Snyder's untimely death in 1907. He was survived by his wife Emma Hauck Snyder and two children, Raymond Jr., and Edith M.

Daniel W. Sitler, Esquire (Adm. 1896), of Mahoning Township, was first a teacher of mathematics and then a lawyer actively involved in community and church affairs in Mauch Chunk. After studying at the Normal Institute, he taught in the Mahoning School district for four years. He then matriculated at Williams College in Massachusetts where he earned his undergraduate degree in 1887. While teaching in a private school in Philadelphia, he decided to change careers and moved to Allentown where he studied law in the office of James S. Biery. He successfully passed the Pennsylvania bar examination and was admitted to both the Lehigh County and Carbon County bars. He opened the first law office in the Borough of Lansford in 1896 and became its borough solicitor. In 1898, as the Republican candidate, he defeated Robert A. Heberling and was elected district attorney for one term.

Sitler moved his law office and residence to Mauch Chunk after his election as district attorney and he remained there for the rest of his life. He served a term as tax collector for Mauch Chunk Borough and was a United States Commissioner for a number of years. His devotion to St. John's Lutheran Church was second only to his service to his family and clients. He was a bible teacher at St. John's for many years. He died at the age of seventy on June 2, 1937 survived by his widow the former Amanda Balliet and two daughters, Helen and Mary.

Ira E. Seidle, Esquire (Adm. 1896) was the Carbon Bar's personification of the Renaissance man in the early decades of the twentieth century. Well educated, well read with a bright inquiring mind, his life was one long passionate and abiding commitment to the law, his church and his community. He was born on December 11, 1869 at Normal Square, Mahoning Township, the home of his maternal ancestors since Revolutionary times. His father, Charles H. Seidle was a self-educated man who had a remarkable multi-faceted career as a school teacher, retail store owner, postmaster at Normal Square, Lehighton banker and for five years an associate judge of Carbon County. A member in the first graduating class of Lehighton High School in 1884, Ira Seidle went on to receive an outstanding education in the best schools of his time. He entered Albright College in 1886; a year later he transferred to Muhlenberg and received a B.S. degree from that institution in 1890, and an M.A. degree in 1892. Seidle also entered the senior class at Yale, where he earned a Bachelor of Arts degree in 1891. He began his legal studies at the Yale Law School, but then transferred to the law school of the University of Pennsylvania where he earned a law degree (LL.B.) in 1895. He and Nathan Balliet were the first Carbon County lawyers to obtain university law degrees.

After practicing law in Philadelphia for a year, Seidle returned to Carbon County and formed a partnership in Lehighton with his brother-in-law, Nathan M. Balliet under the rubric Balliet & Seidle. The firm of Balliet & Seidle was the most prominent firm in the lower part of Carbon County and with a well earned reputation for legal skill and integrity flourished for some forty-seven years. Both Judge Horace Heydt of Lehighton and Albert Prutzman of Palmerton joined the firm for a short time. Studious looking and elegant in his dress and bearing, Seidle was primarily an office practitioner specializing in civil cases and banking law.

Seidle was a prime mover and shaker in the Lehighton business community and many fraternal and charitable organizations. He was manager and treasurer of the

Lehighton Brick Company, and was secretary-director of the Lehigh Valley Building and Loan Association, the first savings and loan association in Lehighton. He was also a director and secretary of the Carbon County Industrial Society which annually sponsored the popular Carbon County Fair at Lehighton. A fervent Mason, he was master of the Lehighton Lodge of Masons, No. 621 and a member of the Lehigh Consistory in Allentown. On June 27, 1941 Balliet and Seidle were honored for their contributions to the Lehighton area at the testimonial dinner featuring Judge McCready as principal speaker. He died October 2, 1943 at the age of seventy-three. He was survived by his wife, the former Elizabeth Gabel, and two daughters, Mrs. Ralph Kreamer and Mrs. William Moyer. His grandson, Ralph E. Kreamer, Jr. was an outstanding reporter for the Allentown *Morning Call.* A knowledgeable local historian, Ralph Kreamer produced a moveable feast of vignettes on Carbon's famous people, places, and events which were published in the *Call* during 1961 and are widely regarded as well-researched and authoritative.

Leighton C. Scott, Esquire (Adm. 1896), a native of East Mauch Chunk, rose from a breaker-boy in Coaldale to become one of the most respected lawyers in his community. Inspired by his father who was a plane engineer with the LC&N Company, he was the embodiment of the self-made man. During his years at the breaker, Scott found time to read and study law in various law offices until he finally took and passed his examinations for admission to practice. He was the only member admitted to the Carbon Bar without a college or high school education.

After his admission, he moved to Lansford where he established his home and his law office. For sixty years, he provided legal services and advice to the citizens of Lansford and Summit Hill. Scott served as solicitor for Lansford Borough, Lansford School District and for the Homestead Building and Loan Association of Summit Hill. For many years he was a member of the Board of Law Examiners of the Carbon County Bar Association. In addition to numerous fraternal affiliations, Scott was an active member of the Trinity Episcopal Church in Lansford.

Senator William Z. Scott of Lansford, a long time member of the Carbon Bar, was a nephew of Leighton Scott and served his law clerkship in Leighton Scott's office before his admission to the bar. He was the brother of Ellsworth Scott, another prominent member of the Carbon Bar, and they practiced together until Ellsworth died in 1919. Leighton Scott died at the age of eighty-six on February 5, 1956. Surviving him was his wife Nettie R. Ross Scott and a son, Attorney Leighton R. Scott.

James M. Breslin, Esquire (Adm. 1896) of Mauch Chunk was a criminal defense lawyer considered by most as quite possibly the finest of his generation at the Carbon Bar. Breslin's appearance in a criminal case immediately added a weight and presence to the defense which were invaluable. He went into every trial with both fists swinging. Every client's cause represented a sacred trust. Supremely skilled in the courtroom and fearless within the bounds of the law, his demeanor in the courtroom belied his humble beginnings and lack of formal education. The son of a coal miner who came from County Donegal in 1833 and lived in Tresckow, Breslin was born January 1, 1870 and worked as a slate picker and miner in his early years. Literally self-educated by reading everything he could get his hands on, he was able to pass the qualifying test to become a teacher at the age of twenty. He taught school in Foster and Banks townships for ten years. In 1894, the lure and excitement of the courtroom drew him to read law in the office of Edward M. Mulhearn. After passing the bar exams he opened his own office in Mauch Chunk and headed for the courtroom to lend his talents to the poor, the oppressed and the downtrodden.

From 1900 to 1935, he appeared on behalf of defendants at every term of criminal court handling adroitly a wide variety of cases. Lacing his arguments to the jury with commonplace observations, puckish wit and homespun aphorisms, he defended some fifteen men charged with murder. "Big Martin" Leskoski was the only client who ever received the death sentence but Breslin eventually obtained a pardon for him from the Governor. He attributed his success to intense preparation, wide knowledge of criminal procedure and his own resourcefulness. His law library was the largest in the county and no lawyer spent more time and energy in investigating the facts and the law so that he could present the best possible defense for his client.

His defense of Palmertonian Lewis Kohut in October of 1915 was vintage Breslin. It was a case[72] most people believed was an open and shut case of first degree murder. Kohut had gone into the Hazard Hotel on April 16, 1915 and fatally stabbed Fedor Klein twice with a large knife in the presence of eleven boarders who were seated with him at the dinner table. An aging Edward Mulhearn was retained to represent Kohut and Mulhearn brought in Breslin as trail counsel. District Attorney Chester Setzer rejected any plea bargain and brought in William G. Thomas, a rising young star in the criminal courts, to assist him. Two hundred jurors, most of whom said they were opposed to capital punishment, were examined over two days before a jury of twelve was selected. Displaying his mastery of criminal procedure, Breslin objected to the proceedings because Judge Barber had not formally closed quarter session court and opened the court of oyer and terminer which had sole jurisdiction over murder cases. He claimed the entire proceedings were

[72]*Commonwealth v. Lewis Kohut, 28 April Term 1915.*

therefore illegal. Judge Barber knew Breslin was right but overruled the objection. Breslin then argued to the jury that the defendant was so intoxicated by the wine and beer he had before the killing, he did not act consciously and with premeditation. The jury convicted Kohut of second degree murder and Judge Barber immediately sentenced him to ten years in prison. Buoyant in victory Breslin exulted to the press after sentence: "Well the prosecution lost five years. We were willing to plead him to second degree murder for a fifteen year sentence."

In one of his more humorous defenses, he represented R. W. Gombert,[73] the paymaster for the New Jersey Zinc Company at Hazard on charges that he embezzled $820 of company funds and made false entries on the company's books. Gombert never denied taking the money but he insisted that he had used the money for the benefit of Palmerton by using it to buy professional baseball players to help the Palmerton baseball team beat Mauch Chunk and other talented teams. After a jury was drawn, Breslin persuaded District Attorney Setzer and his assistant Ben Branch, both baseball fans, to nol pros the false entry charge and agreed to plead his client to the embezzlement. Judge Barber, no baseball enthusiast, was not impressed by Gombert's efforts to bolster Palmerton's baseball team and sentenced him to four months in jail.

Breslin was county solicitor for three years, solicitor for East Mauch Chunk, Beaver Meadow and Banks townships, and served several terms as a school board director in East Mauch Chunk. For ten years he also operated very successfully the old coal mines at Hacklebernie near Mauch Chunk with David Pursell. He died on February 12, 1936 at the age of sixty-six survived by his wife Lizzie, a son James D. Breslin, Esquire and a daughter Elizabeth Breslin.

---

[73] *Commonwealth v. R. W. Gombert*, 12 January Sessions 1915.

Horace DeYoung Lentz, Esquire (Adm. 1896). Born to wealth with an aristocratic name and manner he used his affluence and influence locally as Mauch Chunk's most munificent benefactor after the turn of the century. He provided funds for Mauch Chunk's first children's playground, set up a trust which laid the foundation for Carbon's current county road system and made financial gifts to every school in the county to establish libraries. The Lentz Trail from Jim Thorpe to White Bear was named in his honor because of his life-long work in promoting good roads.

The son of Lafayette Lentz who made a fortune operating a large Schuylkill County colliery, Lentz was born in Mauch Chunk on February 24, 1867. Superbly educated, he attended Adams Academy in Quincy, Massachusetts and then earned his B.A. degree at Harvard University in 1891. Returning to his home town he read law at the offices of Bertolette & Barber and also studied civil engineering. After his admission to the bar, he opened an office in his home at 72 Broadway where he specialized in real estate law. (His home is currently owned by Laura Thomas and was used as medical offices by the late Dr. George P. Thomas). In 1893 he married Jeannie McCreary Alsover the daughter of Jabez Alsover, a prominent Carbon County businessman. They built an impressive summer home on his property in Mahoning Township where the Ukrainian Homestead is presently located. Lentz was the first agent of the Palmer Land Company and played an active role in the establishment of Palmerton. An avid Democrat he ran unsuccessfully for the United States Congress in 1912.

Although he had none of his own, he loved children and actively supported any project which would benefit children educationally or recreationally. He served as a director of the Mauch Chunk Trust Company, vestryman of St. Mark's Episcopal Church and a school director of the Mauch Chunk School District. In 1929, he provided the funds to build Tolman House and also the sexton's house on the west side of St. Mark's Church which was transformed into the handsome corporation room on the first floor and a guild room on the second floor. When he died unexpectedly at the age of sixty-six on November 28, 1933, his good friend James J. Boyle wrote of him in the *Mauch Chunk Times-News*:

> *He was known to every man, woman and child in the community. His common democracy appealed to all. He shared their sorrows and triumphs, was interested in their aspirations and encouraged them by helpful advice and suggestions. Countless are those who owe their start in life to his friendly interest.*

George E. Gray, Esquire (Adm. 1899), a native of Maryland, studied law in the offices of Craig & Loose at Mauch Chunk after graduating from Shippensburg State Normal School and attending the University of Pennsylvania. In 1900, Gray purchased the *Mauch Chunk Daily Times*, and the semi-weekly *Mauch Chunk Coal Gazette*. He served as both editor and publisher of these journals until 1908 when he sold both papers to James J. Boyle, who abandoned the publication of the *Coal Gazette*. In 1895, he married Antoinette Montz and had three children, Margaret S., Charlotte A., and William G. Gray.

Gray was elected district attorney in 1904, and re-elected three years later. He was chairman of the County Republican Committee, director of the First National Bank of Lehighton for two years and superintendent of the sunday school of Zion's Reformed Church in Lehighton where he lived. He was an active member of many Masonic organizations, was one of the local "five minute" speakers during World War I and a member of the local draft board. He ran unsuccessfully for judge as the Republican candidate against James C. McCready in 1939.

Congenial in his public life and unflappable in court, he practiced law in Lehighton for forty-three years. He was solicitor for the Borough of Lehighton, Bowmanstown, Weissport and Franklin Township. He died on September 28, 1947 at the age of seventy-nine.

James Smitham, Esquire (Adm. 1899) was a native of Nesquehoning and a son of Thomas and Anna Maria Meese Smitham, both of whom were born in England. After receiving his primary education in the public schools of his home town, he graduated from Millersville State Normal School in 1891. After teaching school in Nesquehoning for two years, he undertook a year's study at Dickinson College and then earned an Associate Business degree at Eastman Business College. Smitham then decided to pursue a career in law. He entered Princeton University and earned a Bachelor of Arts degree in 1897 and moved on to Harvard Law School where he received his law degree in 1899. After serving a clerkship in the offices of Bertolette & Barber, he opened his own office on the second floor of the Mauch Chunk National Bank Building. He devoted his law practice to real estate transactions and he invested heavily in brick and mortar holdings.

In 1906, he was appointed a referee in bankruptcy for the Middle District of Pennsylvania and served in that office until 1926. At the time, referees were not federal employees; they received no direct compensation from the Government. There was an ethically conflicted arrangement under which they were paid a percentage of the bankrupt estates they administered. Part-time referees like Smitham were permitted to conduct a private law practice while they held office. Smitham presided over the bankruptcies of hundreds of personal and corporate failures during his twenty years on the bench. Despite having to deal daily with economic disasters and fiscal misfortunes, Smitham kept his sense of humor and was known as a witty conversationalist and an engaging story teller.

In the early 1920s he had a controlling interest in the Cornish Arms Hotel, a popular New York City establishment. His title work was meticulous and unerring and it was this reputation which provided the major stimulus to his very successful practice. He died August 19, 1941 survived by his widow and two children, Thomas and Mary F. Smitham.

Philip M. Graul, Esquire (Adm. 1901) of Lehighton used his legal training in both publishing and manufacturing businesses. A native of Hoppenville, Montgomery County, he first came to Carbon County to teach school in Lehighton after receiving his undergraduate education at Ursinus and Muhlenberg Colleges. After graduating from Dickinson School of Law in 1901, he was admitted to the Carbon Bar that same year.

He purchased the *Carbon Advocate*, Lehighton's weekly newspaper from George W. Morthimer in 1902, and operated it for some twenty years until fire destroyed the presses. He also was the general manager of the Lehighton Lace Company, a prime industry in lower Carbon County at the turn of the century.

Graul served as Lehighton Borough solicitor for seven years and was active in the Elks, Masons, Fire Engine Company No. 1 and a major financial supporter of the Democratic Party, locally and nationally. He died on July 18, 1946 at the age of seventy-six and was survived by three sons, Dr. Carl M. Graul, Henry F. Graul and Colonel Donald T. Graul.

Ellsworth E. Scott, Esquire (Adm. 1902), of Summit Hill, son of immigrant parents from Ireland, rose from a slate picker on the boats of the Lehigh Canal at Mauch Chunk to become a successful lawyer, banker and one of the leading home builders in Carbon County.

After a teaching career in Summit Hill, he studied law in the offices of Bertolette & Barber in Mauch Chunk and was admitted to the Carbon Bar in 1902. He joined his brother Leighton C. Scott in the practice of law in Lansford and they practiced together until his untimely death.

Scott organized the Homestead Building and Loan Association in Lansford and the Citizens National Bank of Lansford and is credited with being the prime mover in the building of the old Summit Hill High School. He died December 31, 1919 at fifty-seven years of age. His wife, a daughter, and two sons, L. Pearson Scott and Eldon Scott, survived him.

Chester G. Setzer, Esquire (Adm. 1905). Like many members of the early twentieth century bar, Setzer began as a school teacher and then went on to law school and admission to the bar. Born on November 17, 1880, Setzer grew up in Franklin Township where he received his early education in the public schools, graduating from Mauch Chunk High in 1899. He taught school for three years before he entered Dickinson School of Law where he earned his law degree in 1905. He immediately opened a law office for the general practice of law in Weissport. Following the political footsteps of his father who was the sheriff of Carbon County in 1894, he ran for district attorney as the candidate of the Republican Party in 1911 and defeated Philip M. Graul. Just before his re-election in 1915, he married Florence Costenbader of Emmaus and a former teacher in the Lehighton schools. After he left the district attorney's office, he became a member of the school board of the Franklin Independent District for a number of years and served as its secretary.

Winfred (Fred) D. Lewis, Esquire (Adm. 1908), a native son of Lansford, led the resurgence of the Republican Party in Carbon County as the chairman of the county G.O.P. from 1922 to 1942. With exceptional organizational skills and close personal attention to the minutest of details he built a powerful county organization which propelled Republicans into every office in the courthouse during his leadership years.

Lewis' mother was born in Wales. His father served as a justice of the peace in Coaldale and had a very successful retail coal business and real estate and insurance office there. Born on February 6, 1883, he received his early education in the Lansford public schools and Perkiomen Seminary, Fred Lewis worked his way through Princeton University and earned his Bachelor of Arts (A.B.) degree in 1905. Lack of finances prevented him from completing Dickinson School of Law which he attended for two years, but he successfully took the local bar examination and was admitted to the Carbon and Pennsylvania bars in 1908. He then embarked on his legal career as a sole practitioner, with offices in the Navigation Building, in Mauch Chunk and Lansford. In his two forays into the political arena, he was defeated. In 1910 he ran as the Republican candidate for State Senator and was defeated. In 1912 he was unsuccessful in seeking a seat in the State House. Although he spent a great deal of time developing a large law practice and working for the Republican Party, he also directed his creative energies to a wide range of civic affairs. He founded the Lewis Insurance Agency, the most prominent real estate and insurance firm in the county in the first half of the twentieth century. During World War I, Lewis took a prominent role in raising funds for the war effort as chairman of the four-minute speakers for Carbon County and as chairman and legal advisor of the Carbon County War Chest.

He served as county solicitor from 1936 to 1940, as well as solicitor for the Borough of Summit Hill, and was counsel for the Pennsylvania State Authority. He was also a director of the Dime Bank of Lansford, president of Carbon Finance Corporation, treasurer of the Carbon Loan Company and a founding member of the Mahoning Valley Country Club. He died unexpectedly at the age of fifty-nine on July 25, 1942 at Coaldale Hospital leaving a wife, Arlene Kooser Lewis and two children, Helen Loraine and Winfred D. Jr.

Ben Branch, Esquire (Adm. 1910). Gifted with a photographic memory and a masterful command of the law and the English language, Ben Branch was considered by his peers as one of the best trial lawyers of the Carbon County Bar during the first half of the twentieth century. Prickly, savvy and dramatic, he was equally skilled in marshalling the evidence and in cross-examining witnesses where he searched quietly, but relentlessly, for the evidence which would ultimately win the case. He won a remarkably high percentage of his trials. In 1940, he obtained an acquittal for State Trooper Ben Franklin in a sensational murder case which most experts believed was unwinnable (See **Toy Gun Murder Case**, page 43). In 1943, he convinced the Supreme Court to dismiss homicide charges against Fred Komatowski after a Carbon jury convicted him of "murder in the third degree." (See **Komatowski Case**, page 46).

Born on December 7, 1884 of a Welsh mother, he received his educational foundation in the public schools of his hometown in Nesquehoning. After earning his law degree at Dickinson School of Law in 1910, Branch was admitted to the bar and entered the offices of Freyman & Nothstein in Mauch Chunk. On the death of Nothstein in 1912 he formed a partnership with William Freyman and William Thomas which lasted until 1928 when Thomas was appointed to the Carbon Bench. The firm's offices were located at 78 Broadway. When Frederick Bertolette died unexpectedly in 1915, a number of his corporate clients including the LC&N Company and the New Jersey Zinc Company moved over to Freyman Thomas & Branch.

Branch, a Republican, served as district attorney from 1920 to 1924. When District Attorney David Davis died in office in 1935, President Judge William G. Thomas appointed him to fill his unexpired term.

As the surviving partner in the county's oldest and most respected law firm he inherited a number of prominent clients. His success as a trial lawyer and his banking affiliations attracted many more clients. Three of the largest corporations doing business in Carbon County relied on Branch to solve their legal problems: Lehigh Coal and Navigation Company, New Jersey Zinc Company, and the PP&L Company. He thoroughly enjoyed the prestige of having the important power brokers of business coming to him for legal advice. Stoic and aloof, he kept his bar colleagues at a distance and invited only a few to share his friendship. But aspiring trial lawyers attended his trials and mimicked his courtroom moves. The fact that he could handle jury trials, Supreme Court arguments and corporate legal problems with equal facility was a source of lawyerly awe. He was a charter member of the

Nesquehoning Savings and Loan Association when it was founded in 1913 and served as a director and its solicitor until the time of his death. He was also a director of the First National Bank of Nesquehoning from 1912.

At the time of his death on February 2, 1952 at the age of sixty-eight, Branch also enjoyed a wide reputation as an outstanding authority on Carbon County history. He left a wife, Sadie Grow Branch, and three children, William, John and Richard.

David Davis, Esquire (Adm. 1916), a native of Summit Hill, devoted all of his professional life to public service. Born and reared in Summit Hill, his primary education came from the public schools of Summit Hill and the school of hard knocks at the LC&N Company coal breakers. At a very early age, he set his sights on getting out of the mines and into the political arena.

He prepared for college at Perkiomen Prep School, graduated from Lafayette College in 1912 and obtained his law degree from Dickinson School of Law in 1915. He immediately became active in the County Republican Committee, the Masonic Organization and the Lansford Elks. He was elected district attorney of Carbon County three times and served successive terms from 1926 to 1934. Davis defeated Frank York in 1926. In the election of 1931, he was involved in a hotly contested campaign with George A. Shutack, who had won the Democratic nomination. Accusations swirled around Davis that his county detective, "Butch" Hatrick, was taking payoffs from houses of prostitution. Davis denied any knowledge of such activities, but he distanced himself from Hatrick during the campaign. On election day, he won a third term by a narrow margin. Davis was the first district attorney in Carbon County who made extensive use of the plea bargain to dispose of criminal cases.

Active in the affairs of the Methodist Church and the Masons, he also served as solicitor for the Summit Hill Trust Company, the Workmen's Building and Loan Association, the Summit Hill School Board and the Banks Township School Board. In 1934, Davis was the Republican nominee for State Senator in the 14th District of Monroe, Pike, Wayne and Carbon counties. He was stricken ill while campaigning and died unexpectedly on November 1, 1934 in the Palmerton Hospital just four days before election day. He was survived by his widow.

Raymond F. Smith, Sr., Esquire (Adm. 1916) was the prototypical office practitioner. He drafted contracts, drew up wills and trusts and counseled his clients on how to avoid litigation in their business and financial affairs. He rarely appeared in court during his legal career and only saw the judge at social affairs. He engaged in a low profile but eminently successful estate, real estate and banking practice in the Borough of Palmerton for forty-four years.

After earning his law degree at Dickinson School of Law in 1916, he was admitted to the Carbon County Bar and immediately started a solo practice in Palmerton. After a stint of military service in World War I, he came back to Palmerton and ran unsuccessfully against Ben Branch for district attorney in 1919. In 1926, he succeeded James Smitham as a referee in bankruptcy for the Middle District of Pennsylvania. He was a director and president of the First National Bank of Palmerton, as well as solicitor for the Palmerton Building and Loan Association. Like many other county lawyers, he ran a very successful accident insurance business from his office. He also served as solicitor for the Palmerton School District and the Borough of Palmerton from 1916 to 1955. When his son Raymond was admitted to the bar in 1958, he joined his father in the practice of law. Raymond, Sr. died on March 5, 1960.

Frank X. York, Esquire (Adm. 1918). An outstanding trial lawyer with a bright mind and a retentive memory, he had an impressive collection of municipal clients in the first half of the twentieth century and was considered by his peers an expert in the field of municipal law.

Born in Nesquehoning in 1895 of German immigrant parents, York graduated from Nesquehoning High School and Georgetown University and then went on to Dickinson School of Law where he received his law degree (LL.B.) in 1916. During World War I York entered the United States Army as a private in 1918 and during combat overseas was commissioned as a second lieutenant. He prepared for the bar examinations by reading law in the office of Edward M. Mulhearn. After his admission to the bar, he formed a law partnership with his mentor under the firm name of Mulhearn & York with offices in the Schweiting Building. In 1921, he married Nora Malloy of Lansford and took up residence in Mauch Chunk. After Mulhearn died, York formed a partnership with Daniel P. Dougherty under the firm name of York & Dougherty with offices in the Central Hotel Building in Mauch

Chunk. A fervent Democrat, he was treasurer of the County Democratic Party for fifteen years. In his first and only bid for elected office, he was defeated by David Davis in 1926 as his party's candidate for district attorney. York's activities in the political arena generated a host of clients and a flourishing law practice, including many county municipal bodies. He served as county solicitor from 1924 to 1933. He was solicitor for Mauch Chunk Borough for twenty-six years and served as solicitor for Mauch Chunk Township (now the Borough of Nesquehoning), Kidder Township, Penn Forest Township, Lausanne Township and the Borough of Summit Hill.

In December of 1942, after his partner Daniel Dougherty became ill, he was appointed to take Dougherty's place as a special deputy attorney general for the Commonwealth in the Supreme Court appeal of *Commonwealth v. Fred Komatowski*. It was an appointment he later regretted because the case was hopelessly lost long before he appeared. Komatowski had been charged with first degree murder in the drowning death of Pierce Rehrig, a disabled Lehighton mill operator. It was unquestionably the most bizarre murder case ever tried in Carbon County (See **Komatowski Case**, page 46). There was evidence of police brutality, coerced confessions, deals made with the district attorney to dismiss the murder charges and ultimately a jury verdict of guilty of third degree murder when there was no such charge in existence. The Supreme Court of Pennsylvania threw out the verdict terming it "ridiculous and meaningless" and discharged Komatowski.[74]

York died at the age of sixty on June 28, 1954.

Alan S. Loose, Esquire (Adm. 1925) As the only surviving son of Carbon County's most prominent lawyer Jacob C. Loose, it was expected that Alan Loose would follow in his father's profession and he did, but for only a short period of time.

He received his early education at the prestigious Mercersburg Academy and then went on to Princeton University where he earned his A.B. degree in 1922. The University of Pittsburgh Law School awarded him an LL.B. degree in 1925 and he immediately joined his father in the practice of law in Mauch Chunk. In 1935, he became a director of the Mauch Chunk National Bank and when his father died in 1942, he succeeded to his father's position as the president of the bank. During World War II he was appointed to the County Selective Service Board and served as its chairman.

---

[74]*Commonwealth v. Komatowski, 347 Pa. 445, 32 A.2d 905 (1943).*

In the late 1950s, he built a home in the Virgin Islands and after commuting to Mauch Chunk for a number of years he decided to make the islands his permanent residence. He died in his home at St. Croix, Virgin Islands on September 30, 1975 at the age of seventy-seven preceded in death by his wife the former Ruth Hurst of Louisville, Kentucky and survived by two daughters, Mildred Esterline and Betsy Sugden.

George A. Shutack, Esquire (Adm. 1928) of Nesquehoning personifies the twentieth century rural Pennsylvania lawyer. He handled every type of trial proceeding, from liquor code violations to first degree murder cases. His office practice covered the entire legal spectrum, from preparing simple wills to drafting the most complex real estate transactions. After his family, the law was the love of his life. He practiced law six days a week all year long and never took vacations. During the day, he was either in his law office in Lehighton or trying civil and criminal cases in the courts at Jim Thorpe. At night, he counseled clients in his home office in Nesquehoning. Born in 1900 and still going to his office in 1993, he is a monument to good genes, industry and perseverance.

His legal career is a perfect expression of his coal region roots. Inspired by his brother John, who had become a lawyer, and the challenge and independence which the law offered, he decided early in life to escape the drudgery and hard life of his miner father and to pursue the American dream. Emerging from the coal mines where he toiled as a breaker boy during his teenage summers, he worked his way through Georgetown Law School at night and earned his law degree in 1923. After gaining trial experience in the Washington, D.C. law offices of William C. Sullivan and in the Pittsburgh offices of Weil Christy & Weil, Shutack returned to Carbon County in 1929. After three successive losses as the Democratic candidate for district attorney, he abandoned thoughts of a political career and proceeded to establish himself as the preeminent trial lawyer of his time. For over forty years, his courtroom performances embodied the concept of thoughtfulness and skilled preparation -- in his hands the evidence and the law were masterfully wielded to win his clients cause. His cross-examinations were direct, well-crafted and potent. His summations were particularly compelling, characterized by a skillful and scrupulously fair analysis of the evidence. With James McCready, he served as defense counsel in the controversial murder case of *Commonwealth v. Michael Vladyka* in 1931 and then served as a prosecutor by special appointment of the attorney general in the widely publicized murder case involving Pennsylvania State Trooper Ben Franklin in 1940.

An expert on the law of Eminent Domain, he was a special U.S. Attorney for the Middle District of Pennsylvania in numerous land damage cases during the 1940s. He successfully represented many property owners whose lands were condemned by the Federal Government and the Commonwealth of Pennsylvania during the construction of the Northeast Turnpike and the Beltzville Dam. He achieved the highest verdict ever handed down in a Carbon County condemnation case when a Carbon County jury awarded the Lehighton Water Authority $155,500 against the Pennsylvania Turnpike Commission on April 26, 1963. In the early 1950s, he headed a group of local investors who first brought television to the lower Carbon County area, and after operating the business for several years sold it to Blue Ridge Cable Company. For many years, Shutack chaired the Committee of Bar Examiners, the Law Library Committee and the Committee on Ethics and Unauthorized Practice. He also chaired the Committee of the Bar which installed the Russell Index System in all the row offices.

During his long and productive legal career, Shutack did a great deal of "pro bono" work. He chaired the Unemployment Relief Committee during the Depression, obtained the corporate charter for Gnaden Huetten Hospital, serving as its solicitor free of charge for many years. He was an original member of the Carbon County Recreation Authority and chaired it during the construction of the Mauch Chunk Creek watershed and park which has been credited with saving downtown Jim Thorpe from the devastating floods which marked its history. Shutack served as solicitor for Mahoning Township, Lower Towamensing Township, Beaver Meadows, and for more than thirty-five years, the Lehighton Water Authority.

Shutack married Helen Setar of Nesquehoning on February 9, 1932 and they had two children. His daughter, Marianne Shutack Lavelle, was the first woman admitted to the Carbon County Bar on May 6, 1959. His son, Dr. John G. Shutack is member of the Medical Staff at Hanneman Hospital in Philadelphia, specializing in anesthesiology. In this year of the Sesquicentennial, he is the undisputed Dean of the Carbon Bar.

Martin H. Philip, Esquire (Adm. 1931). Personal injury lawyer, banker, communicator, and at the age of eighty-six, he still actively practices law in his native Palmerton. Born in 1907, he earned a Commerce and Finance degree (1928) at Penn State and his law degree (1931) from the University of Pennsylvania Law School. From the beginning, Philip wanted to be a trial lawyer. He was inspired by the skilled advocacy of Orrin E. Boyle, a prominent Allentown lawyer for whom he worked in his early years. Six months after opening his law office in Palmerton in 1932, he was appointed by Judge Thomas to defend Jacob Hudock,[75] a seventeen-year-old who was charged with first degree murder of another young man who was with him on a deer hunt. In a widely publicized trial, Philip won an acquittal for his client on the murder charge by using an innovative self-defense theory that his client had the right to shoot the man who had, minutes before, shot his brother in order to protect himself from a similar fate. This case was the first of many which Philip tried successfully before juries in Carbon, Lehigh and Northampton counties. After his brother Jacob was admitted to the bar in 1938, he joined Martin in the practice of law as Philip & Philip on Delaware Avenue in Palmerton until 1954.

Philip was always looking for new and imaginative ways to advance his client's cause. He was one of the first trial lawyers in the county to use large mock-ups of accident sites and blown-up photographs of injured plaintiffs. In some of his efforts he was ahead of his time. In 1942, he petitioned on behalf of the putative father to have the unwed mother and child submit to blood-grouping tests in a fornication and bastardy case.[76] This now routine mandatory testing in non-support cases was denied by Judge McCready and on appeal was affirmed by the Superior Court[77] on the grounds that the process was too dangerous an invasion of the body and if done against somebody's will would be a serious assault and battery.

When World War II erupted, Philip answered the call of his country by entering the army as a private. He was placed in security and intelligence and served in duty stations in New York and Philadelphia between 1942 and 1945 when he was discharged as a sergeant.

---

[75]*Commonwealth v. Jacob Hudock*, 13 January Sessions 1932.

[76]*Commonwealth v. Stanley Krutsick*, 4 October Term 1940.

[77]*Commonwealth v. Stanley Krutsick*, 151 Pa.Super 164 (1943)

After his military service, Philip returned to Palmerton and became a specialist in personal injury cases. He derived great pleasure in taking on powerful institutions and insurance carriers on behalf of the working man and woman. He was the first lawyer in Carbon County to obtain a million dollar settlement for his client. As he did with most things, Philip practiced law with vigor and passion, and argued successfully in a number of landmark cases in the Appellate Courts. He convinced the Pennsylvania Superior Court to overturn a long standing practice in Carbon County in entering nominal support orders of $2.00 per week for children born out of wedlock. *Commonwealth ex rel Grace E. Miller v. Jack Ebbert* 184 Pa. Super. 578, 135 A.2d 826 (1957) rejected the "equal guilt" theory adapted by Judge James C. McCready and directed the trial judge to consider the financial resources of both mother and father. In *Focht v. Rabada*[78] the Pennsylvania Superior Court held for the first time that driving while under the influence of alcohol with its great potential for harm and serious injury may under certain circumstances be deemed "outrageous conduct" and support an award of punitive damages in a personal injury case.

In 1954, he was elected a director of the small $5 million Bowmanstown Bank (Tri-County State Bank). The development and growth of this "farmer's bank" to a $70 million bank in collaboration with brilliant banker Carl A. Johnson was one of the crowning achievements of his life. He also represented a wide variety of business corporations such as Blue Ridge Pressure Casters, Inc., Lehighton Brick Company, Orkin Steel and Quakertown Brick & Tile Company.

During his colorful career, he was also active in the field of radio broadcasting. In 1961, he built radio station WYNS on a mountaintop in Ashfield on the outskirts of Lehighton and through his ingenuity and aggressiveness, made it one of the most popular small stations in the Lehigh Valley area where it still operates today.

Martin Philip's offices served as a legal incubator for a long list of young lawyers who received their first professional nurturing in his hard-driving, pressure-packed practice. Many of them are now regarded as outstanding trial lawyers: Maxwell Cohen of Stroudsburg, Joseph H. Foster and Jack E. Feinberg of Philadelphia, Murray Mackson, Richard Director and John M. Yarema of Allentown. Graduates of Martin Philip's law office include the following members of the Carbon Bar: Thomas W. Durnin, Howard R. Moore, Jr., Howard N. Stark, Joseph J. Velitsky, Arnold Sousa, Daniel F. Zeigler, Stephen J. Hartz, John F. Gibbons, Anthony L. Roberti, Michael J. Garfield, George T. Dydynsky, Richard M. Edridge, Marvin O. Schwartz, Barry C. Shabbick, David B. Shulman, and Gerald F. Strubinger, Jr.

[78]217 Pa.Super 35, 268 A.2d 157 (1970).

John G. Cipko, Esquire (Adm. 1932) was a family lawyer for most of his professional life but not in the traditional sense of that specialty. He was counsel to the prominent Fauzio family of Nesquehoning who owned extensive coal lands in the Panther Valley. In that role he served them as legal advisor, investment counselor, family confidante and corporate guru.

Cipko was born in Nesquehoning in 1909 of immigrant parents from Czechoslovakia. His father worked for the old LC&N Company and later operated a grocery store. After receiving his primary education in the Nesquehoning public schools, he earned his undergraduate degree at Dickinson College in 1930 and his law degree at Dickinson School of Law in 1933.

With the country in the throes of the Great Depression he opened a small law office in his Nesquehoning home and using his wife Anne as his secretary, eked out a living drawing deeds for $5 and wills for $10. This bare-bones type of existence chiselled into his character a dogged determination to succeed and an enduring frugality. Like many young lawyers he became involved in the civic and political activities of his community. He was a charter member of the Lansford Lions Club and was the first solicitor for the Panther Valley School District. For almost forty years he was the solicitor of the Carbon County Tax Claim Bureau and the Carbon County Board of Viewers.

From the mid-1950s until the 1980s, Cipko devoted his legal talents to the personal and business interests of James and Frank Fauzio. In 1960 they made the bold move to purchase all the coal lands in the Panther Valley, erected a new "breaker" in Tamaqua and started strip mining. It was Cipko who negotiated the deals, structured the financing and drafted the contracts. Together they revitalized the coal industry in the Panther Valley. As the Fauzio brothers prospered, Cipko's financial prospects grew apace as did his leisure hours. He was able to indulge his passions for tennis, bridge, travel and playing the stock market. Extremely proud of his prowess in tennis, he took on and beat much younger and swifter opponents until late in life. He also found time to serve as a director of the Summit Hill Trust Company which he watched over with the solicitude of a father for a child.

In 1982, he was admitted to the exclusive Fifty-Year Club of the Carbon County Bar on motion of his long time colleague and neighbor George Shutack. He died unexpectedly at the age of eighty-four on March 25, 1993 while on a tennis trip to Jacksonville, Florida. He was survived by his wife Anne.

Albert G. Prutzman, Esquire (Adm. 1932), a Palmerton native, came from a family of lawyers and was the brother-in-law of President Judge Albert H. Heimbach. His brothers Charles D. Prutzman and John Prutzman preceded him into the legal profession. He made his mark in Carbon County as a deputy attorney general of the Commonwealth in numerous hard fought jury trials by vigorously defending land damage claims against the Pennsylvania Turnpike Commission and the Department of Highways in the 1950s and 1960s.

After earning his Bachelor of Arts degree at Penn State University in 1924 and his law degree (LL.B.) in 1927 at Yale Law School, he practiced law in New York City with the Chadbourne Hunt & Jieckelbro law firm. In 1932, he returned to Carbon County where he became associated with the firm of Balliet & Seidle in Lehighton for a short time before opening his own practice. In 1956 he formed a partnership with William B. Quinn with offices on First Street and they practiced law together for seventeen years until Prutzman's death.

An active Democrat, Prutzman served four terms as chairman of the County Democratic Committee. He was county solicitor from 1940 to 1944. An expert in the Pennsylvania School Code, he was legal advisor to the Carbon Area Vocational-Technical School, the Carbon-Lehigh Intermediate Unit and several township school authorities.

He ran twice for public office. In 1942 he campaigned for State Senator and in 1959 for president judge, but was defeated both times. He was more successful in the field of banking. He was elected president of the Bowmanstown Bank (later Tri-County Bank) from 1944 to 1954 and was a director and solicitor of the Home Savings and Loan Association in Lehighton. He died on June 1, 1973 at the age of seventy survived by his wife the former Lottie Tucker, and three children, Captain Albert Prutzman, Charles P. Prutzman, and Jean T. Zimmer.

George M. D. Richards, Esquire (Adm. 1933). He brought to his legal career a wrestler's tenacity and an accountant's passion for detail. Good-natured, jovial and full of the joy of life, George M. D., as he was known at the bar, always seemed to enjoy whatever he was doing whether it was analyzing a legal problem, perusing the *Wall Street Journal* to decide on a stock acquisition or hitting a golf ball down the fairway.

Born in Lansford in 1902, he received his early education in the public schools there and then went on to Penn State where he distinguished himself scholastically by being awarded a Louis Carnegie Scholarship and athletically with a second place medal in the 1923 Eastern Collegiate Wrestling Association Finals. After graduating from Penn State in 1923, he passed the C.P.A. examinations on his first try in 1927 and then earned his law degree at the University of Pennsylvania Law School in 1931. As he looked about after law school the country was in a state of panic and despair. One out of four Americans were out of work. The country's grain prices were at an all time low. Banks in thirty-eight states had closed. There was little legal business for a new lawyer. His father John advised him to stay in Philadelphia and take a position in accounting with the firm of LyBrand Ross Bros. & Montgomery. After two years of auditing debits and credits in the city, however, he yearned to return to his roots. In 1933 he came back to Carbon County, hung his shingle out in Lansford as both a lawyer and C.P.A. and practiced there successfully for fifty years.

Like many of his young colleagues, he left his law practice and went off to war. Enlisting in the Army Air Corp during World War II, Richards served with bravery and distinction in the 449th Heavy Bomb Group in Italy for sixteen months as an intelligence officer with the rank of captain. When he returned from the war in 1946, he devoted himself to his clients, his community and the world of high finance. He became president of the First National Bank of Lansford, a director of the Dime Bank of Lansford and a director of the Panther Valley Building and Loan Association. He served as solicitor for the Borough of Lansford as well as the Lansford-Coaldale Joint Water Authority and the Carbon-Schuylkill Industrial Development Corporation. His legal and financial acumen were always in demand for every public project and he gave it willingly and without compensation.

He is now in retirement in Cocoa Beach, Florida with his wife the former Virginia Andrews.

Jacob Philip, Esquire (Adm. 1936). The quintessential country lawyer, "Jake" Philip has devoted fifty-seven years of his professional career providing legal services to people from every walk of life in lower Carbon and upper Lehigh counties. Born in Palmerton on October 4, 1909 to Solomon and Bertha (Herr) Philip, he received his early education in the Palmerton public schools and Perkiomen Preparatory School. He earned a Bachelor's degree in Commerce and Finance at Penn State in 1932 and his law degree from the University of Pennsylvania in 1935. He immediately joined his brother, Martin Philip, in the practice of law in the Krex Building in Palmerton at the corner of Third and Delaware Avenues. In 1938, the Philip brothers moved their office to 252 Delaware Avenue to the building where their parents operated a clothing store. Jake, in addition to practicing law, helped his father operate the clothing business, known as Philip Brothers. Members of the bar jokingly referred to this arrangement as "Suits on the first floor, lawsuits on the second floor."

In 1943 Jake successfully defended Reuben W. Moyer, a seventy-three-year-old farmer from Parryville who was charged with first degree murder in the shotgun killing of thirty-one-year-old Harry Neeb.[79] As the trial began, Martin Philip, Jake's co-counsel, was called into the service and Orrin Boyle of Allentown replaced him. The case attracted considerable notoriety because Moyer claimed his next door neighbor, Wilma Flyte, was running a brothel which was creating a nuisance. He contended that he shot Neeb in self-defense when Neeb attacked him after he threatened to tell Neeb's wife that he was patronizing Mrs. Flyte. District Attorney Heimbach called Flyte as a witness for the prosecution. Her prancing, fingerpointing, indignant manner proved very unpopular with the jury and was the undoing of the Commonwealth's case. In a verdict the local press said was "not unexpected" the jury found Moyer "Not Guilty."

In 1954, Philip moved his law office to a new building which he constructed at 419 Delaware Avenue, where he maintained a solo practice until 1965 when he was joined by his son-in-law, James A. Wimmer. They formed the partnership of Philip & Wimmer in 1968 and have practiced law continuously together since that time. Philip ran a busy law office. It was not unusual to see his office still filled with clients at eleven o'clock at night. His ability to speak five different languages including Pennsylvania Dutch and his round-the-clock availability made him a much sought after counselor to the senior citizens of Carbon and Lehigh counties.

[79] *Commonwealth v. Reuben W. Moyer*, 3 January Sessions 1943.

During World War II, Attorney Philip served as the solicitor for the Palmerton Selective Service Board. In 1951, he became a director of the Citizens Bank and Trust Company in Palmerton and eventually was elected president and chairman of the board. Under his leadership, the small town Citizens Bank grew from assets of $3.7 million to assets in excess of $110 million by 1993. Philip resides in Allentown with his wife Isabel and has two daughters Linda Wimmer and Audrey Rutman.

W. Joseph Engler, Esquire (Adm. 1937) was as meticulous in the practice of law as he was impeccable in his attire. Acknowledged by his colleagues as an expert in the law of real property, no estate in fee tail confused him, nor complex legal description defied his ability to make it close. To ensure accuracy, he personally typed and checked the descriptions in all the deeds and mortgages produced by his office.

Born in East Mauch Chunk in 1910, he lived to see his hometown change from an industrial transportation center to a tourist community. While he was still a high school student he showed an early flair for advocacy and an amazing prescience by writing a prize winning essay predicting the consolidation of both Mauch Chunk boroughs into a "Bigger and Better Mauch Chunk." In 1956 he had the pleasure of not only seeing his prediction come true but also of being the first solicitor when East Mauch Chunk joined with its arch rival Mauch Chunk and gave birth to the Borough of Jim Thorpe. After receiving his early education at Mauch Chunk Catholic High School, he graduated from Fordham University with a B.A. in 1932 and then earned his law degree at Temple University Law School in 1936. A preceptorship in the office of Ben Branch was followed by opening his own law office in East Mauch Chunk. He remained on the East Side and served the legal needs of his community continuously for over fifty years.

Engler was the first father called in the Carbon County draft lottery during World War II, and he served with the Judge Advocate General's Office in the Army from 1944 to 1945 at Hickman Field in Hawaii.

In 1967, Judge Heimbach appointed Engler to head the court's probation services department. He directed that office for nine years. As solicitor for the Jim Thorpe National Bank he was known as a careful and tenacious title searcher and a skillful drafter of deeds and loan documents. For many years he was solicitor to the Register of Wills' Office and the County Tax Claim Bureau, Jim Thorpe Borough and the Jim Thorpe School District. He was honored by the members of the Carbon Bar in 1987 at the Gourmet Inn upon his entry into the Half-Century Club. Three of his five children joined him in the legal profession, his son W. Joseph Engler, Jr., and daughters Jane Engler Brogan and Jean A. Engler. He died after a lengthy illness on April 2, 1992 at the age of eighty-two survived by his wife Mary and his five children W. Joseph, Jr., John G. II, Jane Engler Brogan, Joan McIlhenny, and Jean A.

Frank D. Llewellyn, Esquire (Adm. 1938) had a great passion for the law and people. From 1938 until his retirement in 1982, he devoted his entire legal career to serving his clients in the Panther Valley.

After attending Summit Hill High School, he worked for a number of years before attending Dickinson College where he earned his undergraduate degree in 1932. It was at that point that he decided to become a lawyer. He entered Harvard Law School and earned his law degree in 1936. World War II interrupted his blossoming law practice and he entered the United States Army where he served thirty-eight months in both the Asia-Pacific theater and the European-African Middle East theater of the war as a radio operator with the 552nd Army Air Force Base Unit. When he returned to his home town of Summit Hill from military service, he opened his law office there, and engaged principally in real estate and municipal law. He was solicitor for the Summit Hill Borough, as well as its secretary and was very active in the Summit Hill American Legion Post 316, for a time as adjutant of the American Legion's Eastern District of the Department of Pennsylvania. He died on December 12, 1984 at the age of eighty-four, survived by his wife Mary Holmes Llewellyn.

Donald L. McCay, Esquire (Adm. 1938). To the casual political observer, McCay simply inherited the political mantle of his father, Republican tyro William D. McCay, when he was elected Carbon County Republican Chairman in 1961. But insiders knew that he really earned it by his many years of unflagging service to the GOP.

A native of Junedale, McCay graduated from Hazleton High School in 1930 and from Bucknell in 1934. His family were among the first settlers of Beaver Meadows. As a young man he worked successively as the operator of a milk delivery route, a mine laborer at Eckley, an insurance claim adjuster, construction superintendent and accountant. He earned his law degree from Harvard Law School in 1937. He opened his law office in Beaver Meadow after his admission to the bar and maintained a practice there until 1957 when he moved his office to his home in Weatherly. In 1943 he ran unsuccessfully for the office of district attorney in the Republican primary against Albert Heimbach.

During World War II he served with the Army Air Corps and discharged with the rank of sergeant in 1945. He was named county solicitor in 1946 and became embroiled in a heated controversy over the politically inspired efforts of Commissioners Nathan Drumheller and Ambrose O'Donnell to surcharge the previous Republican board of commissioners whom McCay served and stoutly defended against any wrongdoing. The imbroglio culminated with the public firing of McCay and seven other Republican employees at the County Home. Ultimately McCay was proven right when the Supreme Court found no evidence to support a surcharge. He was appointed again as county solicitor in 1950 and in 1964.

McCay also served as solicitor for many municipalities and banking institutions. Among them were Weatherly Borough, Weatherly School District, Packer, Lehigh and Lausanne Townships, the Hazleton National Bank and the Anthracite Building and Loan Association. For many years he was an elder of the Weatherly Presbyterian Church, a member of the General Council of the Lehigh Presbytery and the Board of Law Examiners of the Carbon Bar Association. He died after a short illness on June 23, 1966 at the age of fifty-three, survived by his second wife Joanna Skonieczny McCay and two daughters, Jane Malatesta and Constance Pyatt.

Joseph G. Greco, Esquire (Adm. 1939) devoted his life to public service and promoting the Panther Valley, particularly his hometown of Nesquehoning where he resided his entire life. His dedication to his community, the poor and the mentally retarded of Carbon County was recognized by numerous awards and testimonials.

A product of the Mauch Chunk Township (now Nesquehoning) schools, he earned his undergraduate degree from Columbia University in 1933 and his law degree from Fordham Law School in 1936. He was appointed executive director of Public Assistance for Carbon County in 1943 and for thirty years supervised that office until his retirement in 1973. He was a prime mover in establishing and supporting the Nesquehoning Improvement Committee and worked in all the local improvement projects of the Nesquehoning Rotary Club and the Nesquehoning Business and Professional Men's Association. As solicitor and director of the First National Bank of Nesquehoning and the Nesquehoning Savings and Loan Association he urged the investment of their funds in building new homes and renovating old homes in his home town. He and his wife Susan beamed proudly when their son Joseph was admitted to the Carbon Bar in 1974. Greco died on March 13, 1980 at the age of seventy, leaving his wife Susan and son Joseph G. Greco, Jr., a member of the Carbon County Bar.

Carl A. Niehoff, Esquire (Adm. 1941) started his career as a school teacher at Lehighton High School and then decided to pursue a career in the law and public service. Niehoff received a Bachelor of Arts degree in Economics from Lafayette College and returned to his home town of Lehighton to teach history and social studies for five years at the Lehighton High School. He went on to Temple University School of Law and received his LL.B. degree in 1936. His admiration for President Franklin Roosevelt and the Democratic Party's affiliation with the poor and the oppressed led him to take an active role in the local Democratic organization and ultimately a career in politics. He began by running for and being elected district attorney of Carbon County in 1943 over the incumbent Albert H. Heimbach and held that office for four consecutive terms. In 1947, he defeated Frank Llewellyn and in 1951 and 1955, he defeated the Republican standard bearer, George Kerestes.

In 1948, at the request of County Commissioners Ambrose O'Donnell and Nathan Drumheller, he launched a controversial investigation into alleged criminal acts by a former board of commissioners in the construction of a "mystery building" at the County Home for the Elderly at Laurytown (See **Mystery Building Case**, page 50). After a nine month investigation, Niehoff filed a twenty-four-page report with Judge McCready in which he found no evidence of criminal activity on the part of the former commissioners. Judge McCready publicly disagreed with his conclusions. The dispute spilled over into their contest for the judgeship in 1949 which McCready won.

Niehoff served as solicitor to the Carbon County Commissioners from 1939 to 1943 and from 1960 to 1964. In 1949, he became solicitor for the Lehighton Area School District where he served continuously and competently for thirty-four years before retiring in 1982. During his time as legal advisor to the school district, a new high school was built in 1965. Niehoff was one of the leaders in Lehighton's obtaining control of electrical facilities from the Pennsylvania Power and Light Company and was the youngest man to serve on the borough's Light and Power Committee.

Niehoff's deep booming voice could send tremors through the courtroom. It helped make him a feared and effective prosecutor during the '40s and '50s and he lost very few cases. His successful prosecution of Daniel Falcone in the double murder of Mildred Daneker and her husband in Palmerton in 1955 was considered a textbook performance by a prosecutor.

After he left the D.A.'s office and returned to private practice, he never lost his prosecutor's mien. As a counselor, he was stern of countenance and had a brusque straight-from-the-shoulder type of directness. When he advised a client on the law, none doubted that it was correct and should be obeyed. He died in Lehighton after a long illness on September 1, 1984 at the age of seventy-eight survived by his wife Mary, son Donald and daughter Carla. His son, Karl P. Niehoff, a member of the Carbon County Bar, practiced with his father after his admission to the bar in 1964.

Sidney R. Webb, Esquire (Adm. 1941). Lawyer, banker, industrialist, historian, authority on land titles, magician, raconteur, bon vivant and political theorist, Webb was a man of many parts and he enjoyed playing all of them. He was well known in the Palmerton area for his wit, his generous laugh, and entertaining conversation.

Born in Palmerton on January 26, 1915, he traced his roots to his father Algernon's birthplace in Pewsey, England. Webb attended the public schools in his hometown. By entertaining as a professional magician under the stage name of "Sidini," he worked his way to a Commerce and Finance degree at Penn State in 1938 and a law degree at the University of Pittsburgh Law School in 1941. After serving a clerkship in the offices of Albert G. Prutzman and Alan S. Loose, he was admitted to the Carbon Bar and hung out his shingle in Palmerton where he practiced law successfully for thirty-seven years.

As borough solicitor for the Borough of Palmerton from 1956 to 1978, his office was a treasure trove of maps, records and legal documents which he used to resolve many of the borough's title problems. It was also a valuable resource to lawyers and title searchers. One of his deep and abiding interests was the Citizens Bank of Palmerton, and he was its secretary and a director for more than twenty years. With his brother Charles, he also operated the Prince Manufacturing Company in Bowmanstown and from his law offices conducted the business of the Towamensing Mutual Fire Insurance Company.

His most enduring legal legacy to Carbon County is his only son Richard W. Webb, the former four term district attorney and current judge of the Court of Common Pleas. When his son joined him in the practice of law in 1970, he said that it was the happiest moment in his professional career. After his first wife Ellen Williams Webb died in 1966 he married Emma Schlegel who survived him when he died on October 16, 1978 at the age of sixty-three.

George Kerestes, Esquire (Adm. 1942), a Lansford native, had a brief but scintillating legal and political career. After graduating from Lansford High School in 1935, he entered Lafayette College where he excelled as a varsity lineman on the football team and obtained his A.B. degree. Kerestes earned his law degree at the University of Pennsylvania Law School in 1942. Shortly after his admission to the Carbon Bar, he entered the Armed Forces and served overseas until he was honorably discharged in 1946. He then became associated with Alan S. Loose. They maintained a practice, first in the Navigation Building and then, on the second floor of the Jim Thorpe National Bank under the firm name of Loose & Kerestes until Loose retired to St. Thomas in the Virgin Islands in the early '60s.

Kerestes conceived the idea and urged the establishment of the Carbon County Tax Claim Bureau. In February of 1948, Commissioners Nathan Drumheller and C. D. Reinhard created the bureau and appointed Kerestes as its first director. In October of 1949, an unusual Republican-Democratic coalition of Commissioners Nathan Drumheller (R) and Ambrose O'Donnell (D) fired Solicitor Donald McCay and appointed Kerestes to the position. He continued in that post until 1954.

In 1959, after two defeats in seeking the office, he was elected district attorney beating Democrat Frank Llewellyn. He was re-elected district attorney in 1963 over Democratic candidate Russell P. Chaplinsky of Lehighton. He had the distinction of being elected president of the Pennsylvania District Attorneys Association in 1965.

From 1965 through 1967, a crime wave of burglaries and arson swept through Carbon County. Kerestes led the investigation team of local and state police in ferreting out the gang responsible for the crimes. He also directed the prosecution team which obtained their conviction. In addition to his work as district attorney, Kerestes was active in the affairs of the Lutheran Church in America and in many community, fraternal and veteran organizations. He died unexpectedly in his office at the age of forty-nine on January 10, 1967 after successfully prosecuting a criminal case before a Carbon jury. He was survived by his wife Betty, a school teacher, and daughter Peggy Chain.

George Brinley Richards, Esquire (Adm. 1942). One hundred percent Welsh, he was born on May 30, 1920 at 328 West Ridge Street, which the deep coal miners remember as Number Nine Hill which led to the Number Nine and Number Eight operations of the Lehigh Coal and Navigation Company. George Brinley has had not only a distinguished legal career, but he has also achieved high honors in the military, banking and public service phases of his busy life. After receiving his early education in the Lansford public school system, he earned his Bachelor of Arts degree at Temple University and obtained a Bachelor of Laws degree (LL.B.) in 1939 from the Temple University School of Law.

Richards and Michael Lukish of Nesquehoning were the first members of the Carbon County Bar to enter military service in World War II. He had a glittering military career. Entering the service as a private in 1942, he applied for officer candidate school, was accepted and graduated as a second lieutenant. He served in the Army Security and Intelligence Division for over four years and was discharged on September 3, 1946 with the rank of captain and the Army Commendation Ribbon.

He returned to Lansford after the war and opened a law office on the second floor of the Dime Bank Building in Lansford where he practiced law for some thirty-eight years until his retirement in 1984. Active in both the Carbon County Bar and the Pennsylvania Bar, he served on many important committees among which were the Carbon County Board of Law Examiners and the Committee of Legal Biography and History of the Pennsylvania Bar Association. During the term of Judge Heimbach, he served as administrator for the newly mandated magisterial system of Carbon County. He was solicitor to the Carbon County Controller, Lansford School Board, Lansford Borough Council and Carbon County Recorder of Deeds. His commitment and involvement in Lansford civic affairs was deep and diverse. For thirty-three years he assisted his brother, William T. Richards, in running Camp Greenwood, a recreational facility for boys and girls from the Lansford area. He served as a director and solicitor of the Dime Bank for thirty-eight years and was a director and solicitor of the Carbon Telephone Company in Lansford for twenty-one years. He was extremely active in the American Legion and was a fixture as master of ceremonies at all veterans parades in the Lansford area since 1969. Richards also gave many years of service to the American Fire Company No. 1 of Lansford and the Lansford Lions Club where he was a charter member. Proud of his Welsh heritage, he gave many hours of dedicated service to various Welsh societies in Schuylkill and Carbon counties. It would be difficult to find anyone who has given more dedicated service to his home town than George Brinley Richards gave to the Borough of Lansford.

William Z. Scott, Esquire (Adm. 1945) was a World War II military hero and his daring exploits in the Burmese jungles catapulted him into a long and luminous political career. Born on July 4, 1916 in Lansford, the son of the late Dr. William C. and Mellie (Zimmerman) Scott, he was educated at the Lansford High School, Valley Forge Military Academy, Lafayette College and was a member of the class of 1946 at the University of Pennsylvania Law School.

During World War II he served in Burma as an infantry captain with the famous Merrill's Marauders. Wounded in action, he was awarded the Purple Heart, Bronze Star, Presidential Unit Citation and Infantry Combatman's Badge. Shortly after his admission to the Carbon County Bar, he began his political career by getting elected to the House of Representative from Carbon County in 1946 and re-elected in 1948, 1950 and 1952.

In 1949, with Robert Tarleton, William McDonald, Rudy Dubosky and George Bright, Scott became part of the Panther Valley Television Corp. which brought television by cable to the mountainous Panther Valley region and was the first successful television cable system in the country. In 1954 he moved up to the Senate of Pennsylvania from the old Fourteenth Senatorial District which included Carbon, Monroe, Wayne and Pike counties and was re-elected in 1958 and 1962. While serving in the Legislature, many bills which he sponsored were adopted into law including the first to advance the cause of retarded and handicapped children in the State. He was elected Republican Caucus Chairman in the Senate for eight years and chairman of the powerful Judiciary Committee.

In 1966, after the senatorial district was gerrymandered to include Schuylkill County and Carbon County, Governor William W. Scranton appointed him to the Pennsylvania Liquor Control Board and he was reappointed to that position by Governor Raymond P. Shafer. Scott served as chairman of the board for six years. During his tenure, he instituted many new and modern business methods including the first self-service liquor store. He was also active in the affairs of the Republican Party. He was a delegate to the Republican National Convention in San Francisco in 1956 and served on the executive committee for the party for many years. Scott maintained a law office in Lansford with Robert Lazorchick under the firm name of Scott & Lazorchick from 1955 until he moved to Pocono Manor in Monroe County in 1966. He died on November 4, 1993 at the age of seventy-seven and is survived by his wife Marian and two children, Carol and William Z. Scott, Jr., a member of the Carbon County Bar.

John Deutsch, Esquire (Adm. 1948), a product of the Lehighton public schools and Penn State University, graduated from the University of Pennsylvania Law School in 1946. He reveled in the triumphs and endured the defeats of a remarkably long and colorful political career.

After serving his preceptorship under George Shutack, Deutsch opened a law office in a new building which he constructed on First Street in Lehighton and practiced first with Albert Leonzi of Summit Hill until 1952 and then later joined forces with William Wyatt in 1954.

As a young lawyer, he apprenticed in politics by active involvement in many political and civic organizations. He became president of the Carbon County Young Republicans and member of the Lehighton Masonic Organization, the Elks and Lehigh Fire Company No. 1. Deutsch made his first run for public office as a candidate for county commissioner in 1959. Although he was unsuccessful, his enthusiasm, fiery oratory and debating skills brought him to the attention of fellow Republican candidate, George Kerestes. He appointed Deutsch his first assistant when he was elected district attorney in 1959. Deutsch successfully prosecuted many criminal cases the most prominent of which was *Commonwealth v. Edward Eckhart* (See **Eckhart Murder Case**, page 56) in 1966. When Kerestes died suddenly in 1967, Deutsch was appointed district attorney by Judge Albert Heimbach.

A hard hitting trial prosecutor with a big voice and a reputation of going for the jugular vein in cross-examining witnesses, he projected an intimidating presence in the courtroom. Words were his weapons and he wielded them with a deadly mastery to convict a defendant. His rhetoric delivered with great passion, must have appealed to Carbon juries because they returned verdict after verdict of "Guilty." Deutsch did not limit his crime fighting to the courtroom. It was not unusual for him to ride with the police during their patrols and actively engage in the pursuit and capture of criminal suspects. He enjoyed a wide popularity with the electorate which gave him the highest number of votes of all candidates in 1967 when he defeated Thomas W. Durnin and in 1971 when he was unopposed. Richard W. Webb defeated him in his quest for a third term in 1975. Not satisfied with the pedestrian pace of private practice, Deutsch made an unsuccessful bid for public office again in 1977 as an Independent candidate for judge. In 1979, he made his last run for office, but was unable to unseat District Attorney Richard Webb. Deutsch then turned his considerable legal talents and energies to his many business clients in the Lehighton area until his death at the age of sixty-six on October 22, 1987. He was survived by his wife Catherine and two children, John Jr. and James.

William H. Bayer, Esquire (Adm. 1950) is of old Lehighton stock tracing his roots to the early years of this community. A classic paradigm of the professional lawyer, he has woven his law practice around a life of public service and commitment to his hometown. An honors graduate of SS. Peter and Paul's Elementary School and Lehighton High School, he moved on to Penn State University. World War II interrupted his college studies and he entered military service in 1942. Bayer trained at the U.S. Air Force Cadet School where he learned how to fly fighter planes and earned a commission as second lieutenant. As an Air Force pilot, he made many flights over the Pacific Ocean as part of his patrolling duties in the Pacific Theatre until his discharge in 1945. After the war, Bayer returned to Penn State to complete his studies. Then, opting for a legal career, he entered the University of Pennsylvania Law School, where he earned his law degree in 1949.

After admission to the bar in 1950, he practiced law for a short time in Jim Thorpe with Alan Loose and George Kerestes, and in 1952, he opened his own law office in Lehighton where he has provided a wide range of legal services for forty-one years as a sole practitioner. His clients included the New Jersey Zinc Company, Chestnut Hill Railway, Palmer Water Company, Rock Hill Materials, Bright Stores and numerous liability insurance carriers whose interests he protected in the courtroom.

One of Lehighton's most well-known and respected residents, he has served the borough in many different legal capacities. He was solicitor to the Borough Council and the Lehighton Area School Board and is still legal counsel for the Lehighton Zoning Board and Lehighton Planning Commission. He served on the board of trustees at the Gnaden Huetten Memorial Hospital and the Palmerton Hospital. He was actively involved for some forty years as a director and solicitor of the Carbon County Agricultural Association which operated the popular Carbon County Fair until the Lehighton Area School District took over its property by eminent domain in 1992. He promoted and planned for the business and industrial growth of his community as attorney for the Lehighton Industrial Development Corporation and the Central Carbon Industrial Development Corporation. He has also been a leader in many civic, charitable and veterans organizations in Lehighton.

Bayer also found time to lend his talents to a number of committees of the Pennsylvania Bar Association and to serve as solicitor to the treasurer of Carbon County and the register of wills. He presently serves as an assistant county solicitor representing the Office of Children and Youth and the Mental Health Office. He resides in Lehighton with his wife Marion (DeLauretis) Bayer and has five surviving children, Patricia, Gregory, Barbara, Mary Beth and Stephen.

George T. McKinley, Esquire (Adm. 1950). Of the 190 lawyers who have come to the Carbon Bar since 1843, arguably, none has been more popular, wittier or better liked by his peers than "Tom" McKinley. The first born of a distinguished Episcopal priest the Reverend George McKinley and his wife Bessie Roe, he declined to take the cloth, choosing, instead, the life of a country lawyer. The church's loss has been the bar's gain, and he has been providing good-humored support to the bench and bar since his admission. An inveterate spinner of tall stories, he draws them from town and country; they are comic, extravagant and often spiced with self-mockery. Virtually no zany thought that springs into his nimble brain goes unexpressed and there are few lawyers or judges who have not had their funny bones tickled by his wit.

While he was a sophomore at Lehigh University, he was inducted into military service in September of 1942, becoming the first student at Lehigh selected in the nation wide draft. He served with distinction and valor in the United States Army Air Force as a radio gunner on a B-25 bomber seeing action in the Italian Theatre and the China-Burma-India Front. He was discharged in 1945 with the rank of tech sergeant and was awarded the Air Medal.

After the war, he returned to complete his undergraduate studies at Lehigh, where he earned an A.B. degree in Latin and Greek. In 1949, he garnered his law degree at the University of Pennsylvania Law School, and then served his preceptorship in the offices of Alan Loose before admission to the bar. From 1950 to 1960 he practiced law in his hometown of Palmerton and became solicitor for the Carbon County Tax Claim Bureau. When Judge Heimbach became president judge in 1960, he appointed McKinley as his law clerk and then his chief of probation services. At that time the Adult Probation Offices handled the processing of nonsupport cases, juvenile delinquency and dependency cases, as well as adult probation and parole cases. In 1967, George Kerestes appointed him an assistant district attorney, and he prosecuted criminal cases until 1970.

He has been engaged as a general practitioner in Jim Thorpe for thirty-five years first with the law firm of Roger Nanovic until 1977 and since 1978, with Michael Ozalas under the firm name of Ozalas & McKinley. McKinley was solicitor for East Side Borough, Parryville, Lower Towamensing Township, Palmerton Hospital and the Palmerton Library. He is currently an assistant solicitor for Carbon County handling the defence in Mental Health proceedings. He resides in Palmerton with his wife Alice and they have four children, George Louis, Emily Jackson, Michael Albert, and Judith Wilson.

William B. Quinn, Esquire (Adm. 1950) has, for many years, played an important semi-judicial role in the Carbon County Court System. When the new Mental Health Procedures Act was created by the Legislature in 1976, the court appointed him as the Mental Health Review officer for the County of Carbon and he has served continually in that position to the present. Since 1981, Quinn has been the court appointed Custody Hearing Officer. In these positions he has carried out the difficult responsibility of making recommendations to the court on which patients should be confined to mental health units and who should have custody of the children of broken families.

Quinn's family roots go back to the early days of Carbon County. His great-grandparents, James and Katherine Quinn, were natives of Limerick, Ireland and came to the United States in 1845 where they took up residence at Buck Mountain and James Quinn became a miner. His grandfather, John A. Quinn, was one of Lansford's most prominent citizens and operated a drug store there for many years.

Quinn earned his undergraduate degree at Villanova University in 1947 and his law degree at Dickinson School of Law in 1950. After his admission to the bar, he opened up a law office in Lansford. In 1956, he formed a law partnership with Albert Prutzman and they practiced together on the second floor of Prutzman's building on First Street in the Borough of Lehighton until Prutzman's death in 1973. He continues the practice today across the street from his old offices and specializes in estate and real estate work.

Quinn had a number of solicitorships both at the county and municipal level. He was solicitor for Controller Allen D. Kistler from 1958 to 1971. He also served as legal counsel for the Carbon County Vo-Tech, Towamensing Township, Mahoning Township, and Franklin Township, as well as the Borough of Lansford.

He is married to the former Patricia Mason of Jim Thorpe, and they live in Lansford where Quinn has resided his entire life.

Thomas W. Durnin, Esquire (Adm. 1952), a native of Mauch Chunk, spent a great deal of his life in the rough-and-tumble of the county political arena, but he preferred the role of kingmaker to that of a candidate. When he became the chairman of the County Democratic Party in 1970, the Republican Party controlled virtually every office in the courthouse and the statehouse. When he stepped down in 1980, he could rightfully claim that he had revitalized his party and helped elect a Democrat to all the elective offices in the county except the prothonotary and treasurer.

A son of Frank and Laura Durnin, Durnin attended Mauch Chunk Catholic High School where he was a classmate of Joseph Engler and then went on to earn his undergraduate degree at Providence College in Rhode Island in 1932. Like his father, he took a job with the Central Railroad for several years. He also taught in the public schools for a short time until District Attorney Carl Niehoff offered him the position of County Detective in 1943. Spurred on by many lawyers and encouraged by Judge McCready, Durnin entered Dickinson School of Law in 1949 and was awarded a law degree in 1952 at the age of forty-two. His admission to the bar was applauded at a large testimonial dinner by members of the Damien Council of the Knights of Columbus in which he had been active for many years.

His deep involvement in the political life of the county in the years that followed won him many municipal clients. He was for many years solicitor of the Borough of Jim Thorpe, the Jim Thorpe School District, Kidder Township and Penn Forest Township. He also served as a State Motor Vehicle Hearing Inspector. He conducted a private law practice from one of the richly ornamented townhouses of lower Broadway at 80-81 Broadway.

In 1967 he ran unsuccessfully for the office of district attorney against John Deutsch. Ironically that loss propelled him into the chairmanship of the Democratic Party where he led his party to victory after victory for more than a decade. He retired from practice in 1985 to spend more time with his daughter Rose Ann Coffin and his grandchildren.

Robert Lazorchick, Esquire (Adm. 1954) was born May 1, 1925 in the Village of Jeansville, Carbon County, Pennsylvania, the son of Susan Lazorchick and the late George Lazorchick.

Graduating in 1943 from Nesquehoning High School where he garnered All-State Honors as an outstanding football player, he moved on to serve his country in World War II as a member of the Seabees with the United States Navy in the Pacific Theatre of Operations. After military service, he earned his undergraduate degree at the University of Pittsburgh in 1951 and his law degree at the Dickinson School of Law in 1954.

In 1954, Lazorchick began an association with Senator William Z. Scott which ultimately became a partnership in the Borough of Lansford. He maintained an office in that borough until the time of his death. He was the first corporate counsel for Kovatch Corporation, and he devoted a great deal of his talents and energies to protecting its legal interests.

Lazorchick was deeply committed to his profession, his county, and the Republican Party. He was active in the Pennsylvania Bar Association and served a three-year term as the Zone II Governor, the only member of the Carbon County Bar to serve in that capacity. Zone II encompasses the counties of Lehigh, Northampton, Berks, Schuylkill, and Carbon. In that capacity, he was a member of the committee on policy making and also was an associate member of the Philadelphia Bar. Lazorchick served as a member of the board of trustees of the Palmerton Hospital, the Lay Leadership of St. John's Baptist Russian Orthodox Church in Nesquehoning, a member of the Jim Thorpe Masonic Lodge, assisted in forming and was a charter member of the Nesquehoning Lions Club, and he will always be remembered as being instrumental in furthering his avid interest in fishing by forming the Dream Mile Club on the Tobyhanna Creek in Carbon and Monroe counties.

In addition to his active civic calendar, Lazorchick was the solicitor for the prothonotary of Carbon County, was a member of the Advisory Board of the First Valley Bank, solicitor for the supervisors of East Penn Township and the directors of the Lake Hauto Club in Nesquehoning and was, at the time of his death, a candidate for re-election to his seventh two-year term as a state committeeman of the Republican Party.

Lazorchick died at the age of fifty-seven on April 1, 1982, survived by his wife Frances Myers Lazorchick and two children, Susan Lazorchick and Robert B. Lazorchick.

William A. Wyatt, Esquire (Adm. 1954) launched a political career shortly after earning his law degree at the University of Pennsylvania Law School in 1953 and serving as law clerk for the Honorable Chester Rhoades of the Pennsylvania Superior Court. Using a vigorous public speaking campaign before service clubs and veteran organizations on the subject of juvenile delinquency, he became the Republican standard bearer and in the General Election of 1956 surprised the local political establishment by defeating Democratic incumbent, John "Ike" Bonner, of Summit Hill in a very close election. During his years in the Legislature, Wyatt and John Deutsch practiced law together on First Street in Lehighton under the firm name of Deutsch & Wyatt. After four years in Harrisburg, he returned to private practice in Lehighton, and served briefly as chairman of the County Republican Committee. In 1961 Wyatt joined the legal department of RCA in Camden, New Jersey, where he had a distinguished career as a corporate lawyer for twenty-four years. At the time of his retirement in 1985 he held the positions of vice-president and general counsel with RCA. He now resides in Lake Harmony with his wife Barbara Minnich Wyatt. They have two children, Cindy Delaney and Robert Wyatt of New Hill, North Carolina.

Roger N. Nanovic, Esquire (Adm. 1955) has enjoyed a multifaceted and successful legal career first, as a trial lawyer, then, as a corporate counsel and banker. He will be remembered primarily, however, as the progenitor of one of the largest family of lawyers in Pennsylvania. Five of the six children born to Roger and Geraldine Nanovic are currently members of the bar. Roger II, James, Thomas, Susan and Barbara are all, like their father, graduates of the University of Notre Dame and Dickinson School of Law. After their admission to the Carbon Bar, Roger II, James, Thomas and Susan joined their father and today make up *Nanovic Law Offices*, Carbon County's largest law firm with offices in Jim Thorpe and Palmerton.

Born in Palmerton in 1929, Nanovic received his early education in the Zinc town's public schools and inspired by his uncle, Albert Nanovic, matriculated to Notre Dame University for his undergraduate degree which he received in 1951. After earning his law degree at Dickinson Law in 1954 and serving in the United States Army for two years, Nanovic became associated with Albert H. Heimbach, who had developed a successful banking and a civil defense trial practice in Jim Thorpe. When Heimbach was elected to elected to the bench in 1959, Nanovic took over his practice. His active involvement in Republican politics, banking and municipal practice brought him economic and political stature and eventually more clients and legal business. Two fellow Palmertonians became associated with Nanovic in the '70s -- George T. McKinley in 1971 and Michael Ozalas in 1977 -- but they left to form their own law firm in 1978.

In 1960 District Attorney George Kerestes appointed Nanovic an assistant district attorney and he was a top litigator in the district attorney's office until Kerestes' death in 1967. Nanovic then moved into the county solicitor's office from 1967 until 1971. For many years he served as solicitor for Penn Forest Township, Franklin Township, Towamensing Township and Lower Towamensing Township. From the early '60s he has maintained a close association with the Mauch Chunk Trust Company as both a director and solicitor. A stalwart Republican, he participated in many political campaigns as an advisor and financial contributor and counsel for the County Republican Party.

In 1972 he was named corporate counsel for a number of independent bottling companies in the northeastern part of the United States, a position which kept him on the road for a number of years. In April of 1992 Dickinson School of Law honored Nanovic at the President's Dinner for his membership in the John Reed Society, Dickinson's most prestigious donor recognition program. A lifelong resident of Palmerton, he resides in Residence Park with his wife Geraldine.

Thomas S. McCready, Esquire (Adm. 1957). "Innovative", "Dedicated", "Skilled", "Spellbinding" were the adjectives which fellow litigators used to describe his courtroom performances. Although he never held an elective office, public service dominated his legal career. McCready was the first public defender to be appointed by the Carbon County Commissioners when the office was mandated by state legislation.

Born on December 11, 1930 in Palmerton and reared in Summit Hill, McCready received his education at Summit Hill High School and Dickinson College. Following in the legal footsteps of his father, Judge James C. McCready, he entered Dickinson School of Law where he earned his law degree in 1955 and the Walter Harrison Hitchler Award for the senior with the highest overall average. Military service awaited him immediately after law school. He served two years as a sailor with the U.S. Navy in 1955 and 1956 although his duties never took him to sea.

On May 7, 1957, with his father presiding, McCready was admitted to the Carbon Bar. It marked the first time in the history of the county that a sitting judge formally welcomed one of his children to the bar.

In 1969, legislation required the establishment of a public defender's office in each county, and the county commissioners, on recommendation of the Carbon Bar Association, appointed McCready chief public defender for Carbon County. From 1969 to 1990, he represented hundreds of criminal defendants in cases ranging from first degree murder to harassment. In a position which some people feel does not deserve taxpayer support, he received no public encomiums for his twenty-one years as a bright and resourceful public defender. There is no doubt among his peers, however, that he made the office equal to the district attorney's office in quality of performance and set a remarkably high standard for those who follow him.

In the upper echelons of the criminal bar there are trial lawyers and there are "law persons." The trail lawyers are experts in "damage control" -- damaging a witness's credibility while simultaneously confining him to short answers -- and masters of demolishing witnesses and captivating juries. The law person does the legal research, drafts the points for charge, writes the briefs and argues the legal motions. McCready was among the very few criminal defense lawyers who excelled at both.

In 1965 he saved Edward Eckhart from the death sentence winning the grudging respect of the prosecutors with his tenacious defense. In 1969, he persuaded the Supreme Court of Pennsylvania to give Daniel Falcone the right to file an appeal fourteen years after his conviction and paved the way for Falcone's pardon by the Governor in 1972 (See **Falcone Murder Case**, page 51).

Despite his heavy caseload as a public defender, he served simultaneously as solicitor for the Panther Valley School District and the boroughs of Lansford, Summit Hill and Nesquehoning. McCready has been a prominent member of the banking community in the Panther Valley in his role as director and president of the Citizens Bank of Lansford (now merged with Harleysville Bank and Trust Company). Presently, McCready is completing thirty-six years as a solo practitioner in Lansford. He resides in Summit Hill with his wife Sue McCready. They have four children Susann McCready Laverty, Amy, Elizabeth and James Thomas.

Marianne Shutack Lavelle, Esquire (Adm. 1959) of Nesquehoning is a waypaver in the legal profession. She is the first woman admitted to the Carbon County Bar.

The daughter of George A. Shutack, Dean of the Carbon Bar, and Helen Shutack, the office manager in Shutack's firm, Marianne literally grew up in a law office. From her earliest years she heard law discussed daily in her home. She knew the Rule in Shelly's case before she knew anything about the law of gravity. After graduating first in her class from Nesquehoning High School she went on to Bucknell University, where in 1955 she was awarded an A.B. degree in English and Mathematics. In 1958, she received her law degree (J.D.) from Dickinson School of Law. That same year she married John P. Lavelle, the current president judge of Carbon County. Their admission to the Supreme Court of Pennsylvania in May of 1959 was noted on the front page of the *Philadelphia Bulletin* as "historic," since they were the first husband and wife admitted together to the high court. They were admitted to the United States Supreme Court in January of 1963 on motion of Archibald Cox, Solicitor General.

Marianne, her father and her husband practiced law together under the firm name of Shutack Lavelle & Lavelle in the Masonic Building in Lehighton. As the first woman lawyer she quickly became a much sought after public speaker. Many of her talks in local high schools encouraged young women to seek careers in the law. She lent her legal skills, pro bono, to many local civic organizations with which she was associated. Balancing her legal career with family responsibilities, she raised her four children and found time to refine her skills as a specialist in estate and real estate law. When her husband went on the bench in 1978, she took over the firm's practice and then expanded it. She has been solicitor for the Borough of Lehighton, Weissport and a number of municipal authorities. She resides in Lehighton with her husband Judge John P. Lavelle. They have four children, Marianne P., John, Jr., Jacqueline N., and James M.

Murray Mackson, Esquire (Adm. 1959), a native of Wilkes-Barre, came to Palmerton early in his legal career and became a significant player in the justice system and in his adopted community.

Anxious to serve his country during World War II, Mackson enlisted in the Navy at the age of seventeen. His superior performance in various clerical and technical assignments attracted the attention of the Navy brass, and he was invited to attend Officer Candidate's School. The end of the war interrupted his training and he was discharged from the Navy in June of 1946. He immediately entered Penn State University where he earned his Bachelor of Arts degree in February of 1948. Taking advantage of a special accelerated program for veterans, Mackson enrolled at Dickinson School of Law and was awarded his law degree in 1950 after only two years. He passed both the Washington, D.C. Bar and the Pennsylvania Bar and went down to Washington as an attorney for the Wage Stabilization Board investigating and prosecuting violators of the Economic Price Control laws.

In 1952, he returned to Wilkes-Barre where he developed his skills as a trial lawyer and legal counsellor in association with Gifford Cappellini. In 1959, he moved to Palmerton to become an associate in the law offices of Martin H. Philip. After three years, he launched his own law practice there and built a law office at 533 Delaware Avenue in 1964.

State and county government, Lehighton Hospital, and many community projects have had the benefit of his wise counsel and legal talents. After a brief fling in the political arena as a candidate for county commissioner, Governor William Scranton appointed Mackson an assistant attorney general for the Commonwealth of Pennsylvania in 1961. He handled all local litigation matters involving the Commonwealth until 1968. The Carbon County Recreation Authority called on his services in the many land acquisitions and condemnation cases generated by the construction of the Mauch Chunk Lake. He was briefly a board member and has been for many years solicitor for Gnaden Huetten Memorial Hospital. He also served as solicitor for Mahoning Township, and the Borough of Bowmanstown. His involvement in the affairs of his community included membership on the board of directors of PACE, a local industrial development group and service as Commander of the Palmerton Veterans Organization.

His most conspicuous trial work was during his tenure as first assistant district attorney from 1966 until 1975 under John Deutsch, particularly the prosecution of Robert W. Snyder for the shotgun murder of his wife in 1973.

Mackson is presently "of counsel" with the law firm of Weaver, Mosbach, Piosa, Hickson & Marles in Fogelsville, Pennsylvania. His son Lee Mackson, practices law in Miami, Florida and his daughter Lisa is a photographer in London, England.

John F. Gibbons, Esquire (Adm. 1973). His brilliant career as a successful criminal defense lawyer ended abruptly and tragically when the ultralight aircraft he was flying plummeted into a field on March 31, 1983. The aircraft, which Gibbons had built himself, developed mechanical trouble, lost some parts and then nose-dived to the ground near his home located in the Big Creek Valley area of Towamensing Township killing him instantly. He was only thirty-five years of age.

A graduate of Penn State University, Gibbons earned his law degree from Temple University School of Law in 1973. He began the practice of law as an associate in the offices of Martin Philip and then moved on to establish his own practice in April of 1975 at 119 South First Street in Lehighton. On December 18, 1975 the Carbon County commissioners appointed him an assistant public defender to Thomas S. McCready, chief public defender. For eight years his All-American-boy good looks, engaging personal charm and interesting defenses made him a consistent courtroom winner.

At his memorial service held in court in May of 1983, Judge Lavelle eulogized the youthful defender: "I experienced his talents in court many times, but more remarkable than his legal talents was his enormous zest for legal combat. His loyalty was complete and undiluted. I am sure his clients felt that never had they experienced anyone more on their side than John Gibbons."

His two daughters Jennifer and Christina survived him.

CHAPTER XIV

CONSUMMATE COURT JOURNALIST: JOSEPH L. BOYLE

by
Kathleen McBride[80]

Joseph Lawrence Boyle was literally born into the newspaper business. Not only was he the son of the owner-publisher of the *Mauch Chunk Daily Times*, but he was actually born right in the newspaper building itself. On March 11, 1915 Annie E. Boyle (formerly Annie Boyce) gave birth to Joe in the family's living quarters, under the same roof as the newspaper presses. From that day on, Joe lived and breathed, not to mention, loved, the newspaper profession.

Joe's father, James J. Boyle, was his prime inspiration and first teacher. James Boyle, known to his friends as Jim, was born at Seek, near Coaldale, Schuylkill County in 1872. Just out of school, he was doing technical and mechanical work in the Beaver Meadow mines when he first ventured into journalism. The article he wrote detailing the dedication of a school building in Beaver Meadows was received by the *Plain Speaker* with great favor; as a result, Jim soon became a reporter for this Hazleton paper.

Six years later, on February 21, 1908, Jim purchased the *Mauch Chunk Daily Times* (founded on April 2, 1883, and originally called the *Lehigh Pioneer-Courier*) from Attorney George E. Gray of Lehighton. He and his wife Annie, along with their two children, Gertrude and Grace, moved to Mauch Chunk to live above the newspaper offices and presses at 25 Race Street, where the family quickly learned their new occupation.

During this new venture, the methods used in the newspaper business gradually changed. Linotype replaced the former practice of setting type by hand. To keep up with the competition, new machinery had to be bought. The machinery was purchased, the new process mastered and the Boyle family kept right on moving along with the times. In 1927, the *Mauch Chunk Daily Times* absorbed the *Mauch Chunk Daily News* to become the *Times News*.

But Jim didn't do it alone. The *Mauch Chunk Daily Times* was a family paper. Annie Boyle helped her husband by doing a little of everything. She even gave the paperboys money for supper when the paper was running late. That was one thing that

---

[80]Kathleen McBride of Jim Thorpe is a 1993 graduate of Kings College where she majored in journalism.

distinguished the Boyle's paper from other newspapers, both then and today. If there were a late breaking story, Jim would do something almost unheard of -- stop the press. The newspaper never missed an edition -- sometimes it was a bit late -- but it always contained all the day's stories. Jim served as publisher, reporter, editor, compositor and printer. In the mornings and afternoons, he would prepare the contents of the papers for press and then in the evenings he would see the papers printed and delivered. He was in charge of it all -- from the conceptualization of the story right down to seeing the last newspaper dropped off on a doorstep.

Joe, Jim, and Gertrude Boyle

As they were growing up, Gertrude, Grace, Elizabeth and Mary had the job of going door-to-door to collect the money for the paper. The eldest daughter Gertrude, who at the tender age of nine had minded her younger sisters and brother while her mother was downstairs working on the newspaper, learned the business side of the newspaper. From day one she, being the oldest, was destined to have a career of working with the newspaper. Grace went on to become a nurse and Elizabeth an English and French teacher. The fourth daughter, Mary, entered the field of dental hygiene.

And then there was Joe. Joe, the youngest child and only surviving boy of the family (Lawrence had died when he was only a few weeks old and James had died of diphtheria at the age of two and one half years), followed closely in his father's footsteps.

As a boy, Joe worked with and learned a great deal from his father and while in high school he wrote a column entitled "Sports Pickups." In 1937, when he graduated from Mt. St. Mary's College in Emmitsburg, Maryland, Joe began his official career as a newspaper man. Upon Joe's return to Mauch Chunk, Jim Boyle started to take things a bit easier and left many of his jobs in Joe's capable hands. One such job included the "courthouse beat."

Joe spent more time in the Carbon County courtroom than any judge, lawyer or juror. Like his father before him, Joe was proud to be solely responsible for covering the "courthouse beat," a beat he covered for most of his sixty year journalistic career.

He covered every trial, including about twenty murder trials. Joe produced a story for every one -- even when there wasn't really a story. His coverage always made the trials seem interesting. He spent over fifty years in the Carbon County courthouse and courtroom and witnessed the Court's progression through three court judges, James C. McCready, Albert H. Heimbach and John P. Lavelle. Joe covered trials ranging from larceny to prostitution, from fender benders to rapes, and from non-support charges to charges of illegal riding on a Lehigh Valley Railroad train.

He also attended the Carbon County commissioners' meetings, which are held once a week. Over fifty years this adds up to about 2400 meetings! Joe never tired of his courthouse duties, in fact, he loved them. He loved everything having to do with his hometown of Mauch Chunk and the surrounding area.

In December of 1951, Jim Boyle contracted an illness and two weeks later, on December 15, died in the home of his daughter Gertrude and her husband Cy Apfelbaum. Up until the time of his illness, he had been actively engaged in the management of the newspaper; now the *Times News* was left in the hands of Gertrude and Joe. Annie Boyle had died on April 3, 1934.

Joe and Gertrude continued where their father had left off, assuming the position of co-publishers. Gertrude, who was in charge of the books and other office duties, in addition to her writing for the paper, pleased the readers with her popular "Strictly Personal" column. Joe penned such favorites as "A'Chording to Boyle," a column that recounted anecdotes from the past about local people and places, and an annual April Fool's Day story. These front page spoofs related a well-planned, highly feasible project. In fact some of them, like the Mauch Chunk watershed that stopped the flooding of the downtown area while creating a recreational park, were prophetic with the results coming just as Joe had predicted.

Joe Boyle meeting a deadline

Besides working with the newspaper, Joe was deeply involved in community activities. He was instrumental in organizing the VFW Post, served as community chairman of the American Legion and was the member of the Jim Thorpe Lions Club instrumental in encouraging the club to restore the Asa Packer Mansion. During the years, Joe was a district chairman of the Boy Scouts of America, served as president of the Rotary Club, executive secretary of the Industrial Association, one of the founders and the first president of the Men of Marian and an executive director of the Lehighton Chamber of Commerce. He also served a two-year term as a member of the Jim Thorpe Borough Council. And for over fifteen years, Joe was a member of the Carbon County Planning Commission, the Carbon County Recreation Authority and the Carbon Tourist Promotion Agency of which he was the first chairman.

One of Joe's biggest accomplishments was the merger of the Boroughs of Mauch Chunk with East Mauch Chunk to become the Borough of Jim Thorpe. Joe was the driving force behind the merger and devoted a tremendous amount of his time, energy and persuasive skills to the effort which had gone aborning for many years before he entered the picture.

In his seventy-seven years of life, Joe received more honors and awards than the average person would ever dream of receiving. In 1954, as a result of his "Nickel-a-Week" fund-raising campaign, he received a Freedoms Foundation Award. A year later he earned the prestigious Distinguished Service Award presented by the Newspaper Editors and the Pennsylvania Newspapers Publishers Association. He received the Marian Award, the

American Legion National Press Award and Meritorious Service Award and the Panther Valley Irish-American Association Shamrock Award. Recipient of the Man of the Year of the Jim Thorpe Olympian Booster Club, Joe also received awards of appreciation from Carbon County Conservation District, Carbon County Recreation Authority, Jim Thorpe Area School District, St. Joseph's CYO Program, YMCA Youth Programs, and District 18 Little League. And these were just some of Joe's many awards.

Joe always gave his parents, Jim and Annie, praise for his success. The parallels between Joe and his father were outstanding as can be seen by the similar articles written about them upon their deaths. A part of Jim's read:

> *. . . a deeply humble individual whose greatest enjoyment came in helping others. He was a true friend, a kindly neighbor and a devoted father. In the realm of journalism, he attained high rank and was respected and emulated by those of his profession. He was recognized as a forceful, dynamic, intelligent man, loved by all who saw in him the highest attributes of Christian charity.*

An editorial eulogy about Joe stated

> *Not many can match the impact he made on the people and community surrounding him. Those of us who worked with Joe over the years admired him as a journalist blessed with great talent, intelligence, sense of humor, packaged into a bundle of energy and determination. . . Boyle's fire burned with its most intensity in three areas -- on his love for his wife and confidant of 46 years, Rita, and their children [Rita (Huggler) and Joseph]; his appreciation for his Catholic faith and upbringing; and his almost blind loyalty to his hometown of Jim Thorpe.*

Joe met his death suddenly and tragically on May 25, 1992 while riding on a float in Jim Thorpe's Memorial Day Parade with the seventh and eighth grade students from St. Joseph's Regional School. Joe had been teaching the students about journalism and local history, while acting as the moderator of their school newspaper. Moments after waving to his wife Rita while taking his last trip through the town that he loved so deeply, Joe was thrown from the float, struck his head on a tree and died instantly. How ironic that Joe Boyle should die in a way that symbolized his entire life -- lovingly and loyally serving the residents of Jim Thorpe.

Joe was a newspaper man right up to the very end. The last article ever written by Joe Boyle appeared in the *Morning Call* the very same day they ran his obituary.

CHAPTER XV

THE "MOLLIE MAGUIRE" TRIALS (1876)

Did the "Mollies" Have a Fair and Impartial Jury?

From January through December of 1876 -- in the Commonwealth of Pennsylvania where William Penn one hundred fifty years before had guaranteed to all citizens the right to a fair trial -- Michael Doyle, Edward Kelly, John Donahue, Alexander Campbell, Thomas P. Fisher and Patrick McKenna were successively put on trial for their lives in the small red brick courthouse in Mauch Chunk, the seat of Carbon County.

Their odyssey to the Mauch Chunk courtroom began with two killings in the Carbon County mining towns of Summit Hill and Lansford. Morgan Powell, an assistant mine boss, was shot in the chest with a single bullet on December 2, 1871, at about 7:00 P.M. as he was leaving Henry Williamson's store in Summit Hill. Three men fled from the scene without being recognized. Powell died of his wound two days later (See page 390 for the Mauch Chunk ***Gazette's*** coverage of the killing).

On September 3, 1875, John P. Jones, a mine boss of the Lehigh and Wilkes Barre Coal Company, was shot to death at 7:00 A.M. as he walked from his home on Storm Hill to the Lansford train depot. At least fifty people on or near the train which had just arrived from Tamaqua saw two men firing pistols at Jones and watched three men flee from the murder site. Coal company security forces and an angry horde of armed citizens pursued the men through woods and over mountains to a waterhole near Tamaqua. Perspiring and near exhaustion, they were taken into custody, without incident, within three hours of the shooting. When questioned, the men identified themselves as Michael Doyle, Edward Kelly, and James Kerrigan. They were quickly taken by coal company police on a train through hostile mobs shouting "Lynch them!" in Lansford and Mauch Chunk to the Carbon County Jail where they were charged with Jones' murder. Three pistols and a billy club were found near the waterhole. Bullet cartridges, similar to the one which killed Jones, fell from their pockets as they were being taken to jail. Inside the lapels of their coat police found badges emblazoned with the letters AOH. The Mauch Chunk ***Democrat*** headlined the murder and the chase in its September 4, 1875 edition which is reproduced on page 391.

In late January of 1876, while he was in jail awaiting trial for Jones' murder, James Kerrigan decided to become a witness for the prosecution. In a written statement, he told the prosecutors that Alexander Campbell, a well known Lansford hotel owner, not only planned Jones' murder, but that he was the ringleader of the "Mollie Maguires" in Carbon County. He gave them a detailed account of the Jones' killing, fingering Doyle and Kelly as the shooters. Kerrigan also gave a statement that John "Yellow Jack" Donahue had told him that he, Donahue, with the assistance of Thomas Fisher and Patrick McKenna and two others, had killed Morgan Powell for $100 upon orders of Alexander Campbell. Based on Kerrigan's accusations, Campbell was arrested on February 4, 1876 and charged with the murder of Jones and Powell. Donahue was also arrested with Thomas Fisher, Patrick McKenna, Patrick O'Donnell, and John Malloy and they were all charged with Powell's murder.

National origin, employment, and membership in a fraternal organization brought Doyle, Kelly, Donahue, Campbell, Fisher and McKenna together. They all had their roots in Ireland, all had worked in the coal mines of Schuylkill County and all were members of the Ancient Order of Hibernians (AOH). The press and their prosecutors called them "Mollie Maguires." They were all charged with first degree murder and the prosecution sought the ultimate penalty -- death by hanging.

Over the years, these "Mollie" trials have sparked a firestorm of troubling questions about power, justice and money in the hard coal regions in the latter part of the nineteenth century. Using the newspaper reports of the time and Pinkerton Detective Agency files, many historians and writers have reconstructed and analyzed the crimes, the trials of the six Irishmen and their coal region backdrop. Almost unanimously, they conclude that the men were "Mollie Maguires" and members of the Ancient Order of Hibernians (AOH) whose secret purpose was to threaten, burn, maim and murder those who deprived members of jobs or who were perceived as committing wrongs against the members. To accomplish these ends, Alexander Campbell, the Carbon County leader of the AOH, planned the murders of the two coal mine supervisors. Many witnesses took the stand at the murder trials to support these conclusions and Carbon County juries heard their testimony and convicted all six men. On June 21, 1877, sheriff's deputies led Doyle, Kelly, Campbell and Donahue to the gallows built inside the Carbon County prison, where they were hanged simultaneously.[81] Fisher was hanged on March 28, 1878 and McKenna was sentenced to the state penitentiary for nine years.

Alfred Mathews and Austin Hungerford, in their *History of the counties of Lehigh and Carbon in the Commonwealth of Pennsylvania, 1884* extolled the Carbon prosecutors as purgers of an outcast band of outlaws:

> *In the history of what is judicially known as the Mollie Maguire trials Carbon County occupies a most conspicuous position. It was here the first trial resulting in conviction and execution took place. The evidence elicited on this trial unlocked the mysteries of an organization of criminals, and led to the conviction and execution of upwards of twenty persons charged with murder, the incarceration in the penitentiary of many others, and making great numbers*

[81]On this same day, McGeehan, Boyle, Carroll, Roarity, and Duffy were hanged in the Schuylkill County prison for the murder of Patrolman Benjamin Yost of Tamaqua.

> *fugitives from justice.*
>
> *The members of the Mollie Maguire organization having been denounced and excommunicated by the Roman Catholic Church, and the branches of the order in the counties where trials and convictions have taken place having been suspended by the Ancient Order of Hibernians of Pennsylvania, it is hoped that this power for mischief is gone forever.*

Fred Brenckman's *History of Carbon County* opened his chapter on "The Mollie Maguires" in similar fashion:

> *While Carbon county, by reason of its smaller area and population, contained fewer Mollie Maguires than either of the neighboring counties of Luzerne and Schuylkill, it nevertheless occupies a position of equal importance to these in the popular mind when the memory of the crimes and outrages perpetrated by the members of that dark and blood-stained organization are recalled.*
>
> *It was at Mauch Chunk, after the most fearless and resolute of the law-abiding members of society in the coal regions had begun to despair of ever being able to bring a Mollie Maguire to justice for the commission of crime, that the first conviction and execution of one of this lawless and murderous band took place.*

But Harold W. Aurand, in his thoughtful study, *From the Molly Maguires to the United Mine Workers*, expressed an entirely different view of the Carbon proceedings:

> *The Molly Maguire investigation and trials was one of the most astounding surrenders of sovereignty in American history. A private corporation initiated the investigation through a private detective agency; a private police force arrested the alleged offenders; the coal company attorneys prosecuted them. The state provided only the Courtroom and the hangman.*

Unquestionably, the trials of these men in Mauch Chunk (now Jim Thorpe) were the most sensational in the history of the Bench and Bar of Carbon County. Every local and major national newspaper covered the legal proceedings. What was most important about the trials was something that had nothing to do with the law, something that never appeared in the newspaper accounts of the trials, but was always there between the lines: the future of trade unionism in Northeast Pennsylvania hung on the outcome.

A local history devoted to lawyers and judges sworn to uphold the right of every citizen to a fair trial would be incomplete without some analysis of these notorious trials.

William Herman Rau photo of Mauch Chunk, circa 1891. In 1870, Mauch Chunk probably had the highest mean per capita income of any city in the United States.

Recently, the original transcripts and pleadings of the pretrial proceedings and the trials of the six defendants were discovered in the basement of the Carbon County Courthouse.[82] Although handwritten with pen and ink, they are in extraordinarily good condition. These original court documents offer an unusual opportunity to examine the trials, not only with the clearer hindsight of over one-hundred years, but also, for the first time, in the light of current concepts of due process.[83]

Our examination, then, will not concentrate on the quantity or quality of the evidence presented at the trials. Many books and articles have scrutinized the newspaper reports of the testimony and debated the credibility and weight to be given to the "informer" James McParlan and the "squealer" James Kerrigan.[84] Instead, we shall examine the trials from a due process perspective and endeavor to find out whether the defendants had fair and impartial juries. Our analysis will focus on three areas: (1) the composition of the jury pool selected for the "Mollie" trial, (2) the procedures used to pick the juries, and (3) whether the cases should have been tried in Carbon County. We shall consider these issues under the law of 1876 and 1993.

Social, Economic, and Political Background

We begin our fair trial-due process analysis, as we must, by examining the local demographics as well as the social and political climate of Carbon County at the time of the trials.

In 1876, Carbon County was still an agricultural area with a teeming industrial core. Farming, lumbering, mining and railroading were the principal occupations. Two-thirds of the county was farmland and the Pennsylvania Dutch predominated. According to the 1870 Census, it had a total population of about 28,144. Of the 6,964 foreign born citizens of the county, there were 3,577 Irish born, 1,456 English and Welsh natives, 109

[82]The original transcripts are kept in the archives of the Carbon County Courthouse in Jim Thorpe, Pennsylvania. Copies of the transcripts are available at the Pennsylvania Historical Museum in Harrisburg, Pennsylvania.

[83]These original trial transcripts and the pleadings were an invaluable resource in writing this chapter. They were essential to our voir dire analysis because they enabled us to examine what was actually taking place in the courtroom at the time the trials were going on. We did not have to rely on second and third hand reports from the newspapers of the time.

[84]See Bimba, Anthony. The Molly Maguires. International Publisher, 1932., Broehl, Wayne G. Jr. The Mollie Maguires. Cambridge: Harvard University Press, 1964., Campbell, Patrick. A Molly Maguire Story. Lawrenceville, NJ: Princeton University Press, 1992., Coleman, James W. The Molly Maguire Riots: Industrial Conflict in the Pennsylvania Coal Region. Richmond, VA: Garrett, 1937., Dewees, Francis P. The Molly Maguires. Lippincott, 1877., Pinkerton, Allan. The Molly Maguires and the Detectives. G. W. Dillingham, 1905.

Scottish born, and 1,651 German born.[85] The Irish made up thirteen percent of the total county population and fifty percent of the foreign born population. The Welsh-English comprised five percent of the total population and the German born made up six percent of the population.[86]

Mauch Chunk Township, Mauch Chunk Borough, and Banks Township were the population centers of the county. The coal mining areas were Mauch Chunk Township (now Summit Hill, Lansford, and Nesquehoning), Lausanne Township, Banks Township, and parts of Kidder Township. Because over ninety percent of the Irish males worked in the mines, the Irish population lived primarily in these four areas in patch towns next to the collieries. Coal companies owned everything -- the land, streets, houses, stores, schools, churches, and public buildings.[87] The Irish were Catholic and registered Democratic; the rest of the population was Protestant and evenly divided as Democrats and Republicans.

The county seat was Mauch Chunk or "Bear Mountain" which was what the native Indians called the east slope of mountain next to the Lehigh River. Its meaning, like all Indian namings, is poetically exact. From a high view the encircling mountain appears remarkably like a gigantic sleeping bear, its broad back rippling across the horizon.

A visitor to Mauch Chunk in 1876 looked at the rough terrain and towering mountains which surrounded the town and gasped, "How did the people here ever find this place?" The answer, of course, was that God had bestowed on the area more than mountains. To the north in Summit Hill, Lansford, and Nesquehoning were rich deposits of low-sulphur anthracite. Also winding through the rough terrain from White Haven to Easton, like a thread of quicksilver, was the swiftly moving Lehigh River. Mauch Chunk was a by-product of these two natural resources. It first lured Josiah White and Erskine Hazard who saw the potential of mining the coal and of building canal boats to transport it on the Lehigh River to the Lehigh Valley and of establishing there the headquarters of their Lehigh Coal and Navigation Company. It also attracted Asa Packer, who had the vision to see that a better way to bring the coal to the eastern markets was to build a railroad along the Lehigh River from Mauch Chunk to Easton. These men and their companies took the secluded river outpost out of the wilderness, made it a huge transportation center for the coal industries of the Northeast, and transformed it into an extraordinarily stimulating and interesting place.

---

[85]Bureau of Census records for 1880 reveal that the population of the County increased to 31,377. The breakdown of the foreign born population did not change much. Of the total population, German born residents made up 5.9%, English/Welsh born residents comprised 3.9%, and Irish born residents made up 13%.

[86]Ninth Census of U.S., Statistics of Population, 1870, I, pp. 369-370.

[87]Miller, Donald L. and Richard E. Sharpless. *The Kingdom of Coal.* Philadelphia: 1985, p. 142.

By the mid-nineteenth century, Mauch Chunk had become a company town made wealthy by the exploitation of anthracite coal and by the railroads that hauled it to urban areas and to steel and iron factories. Professors Donald L. Miller and Richard E. Sharpless of Lafayette College in their definitive work on the development of the coal industry in Northeast Pennsylvania described Mauch Chunk's prosperity:

> *It boasted more concentrated wealth than any other town in the Lehigh field; in 1870 it probably had the highest mean per capita income of any city in the United States. Fifty of its residents were each worth more than $50,000; Packer's holdings and personal wealth exceeded $10 Million. Money flowed in from coal, transportation, and services. It built impressive new buildings, including Lehigh Coal's massive brick headquarters and a collection of fine homes along "Millionaire's Row" on a ridge overlooking the town. Mauch Chunk's scenic location added to its attraction. The railroad brought affluent tourists from New York and Philadelphia to this "Switzerland of America." They disembarked from the train at the foot of the new resort hotel, eager to take the mountain airs, ride the scenic gravity railroad, see and be seen in the new opera house, and bask in the warm, self-congratulatory atmosphere of capital gains.*[88]

In Northeast Pennsylvania, coal was king for most of the 1800s. It heated the homes and fueled the Industrial Revolution. In 1870, the first year state mining records were compiled, northeastern Pennsylvania produced fourteen million tons of anthracite and employed 35,600 men. In the years from 1843 to 1880, the Lehigh Coal and Navigation Company, Carbon's largest employer, alone produced over twenty-one million tons of coal and carried it on the famous Switchback gravity railroad line to Mauch Chunk. The Lehigh Valley Railroad and the Central Railroad of New Jersey, with their headquarters in Mauch Chunk, had their trains rolling night and day transporting the anthracite to Easton and then to Philadelphia and New York markets. Between 1855 and 1875, the Lehigh Valley Railroad shipped 39,298,921 tons of coal while during the same period, the Lehigh and Susquehanna Railroad and its lessee, the Central Railroad of New Jersey, hauled 13,741,384 tons.[89]

Not well known and almost ignored by the press, was the fact that the coal came from mines which were owned by the railroads through holding company operations. The Reading Railroad Company, led by its President Franklin B. Gowen, was the largest and most powerful company having these combined interests in the anthracite region. In a smaller way, Carbon's LC&N Company and the Lehigh Valley Railroad enjoyed similar

[88]Miller, Donald L. and Richard E. Sharpless. *The Kingdom of Coal.* Philadelphia: University of Pennsylvania Press, 1985, p. 72.

[89]Eckhart, Thomas D. *The History of Carbon County.* Lehighton, PA: TN Printing, 1992, p. 140.

monopolies. The Philadelphia and Reading Coal and Iron Company, a subsidiary which the Reading Company spawned in 1871, purchased some 100,000 acres of coal lands (almost one-third of all the coal lands in Northeast Pennsylvania) between 1871 and 1875 at a cost of nearly $40 million. By price fixing and superior technology, those railroads could force most of the independent coal operators to deal with them or go out of business. The railroads then took over the hard coal industry. Since the Reading Company was the largest of the monopolies, Franklin Gowen was the man in control when it came to dictating wages, prices and allocation of coal production.[90]

About half of the Carbon County labor force worked on the railroads or in the mines. The Irish pick-axed and blasted the coal from the mines which deep pocketed Summit Hill, Lansford and Nesquehoning; Welsh and English bosses decided when and where they would work. Conditions in the mines were atrocious. Miners contended with poorly ventilated mine shafts and constant exposure to gas leaks, suffocation and explosions causing hundreds of deaths and permanent disabilities. They worked long hours, lived in shoddy wooden shacks without sanitary facilities in "coal patches" which the companies rented to them at unconscionable rates. They also drank hard to blot out their miserable existences. Alcoholism was a severe problem. Worse yet were the miners' wages. They earned $1.25 a day and had to buy food and goods at the company store where prices had been inflated from ten to fifty percent more than at an independent store.

And then there was the Coal and Iron Police. Organized by an act of the Legislature in 1866, this private and highly paid company police system ruled not only the mine and mill properties, but the company towns as well. Their brutal treatment and invasions of the privacy rights and constitutional liberties of the workers made the "patch towns" seem like Soviet gulags. When a crime was committed, it was not unusual for the Coal and Iron Police to enter a suspect's home by force and remove him to the county jail, where they guarded him, extracted his "confession," and then testified against him in court.

There was another factor that cannot be overlooked. A deep-seated and pervasive prejudice against Irish Catholics smoldered in the anthracite region. Fear and a native abhorrence of the outsider produced this enmity. Growing numbers of Irish immigrants coming into Carbon and Schuylkill counties aroused fears in the older inhabitants that they would lose their jobs, money, and power. Between 1860 and 1870 the Irish population had increased by more than sixty percent. The nationwide Native American political movement which opposed electing anyone who was not American born and Protestant capitalized on these local fears and promoted anti-Irish bigotry. Beginning in the late 1850s, Benjamin Bannan, the nativist editor of Pottsville's *Miner's Journal*, began to pour

---

[90] Miller, Donald L. and Richard E. Sharpless. *The Kingdom of Coal.* Philadelphia: University of Pennsylvania Press, 1985, p. 81.

out a venomous stream of complaints against Irish Catholics for their political activities. But as time went on, Bannan blamed almost every crime in Schuylkill County on the local Irish and connected them to the "Mollie Maguires." The first time the term "Mollie Maguires" appeared in print in the coal regions was in one of Bannan's diatribes accusing the Irish of voting irregularities in 1857.[91] Bannan's bile spilled over into the newspapers of neighboring Carbon County. Joseph Lynn, the owner and publisher of the *Carbon Democrat*, wrote a satirical column in his July 3, 1869 edition which evoked the bias prevalent against the Irish:

Those Irishmen.

> *Irishmen of Carbon have now a fine opportunity to join the Republican party by special invitation of the* ***Gazette****. The exortation [sic] is elaborate and chaste, and we have no doubt they will all hasten to obey it -- they all love oppression so fondly. The* ***Gazette*** *thinks they fled the Green Isle to escape the excessive freedom that was being forced upon them. Well, the dear fellows, they make worthy efforts; they try hard to make "water and goose-oil" mix. Our neighbors don't know their own party; nine hundred and ninety-nine out of every thousand Irishmen in Pennsylvania can "read it like a book." For the* ***Gazette's*** *benefit we give the following very concise facts for it [sic] study:*
>
> *In the Pennsylvania Legislature, about a year ago, John Hickman, the Republican member from Chester county, said:*
>
> *"I may see the day that I may walk side by side with a Black woman. I have seen a great many colored women that I would rather walk with than a great many white men. I know a great many negroes who I think are better entitled to vote this moment than a great many white men who do vote, and have long exercised the francise [sic]. An intelligent negro is better than an Irish Catholic and is entitled to a vote."*

The "No Irish Need Apply" signs appearing on the front doors of many company offices in Carbon and Schuylkill counties also reflected the widespread anti-Irish feeling. The February 19, 1876 edition of the *Mauch Chunk Democrat*, two days before Michael Doyle was brought into court for sentencing, acknowledged the local bias and told the Irish how to end it:

> *For many years a feeling of dislike has been regnant in the hearts of many that claim to be citizens of this Republic against those of Irish extraction. No matter what their services may have been in sustaining the country throughout her varied trials -- and that such services have been of vast consequence no one can*

[91] Gunderlunas, William and William Shade. Before the Molly Maguires. New York: 1976.

> *successfully contradict -- the name of "irishman" and "Catholic" has been sufficient in the minds of the narrow minded and bigoted to condemn them; that all infringements of the law committed by some desperado was sustained by the silent assent of his compatriots. This feeling is, of course, wrong but it prevails. Now we hold that it is the duty of our Irish friends to aid in sustaining the laws to help the course of justice and in so doing clear away this stigma and thus inaugurate a better feeling among our citizens, both native born and adopted.*

The primary sources for news at this time were small weekly newspapers which, besides making a profit, had two main goals: (1) to promote the interests and policies of the industrial leaders who controlled the wealth, power and employment in their communities, and (2) to serve as a political pulpit from which their publisher-owner could extol the virtues of his party and candidates. Newspapers were printed in a narrow, multi-decked style which, because of its visual effect, was called a "tombstone." The *Mauch Chunk Gazette*, *Mauch Chunk Democrat*, *Carbon Advocate*, and *Weekly Intelligencer* were the local newspapers feeding the news and the publisher's views to the people of Carbon County. There were about 5246 households in the county in 1876 and eighty percent of the households subscribed to or bought at least one of these newspapers. The *Gazette* was the organ of the Republican Party; the *Democrat*, as its name proclaims, was the political tract for the Democratic Party; the *Carbon Advocate*, a Lehighton newspaper, also followed the line of the Democratic Party; the *Intelligencer* published in Summit Hill by Robert Harris and Eveland Harris, who also owned the *Tamaqua Courier*, was Republican in its editorial policy. They were all pro-coal operator and pro-railroad. They were anti-labor, anti-Catholic and anti-Irish. Featuring a quick-on-the-draw sense of outrage, their news reports vilified those they opposed and deified those they supported. For $1 you could have a one-year subscription.

There was also the threat of a new force on the area's industrial horizon -- unionization of the miners. In 1868, John Siney, a native of Ireland who came to St. Clair in Schuylkill County during the Civil War, succeeded in organizing the Workingmen's Benevolent Association (WBA) to combat the low wages and the intolerable working conditions which the coal operators foisted on the mine workers. Strikes became their most effective weapon. But there was also violence, most of it in Schuylkill County. Mine bosses were beaten and killed, homes were burned, collieries were dynamited, coal cars were overturned and trains derailed. Not surprisingly, the coal operators retaliated against union leaders and their families. They were fired from their jobs and blacklisted. Several of them and their families were assaulted and killed.

As early as 1870, the coal operators decided to recognize the WBA as a legitimate bargaining agency and grudgingly agreed to a sliding scale of wages based on the prevailing price of coal, and to a $2.50 per day minimum wage. Unfortunately for the miners, the combination of a nationwide economic depression and a glutted coal market sent

Franklin B. Gowen, President of the Reading Railroad Company

the price of coal plummeting in 1873. The coal operators, led by Franklin B. Gowen, decided to take advantage of this economic crunch and simultaneously destroy the union. They refused to renew the collective bargaining agreement and announced a twenty percent wage cut and "no minimum wage." In December of 1874, the union called a strike. This "Long Strike," as it is now called, became the most disastrous walkout in labor history. Within two months, the miners' pockets were nearly empty. Burning buildings, riotous demonstrations and train wrecks were widespread in Schuylkill and Carbon counties as union members tried to force Gowen and the coal operators to the bargaining table. Privately, Gowen used his strong personality and threats of retaliation to hold the individual mine operators in line in refusing to make any concessions to the union. By July of 1875, the miners, driven to the brink of starvation, called off the strike and begged to get back to work. Gowen extracted a humiliating price. The miners had to agree to disband the WBA and take the twenty percent wage cut.

Long before the coal operators crushed their union, however, the miners had found another organization to wage their battle against Gowen and the allied coal companies. Many miners of Irish ancestry were already members of a national Irish fraternal society, the Ancient Order of Hibernians (AOH). Its purpose was to promote their interests and raise funds to take care of injured miners and their families. The Hibernians had local divisions in every county in the hard coal regions and were very active in getting their members elected to public offices. It was a natural move to have the county chapters of the AOH serve as their union. Men like Jack Kehoe, a Girardville miner and local delegate of the Hibernians, and Alexander Campbell, a former miner and bodymaster (local chairman) from Lansford, encouraged this strategy. Some of the local AOH chapters, then, became temporary labor unions until the miners could muster the strength and resources to form a permanent union organization again.

Late in 1872, it had become apparent to Reading Company stockholders that Gowen's voracious purchasing of coal lands in the anthracite region, and his hard line with WBA, had brought the company to the brink of bankruptcy. The "Road," as it was commonly called, was sustaining huge losses, its stock was nosediving and there were large numbers of layoffs. A barrage of criticism descended upon Gowen from all quarters -- from stockholders, consumers, mine owners and laborers. The State Legislature launched an investigation into what his critics called "ruthless and spendthrift activities." Gowen needed a strategy to take the harsh spotlight of public scrutiny from him, and a scapegoat that he could blame for the Reading's rapidly deteriorating financial condition. He saw the AOH as an ideal scapegoat and one that would make an excellent whipping post.[92] But he had no proof to connect the organization to the violence. As a former prosecutor, Gowen knew that swaying the public mind would go a long way toward making the connection. Because the Irish were already widely disliked and social pariahs, it would not be too difficult to persuade the public that the miners and their labor leaders were all criminals. Drawing on his experiences as a district attorney and his battles for control of the Reading Company, Gowen conceived and launched a three-part plan to destroy the AOH. First he would demonize the organization; he would then infiltrate it and gather evidence; finally, he would bring the leaders to trial before juries who were programmed to convict and a court certain to execute.

Early in 1873, he created the factoid that if you were Irish you had to be a "Mollie Maguire" or "Mollie" sympathizer. Taking full advantage of the bias against the Irish, he began to issue press releases and circulating handbills through the Coal and Iron Police blaming the coal region violence on the AOH and publicly branding all its members as "Mollie Maguires." Although there was no society in Pennsylvania or anywhere in the United States called "Mollie Maguires," Gowen reasoned that calling someone a "Mollie" (like the term "Mafia" today), if repeated often enough, especially in the local newspapers, would give credibility to his factoid. The name "Mollie Maguires" had been brought to America from Ireland and the story behind the name was well known throughout the hard coal regions. Mollie Maguire was a legendary, albeit apocryphal, Irish heroine. In the 1840s, she was said to have led poverty-stricken farmers in Ireland in secret violent attacks against the brutal bailiffs, who collected house and cattle rents for absent English landlords. It was a name that symbolized lawlessness and violence to the average law-abiding citizen.

Gowen's propaganda campaign contained a germ of truth. There was indeed a small band of leaders who organized a secret group of men within the AOH to fight the mine owners. These "bodymasters" planned retaliatory actions against the mine superintendents and work-sabotage. Then, from within this inner circle, they solicited men from another lodge to execute their plans. Most Hibernians were unaware of these clandestine activities and if they were aware, they looked the other way.[93]

Gowen had an eager ally in the newspapers because they were controlled by the coal operators who in turn were controlled by the railroads. A continuous flow of newspaper articles carrying the Gowen press releases streamed off the local presses accusing the "Mollies" of one act of violence after another.

---

[92]Broehl, Wayne G. *The Molly Maguires*. Cambridge: Harvard University Press, 1964.

[93]Miller, Donald L. and Sharpless, Richard E. *The Kingdom of Coal*. Philadelphia: University of Pennsylvania Press, 1985, pp. 155-163.

Gowen realized that the Irish would support and defend their fellow Irishmen if they were prosecuted. He told his friends that many good Irish people had taken the witness stand and perjured themselves by providing "alibis" to Irish defendants who were prosecuted unsuccessfully in the past. But he had a bold new plan to suppress any Irish "alibiing." He would shake their souls with the one threat he knew every Irish Catholic dreaded -- excommunication from the Church and eternal damnation. Archbishop James F. Wood, the head of the Archdiocese of Philadelphia which included Carbon and Schuylkill counties, was a close friend and confidant of Gowen. Gowen convinced Archbishop Wood that the Hibernians were responsible for the "reign of terror" in the coal regions and threatened the economic destruction of his railroad. Archbishop Wood, perhaps naively and unwittingly, became one of Gowen's most powerful allies. He issued a pastoral letter on December 15, 1875 condemning the AOH:

> . . . *As we know from most reliable sources and indeed of our own personal knowledge, that most insidious efforts have been, and are being made, in many parts of our Diocese, and probably throughout the whole country, to blind and deceive the faithful, and to entangle them in the meshes and shackles of these unlawful and forbidden societies, it becomes our duty to call to the minds of our people, the action of the Church in this matter; to warn them to refrain from any alliance with them; and earnestly to exhort all who may have violated this prohibition of the Church, to leave these evil associations, and by a speedy and sincere penance, to seek reconciliation with the Church.*
>
> *To say nothing of the "Masons," "Odd Fellows," "Sons of Temperance," etc. about whose condemnation no doubt can exist, these societies are known by various other appellations; such, for example, as the "National Brotherhood." condemned by the Bishops of Ireland; the "Fenian Brotherhood," whose efforts to aggregate members to their association in this country are unscrupulous and unceasing, and, in addition to these, the "Molly Maguires," otherwise the "Ancient Order of Hibernians," or the "Buckshots," and others, whose spirit is equally objectionable, and whose names seem to be selected rather to conceal, than to indicate the object of their associations.*
>
> *We admonish, also, our Reverend Clergy affectionately to instruct and warn their flocks, calling to their minds the spirit of docility and obedience, which should animate them, and the holy alacrity with which they should labor to conform themselves in all things to the commands and desires of the Church, and to avoid, with the most scrupulous care, all that she disapproves and condemns -- to place before them, on the one hand, the rewards and blessings which will follow such a course, and on the other hand, the true character of the extreme ecclesiastical censures which a contrary mode of action will precipitate upon them.*

He followed that with an announcement that he would excommunicate any Irishman who was a member of the AOH.[92] On April 6, 1876, the *Philadelphia Times*, in an editorial undoubtedly prompted by Gowen, connected the AOH with the "Mollie Maguires" and noted Wood's condemnation of the AOH:

> ***An Order of Assassins***
>
> *Kerrigan's confession, which has been often referred to, and the substance of which was given in The Times specials from Pottsville some months ago, is at last made public, and it is a startling document. Kerrigan, it will be remembered, is one of the Mollie Maguires indicted for the murder of Jones, a mine boss, in Carbon county. Doyle has already been convicted for the part he played in that murder, and Kelley, another of the indicted parties, is now being tried at Mauch Chunk. This confession merely confirms what intelligent persons in the coal region have long suspected, but the public elsewhere will not be prepared to believe that a widespread and influential society, which has usually been considered entirely respectable, contains within itself a carefully perfected system by which arson and assassination are planned and committed with almost perfect impunity in communities like the mining regions, where the organization is strong in numbers. In fact, it will require something more than the statement of one confessed murderer to convince people generally that the Ancient Order of Hibernians is everywhere an association of assassins as reckless of human life as the Carbonari of Italy. The Mollie Maguires are indisputably a set of Thugs. They have produced a real reign of terror in the anthracite districts of Pennsylvania, and it is more than likely that they comprise the most lawless members of the Hibernian Order, who, protected by their oaths of membership, have banded themselves together, and taken a sort of murderers' degree. Archbishop Wood, of this city, condemns the Ancient Order itself for the multiplied outrages of the cut-throat Mollies, and some time since issued an address excommunicating its members, an action which the Hibernians in other parts of the country bitterly resent. Whatever the connection of the Mollies with the larger and more respectable order, the latter is responsible for the atrocities in the coal regions by tacitly aiding to hide the culprits. It must rid itself of these bloodthirsty scoundrels and give them up to justice, or share their infamy.*

---

[92]Historians have speculated as to why Archbishop Wood would get so involved with Gowen and lash out so strongly against the AOH. Some said that his English ancestry and education and years in the banking business before he became a priest might have hardened his attitude toward the Irish miners (See Broehl, Wayne G., Jr. *The Mollie Maguires*. p.79). There were also reports that the Archdiocese of Philadelphia owned stock in the Reading Railroad which, of course, would be a much more plausible motive for the Archbishop's active involvement in these secular matters.

Gowen kept in close contact with Archbishop Wood, even during the Pottsville trials of the "Mollies," briefing him on developments, thanking him for his assistance and seeking his help:

Pottsville May 11 1876

Most Reverend James F. Wood, D.D.

My Dear Sir

I will send you to day copies of a Pottsville paper containing the evidence in the trial of the murderers of Yost, which is I think without exception the most remarkable criminal trial I have ever had knowledge of. Our secret detective who was for over two years a member of the Molly Maguires has been upon the stand for four days and his testimony proves the existence of the most infamous, cowardly and diabolical secret society of murderers of which I have ever heard of in a civilized country.

His testimony will be followed by the confessions of one of the guilty parties who has turned States Evidence & will be corroborated by so many independent facts & circumstances as to make the case an impregnable one. If you will read the testimony or have it read to you will find that the true character of the detective became known through Father O'Conner who in his eagerness to save young men from joining the secret society of thugs, warned them publicly from his pulpit of the true character of our officer -- & you will also see how easily some of the worst men of the order deceive & ingratiate themselves with, the priests by reading in the testimony that Father O'Conner who has behaved so well, and done so much to break up the order, was in communication with Jack Kehoe & gave the latter the information about the detective which led Kehoe to attempt to have him assassinated, & which forced him to withdraw from the County.

It seems to me that the Lord is on our side, for if it had not been for Father O'Conner we could never have had the success we are now meeting with in our efforts to crush out this society.

When our detective understood his mission he was promised that he should never become a witness, or be known in his true character -- & had it not been for Father O'Conner making his mission known we could not have used him as a witness -- but when his true character was discovered there was no longer any object in secrecy & by using his testimony we have been enabled to arrest all the leaders of the organization except those who ran away when Kerrigan turned informer & we will undoubtedly be able to break up the whole society. I know you will rejoice at this & I would be under many obligations to you if you would urge the priests in the county to take advantage of the present opportunities to denounce the association & to save other innocent young men from joining it.

Very Sincerely -- F. B. Gowen

In a letter three days later, Gowen asked the archbishop to allow him to state publicly that the bishop wanted the "Mollies" (AOH) destroyed and to direct the pastors from churches in Lansford and Tamaqua to go to the Pottsville trial and try some silent persuasion on their Irish women parishioners:

Phila May 14, 1876

My Dear Sir,

As I am now so constantly engaged at Pottsville, and as I must return to that place tomorrow morning at six o'clock, I took the liberty of calling upon you today to say that Father O'Conner was upon the witness stand yesterday at his own & my request & that in my speech to the Jury I will fully vindicate him upon any intentional association with the Molly Maguires. To do this effectually however & to put at rest all suspicions as to his position & that of the Church I would like to have your permission to state publicly that you have been for some time cognizant of the means I had taken to break up the association of Molly Maguires & that you had most earnestly desired to destroy and disperse their organization.

There is another matter of grave importance to which I desire to call your attention. We know from our detectives who have been among the friends of the prisoners that arrangements have been made to procure quite a number of people including many women, to swear to an ***alibi*** *which is of course entirely false & which if sworn to in court, will inevitably lead to the arrest & punishment of these poor misguided women for perjury. It has struck me that possibly the presence in court of the parish priests known to these women as their pastors might have some restraining influence upon them, & prevent the commission of a high crime which must necessarily be followed by punishment. These witnesses are from the mining town of Lansford or Storm Hill near Summit Hill, midway between Tamaqua & Mauch Chunk -- & if you take the same view of this case that I do & see no objections to what I suggest I would be much obliged to you if you would telegraph the priest of the parish in which Lansford is situated, as well as the priest of Tamaqua to go to Pottsville tomorrow and report to me there in the court house.*

Believe me my dear Archbishop -- that I make this suggestion entirely to preserve the ends of Justice and to prevent unthinking people committing a heinous crime. I will be obliged to you if you will drop me a line in answer to this directed to Pottsville.

With great respect
Very Truly Your Friend
Most Rev. James F. Wood D.D.

Franklin B. Gowen

On May 16, 1876 Gowen again wrote to the Archbishop thanking him for sending the priests but lamenting the fact that the women testified anyway:

Philadelphia & Reading Rail Road Co.
Philad. May 16th 1876

Most Rev. James F. Wood, D.D.

My dear sir,

I am very much obliged to you for your favor of 14th inst., which I received yesterday.

Father Brehoney and Father McEnroe have both been in court today, but I regret to say that their presence has not had the effect of restraining three or four witnesses from testifying to an alibi, in the case of one of the prisoners, who, beyond any peradventure, was one of the guilty agents in the commission of the murder.

With great respect,
Yours very truly,

Franklin B. Gowen
Prest.

The lethal core of Gowen's master plan was the use of an informer. Gowen was convinced that the best way to destroy the AOH was by hiring a private detective who would join the organization, learn its secrets and gather enough evidence to hang its leaders. In October of 1873, he arranged with Pinkerton's National Detective Agency to have one of its detectives infiltrate the Schuylkill County AOH organizations and obtain evidence which would implicate its leaders in crime. This agency had gained a reputation for being the most powerful organization in the United States for catching criminals. In his first meeting with Allan Pinkerton, the head of the agency, Gowen laid out his undercover plan and denounced the "Mollies":

> *The coal regions are infested by a most desperate class of men, banded together for the worst purposes -- called by some, the Buckshots, by others the Mollie Maguires -- and they are making havoc with the country. It is a secret organization, has its meetings in hidden and out-of-the-way places, and its members, I have been convinced ever since my residence in Pottsville and my connection with the criminal courts as District Attorney in the county of Schuylkill, are guilty of a majority of all the murders and other deeds of outrage which, for many years, have been committed in the neighborhood. I wish you to investigate this mysterious order, find out its interior workings, expose its evil transactions, and see if the just laws of the State cannot again be made effective in bringing criminals to justice. At present, whenever an assassination is consummated, and, as a consequence, a trial is instituted, a convenient alibi steps forward and secures for the prisoner his freedom. Municipal laws are thus incapable of execution; sheriffs of counties are powerless, and the usual run of detectives are of as little value as the open, uniformed police of the different cities. All of these have been tested, and all have failed.*[95]

Pinkerton selected one of his top detectives, James McParlan, a twenty-eight-year-old Irishman, to be the "mole." He assured McParlan that he would never have to take the witness stand and testify. Within six months, using the name James McKenna, McParlan became a member of the Shenandoah division of the Hibernians and began his undercover work as a labor spy.

Gowen's media-church strategy to exalt himself and excite public opinion against the Hibernians proved successful. The *Mauch Chunk Democrat*, the *Carbon Advocate*, the *Weekly Intelligencer* and the *Mauch Chunk Coal Gazette* regularly denounced the members of the Ancient Order of Hibernians as terrorists and "Mollies."[96] By 1876, even the prestigious *New York Times* was connecting any violence in the hard coal regions to "the notorious Mollie Maguires." Public perception that the Irish were untrustworthy and dangerous was epidemic. In three short years, Gowen had also transformed himself in the minds of Reading Company stockholders and average citizens from a financial plunderer to a law-and-order hero---and a man to be trusted.

---

[95]Pinkerton, Allan. *The Molly Maguires and the Detectives*. New York: 1877, pp. 13-14.

[96]*Mauch Chunk Democrat*: 4/6/76, 4/8/76, 2/19/76, 6/30/76; *Carbon Advocate*: 6/18/77; *Weekly Intelligencer*: 2/17/76

Rear View of Courthouse II in 1876

And so it was in this heated, emotionally charged climate, stirred by the ill winds of racial and religious bias, labor violence and Gowen's propaganda campaign against the AOH, that Doyle, Kelly, Campbell, Donahue, McKenna and Fisher were brought to trial in 1876. The battle lines were clearly drawn -- capital against labor, Republicans against Democrats, immigrants against native born Americans, employers against employees, Protestants against Catholics, the haves against the have-nots. For the news media, the Carbon County courtroom had become an Armageddon between the forces of good and evil. They came face to face in a life and death engagement.

Asa Packer

Looming sphinx-like and powerful in his elegant Victorian mansion on the hill above the courthouse where the trials were to be played out was Carbon County's wealthiest and most prominent citizen -- Asa Packer. In 1868, the Pennsylvania Delegate gave him its vote for President at the National Democratic Convention. In 1869, he opposed Republican John White Geary in a spirited campaign for the governorship of Pennsylvania and lost by a narrow margin. His company built the stately red brick Lehigh Valley Railroad Building (now called the Navigation Building) directly across from the courthouse and several other large commercial buildings on Broadway. He was by far the largest taxpayer in Mauch Chunk. For the three-year period from 1866 through 1868, the Borough of Mauch Chunk levied taxes totalling $189,987. Asa Packer himself paid $127,750 in taxes or sixty-eight percent of the total tax levy.[97] He owned several coal mine operations along the Nesquehoning Creek, and by 1855 he had completed construction of his forty-six mile Lehigh Valley Railroad line from Mauch Chunk to Easton. The success of Packer's railroad, whose construction had brought him to the brink of bankruptcy, depended on a continuous flow of coal from the mines. The strikes not only closed down the mines but also shut down his railroad's most profitable business.

It would be naive to assume that Asa Packer, the man who almost single-handedly brought Carbon County into existence, remained a passive observer while serious economic losses threatened his enterprises. As surely as Gowen, he recognized that the conviction and execution of these men could go a long way to stifle the miners' propensity to strike. His role in the "Mollie" trials was secret, subtle, but stunning in its impact. As the trials began, a prosecution team closely tied to Packer suddenly emerged to represent the Commonwealth.

[97] *Carbon Democrat*. September 18, 1869.

Allen Craig, Packer's personal attorney and chief counsel for his Lehigh Valley Railroad was the prosecutor's expert on the law. Craig had served as Carbon County's district attorney for three years in the late 1850s. General Charles Albright and William G. Freyman, his law partner, also appeared. Albright, Carbon County's highest ranking soldier and hero of the Civil War, was a close friend of Packer and chief counsel for the Lehigh and Wilkes Barre Coal Company. Crafty, energetic, with a dynamic presence, he was the chief architect of the Commonwealth's cases against the defendants and was the lead prosecutor. Dressed in his Union Army uniform with full regalia, including sword, he would stride up and down in the front of the jury box during the trials as though he were leading a charge at Antietam. Frank W. Hughes of Pottsville, chief counsel of the Reading Railroad, was sent to Carbon County by Franklin Gowen as his personal representative on the prosecution team. Hughes was sixty-three years of age, had been Attorney General of the Commonwealth, district attorney of Schuylkill County for twelve years and had also served in Congress. His massive head covered with white locks of hair and sharp piercing eyes made him a striking presence in the courtroom.

It was not unusual at this time for lawyers who represented a victim's family to assist the district attorney in trying the case against the defendant. There were no previous cases, however, where lawyers for the victim completely took over the prosecution. There can be little question as to why they did so. Siewers was a young and inexperienced district attorney. Admitted to the Carbon Bar just two years before the trials began, he had not done well in the only three first degree murder cases which he prosecuted. In *Commonwealth v. Eckley Farrow*[98] and *Commonwealth v. William Gouldstraw,*[99] tried in 1874, the defendants were found not guilty by Carbon juries. In *Commonwealth v. Neal Paul,*[100] the jury returned a reduced verdict of guilty of voluntary manslaughter. Franklin Gowen and Asa Packer surely did not want the most important criminal cases in the history of their counties to be left in the hands of a questionable prosecutor. Gowen was already preparing to try several "Mollie" cases in Schuylkill County, but it is clear that he was choreographing the death dance that would lead the "Mollies" to the gallows in Carbon County The *Democrat* and the *Gazette* during this period contained "insider" reports of many train trips to Pottsville and Philadelphia by General Albright and District Attorney Siewers. It is reasonable to infer that they were having frequent strategy sessions with Gowen about how to try the cases in Carbon, how to handle the anticipated "alibi" defense, and which case should be tried first. The Lehigh and Wilkes Barre Coal Company

---

[98]25 January Term 1875.

[99]8 January Term 1875.

[100]13 March Term 1874.

Alexander Campbell on trial in the Carbon County Courtroom. Edward Fox (with hand raised) cross examines James "Powderkeg" Kerrigan. Sitting at defense counsel table (left to right) Daniel Kalbfus, Fox, Edward Mulhearn and defendant Alex Campbell. At prosecutors' table (left to right) Frank Hughes, Edward R. Siewers, General Charles Albright and Allen Craig. Presiding is Judge Samuel Dreher flanked by Associate Judges Levi Wentz, to his left and James Huston on the right.

Gen. Charles Albright

Defendant Alexander Campbell

The Hon. Samuel S. Dreher

Detective James McParlan

James "The Squealer" Kerrigan

announced that it would pay the legal fees for the corporate counsel prosecuting the cases because John P. Jones was employed by the company. Under the law, only the district attorney could appoint associate prosecutors. The trial transcripts clearly show that although Edward Siewers was present during the trials, his role was strictly a minor one. He argued some of the pretrial motions and made some of the opening statements. Albright was the chief prosecutor, and Craig and Hughes were in the first and second chairs for the prosecution.

Lin Bartholomew of Pottsville was lead defense counsel for Doyle and Kelly. Forty-two years of age, he was well known throughout the Commonwealth for his eloquence. He had tried seventy-seven homicide cases during his eighteen years of practicing law. John W. Ryon, a former district attorney of Tioga County and one of Pottsville's leading trial lawyers, and young U. S. Congressman James B. Reilly, a former district attorney of Schuylkill County, assisted Bartholomew. The *Mauch Chunk Coal Gazette* described the Pottsville defense team:

> *Mr. Ryon is a man of medium height. His face is of the round English pattern, and it is covered with short bristling iron gray whiskers. He has a full, resonant voice which is very powerful. At first sight one would take Mr. Ryon for a heavy, dull lawyer, but it would be a great mistake. He is as droll as he looks solemn, and he adds greatly to the effect of his sharp, dryly pungent thrusts by the grave manner of his delivery.*
>
> *Mr. Reilly has the reputation of being one of Pennsylvania's handsomest congressmen. He is a brilliant young lawyer and a fluent talker.*

Carbon County lawyers Daniel Kalbfus and Edward Mulhearn of Mauch Chunk also lined up for the Doyle defense. Prominent in Democratic Party politics, passionate and mercurial, Kalbfus had gained considerable recognition as a successful criminal defense lawyer in the *Paul* and *Gouldstraw* murder cases and as a fiery orator. As the trials began, he was already being heralded as his party's candidate for Congress. Young Edward Mulhearn had studied law in Kalbfus' office and was just admitted to the bar in 1873. As the only local Irish Catholic who made it to the bar, he enjoyed the confidence of the Irish population. Mulhearn was yet untested in any major trials. The Carbon and Schuylkill AOH chapters had raised a defense fund for Doyle and Kelly and the funds were given to the families of Doyle and Kelly to retain the best legal talent available. After their convictions, however, defense funds quickly dried up and the other defendants were left to fend for themselves. Alexander Campbell retained the services of Edward J. Fox of Easton and Kalbfus and Mulhearn with his own funds. Edward J. Fox was widely known as a skilled trial lawyer with a golden tongue. He had already tried many important cases throughout eastern Pennsylvania and in the courts of Philadelphia. McKenna and Fisher, through friends and relatives, raised the money to hire Fox and Ryon. By the time Donahue appeared before the court for trial, he told the court he had no funds to hire a lawyer.

Judge Dreher appointed four young and inexperienced Carbon lawyers to represent him: Frederick Bertolette, P. J. Meehan, James S. Loose and William M. Rapsher.

Presiding over the trials was the popular fifty-two-year-old President Judge Samuel S. Dreher. In his sixth year on the Bench of Carbon and Monroe counties, he had been elected without opposition, a rare compliment in a district where partisan politics was very strong. A resident of Stroudsburg in Monroe County where he was once district attorney, Dreher was trying his first capital cases in the glare of the national press. Deliberate and dignified, he ran a taut courtroom but made a point of being polite and courteous to counsel and litigants. His patience appeared limitless as he allowed lawyers to argue their positions at length and often to the point of exhaustion, a practice common among the lawyers of the times.

Months before the trials began, however, a process had been carried out in secret which would have a much greater impact on the defendants' guilt or innocence than the judge or the lawyers or the evidence presented in the courtroom. In October of 1875, a pool of jurors had been selected for the "Mollie" trials in a way which violated their constitutional rights to a jury of their peers. Subtly but surely, the scales of justice had already been tipped against them.

Composition of the Jury Array

In the 1870s, Pennsylvania Legislative Act No. 41 of April 10, 1867 required that all juries -- petit, traverse and grand -- be selected from the county voter lists by two (2) jury commissioners and the president judge or a majority of them. In actual practice, it was the two (2) jury commissioners who did the selecting. Six-hundred (600) names, apportioned among the county election districts, were required to be placed into the jury wheel. Since women did not yet have the right to vote, only men served on juries. The names and addresses of the jurors placed in the "wheel" were given to the local newspapers for publication.

Because voter registration lists were kept in the offices of the local tax assessor, the jury commissioners could not, without great effort, obtain these voter lists. It was the customary practice for the jury commissioners to ask their friends, relatives, and political committee people living in different parts of the county to give them the names of about sixty (60) men whom they believed would make good jurymen. Using these lists, the two (2) jury commissioners would meet in the courthouse, be sworn and then alternately select jurors for the annual pool of jurors called the "array." The jurors' names were written upon separate slips of paper, folded and placed in a cylindrical box called a "jury wheel." The sheriff was the official custodian of the key to this "wheel." Before each term of court, the judge would tell the jury commissioners how many jurors were needed for the case or cases to be tried. Two (2) jury commissioners then drew from the "wheel" the names of those who were to serve as jurors for the following court term and these jurors were then subpoenaed to appear by the sheriff.[101]

THE JURY WHEEL

On October 23, 1875, Judge Dreher initiated this selection process for the "Mollie" trials by ordering the jury commissioners to select six-hundred (600) "sober, intelligent and judicious persons" as grand and petit jurors. In the middle of November 1875, Jury Commissioners A. D. Christman and Charles Lentz selected the six-hundred (600) jurors. Their names, address and occupation appear in the official court venire list for 1876 and are reproduced as **Exhibit 1** to this chapter at pages 326 to 345. Judge Dreher directed that none of the jurors' names be published in the local newspapers because "murder cases would be on the trial list."

We have examined each name in the 1876 jury pool to find out the origin of the family name. The naturalization and immigration records for Carbon County, which contains birth information on all foreign born citizens, were searched to see if any of the six-hundred (600) jurors, or the forty (40) additional jurors brought in for the *Doyle* trial (See **Exhibit 1A**, pages 346 to 347), appear in those records as foreign born and if so, whether they were Irish born. The U.S. Census reports of 1870 and 1880 were also reviewed and

[101]Wagner, Charles. History, Government and Geography of Carbon County. Pennsylvania: 1910.

analyzed to determine if any of the surnames on the jury array were descendants of Irish immigrants or were Irish immigrants. Because of the difficulty in determining from the census reports whether a particular name was Irish or Scottish, a cross-check was made by looking up the surname of each juror and identifying his ancestry.[99] If there was a question about whether the juror's ancestry was Scottish or Irish, we determined the juror's residence and occupation from the jury list. The juror was then classified as Scottish or Irish based on the assumption that the Irish lived in the mining towns of the county and were laborers in the mines.

Astonishingly, this analysis revealed that, of the six-hundred and forty (640) prospective jurors selected by the jury commissioners, only two (2) prospective jurors were Irish: Dominick McFadden and John R. McGinley. The Irish representation on the 1876 jury array was less than one percent (1%) or thirty-one hundredths percent (.31%) of the total number selected. As we have previously noted, the Irish made up thirteen percent (13%) of the county population. On its face, the 1876 jury array showed a selective limitation of Irishmen on the juries which would try the "Mollie" cases.

Although the defense made several motions to quash the array of jurors, none addressed the purposeful or deliberate limitation of Irishmen in the jury pool. Even if this issue had been raised at that time, there was no case law or statutory law prohibiting this shameful practice.

Today, the selection procedures would not pass constitutional muster. Both the Federal and the Pennsylvania Constitution guarantee the accused the right of trial by his peers. U.S. Const., Amend.VI; Pa. Const., Art.II Sec.9. It has long been the law of this land that a defendant in a criminal case is not constitutionally entitled to demand a proportionate number of his race, sex, religion or national origin in the jury pool or on the jury which tries him. But, in *Williams v. Florida*, 399 U.S. 78, 100, 90 S.Ct. 1893, 1906 (1970) the Supreme Court of the United States held that the Sixth Amendment's guarantee of trial by jury encompasses the "fair possibility for obtaining [on the jury] a representative cross section of the community." The court later said that a criminal defendant had the burden of proof on this issue and to make out a prima facie case of a discriminatory jury selection process which violates the Sixth Amendment, the defendant must establish two factors: (1) a statistical improbability of inclusion of a particular segment of the community and (2) an inherently non-neutral, i.e. discriminatory selection procedure. See *Alexander v. Louisiana*, 405 U.S. 625, 92 S.Ct. 1221 (1972). The Pennsylvania Supreme Court adopted similar guidelines when it spelled out the evidence necessary to establish a prima facie case of purposeful discrimination in jury selection:

---

[99]Hanks, Patrick and Flavia Hodges. *A Dictionary of Surnames*. New York: Oxford University Press, 1988; Smith, Elsdon C. *New Dictionary of American Family Names*. New York: Harper & Row, 1973.

> *The facts must provide evidence indicating either that the procedures as designed or implemented are likely to result in juries unrepresentative of a cross-section of the community, or that the procedures have in fact continuously failed to represent certain identifiable population groups over a period of time. These are facts concerning the proportion of the county's population represented by various specified population groups . . . . the frequency with which persons from these groups appear on the jury lists, and the methods by which these lists are selected (See* ***Commonwealth v. Butler****, 448 Pa. 128, 291 A.2d 89 (1972); see also* ***Commonwealth v. Martin****, 465 Pa. 134, 348 A.2d 391 (1975)).*

In 1980, the Pennsylvania Legislature acknowledged the importance of this case law when it declared:

> *It is the policy of this Commonwealth that:*
>
> > *(1) All persons entitled to a jury trial in a civil action or criminal proceeding shall have the right to jurors selected at random from a representative cross section of the eligible population of the county.*
> >
> > *(2) All qualified citizens shall have the opportunity to be considered for service as jurors in the courts of this Commonwealth and shall have an obligation to serve as jurors when summoned for that purpose.*
> >
> > *(3) A citizen shall not be excluded from service as a juror on the basis of race, color, religion, sex, national origin or economic status.*
> >
> > *1980, June 26, P.L. 266, No. 78, Sec. 3, imd. effective.*

The case law of *Alexander* and *Butler* would permit the defendants to easily establish, at a pretrial hearing, a prima facie claim of purposeful discrimination in the Carbon County jury selection process:

(1) The United States Census report of 1870 would show that the Irish made up thirteen percent (13%) of the total population of Carbon County.

(2) The jury commissioners could be subpoenaed to court to testify as to their usual practice of using friends, relatives and political allies to supply them with names of prospective jurors rather than randomly selecting them from voter lists as the law required. Because it was a matter of common knowledge that the Irish lived exclusively in the mining communities of Mauch Chunk, Lausanne, and Banks Township, this selection practice

provided the jury commissioners with a clear and easy opportunity to exclude the Irish from the jury pool by simply not taking any lists of names from those areas. This procedure also made it possible for the jury commissioners to examine the names on the lists sent to them and exclude or limit those with an Irish surname. Since the Irish were all Catholics and the rest of the county Protestant, the jury commissioners were also able to discriminate, in the selection process, on the basis of religion. The most pernicious part of the process was that the selection of both the jury pools and the jury panels took place in secret. The system was an open invitation for the jury commissioners to practice discrimination and the record shows that they did.

(3) The following statistical survey of the jury arrays selected in Carbon County from 1865 to 1875 could be produced and show that for ten years Carbon County juries were not truly representative of a cross section of the community because of the limitation on the number of Irish jurors.

1865-1875 Survey of Carbon Jury Arrays by National Origin

Year	Jury Array	Irish Jurors	Scots-Irish/ Scots Jurors	English/ Welsh Jurors	Penna. Dutch/ German Jurors	French/ Other Jurors
1865	335	11 (3.28%)	24 (7.16%)	74 (22.09%)	219 (65.37%)	7 (2.09%)
1866	444	7 (1.58%)	40 (9.01%)	101 (22.75%)	280 (63.06%)	16 (3.60%)
1867	372	18 (4.84%)	30 (8.06%)	78 (20.97%)	238 (63.98%)	8 (2.15%)
1868	252	16 (6.35%)	29 (11.51%)	63 (25.00%)	138 (54.76%)	6 (2.38%)
1869	288	11 (3.82%)	19 (6.60%)	73 (25.35%)	177 (61.46%)	8 (2.78%)
1870	324	26 (8.02%)	35 (10.80%)	96 (29.63%)	160 (49.38%)	7 (2.16%)
1871	288	16 (5.56%)	21 (7.29%)	50 (17.36%)	197 (68.40%)	4 (1.39%)
1872	360	29 (8.06%)	25 (6.94%)	77 (21.39%)	223 (61.94%)	6 (1.67%)
1873	359	18 (5.01%)	34 (9.47%)	72 (20.06%)	231 (64.35%)	4 (1.11%)
1874	396	17 (4.29%)	35 (8.84%)	95 (23.99%)	240 (60.61%)	9 (2.27%)
1875	432	11 (2.55%)	40 (9.26%)	93 (21.53%)	280 (64.81%)	8 (1.85%)
Mean	350	16 (4.57%)	30 (8.57%)	79 (22.57%)	217 (62.00%)	8 (2.29%)

The mean average of the number of Irish jurors chosen for jury duty in the jury pools from 1865 to 1875 was sixteen (16), or a lowly four and fifty-seven hundredths percent (4.57%). Interestingly, this study also reveals that, although the English-Welsh population of the county was three and nine tenths percent (3.9%), English-Welsh surnamed jurors made up twenty two and fifty seven hundredths percent (22.57%) of those called to jury duty.

(4) A close analysis of the 1876 jury pool reveals further evidence of the discriminatory selection process. The following statistical survey taken from 1870 census data shows a breakdown of the county's population by municipality and by native and foreign born citizens. It also shows the breakdown of the 1876 jury array by municipality. It then compares the numbers and percentages of the prospective jurors with the numbers and percentages of each municipality's total population and foreign born population.

Comparison of 1870 Population and Foreign Population to 1876 Jury Array by Municipality

Municipality	Population	Population in percent	Foreign born pop.	Foreign born pop. in percent	Jurors from each municipality	% of jurors from each municipality
Banks Township	3982	14.15%	1759	44.17%	26	4.13%
East Penn Township	862	3.06%	21	2.44%	48	7.62%
Franklin Township	1912	6.79%	132	6.90%	67	10.63%
Weissport Borough	359	1.28%	36	10.03%	15	2.38%
Kidder Township	1417	5.03%	181	12.77%	27	4.29%
Lausanne Township	1416	5.03%	529	37.36%	6	.95%
Weatherly Borough	1076	3.82%	172	15.99%	39	6.19%
L. Towamensing Township	1552	5.51%	86	5.54%	56	8.89%
Mahoning Township	1589	5.65%	119	7.49%	55	8.73%
Lehighton Borough	1485	5.28%	142	9.56%	59	9.37%
Mauch Chunk Township	5210	18.51%	2029	38.94%	38	6.03%
East Mauch Chunk Borough	1585	5.63%	504	31.80%	26	4.13%
Mauch Chunk Borough	3841	13.65%	1089	28.35%	101	16.03%
Packer Township	441	1.57%	42	9.52%	12	1.90%
Penn Forest Township	504	1.79%	52	10.32%	20	3.17%
U. Towamensing Township	913	3.24%	71	7.78%	35	5.56%

This comparison shows that the two most populous municipalities, Mauch Chunk Township and Banks Township, where the Irish lived, were among the lowest in jurors selected for the pool. It is also clear from this comparison that while the jury commissioners were limiting their selection of jurors from Banks, Lausanne, Mauch Chunk Townships, the mining areas of the county, they were choosing most of the jurors from the business and agricultural areas. The comparison also shows that, except for Mauch Chunk Borough, the jury commissioners picked few jurors from those municipalities where there was a large foreign born population. The largest group of jurors came from Mauch Chunk Borough where most of the population either worked for the railroads or depended on the railroads for their livelihood. These jurors would be inclined to be pro-prosecution in cases which were being prosecuted by the leading railroad and coal company lawyers of Carbon County against defendants accused of killing coal mine bosses.

(5) The following nationality comparison of the 1876 jury pool shows that the jury selection process in 1875 was not neutral. Only two Irishmen, Dominick McFadden and John R. McGinley, were selected for the 1876 jury array. By limiting the number of Irishmen in the six-hundred (600) man jury pool to two (2), the odds against selecting an Irish juror for a panel were overwhelming. It is not surprising that of the two-hundred and eleven (211) jurors who were selected from the jury wheel for the panels of Doyle, Kelly, Campbell, Fisher, McKenna and Donahue, there was only one (1) Irishman. Of the seventy-two (72) jurors who were eventually seated, there was no Irishman among them.

Comparison of Nationality of 1876 Jury Array by Municipality

Municipality	Irish Jurors	Scots-Irish/ Scots Jurors	English/ Welsh Jurors	Penna. Dutch/ German Jurors	French/ Other Jurors
Banks Township	0	3	17	6	0
East Penn Township	0	2	1	41	3
Franklin Township	0	6	13	50	0
Weissport Borough	0	0	4	15	0
Kidder Township	0	4	7	16	0
Lausanne Township	0	0	2	4	0
Weatherly Borough	0	4	8	27	0
L. Towamensing Township	0	4	3	48	1
Mahoning Township	0	3	9	61	0
Lehighton Borough	0	1	7	36	0
Mauch Chunk Township	0	2	13	23	1
East Mauch Chunk Borough	0	1	8	17	0
Mauch Chunk Borough	2	7	39	51	3
Packer Township	0	0	5	7	0
Penn Forest Township	0	0	0	20	0
U. Towamensing Township	0	1	1	33	0
Totals	2	38	137	455	8
Totals in Percent	(.31%)	(5.94%)	(21.41%)	(71.09%)	(1.25%)

In summary, the body of evidence convincingly shows that, in the jury selection procedures which were in effect in 1876 and for many years before, the jury commissioners of Carbon County were aware of the national origin, religion and political affiliation of the persons whose names were on the lists used to pick jurors and that they had the opportunity to select potential jurors on the basis of such characteristics and affiliations. Such a procedure was discriminatory in nature. The evidence also demonstrates that this jury selection process as implemented by the jury commissioners continuously failed to produce a representative cross section of the Irish community, and in 1876 produced virtually no representation of the Irish community. Clearly, this would be more than sufficient evidence to establish a case of invidious discrimination in the jury selection process. The trial judge today would have to quash the jury array.

If the trial court failed to do so, an appellate court, having the benefit of this evidence and the undisputed fact that not one (1) Irishman was on any of the six (6) juries would find that the defendants did not have the fair possibility for obtaining on their juries a representative cross section of the Irish community and would set aside their convictions.

Motion to Quash Array of Petit Jurors

Two identical defense motions, a Motion to Quash the Indictment and a Motion to Quash the Array of Jurors, were filed in all defendants' cases. The motions claimed that the jury commissioners were not sworn, "as the Act of the 10th of April 1867 prescribed," before they selected the grand jurors and the petit (criminal) jurors.

The 1867 law required jury commissioners to take and subscribe an official oath before selecting the jury array. Failure to do so made the jury selection fatally defective.

Official court documents revealed that Jury Commissioners A. D. Christman, Charles Lentz and Sheriff Oliver Breneiser, took their official oaths and subscribed their names before Clerk of Courts Kemmerer on *November 17, 1875*. The certified list of jurors selected for 1876 filed in the clerk's office by the jury commissioners, however, showed that the jury commissioners selected the jurors on *November 16, 17, 18 and 19, 1875*. On its face, the record showed that the jury commissioners were sworn after jury selection had begun, and the jury selection was not according to the law.

Judge Dreher decided to conduct a hearing on the defense motions and let the Commonwealth explain this defect in the jury selection. At a brief hearing on June 20, James Dinkey, clerk to the jury commissioners, testified that although he and the jury commissioners met to select jurors on November 16, he thought they did not write any names on the ballots until the morning of November 17, 1875 between 8:00 A.M. and 11:00 A.M. and did not place any names in the jury wheel until November 18 and 19. He could not remember what time on the 17th the jury commissioners actually began to write the names on the ballots. Sheriff Breneiser testified that he thought that the oath was administered to him and the jury commissioners on the afternoon of November 17. Neither the jury commissioners, nor the Clerk of Courts Kemmerer testified, a fact which the Supreme Court of Pennsylvania found worthy of note. Defendants' motion placed Judge Dreher on the horns of a dilemma. If he granted the motion to quash the jury array, no trials could be held in 1876 because there would be no jurors and obtaining a new venire of six-hundred (600) jurors on an emergency basis was fraught with legal problems. On the other hand, there was no evidence that the jury commissioners were sworn before November 17, and names were being written on ballots during the morning of November 17. Neither Dinkey nor Sheriff Breneiser had any clear recollection of when the oath was taken. Both "thought" what they testified to was correct.

Judge Dreher resolved the dilemma by making a legal conclusion which ignored the evidence and defied logic. Finding that everything which was done on November 16 was "preliminary," Judge Dreher ruled, in a written opinion, that "no actual selection of names was made until after the oath was administered and subscribed," and denied both motions.

His opinion completely ignored the conflicts and inherent weaknesses in the witnesses' testimony. Nor did he even mention the official court documents before him, or the curious fact that the jury commissioners, who could have given the most reliable evidence about when they took their oath, did not testify. The facts before him clearly showed that the jury commissioners were picking names for the jury pool for a full day before they took the oath. So he interpreted the law to suit the facts before him by holding that jury selection does not begin until the juror's name is written on the ballot. Judge Dreher made the only finding which would make the jury selection legal and more important would permit the trials to go on.

When this point was raised on appeal, the Supreme Court of Pennsylvania, although it noted the failure of the jury commissioners to testify and expressed reservations about the credibility of the witnesses, deferred, as usual, to the factual findings of the trial judge who saw and heard the witnesses and affirmed Judge Dreher's ruling on the Motions in *Campbell v. Commonwealth*, 84 Pa. 187 (1877).

Motion for Change of Venue

On January 16, 1876, Doyle, Kelly and Kerrigan, shackled and guarded by a detachment of Coal and Iron Police, were brought into a packed Carbon County courtroom for trial. No sooner had Judge Dreher and his associate judges taken their seats than Attorneys James B. Reilly and Lin Bartholomew rose to their feet and informed the court that they wished to present, on behalf of the three (3) prisoners, a petition for a change of venue to move their cases to another county.[103]

The petition alleged that such "undue excitement" existed in the county against the defendants that they could not get a fair trial; that the jail was surrounded by armed guards to protect them from an "excited populace"; that because of certain inflammatory articles appearing in the newspapers of Carbon County, there was so great a prejudice against them as to render it impossible for them to get a fair trial; that the Lehigh and Wilkes Barre Coal and Iron Company, the Philadelphia and Reading Railroad Company and

[103]On October 19, 1875, the defendants presented to the court similar applications which were denied. Campbell, Donahue, Fisher and McKenna all filed petitions for change of venue at the time their cases were called to trial.

others had formed a conspiracy to secure convictions and were expending large sums of money to secure their conviction; that the private counsel retained to assist the district attorney were employed by these companies and these lawyers had employed special police who were "working up" the prosecution against them; that these lawyers had secured free trips on the railroads for witnesses who would testify against them; that these companies had large and extensive operations in the county, a large number of the Carbon County work force is directly or indirectly dependent on these companies, and a number of the jurors on the panel worked for these companies; and that the totality of these circumstances would prevent them from getting a fair trial.

Reilly presented to the court written certifications from local defense attorneys Daniel Kalbfus and Edward Mulhearn that they believed the defendants could not get a fair trial in Carbon County. He read a number of excerpts from the *Mauch Chunk Democrat* and *Coal Gazette* to show that excitement in the county over the Jones murder had reached a fever pitch and that there was palpable prejudice against the defendants. Reilly argued that these were exactly the kind of cases to which the new change of venue statute applied.

District Attorney Siewers had filed a written answer to the Venue Petition in which he denied all defendants' allegations as "false and unfounded." Siewers admitted that the jail was armed but disingenuously alleged that it was to prevent a rescue of the prisoners, not to preserve their lives from an excited populace. He alleged that there was no popular uprising against the prisoners; that the Lehigh and Wilkes Barre Coal Company had "pushed" the prisoners no more than was necessary. The Commonwealth's attorneys also handed up to the court several "certificates": (1) W. D. Zehner, superintendent of the Lehigh and Wilkes Barre Coal Company wrote that there was no combination by his company against defendants; (2) Sheriff Oliver Breneiser stated that Coal and Iron Police were at the jail to prevent rescue of prisoners; (3) thirty (30) citizens from Mauch Chunk signed a certificate over the following statements:

> *We desire to give it for our opinion from an intimate knowledge of the people of the county that there is no such undue excitement or prejudice in the county, or combination of influential persons or confrontation against the defendants above named or will prevent them from having a perfectly fair and impartial trial.*
>
> *We further express it for our conviction that nothing published in the newspapers of the county has so affected the minds of the public or will prevent the defendants from having a fair and impartial trial;*

and (4) Allen Craig and General Albright swore that no prejudice against defendants existed in the community and, in their opinion, defendants could get a fair trial.

General Albright responded by arguing (1) that it was not unusual for newspapers to report extensively on a murder and the jurors should not be "condemned" for reading the press reports, (2) that the law guarantees the defendants a fair trial, (3) that the best evidence that law and order prevail in Carbon County is the presence of the defendants in court and that they have not been harmed throughout all the excitement, and (4) the widespread newspaper coverage would likely influence jurors in other counties.

Bartholomew, Kalbfus and Reilly presented lengthy and forceful arguments that the newspaper articles, which they read to the court, connecting the defendants with the "Mollie Maguires" and a series of killings in the coal regions reflected public opinion; that the defense's allegations that the Lehigh and Wilkes Barre Coal Company retained the prosecutors had gone unrefuted and proved that there was a combination against them; that eight (8) of the jurors on the panel were from Summit Hill and worked for the coal company; that the defendants could not get a fair trial in any county which produced anthracite coal; and that the newspaper reports that peace was restored in Carbon County really showed that "we are sitting on a volcano in this county."

Albright countered by contending that only jury selection would show whether a fair jury could be obtained. Showing his failure to grasp the issue, Siewers argued that the defense read extracts from only local newspapers which he admitted were sensational; that he could bring into court city newspapers which were in favor of fair and impartial trials. Allen Craig pointed out that the court must be satisfied that the defense allegations are true and defendants have the burden of proof.

After a noon recess, Judge Dreher announced the court's decision in a one line sentence: "After due consideration of the motion the court finds insufficient evidence to order a change of venue and denies the motion." As we shall demonstrate, this ruling completely ignored the law and the evidence.

Under the law which controlled these proceedings in 1876 it would be difficult to imagine more compelling cases for removal than those of *Doyle*, *Kelly*, *Campbell*, *Donahue*, *McKenna* and *Fisher*.

On March 18, 1875, Governor Hartranft had signed into law Pennsylvania's first change of venue statute. Act 34 of the Session of 1875 provided that

> *in criminal prosecutions, the venue may be changed, on application of the defendant or defendants in the following cases. . . . Second: When, upon the application of the defendant in a felony, it is made to appear to the satisfaction of the court, that from undue excitement against the prisoner, in the County where the offense was committed, a fair trial cannot be had or that there exists*

> *in that County so great a prejudice against him that he cannot obtain a fair trial, or that there is a combination against him, instigated by influential persons, by reason of which he cannot obtain a fair trial.*

By its use of the words "venue may be changed" and "made to appear to the satisfaction of the Court," this act gave the court broad discretion in deciding whether to move the case to another county. Therefore, the standard to be applied in any appellate review of Judge Dreher's decision is whether there was a clear abuse of discretion. When a court fails to consider unrefuted credible evidence in making findings of fact, it abuses its discretion.

There was substantial evidence right in the courtroom that a coordinated, well-planned effort had been mounted against the defendants by influential persons which would prevent a fair trial. District Attorney Siewers had relinquished his authority and permitted non-elected private corporate lawyers to prosecute the defendants. Albright, Craig and Hughes were chief counsel for the leading mining and railroad interests in the hard coal region. It was widely known and unrefuted in the change of venue proceedings that the investigation and prosecution were being financed by the Lehigh and Wilkes Barre Coal Company. Not only did this company pay the prosecutors, but also transported their witnesses to the courthouse. The court could also see, if it looked about, that the community was emotionally stirred, and that there were intense feelings against the defendants. Capacity crowds filled the courtroom for every trial. The defendants were being closely guarded by Coal and Iron Police while they were in the courtroom. Moreover, Coal and Iron Police surrounded the jail and marched up and down the main street in Mauch Chunk. Cannons had been strategically placed around the jail. Judge Dreher and the two lay judges closed their eyes and their minds to this salient evidence.

Additionally, the evidence presented to the court by the prosecution to refute the defense allegations was at best suspect and fanciful; at worst, it was pure fabrication. All of the "certificates" were signed by people who had a vital interest in the outcome of the trials. W. D. Zehner was the employer of the murder victim, John P. Jones. Allen Craig and General Albright were the leaders of the prosecution team. Incredibly, eighteen (18) of the thirty (30) people who signed the "citizens certificate" were members of the jury array who had already been summoned for the trials. All of the signers were from Mauch Chunk where hostility against the "Mollies" had transformed the community into an armed camp.

Seven (7) of the signers were selected as potential jurors during the trials and, when they were voir dired, directly contradicted their "certificates" that there was no bias in the community against the defendants,and had to be removed from the jury panels by defense challenges:

1) General William Lilly was a coal operator, congressman, and the county's most prominent citizen. In the *Kelly* case, he said he read the newspaper reports, attended the *Doyle* trial, and formed an opinion about the defendant.

2) Josiah Sandel, in the *Fisher/McKenna* case, indicated he was biased against the "Mollies."

3) Daniel G. Bertsch, in the *Kelly* case, said he had a fixed opinion about Kelly.

4) James Heberling was a prominent merchant and later an associate judge. In the *Fisher/McKenna* case, he said he had conversed about the evidence and expressed opinions against the "Mollies."

5) George W. Esser, in the *Donahue* case, admitted he had an opinion on the guilt of the prisoner which would require evidence to change.

6) Franklin Hazard, manager of the LC&N Company, was on the *Campbell I* case. He boasted that he had a strong opinion about the prisoner's guilt after reading "Kerrigan's Confession," and then publicly lamented, "There ought to be more hangings than there is."

7) James Belford, in the *Campbell I* case, told the court that he had read about the *Doyle* and *Kelly* cases and Kerrigan's Confession and formed an opinion about the prisoner's guilt.

Furthermore, the newspapers were reporting regularly that hostility toward the "Mollies" and fear and rumors had so permeated the community that additional security measures were being taken and citizens were ready to use deadly force.

The *Carbon Democrat* of February 19, 1876, under the headline "Rumors of War" reported on the tensions observed in Mauch Chunk:

> *During last evening considerable uneasiness was manifest on the streets, a report having gained currency that an attempt would be made by the "Mollies" to take Kerrigan from the jail. This would ordinarily be a difficult job; but it was stated that some of our most prominent citizens would be taken and held in front, so that if resistance was attempted they would be the first to fall. Whether or no such an idea was thought of we cannot say; but if so, and had such a bold, devilish scheme been carried into effect a terrible vengeance would have been exacted, as our citizens easily took the alarm and were prepared to support the authorities. An extra force of police was sent for, who remained on duty,*

> *throughout the night, and to-day such measures will be taken as will insure Kerrigan's safety.*

C. O. Ziegenfuss, a reporter for the *Bethlehem Daily Times*, who came to Mauch Chunk to report on the trial of Edward Kelly, observed in its April 3, 1876 edition that Mauch Chunk was filled with "minute men" and hostility towards the prisoners was escalating:

> *I have already alluded to the interest that each and every inhabitant of this place takes in this trial. Except an occasional beer and a little "penny ante," now and then, nothing will persuade them from their favorite topic -- the dreadful "Molly Maguires." All sorts of horrible things are imagined as possible to befall this magnificently located borough, and some of the experiences of a stranger here are exceedingly funny. In calling on friends, since our sojourn here, we have seen drawn from their hiding places complete arsenals of muskets, revolvers and ammunition. And they show you these articles only in strictest confidence -- and that to every friend that may chance to call. These stores of war implements, you are informed, sotto voce are kept on hand to repel the invasions of the "Molly Maguires." Your host is a*
>
> *"MINUTE MAN."*
>
> *And he feels the importance of the situation. In half an hour he can tell you more about the "Molly Maguires" and their terrible crimes than could Kerrigan and the whole gang in half a century. And your host will mean, and himself firmly believes, everything he tells you. But he is a good citizen, and means to protect the good name of his county and State. The arms and ammunition have been sent here upon the request of the citizens by the Governor. A majority of the prominent citizens of the town belong to the "minute men."*

The same reporter on March 31, 1876 came to the same conclusion as many other impartial observers:

> *Mauch Chunk is absorbed in the trial. Outside of it you hear nothing. The town and its people feel the importance of the occasion, and they will hear of nothing else.*

The court was also well aware that the cases before them were not ordinary homicides. The killings were committed during a time of great labor unrest and violence in the coal regions which the press repeatedly referred to as a "reign of terror." The defendants were miners. The victims were mine superintendents. Capital was arrayed against labor. The defendants had been labeled as "Mollies," a name which engendered fear and loathing in the heart of every non-Irish citizen in Carbon County. Sullen, hostile supporters on both sides vied for seats every time the courtroom doors opened. It strains credulity to the breaking point to believe that a fair and impartial trial could take place in a county where only a few months before citizens were threatening to lynch the defendants and armed, fearful Mauch Chunkers were poised to battle supporters of the defendants.

This evidence was more than sufficient to warrant a change of venue under the 1875 Statute. The court's failure to consider this evidence and move the case out of Carbon County was a clear abuse of discretion.[104] Incredibly, this issue was never raised on any appeal to the Supreme Court of Pennsylvania.

Change of Venue under Current Law

We now turn to an examination of the venue issue under the law today and based on the evidence available to the defense. Just as in 1876, current Pennsylvania law provides that the grant or refusal of a Motion for a Change of Venue is within the sound discretion of the court. Today, however, the moving party has the right to a hearing to show the prejudicial nature of pretrial publicity. *Commonwealth v. Casper*, 481 Pa. 143, 392 A.2d 287 (1978). Proof by affidavits will not suffice and is not permitted.

The constitutional standard of fairness requires that a defendant have a panel of impartial, indifferent jurors regardless of the malevolence of the crime or the strength of the case against the accused.[105] In a long line of Pennsylvania cases, it has been held that where jurors are exposed to evidence outside the judicial process by pretrial or trial reports and are prejudiced by it in reaching a verdict, the publicity itself may constitute a denial of due process.

In the ordinary case, one who claims he has been denied a fair trial because of prejudicial pretrial publicity must show actual prejudice in the empaneling of the jury to a degree that would render a fair trial impossible (See *Murphy v. Florida*, 421 U.S. 794, 95 S.Ct. 2031 (1975); *Commonwealth v. Rolison*, 473 Pa. 261, 374 A.2d 509 (1977)). This rule, however, is subject to an important exception. Where the pretrial publicity is inherently prejudicial, that is, it is sustained, pervasive, inflammatory, and inculpatory, then prejudice

---

[104]Ironically, some twenty five years later, Judge Horace Heydt although outvoted by two associate Judges, ruled that non union strike breaker defendants charged with killing an activist union mine leader could not get a fair jury in Carbon County because of the hostility between capital and labor. The Supreme Court of Pennsylvania reversed the decision of the two associate Judges and affirmed Judge Heydt's decision to move the cases out of Carbon County. Commonwealth v. Ronemus, 205 Pa. 420 (1903).

[105]Irvin v. Dowd, 366 U.S. at 722, 81 S.Ct. 1639, 6L.Ed 2d 751 (1961).

is presumed and defendant does not have the burden of establishing a nexus between the publicity and actual jury prejudice. *Commonwealth v. Frazier*, 471 Pa. 121, 369 A.2d 1224 (1977). If the publicity was inherently prejudicial, and if it saturated the community and if there was insufficient time for the community to cool down from the effects of the publicity, then a change of venue should be granted and if not a new trial is required. *Commonwealth v. Breakiron*, 524 Pa. 282, 571 A.2d 1035 (1990); Cert. denied, *Breakiron v. Pennsylvania*, 498 U.S. 881, 112 L.Ed 2d 179 (1990).

In the *Casper* case, the Pennsylvania Supreme Court laid out the factors that should be examined in order to determine whether material is inherently prejudicial:

> *. . . whether the pre-trial publicity was, on the one hand, factual and objective, or, on the other hand, consisted of sensational, inflammatory and "slanted articles demanding conviction,"* ***United States v. Sawyers****, 423 F.2d 1335, 1343 (4th Cir. 1970); whether the pre-trial publicity revealed the existence of the accused's prior criminal record; whether it referred to confessions, admissions or reenactments of the crime by the defendant; and whether such information is the product of reports by the police and prosecutorial officers. Should any of the above elements be found, the next step of the inquiry is to determine whether such publicity has been so extensive, so sustained and so pervasive that the community must be deemed to have been saturated with it. In this connection the size and character of the area concerned, and more particularly the pervasiveness of the media coverage in the community, warrant consideration.* *Commonwealth v. Casper, supra*, 481 Pa. at 152-53, 392 A.2d at 292 (footnotes omitted).

It must also be remembered that

> *[A] motion for change of venue . . . shall be granted whenever it is determined that because of the dissemination of potentially prejudicial material, there is a substantial likelihood that in the absence of such relief, a fair trial cannot be had. This determination may be based on such evidence as qualified public opinion surveys or opinion testimony offered by individuals, or in the Court's own evaluation of the nature, frequency, and timing of the material involved. A showing of actual prejudice shall not be required. ABA Standards Relating to Fair Trial and Free Press, supra*, at Std. 8-3.3(c) (2d ed. Approved draft, 1978). *Id.*, 481 Pa. at 153-54, 392 A.2d at 292-93.

Another important factor to consider in exercising the court's discretion to grant or deny a change of venue is how much "cooling off" time has passed from the peak of the publicity until the time of trial. *Commonwealth v. Nahodil*, 462 Pa. 301, 341 A.2d 91 (1975).

Inflammatory and Emotional Publicity

From arrest to trial, Carbon newspapers extensively covered every aspect of the defendants' cases. There were thirty-six large headlined newspapers articles which directly featured aspects of the cases. The bold headlines had to attract the attention of even the most casual reader of the newspaper. They immediately and directly called the defendants the killers of Jones and Powell.

All of the elements of inherently prejudicial material referred to in the *Casper* case appear in the pretrial publications of the "Mollie" cases.

First, it demanded conviction. At the time Doyle, Kelly, and Kerrigan were arrested in early September 1875, the *Mauch Chunk Gazette*, *The Carbon Advocate* and *Mauch Chunk Democrat*, and the *Weekly Intelligencer*, which were published once a week, carried similar reports on the Jones' murder. All four newspapers proclaimed that Doyle, Kelly and Kerrigan were the "ASSASSINS" and "MURDERERS" who killed Jones at the direction of the "Mollie Maguire" organization. They demanded swift conviction and execution.

Secondly, it was slanted. The *Mauch Chunk Democrat* of September 4, and September 11, 1875 gave detailed accounts of the Jones murder and the capture of the accused. It was the first county newspaper to describe them. Under the bold caption "The Murderers" the text left no doubt in the mind of the reader that they were criminal types:

> *Edward Kelly is a young man about 30 years of age, smooth face, florid complexion, reddish hair, and wore a black railroad cap. He hails from Schuylkill County and is unknown at Summit Hill.*
>
> *The principal, who is supposed to be the one who fired the fatal shot, gave his name as Michael Doyle, and his residence at Mt. Laffee, Schuylkill Co. He is about 28 years of age, a tall, heavy set fellow, dark moustache, and wears the countenance of a determined, villainous desperado. He wore a dark suit, no vest, white shirt with no collar.*
>
> *James Carrigan [sic], the smallest of the three, who did the signaling to get his comrades out of harm's way, is a repeated hard case from the vicinity of Tamaqua, where he has an unenviable reputation. He is quite small in stature, has small and ill-looking eyes, and a countenance that would be singled out in a crowd as that of a treacherous, cunning villain. His features are sharp, wears dark side whiskers, and appeared the most nervous of the three. He is older than a glance at him would indicate, evidently about 35 years of age.*

Thirdly, it was sensational and inflammatory. The *Democrat* reported that excited mobs tried to lynch the men as they were brought to jail in Mauch Chunk:

> *The men arrived via L.& S.R.R. at 6:30 guarded by a strong party of men armed to the teeth. The three prisoners were hand-cuffed together, and on being assisted from the open car, a procession was formed which was soon turned into a tumult of excited citizens, who, as the officers proceeded towards Squire Yeager's office, excitedly demanded that they be hung. The crowd in a moment increased to several hundred and shouts of "hang them" "lynch the scoundrels" greeted the prisoners, who, not withstanding the peril they were in, kept quite cool. The scene in front of the Squire's office on Broadway was exciting, the crowd demanding that they be lynched, while some of our prominent citizens appealed to the crowd to let the law take its course, which advice, backed by the carbines and drawn revolvers of the officers, was heeded, though it needed but a rope, and in a moment the three would have been dangling from the awning in front of the justice's office . . . .*
>
> *A cordon of policemen was formed about the prisoners and they were marched to the depot, followed by an immense and exciting throng who yelled "hang them," "hang them," and were it not for the officers surrounding and protecting them they would have been lynched. They were put on a flat car, hand-cuffed, the engine steaming off amid hideous yells. Nothing occurred until they arrived at Lansford, where fully five hundred people were awaiting the murderers to inflict summary vengeance upon them. Those in charge very prudently ran the train through without stopping to Mauch Chunk, where it not being generally known when they would arrive, not more than a hundred had gathered to see the desperados.*

Lehighton's only newspaper, the *Carbon Advocate*, in its bold September 11, 1875 headlines, pronounced the three suspects guilty of Jones' murder:

MURDER!

JOHN P. JONES SHOT DOWN IN OPEN DAY BY MOLLIE MAGUIRE ASSASSINS!

THE MURDERERS PURSUED BY HUNDRED OF CITIZENS, OVER MOUNTAINS AND THROUGH VALES, FROM CARBON COUNTY TO SCHUYLKILL

THE ASSASSINS CAPTURED ON A MOUNTAIN NEAR TAMAQUA AND BROUGHT TO MAUCH CHUNK

THE UPRISING OF THE PEOPLE AND THEIR DEMAND FOR SUMMARY EXECUTION

SENTINELS PLACED IN AND AROUND THE JAIL, TO GUARD AGAINST ANY ATTEMPT EITHER TO LYNCH OR FREE THE ASSASSINS

In the report that followed, the newspaper urged its readers to form vigilante groups to lynch the "murderers":

> *. . . Now let us rise up and form vigilante committees if ever the dream of peace and protection is to be realized, it can only be possible by the general acknowledgment of this one power raised above all others, to investigate, string up and smooth the way in the strifes of the people.*

The *Mauch Chunk Gazette*, the *Intelligencer*, the *Tamaqua Courier* and the *Shenandoah Herald*, all of which had circulation in Carbon County, carried similar reports.

Anyone reading these slanted and inflammatory articles would have to conclude, as did the newspapers, that Doyle, Kelly and Kerrigan were indeed the killers of Jones. The reports, however, went beyond convicting the accused of Jones' murder. They connected them to other killings and portrayed them as "Mollie" outlaws using every tactic to evade justice and openly advocated lynching them before trial.

The *Democrat* disclosed in its September 4, 1875 edition that "Policeman Brink of the Coal and Iron Police, from the description sent him, is of the opinion that Doyle is the man who killed the boss at Hesson's Colliery, Raven Run."

Most prominent among the subjects of this extensive press coverage was that the defendants were members of the "Mollie Maguires," a group which was randomly, indiscriminately and repeatedly characterized as an association of outlaws. The articles connected the "Mollies" to many of the killings which took place in Schuylkill County and implied that the security and way of life of each citizen were personally threatened by what the defendants had done. Twenty (20) subsequent newspaper stories reporting through the period up to the time of the *Doyle* trial carried what became standard reference -- that a "Mollie Maguire" killing was involved. No source was given for this conclusion nor was any rationale offered.

Special media attention was given to the fact that none of the defendants could obtain pretrial release on bail. The press also reported that no one was permitted to visit the defendants in the county jail. These reports could not help but heighten the notion that these men were so dangerous that they required special security.

Carbon County's press also gave considerable attention to the defendants' pretrial application for a Change of Venue and Motion to Strike the Array of Jurors. The *Democrat* of October 23, 1875 devoted two columns to the "debate." In reporting on these pretrial applications, the *Democrat* of April 1, 1876 referred to them as "anything to gain time."

Alexander Campbell was arrested and jailed on January 23, 1876. On February 5, 1876, the *Mauch Chunk Democrat*, under the headline, "MURDER WILL OUT, One of the Trio 'Squeals!," reported Campbell's arrest with unrestrained glee and relief. It proclaimed that an unnamed member of the three arrestees implicated Campbell in the Jones killing and then told of Campbell's "Mollie Maguire" connection:

> *If a bomb-shell had suddenly been thrown into and exploded in this usually so quiet town, it would not have created a greater sensation than the unexpected announcement that one of the trio now held in confinement for complicity in the Jones murder had "squealed", and that in consequence Alexander Campbell, of Ashton, had been arrested as an additional accomplice in the taking off of Jones, and five arrests in Schuylkill County for the assassination of officer Yost, of Tamaqua, on the morning of the 5th of July last. When the news first reached us, we hardly knew whether to credit it or not. Indeed, it seemed too good to be true. But "murder will out," and, for once, we were gratified to find that Dame Rumor had told the truth.*
>
> *How the confession was obtained, or who of the trio it was that "squealed" we are not a liberty at present to state, but may add that the confession has been made voluntarily, and without the holding out to the culprit of any inducements by the gentlemen connected with the prosecution of the case. Aleck Campbell "the greatest Roman of them all" is a liquor dealer, a resident of Ashton, and has, heretofore, been held in good repute, although for some time suspected of keeping a general head-quarters of that gang of out-laws yelept Molly Maguires. Yet, although suspected, he would hardly have been arrested had it not been for the confession above referred to. To what extent he may be implicated, his trial will demonstrate. Any one, little acquainted with Aleck, would hardly believe him to be the villain, those better acquainted with him now represent him to be.*
>
> *The importance of both, arrests and confession, can hardly be overrated. It will knock the bottom out of the tactics of the defense, prevent some of the limbs of the law from spreading themselves beyond reasonable proportions, expedite the trials, save the tax-payers thousands of dollars, and may render life and property more secure than they have hitherto been.*

On February 19, 1876 the *Mauch Chunk Democrat* revealed to its Carbon readers the name of the "squealer" against Campbell -- James Kerrigan who had been brought from Mauch Chunk to Pottsville by General Albright. According to the story, in a closed-door habeas corpus proceeding in Schuylkill County Court, Judge Cyrus Pershing[106]

[106] Franklin Gowen persuaded Cyrus L. Pershing, a native of Cambria County and an attorney for the Pennsylvania Railroad for twenty years, to accept the Republican nomination even though he never stepped into Schuylkill county before the campaign. The support given Pershing by the railroad and mining magnates gave him an easy victory. (Coleman, *The Molly Maguire Riots*, pp. 67-68).

permitted the press to remain during the hearing, but directed them not to publish anything unless it was approved by the prosecutors. The *Democrat* then went on to give its readers its report of the closed hearing which had been sanitized by the prosecution: that Kerrigan testified that Alexander Campbell wanted John P. Jones killed and made arrangements with AOH members in Schuylkill County to get the job done; that Doyle and Kelly were sent to do the killing; that Campbell told Kerrigan to take Doyle and Kelly to Lansford and point out John P. Jones because they did not know him and Kerrigan did; that he (Kerrigan) led Doyle and Kelly to Lansford but refused to participate in the killing of Jones; that he was a member of the "Mollie Maguires"; and that the "Mollies" had a rule requiring members to commit murder when directed by its leaders.

The Schuylkill County courtroom depicted here was the scene of the habeas corpus proceedings described above and other "Mollie" trials

The reporter concluded his "exclusive" report by telling his readers that, although there was a limited "gag" order, testimony at the hearing revealed that Campbell was involved in many other murders:

> *As we before stated we are allowed to publish only a small portion of the testimony, but such extraordinary developments having been made the blows will strike like lightening "[sic]", and men heretofore above suspicion but now inculpated will have the law's vengeance meted out to them that they so richly deserve.*

> *The statements made go to show that Alexander Campbell, now incarcerated in our county jail, is a notable villain, he being implicated in something like a dozen murders. Apparently he is one of the leaders, being a man of intelligence. It would seem that he was the chief planner of these horrible murders, the demand being made on him and he furnishing the instruments. The recital of this testimony is terrible and such a burden of guilt resting on one man we should think would be more than could be borne.*

On Saturday, February 26, the *Carbon Advocate* in Lehighton republished the foregoing *Democrat* report with the headline "More on the Mollies" and referred to the Pottsville proceedings as a "case of the Mollie Maguire murderers."

These reports on the Pottsville proceedings were particularly damaging to the fair trial rights of Kelly, Campbell and the other defendants because Kerrigan's testimony was totally irrelevant in the habeas corpus proceedings in Schuylkill County and could have only one purpose -- to bias potential jurors and intimidate the defense. The only issue before the Schuylkill Court was whether bail should be set for the Schuylkill County defendants who were charged with the murder of Officer Yost in Tamaqua. Kerrigan's testimony about the involvement of Kelly, Doyle and Campbell in the killing of John P. Jones had nothing to do with that issue. It did, however, let the public know that the rumors about Kerrigan's talking to the prosecutors were true, and that he was now telling his story under oath in court. More importantly, it gave the prosecutors an opportunity to broadcast from a court setting their main trial theme that the Jones' murder was a killing planned and carried out by the "Mollie Maguires."

Campbell's failure in his bid to be released on bail prompted another report that Kerrigan was testifying under oath, and that Judge Dreher was so impressed by his testimony that he denied Campbell bail. The February 26 edition of the *Carbon Advocate* reported that at a closed hearing on February 25, the court, after hearing testimony from Kerrigan and others which "seemed to tell on him (Campbell) as a terrible bombshell thrown into camp, denied bail and remanded Campbell back to jail."

About a month later, on April 6, 1876, just after a Carbon jury convicted Edward Kelly of first degree murder, all four Carbon newspapers printed Kerrigan's lengthy two column statement to the prosecutors.[107] It appeared under the headline "KERRIGAN'S CONFESSION." The statement laid out with painstaking detail how Alexander Campbell plotted not only the murder of Jones, but also the murder of Tamaqua policeman Benjamin Yost. It downplayed Kerrigan's role in the Jones murder almost to the

[107] On this same date, Kerrigan's confession also appeared in the *Philadelphia Times*, *Bethlehem Daily Times*, *Tamaqua Courier*, *Shenandoah Herald*, and *Miner's Journal*.

point of non-involvement. Kerrigan said that, although Alex Campbell told him to help kill Jones and gave him a pistol, he rejected the pistol and when Jones was shot by Kelly and Doyle he, Kerrigan, was sound asleep near Randall's colliery in Lansford.

The only possible source for the press reports of Kerrigan's "squealing" on Alexander Campbell was the prosecutor. Kerrigan gave his statement to Sheriff Oliver Breneiser and Daniel Shepp, a Tamaqua mine owner, and it was turned over to prosecutors Siewers and Hughes. It is also undisputed that the prosecutors, with the Schuylkill County Court's blessing, told the press what to report from the habeas corpus proceeding in Pottsville.

The *Democrat* lost no time in letting the public know that Kerrigan's "confession" was worthy of belief and that no deals were made with the prosecution for the "confession." In his February 19, 1876 editorial Joseph Lynn wrote:

> *For in our mind we believe the man Kerrigan would never have made the confession attributed to him -- no inducements whatever having been held out to him -- but for fear of the dread hereafter.*

There was no "cooling-off" period where the publicity abated and could fade from the public awareness. The first trial began within four months of the first barrage of publicity and the extensive coverage continued throughout the entire year of the trials.

Additionally, the pretrial publicity revealed that the accused were involved in other killings and one of them, Kerrigan, had given a written "confession" to the prosecution implicating the defendants in the crimes charged and other crimes. This information was the product of the prosecution and the Coal and Iron Police, a practice that was condemned and proscribed by the Pennsylvania Supreme Court in *Commonwealth v. Pierce*, 451 Pa. 190, 303 A.2d 209, Cert. denied, 414 U.S. 878, 94 S.Ct. 164 (1973).

As we have demonstrated, the pretrial publicity made it highly unlikely that a "panel of impartial indifferent jurors"[108] could be chosen from the Carbon County community. The extensive and slanted coverage of the defendants' trials, however, virtually foreclosed any possibility of a fair and impartial jury for any defendant tried after Doyle.

The trial coverage of the defendants' cases began on January 18, 1876 with the voir dire of the jury in the *Doyle* case and continued until the jury returned their verdict on December 21, 1876 in the second *Campbell* trial. For each trial local newspapers, using

[108]*Irvin v. Dowd*, 366 U.S. 717, 722, 81 S.Ct. 1639, 6 L.ED.2d 751 (1961)

hired speed writers, printed every statement and speech of counsel, a summary of the testimony of every witness, the charge of the court to the jury and their own analysis of the impact of the evidence on the jury. While not excessively emotional, it left no doubt, as they reported trial after trial, that any reasonable person would convict on the evidence presented and that the defense attorneys had hopeless cases and no defense. Typical of the slanted reporting is the trial coverage of the end of the *Doyle* case which is appended to this chapter as **Exhibit 2**, page 348.

In summary, the newspaper coverage, both pretrial and trial, meets all the elements of what the law today calls *inherently prejudicial reporting.* It was slanted; it was inflammatory; and it demanded conviction. It could only lead jurors to believe that the violent crimes which they said the "Mollies" committed were, in reality, attacks on them, and implied that their families might be the next victims. So far as the press was concerned, the defendants were the "Mollies" who were perpetrating violence and death in the coal regions. The publicity was calculated to fill potential jurors with a high sense of duty to end a "reign of terror" and not just bring some petty criminals to justice. In effect, the press became the voice of the prosecutors and made emotional arguments to find the defendants guilty.

Prejudicial Material Widely Disseminated

Having concluded that the nature and content of the press coverage was inflammatory and emotional, we next turn to the question whether the publicity was pervasive, i.e. that there was a likelihood that a significant portion of the population was exposed to such publicity. As we have previously noted, the major sources for news in Carbon County at the time of the "Mollie" trials were the *Mauch Chunk Democrat*, the *Mauch Chunk Gazette*, the *Carbon Advocate*, and the *Weekly Intelligencer.* Eighty percent (80%) of the households in the county either subscribed to or bought these newspapers.

The only jurors who did not read the newspapers were either illiterate or did not read English. They were the jurors chosen to decide the guilt or innocence of the defendants.[109] Even the *Mauch Chunk Democrat*, which cheered the prosecution throughout, in its January 22, 1875 edition shook its journalistic head in disbelief at the Doyle jury:

> *Court being rather slow in coming to time, gives us a chance for a stray look into the jury-box, and to find that eleven jurors have been accepted. Who'll be the twelfth? Will it be the aged countryman concerning whom counsel have thus far spent so much legal ammunition? We soon shall see, as he is still held*

[109]Under existing Pennsylvania law, a juror shall be disqualified if he or she is unable to read, write, speak and understand the English language. 42 Pa. C.S.A. 4502, 1980, June 26, P.L.M. 78 Sec 3.

> *in reserve, and the defense have hitherto striven to fill the jury-box with all the self-confessed ignorance they could possibly lay their hands on. A casual glance at the eleven thus far chosen would be sufficient to convince the most skeptical that there isn't much intelligence there. But "Honi soit qui mal y pense," and since the eleven unmeaning countenances are there to represent the law and majesty of the "people," the less there is said or thought about it the better.*

The reporter for the *Bethlehem Times* at the *Kelly* trial, on April 3, 1876, observed that the only jury which could be impanelled was an illiterate one which was certain to convict:

> *For two days hundreds of people have been kept idle in this town, while 12 men were being selected -- by painful stage -- to try this alleged murderer of the mine boss, John P. Jones. The process was a tedious one. Yet, when the qualifications required in a first class juryman are considered, the wonder is not that so much difficulty was encountered in securing a jury, but that it was possible to get one at all. Illiteracy is the password to the jury box. There was, in this case, a panel of 57 jurors -- out of 55 called 12 were found who did not read newspapers, and who swore they had never heard of the Doyle or the present case. They are the men who will try Edward Kelly.*
>
> *From this showing it would appear that 22 per centum of the people of this (Carbon) county do not read newspapers! And further, that it is an excellent county in which to find a jury -- "sure pop."*

Jury Voir Dires[110] Confirm Pervasive Publicity

A careful examination of the individual voir dires of the jurors confirms that the newspaper reports had been widely disseminated and read and were in the minds of most of the potential jurors. It is also clear that if the juror had not read or heard about the newspaper coverage, he was exposed to his fellow jurors' opinions about the defendants' guilt during the voir dire questioning.[111]

Unlike today's statewide practice of a sequestered individual voir dire, all of the jurors in the "Mollie" trials sat in the courtroom during the questioning of the other

[110] VOIR DIRE L.Fr. To speak the truth. This phrase denotes the preliminary examination which the court or counsel may make of one presented as a witness or juror, where his competency, interest, bias etc., is evaluated. State v. McRae, 200 N.C. 149, 156 S.E. 800,803. (Black's Dictionary).

[111] Today, Pennsylvania Rule of Criminal Procedure 1106 requires that jurors in capital cases be questioned individually. It is the common practice in Pennsylvania to conduct the questioning of individual jurors separately from the other jurors in order to avoid an entire panel being exposed to expressions of opinions of guilt or prejudices of jurors against the defendant.

prospective jurors. They therefore could hear the lawyers' questions and the answers of each juror. When the questioning of a juror was completed, the lawyers would loudly accept or challenge the juror. Then as now, Pennsylvania law permitted both peremptory challenges and challenges for cause. Peremptory challenges permit the excusal of a juror without giving a reason. In capital cases, the Commonwealth and the defense were each allowed twenty challenges. Challenges for cause allow the judge to excuse a prospective juror whose answers indicate he cannot be impartial or irrespective of his answers the court should presume the likelihood of prejudice on his part. Judge Dreher's public rulings on the challenges for cause educated the remaining jurors in the courtroom on the answers which would keep them on the jury panel, and gave them ample time to "tailor" their responses accordingly. More devastating to the defendants was that the prospective jurors heard a majority of those voir dired say that they had fixed opinions against the defendants and, in some instances, what those opinions were.

The best evidence of the pervasiveness of the newspaper publicity appears in the voir dire examination of the various jury panels. The following analysis of the juror's answers on voir dires shows that large numbers of jurors in each of the trials had read the newspaper reports and already prejudged the defendants because of the prejudicial newspaper material.

Commonwealth v. Michael Doyle[112]

Michael Doyle, who was selected to be tried first, came to trial on January 18, 1876, a little more than four (4) months after the homicide. It took five (5) days to pick his jury. Sixty (60) jurors were originally summoned for voir dire questioning to determine whether they could be fair and impartial jurors. A jury of twelve (12) could not be selected from the original sixty (60) and Judge Dreher directed the sheriff to summon an additional forty (40) jurors. The sheriff could bring in only thirty (30) additional "talesmen."

Seventy-two (72) men were called for the Doyle panel (See **Exhibit 3**, pages 349 to 358). Nineteen (19) were excused for physical defects, or because they did not understand English or were opposed to capital punishment. All fifty-three (53) members of the remaining panel revealed on voir dire that they had read or heard of the homicide for which Doyle was on trial. Of the fifty-three (53) who read or heard about the case, thirty (30) or fifty-six percent (56%) of the jurors were challenged for cause by the defense because they stated that they had formed a fixed opinion of defendant's guilt based on the newspaper articles -- an opinion which could not be put aside or which would take evidence to overcome. Twenty-two (22) of the defense challenges were sustained by the court and

[112] 34 October Sessions 1875.

the jurors were removed. Eight (8) of Doyle's challenges for cause (based on a juror's statement that he had formed an opinion as to defendant's guilt as a result of the newspaper articles) were refused by Judge Dreher, and Doyle was required to use peremptory challenges to keep six (6) of those prospective jurors from being seated. Doyle had to use an additional nine (9) peremptory challenges to remove jurors who had read or heard about the case or had formed opinions about the defendant's guilt. Therefore a total of thirty-seven (37) or sixty-nine and eight tenths percent (69.8%) of the jurors questioned for bias were removed because of prejudgment.

All twelve (12) jurors who were eventually seated recalled having heard or read of the Jones murder and the pending case; one (1) of the twelve (12) had an opinion which would require evidence to change; five (5) or forty-two percent (42%) of the twelve (12) jurors had a poor understanding of the English language.

Commonwealth v. Edward Kelly[113]

The trial of Edward Kelly began on March 29, 1876. His jury was picked in two (2) days. Fifty-two (52) prospective jurors were interviewed during the voir dire examination (See **Exhibit 4**, pages 359 to 365). Seven (7) were excused for physical defects, opposition to capital punishment or not understanding English. Of the remaining forty-five (45) questioned for bias, thirty-eight (38) or eighty-four percent (84%) of the panel, said that they recalled hearing or reading newspaper articles about the case. (According to the trial record, nineteen (19) of the forty-five (45) attended some or all of the trial of Michael Doyle.) Of the forty-five (45) questioned about bias, twenty-eight (28) said that they had formed fixed opinions about the defendant's guilt and it would take evidence to change their opinions. The court granted twenty-five (25) defense challenges for cause because the prospective juror stated that he had formed a fixed opinion of defendant's guilt based on his recollection of the newspaper articles -- an opinion which could not be put aside. Judge Dreher refused one (1) of Kelly's challenges for cause (based on a juror's statement that he had formed an opinion as to defendant's guilt as a result of the newspaper articles), and Kelly had to use a peremptory challenge to keep this prospective juror from being seated. Five (5) additional defense peremptory challenges were exercised to remove jurors who had read about the case and said they had not formed an opinion. Therefore, thirty-one (31) or sixty-eight and eight tenths percent (68.8%) of the jurors questioned for bias were removed for prejudgment.

Of the twelve (12) jurors who were eventually seated, eight (8) recalled having heard or read of the Jones murder. Four (4) of the jurors admitted to a language problem which would prevent their understanding of the court proceedings.

[113] 34 October Sessions 1875.

Commonwealth v. Alexander Campbell[114]

In the first *Campbell* case for the Jones murder, which went to trial on June 21, 1876, thirty-six (36) jurors were voir dired in one (1) day (See **Exhibit 5**, pages 366 to 372). Eight (8) were disqualified because they did not understand English or were sick or were opposed to the death penalty and were not questioned on the merits. Of the twenty-eight (28) remaining jurors questioned for bias, twenty-seven (27) had read or heard about newspaper articles concerning the case and one (1) had attended Doyle's trial. Twenty (20) members of Campbell's jury panel said they had strong opinions about defendant's guilt. Twelve (12) of the prospective jurors who had formed fixed opinions about the case were successfully challenged for cause by the defense. Judge Dreher overruled three (3) of Campbell's challenges for cause because of fixed opinions and Campbell had to use three (3) peremptory challenges to keep these individuals from the jury. Campbell used an additional four (4) peremptory challenges to remove jurors who formed opinions or knew of the cases as a result of what they read in the newspapers. Therefore, nineteen (19) jurors or sixty-seven and eight tenth percent (67.8%) of the panel questioned for bias were removed because of prejudgment.

Curiously, two (2) of the jurors removed for cause were Fisher Hazard and Joseph Lynn, both powerful Mauch Chunk citizens and well known throughout Carbon County. Hazard was a member of the board of directors of the Lehigh Coal and Navigation Company, the leading coal producer and employer in the county. Lynn was the owner and publisher of the *Mauch Chunk Democrat* and an avowed enemy of the AOH and the Irish. Hazard told the court that based on what he read in the newspapers, he had a fixed opinion about Campbell's guilt and that "there ought to be more hangings." Lynn proudly told the court that he had written editorials about Campbell's guilt and believed that Campbell was guilty. Their removal from the jury panel could not possibly erase their words and opinions from the minds of the remaining jurors who sat in the courtroom while they were questioned.

The twelve (12) jurors selected for the *Campbell* trial included eleven (11) thoroughly familiar with Campbell and the *Doyle* and *Kelly* cases. Four (4) of the jurors confessed to opinions of varying degrees about Campbell's guilt but said they would follow the evidence. Seven (7) jurors admitted reading "Kerrigan's Confession."

[114]June Term 1876.

Commonwealth v. John Donahue[115]

John "Yellow Jack" Donahue, represented by four court appointed lawyers, went before a jury of his peers on October 19, 1876 for the murder of Morgan Powell in 1871. Thirty-six (36) jurors were voir dired (See **Exhibit 6**, pages 373 to 377). Jury selection consumed two (2) days. Eight (8) were excused for physical defects, because they were opposed to the death penalty or did not understand English and were not questioned on the merits. Of the twenty-eight (28) remaining jurors, sixteen (16) had read or heard about newspaper articles concerning the case; two (2) attended other trials of the defendants. Nine (9) of the members of Donahue's panel had fixed opinions of Donahue's guilt. Six (6) of the prospective jurors were challenged for cause by the defense because they had formed fixed opinions about the defendant and five (5) of these challenges were sustained. One (1) of Donahue's challenges for cause based on the juror's courtroom presence during the related perjury cases was overruled by Judge Dreher and the juror was sworn. Defendant used ten (10) peremptory challenges to remove jurors who had heard or read about the case or formed opinions. Therefore, fifteen (15) or fifty-three percent (53%) of the panel was removed because of prejudgment.

Of the twelve (12) jurors selected to try Donahue, four (4) recalled reading or hearing about the case. All twelve (12) said they had not formed opinions about Donahue. Two (2) of the jurors hedged their responses indicating they "think" or "guess" they could render a verdict on the evidence. Four (4) of the twelve (12) had a poor understanding of the English language.

Commonwealth v. Thomas Fisher and Patrick McKenna[116]

Thomas Fisher and Patrick McKenna were tried together for the murder of Morgan Powell. On December 5, 1876, thirty-one (31) jurors were voir dired (See **Exhibit 7**, pages 378 to 383). Their jury was selected in one (1) day. Poor health and lack of understanding of the English language disqualified three (3) jurors from the panel. Of the twenty-eight (28) jurors remaining, twenty-seven (27) heard or read of the "Mollie" cases. Eleven (11) jurors had formed opinions about the defendants or the "Mollie Maguires" as an organization. Fisher and McKenna successfully challenged six (6) jurors for cause. The court overruled two (2) of these challenges and defense counsel used two (2) peremptory challenges to keep these individuals from the panel. The defense used an additional nine (9) peremptory challenges to keep those who read or heard about "Mollie" cases and said they had no opinion from the jury. Therefore, seventeen (17) jurors or sixty-seven percent (67%) of the panel were removed because of prejudgment.

---

[115]31 June Term 1876.

[116]57 October Term 1876.

The entire jury of twelve (12) had read or heard about the Powell murder and defendants. However, none of the jurors admitted having an opinion as to the guilt or innocence of the defendants. Two (2) jurors expressed difficulty in understanding the English language, and one (1) juror admitted to a hearing problem preventing him from hearing everything in the courtroom.

Commonwealth v. Alexander Campbell[117]

On December 18, 1876, Alexander Campbell went on trial again, this time for the murder of Morgan Powell in 1871. His jury was picked in less than two (2) hours. Counsel questioned thirty-two (32) prospective jurors (See **Exhibit 8**, pages 384 to 388). Three (3) jurors were removed for reasons of health, age, or opposition to capital punishment. Of the remaining twenty-nine (29) jurors questioned for bias, only six (6) admitted hearing or reading about the case previously and another sixteen (16) jurors were never asked if they had previous knowledge of the case. Eleven (11) jurors indicated they had an opinion about the prisoner or the "Mollie Maguires," and only three (3) of these eleven (11) with opinions said they had read or heard of Campbell's first trial. The remaining eight (8) with opinions were not asked if they knew of the first trial.

The defense successfully challenged ten (10) of the twenty (29) remaining jurors for cause, because they had an opinion of the defendant's guilt or were biased against the "Mollie Maguires" in general. Judge Dreher overruled two (2) of these challenges, forcing the defense to use two (2) peremptory challenges to remove these individuals from the panel. Five (5) additional peremptory challenges were required to remove other biased individuals from the panel. Therefore, seventeen (17) jurors or fifty-nine percent (59%) of the panel questioned for bias were removed because of prejudgment. The twelve (12) selected jurors included two (2) who admitted they heard or knew about the first *Campbell* case, and one (1) who claimed he did not know whether he had formed or expressed an opinion, but there was no information from him about whether he read or heard about the case. One (1) of the jurors expressed difficulty in understanding the English language.

Overview of Jury Voir Dires

Better than any public opinion survey, the voir dires of the various jury panels show that the news coverage which began at the time the defendants were arrested and continued during the trials had reached a high proportion of the homes of potential jurors. They also show that this publicity was vividly in the jurors' minds at the time of the trials. One hundred and sixty-seven (167) or seventy-nine percent (79%) of the two hundred and eleven (211) jurors who were asked whether they read or heard about the defendants' cases responded affirmatively. One hundred and thirty-six (136) or sixty-four percent (64%) of the

[117] December Term 1876.

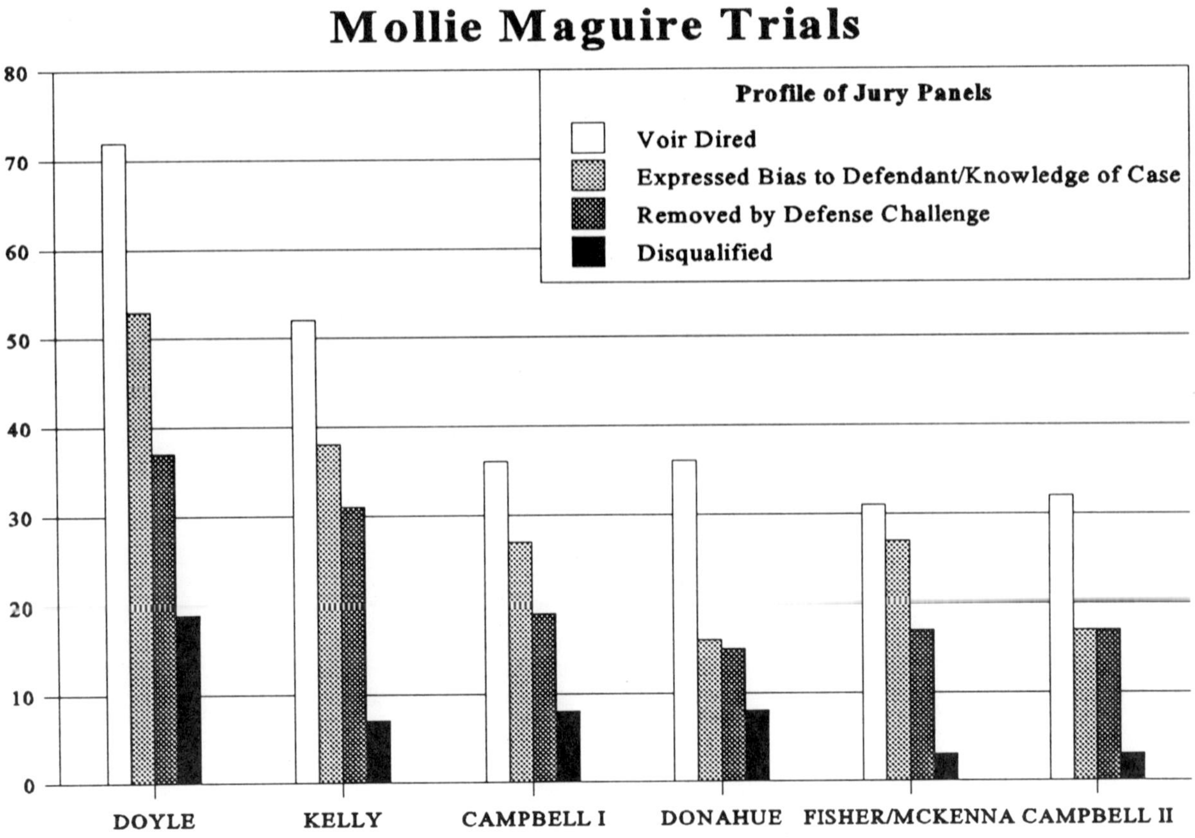

Profile of Jury Panels

jurors questioned about bias were stricken from the panels because they had prejudged the defendants. Of the seventy-two (72) jurors who were eventually seated, forty-nine (49) or sixty-eight percent (68%) had read or heard about the murders.

Additionally, the potential for prejudice resulting from the nearness of the news articles to the trials was extremely great, particularly those alleging the defendants were "Mollies" who killed many people, publicizing Officer Brink's statement that Doyle had killed another man and reporting that Alexander Campbell was involved in other killings. This potential for prejudice existed despite the statements by the prospective jurors that they could put aside any opinions about the defendants which they had formed after reading the newspaper articles. *Commonwealth v. Price*, 463 Pa. 200, 344 A.2d 493 (1975) and *Commonwealth v. Harkins*, 459 Pa. 196, 328 A.2d 156 (1974).

On the basis of this evidence, a court today would undoubtedly conclude that the publicity was so sensational, inflammatory, and pervasive that the court would presume that the jury had been biased (See *ABA Project on Minimum Standards for Criminal Justice, Standards Relating to Fair Trial and Free Press*, Section 342(C) 1956). Defendants' right to be tried by an impartial jury, as guaranteed by the Sixth Amendment to the United States Constitution and by Article I, Section 9 of the Constitution of the Commonwealth of Pennsylvania was violated because the nature of the publicity was such that one exposed to it would be unable to serve as an impartial juror and because the extent of that publicity was such that not only seventy-nine percent (79%) of the prospective jurors were exposed to it but also sixty-four percent (64%) of the jurors questioned had prejudged the defendant.

Where sixty-two percent (62%) of the jurors had an opinion on the defendant's guilt and fifty-three percent (53%) of those questioned were removed on the ground of irrevocable prejudgment of the merits, pretrial publicity was shown to have prevented the defendant from selecting an impartial jury and refusal to grant a change in venue was an abuse of the trial court's discretion. *Commonwealth v. Cohen*, 489 Pa. 167, 413 A.2d 1066 (1980), cert. *denied*, 449 U.S. 840, 101 S.Ct. 118.

In *Commonwealth v. Frazier*, 471 Pa. 131, 369 A.2d 1224 (1977), sixteen (16) or fifty percent (50%) of the thirty-two (32) prospective jurors questioned on bias were removed from the panel by the court or defense counsel because of prejudgment and eighty-seven percent (87%) of the panel recalled reading or hearing about the murder four (4) months after the homicide. The Supreme Court ruled that such evidence showed that the news coverage publicizing defendant's prior criminal record and his admission of guilt potentially prejudiced the defendant by depriving him of a fair and impartial jury, reversed his conviction and ordered a new trial.

These cases are predictive that a Pennsylvania Appellate Court today would find that the trial court abused its discretion in refusing the request for change of venue, would reverse the defendants' convictions and grant new trials.

Conclusion

There are many other aspects of the "Mollie" trials which raise serious questions about whether the defendants received fair trials. Were their defense counsel ineffective (1) in failing to challenge their prosecution by coal company and railroad lawyers, (2) in failing to suppress any evidence about the secret purposes of the AOH, (3) in neglecting to raise the change of venue issue on appeal, (4) in not perfecting appeals to the Supreme Court of Pennsylvania for some of the defendants who were sentenced to death, and (5) in failing to put Alexander Campbell on the witness stand to repudiate the testimony of McParlan and Kerrigan, the only witnesses to his alleged conspiracy to murder Jones.

Both of these witnesses had nothing to lose and everything to gain. McParlan was a coal company undercover detective paid to bring down the leaders of the AOH; Kerrigan, who was caught fleeing from the Jones' murder site, was testifying to save his own life.

Additionally, was there prosecutorial misconduct in the prosecutors' summations to the jury in which they linked the defendants to many other killings in the coal regions which were not in evidence? Was there prosecutorial overreaching when the attorneys for the Commonwealth released Kerrigan's confession to the press?

Was there prosecutorial misconduct in their using McParlan to obtain the defense lawyers' strategy? It is uncontroverted that James McParlan, the Pinkerton detective who was the Commonwealth's star witness in the *Campbell* case, sat in on defense counsel strategy sessions during the *Doyle* and *Kelly* cases and then reported the defense strategy to the prosecutors.[118] Standing alone, this spying upon and intrusion into the relationship between Doyle and Kelly and their counsel would invalidate their trials. In *Caldwell v. United States*, 205 F.2d 879 (1953) where an undercover government agent gained free access to the planning of Caldwell's defense and reported the information to the prosecutors, the D.C. Circuit Court reversed this conviction and granted a new trial with this observation:

> *The Constitution's prohibitions against unreasonable searches, and its guarantees of due process of law and effective representation of counsel, lose most of their substance if the Government can, with impunity, place a secret agent in a lawyer's office . . . to listen to their conversations and to participate in their counsels of defense . . . If it does occur a conviction tainted by it cannot stand. See* ***Caldwell v. United States*** *at page 880.*

In a history of this size, it is not possible to treat these issues adequately. They should be examined in depth and on a case by case basis. We hope that this chapter will spur others to examine these questions and shed the light of due process upon them.

Of course nothing can change the cold hard reality that Doyle, Kelly, Campbell, Donahue, McKenna, and Fisher died ignominiously on the gallows. But any objective study of the temper of the times and the entire record of these cases must conclude that they should not have been tried in Carbon County and did not have fair and impartial juries. They were, therefore, denied one of the fundamental rights that William Penn guaranteed to all of Pennsylvania's citizens.

[118] Dewees, F.P. *The Molly Maguires*. New York: Burt Franklin, 1876, p. 247.

The Mollie Maguire Trials (1876-1878)

The Cases

Defendant	Arrest Date Charge/Victim	Jury Trial Dates/Verdict	Sentencing & Execution Dates
1. MICHAEL J. DOYLE of Mount Laffee, Schuylkill County, PA Miner age 26	September 3, 1875 1st Degree Murder in killing of JOHN P. JONES on September 3, 1875	January 18, 1876 to January 31, 1876 GUILTY (Jury out 2 hrs., 15 min.)	2/22/76: Death by Hanging 6/21/77: Hanged in Carbon County Prison
2. EDWARD KELLY of Mount Laffee, Schuylkill County, PA Miner age 18	September 3, 1875 1st Degree Murder in killing of JOHN P. JONES on September 3, 1875	March 29, 1876 to April 6, 1876 GUILTY (Jury out 2 hrs., 15 min.)	4/12/76: Death by Hanging 6/21/77: Hanged in Carbon County Prison
3. ALEXANDER CAMPBELL of Summit Hill, Carbon County, PA Bodymaster of Ancient Order of Hibernians; Hotel Owner age 40	1st Degree Murder in killing of JOHN P. JONES on September 3, 1875	June 20, 1876 to July 1, 1876 GUILTY (Jury out 2 hrs., 15 min.)	8/28/76: Death by Hanging 6/21/77: Hanged in Carbon County Prison
4. JOHN (Yellow Jack) DONAHUE of Tuscarora, Schuylkill County, PA Bodymaster of Ancient Order of Hibernians of Tuscarora; Miner	1st Degree Murder in killing of MORGAN POWELL on December 2, 1871	October 19, 1876 to October 24, 1876 GUILTY (Jury out 6 hrs.)	12/18/76: Death by Hanging 6/21/77: Hanged in Carbon County Prison
5. THOMAS P. FISHER of Summit Hill, Carbon County, PA Owner of Rising Sun Hotel; Miner age 40	1st Degree Murder in killing of MORGAN POWELL on December 2, 1871	December 5, 1876 to December 16, 1876 GUILTY (Jury out 4 hrs.)	6/14/77: Death by Hanging 3/28/78: Hanged in Carbon County Prison
6. PATRICK MCKENNA of Summit Hill, Carbon County, PA	1st Degree Murder in killing of MORGAN POWELL on December 2, 1871	December 5, 1876 to December 16, 1876 GUILTY of 2nd Degree Murder	9 years in state penitentiary
7. ALEXANDER CAMPBELL (see above)	1st Degree Murder in killing of MORGAN POWELL on December 2, 1871	December 18-21, 1876 GUILTY (Jury out 1 hr.)	Date unknown: Death by Hanging 6/21/77: Hanged in Carbon County Prison
8. PATRICK O'DONNELL of Tuscarora, Schuylkill County, PA Miner	1st Degree Murder in killing of MORGAN POWELL on December 2, 1871	April 10-12, 1877 (mistrial) October 9-11, 1877 GUILTY of 2nd Degree Murder	4 years in state penitentiary
9. JOHN MALLOY of Tuscarora, Schuylkill County, PA Miner	1st Degree Murder in killing of MORGAN POWELL on December 2, 1871	April 13-16, 1877 GUILTY of 2nd Degree Murder	5 years in state penitentiary
10. JAMES (Hairy Man) MCDONNELL of Tuscarora, Schuylkill County, PA Miner	1st Degree Murder in killing of GEORGE K. SMITH on November 5, 1863	April 11-16, 1878 GUILTY	Date unknown: Death by Hanging 1/14/79: Hanged in Carbon County Prison
11. CHARLES SHARP of Tuscarora, Schuylkill County, PA Miner	1st Degree Murder in killing of GEORGE K. SMITH on November 5, 1863	April 16-20, 1878 GUILTY	Date unknown: Death by Hanging 1/14/79: Hanged in Carbon County Prison

Honorable Samuel Stokes Dreher, President Judge of Carbon County, presiding

The Principles

Defendant	Number of Witnesses	Defense Attorneys	Prosecuting Attorneys
1. MICHAEL J. DOYLE	Commonwealth - 120 Defense - none	Edward M. Mulhearn Daniel Kalbfus John W. Ryon Lin Bartholomew James B. Reilly	General Charles Albright, Chief Prosecutor Edward R. Siewers, D.A. Frank W. Hughes Allen W. Craig
2. EDWARD KELLY	Commonwealth - 111 Defense - none	Daniel Kalbfus Lin Bartholomew Edward M. Mulhearn	General Charles Albright, Chief Prosecutor Edward R. Siewers, D.A. Frank W. Hughes
3. ALEXANDER CAMPBELL (case 1)	Commonwealth - 60 (including James McParlan & James Kerrigan Defense - 24 (Def. did not testify)	Daniel Kalbfus Edward T. Fox Edward M. Mulhearn	General Charles Albright, Chief Prosecutor Edward R. Siewers, D.A. Frank W. Hughes Allen W. Craig
4. JOHN (Yellow Jack) DONOHUE	Commonwealth - 46 (including James McParlan and James Kerrigan Defense - none, but 2 statements were read	(all court-app'ted on trial's 1st day) Frederick Bertolette P. J. Meehan James S. Loose William M. Rapsher	General Charles Albright, Chief Prosecutor Edward R. Siewers, D.A. Frank W. Hughes Allen W. Craig
5. THOMAS P. FISHER	Commonwealth - 33 (including James McParlan and James Kerrigan Defense - 24	Edward T. Fox John W. Ryon John D. Bertolette	General Charles Albright, Chief Prosecutor Edward R. Siewers, D.A. Frank W. Hughes Allen W. Craig
6. PATRICK MCKENNA	(trial consolidated with <u>Com. v. Thomas Fisher</u>)	(trial consolidated with <u>Com. v. Thomas Fisher</u>)	(trial consolidated with <u>Com. v. Thomas Fisher</u>)
7. ALEXANDER CAMPBELL (case 2)	Commonwealth - 35 (including James McParlan and James Kerrigan) Defense - 3	Daniel Kalbfus	Edward R. Siewers, D.A. Frank W. Hughes
8. PATRICK O'DONNELL	Commonwealth - 20 (including James Kerrigan) Defense - 13	Daniel Kalbfus	Allen W. Craig
9. JOHN MALLOY	Commonwealth - 20 Defense - 4	(all court-app'ted on trial's 1st day) Frederick Bertolette P. J. Meehan James S. Loose	General Charles Albright, Chief Prosecutor Edward R. Siewers, D.A.
10. JAMES (Hairy Man) MCDONNELL	Commonwealth - 20 Defense - 6	P. J. Meehan Francis P. Longstreet	General Charles Albright, Chief Prosecutor Edward R. Siewers, D.A.
11. CHARLES SHARP	Commonwealth - 2 (including James Kerrigan Defense - 1	P. J. Meehan Francis P. Longstreet	General Charles Albright, Chief Prosecutor Edward R. Siewers, D.A.

LIST OF PERSONS WITH THEIR OCCUPATIONS, AND RESIDENCES, SELECTED AND PLACED IN THE JURY WHEEL OF CARBON COUNTY, IN THE STATE OF PENNSYLVANIA, FOR THE YEAR 1876.

NO.	NAME	OCCUPATION	RESIDENCE	VOIR DIRE RESULT**	
134.	Acker, Manasses	Laborer	Franklin Tsp.	Doyle	CC
159.	Albright, D. B.	Merchant	Weissport		
211.	Albright, Jacob H.	Laborer	East Penn Tsp.		
547.	Allen, Joseph A.	Engineer	Beaver Meadow		
197.	Andreas, Josiah	Farmer	East Penn Tsp.	Campbell II	DP
1.	Andrews, Edwin	Laborer	Lower Towamensing	Campbell II	Juror
98.	Anthony, George F.	Agent	Parryville	Campbell I	DC
132.	Anthony, Joseph	Farmer	Franklin Tsp.	Donahue	DP
106.	Anthony, Robert	Huckster	Franklin Tsp.		
404.	Armbruster, Lewis	Saloon Keeper	Mauch Chunk		
221.	Arner, Ammon	Merchant	Mahoning Tsp.		
293.	Arner, David	Laborer	Lehighton		
573.	Arner, Jacob D.	Merchant	Summit Hill		
220.	Arner, John H.	Clerk	Mahoning Tsp.		
569.	Arner, Thomas	Carpenter	Summit Hill		
131.	Arner, Thomas F.	Teacher	Franklin Tsp.		
294.	Arner, Tilghman	Gentleman	Lehighton		
568.	Arner, William H.	Carpenter	Summit Hill	Doyle	DC
219.	Auge, David	Farmer	Mahoning Tsp.		
200.	Bailey, D. C.	Huckster	East Penn Tsp.		
199.	Balliet, James D.	Farmer	East Penn Tsp.		
9.	Balliet, John	Merchant	Lower Towamensing		
161.	Bartholomew, Elias	Carpenter	Weissport		
160.	Bartholomew, Philip	Painter	Weissport		
439.	Bauer, Elven	Merchant	East Mauch Chunk		

*Jurors of Irish Heritage
**DP=Defense Peremptory
CP=Commonwealth Peremptory
DC=Defense for Cause
CC=Commonwealth Challenge Cause

EXHIBIT 1

224. Beck, Daniel	Farmer	Mahoning Tsp.		
196. Beck, Jonas	Laborer	East Penn Tsp.	Doyle	Juror
515. Becker, Benjamin	Laborer	Lehigh Tsp. P. Haven	Donahue	DC
451. Beckhart, Simon	Justice	East Mauch Chunk		
50. Beer, Alexander	Merchant	Lower Towamensing		
79. Beer, Benjamin	Farmer	Towamensing		
71. Beer, George	Laborer	Towamensing	Kelly	CC
62. Beer, Jonas C.	Laborer	Towamensing	Campbell I	DC
346. Beers, Asa R.	Merchant	Mauch Chunk	Campbell I	DP
138. Begle, Adam	Huckster	Franklin Tsp.		
428. Behler, John	Inn Keeper	Mauch Chunk	Campbell I	DC
109. Behler, Levi	Farmer	Franklin Tsp.		
66. Behler, William	Inn Keeper	Towamensing	Donahue	DP
323. Behrens, Francis	Sawyer	Penn Forest	Doyle	CC
128. Beiber, James	Farmer	Franklin Tsp.		
450. Beighe, John	Bt. Builder	East Mauch Chunk		
444. Beinamen, Henry	Brick Maker	East Mauch Chunk		
392. Belford, Charles	Gentleman	Mauch Chunk		
390. Belford, James	Gentleman	Mauch Chunk	Campbell I	DP
393. Belford, Nathan	Gentleman	Mauch Chunk		
107. Beltz, David	Inn Keeper	Franklin Tsp.	Campbell II	Juror
7. Beltz, Henry	Teacher	Lower Towamensing	Doyle	DC
52. Beltz, William	Farmer	Lower Towamensing		
452. Bennyhoff, Jonas	Carpenter	East Mauch Chunk		
300. Berger, Elias	Laborer	Lehighton	Campbell I	Juror
222. Berger, George	Farmer	Mahoning Tsp.	Campbell II	Juror
155. Berlin, Joel	Inn Keeper	Franklin Tsp.		
427. Bertsch, Abraham	Merchant	Mauch Chunk		
350. Bertsch, Daniel G.	Merchant	Mauch Chunk	Kelly	DC
198. Bittenbender, William	Laborer	East Penn Tsp.	F/Mc	Excused
530. Bittner, John	Farmer	Packer Tsp.	Kelly	DC

*Jurors of Irish Heritage
**DP=Defense Peremptory DC=Defense for Cause
CP=Commonwealth Peremptory CC=Commonwealth Challenge Cause

EXHIBIT 1

510. Blakeslee, W. W.	Merchant	Weatherly	Kelly	DC
511. Bleckley, John F.	Inn Keeper	Lehigh Tsp. P. Haven		
41. Bloss, Oliver	Teacher	Lower Towamensing	Donahue	Juror
11. Bloss, Simon	Farmer	Lower Towamensing		
10. Bloss, William Jr.	Laborer	Lower Towamensing	Doyle	Juror
72. Bock, Paul	Farmer	Towamensing		
540. Boose, Jacob	Inn Keeper	Nesquehoning	F/Mc	DP
299. Bower, C. H.	Agent	Lehighton	Doyle	DC
38. Bowman, Henry	Contractor	Lower Towamensing		
56. Bowman, Josiah	Farmer	Lower Towamensing		
49. Bowman, R. D.	Clerk	Lower Towamensing		
115. Boyer, Daniel Jr.	Carpenter	Franklin Tsp.	Doyle	DC
31. Boyer, Daniel Sr.	Gentleman	Lower Towamensing		
377. Boyle, E. Mell	Printer	Mauch Chunk	Doyle	DP
356. Bradley, Samuel	Machinist	Mauch Chunk	Campbell II	DP
589. Branch, Richard	Merchant	Nesquehoning		
384. Brelsford, John	Manufacturer	Mauch Chunk		
297. Bretney, Clinton	Cordwainer	Lehighton		
223. Bretney, Henry	Farmer	Mahoning Tsp.	F/Mc	Excused
144. Brian, David O.	Lock Tender	Franklin Tsp.		
403. Brighton, John	Saloon Keeper	Mauch Chunk		
298. Brinkman, Fred	Stone Cutter	Lehighton		
556. Britton, John	Machinist	Jeanesville		
296. Brodhead, Abraham C.	Supt.	Lehighton		
454. Brodhead, A. J.	Coal Dealer	East Mauch Chunk	Doyle	CC
286. Brodhead, F. W.	Clerk	Packerton		
111. Brown, James	Farmer	Franklin Tsp.		
295. Buchman, Adam	Coach Maker	Lehighton		
471. Buckalew, William	Clerk	Kidder Tsp. N. D.		
136. Bush, John	Carpenter	Franklin Tsp.		
369. Butler, Robert Q.	Gentleman	Mauch Chunk		

*Jurors of Irish Heritage
**DP=Defense Peremptory
CP=Commonwealth Peremptory

DC=Defense for Cause
CC=Commonwealth Challenge Cause

EXHIBIT 1

368. Butler, William	Gentleman	Mauch Chunk		
468. Butz, Isaac	Merchant	Kidder Tsp. N. D.	Campbell I	Excused
585. Bynon, John	Miner	Summit Hill		
420. Calvin, Robert	Carpenter	Mauch Chunk		
486. Campbell, Alexander	Contractor	Kidder Tsp. S. D.	F/Mc	Juror
129. Campbell, Henry	Merchant/Merchant	Franklin Tsp.		
99. Campbell, Robert	Merchant/Farmer	Parryville	Campbell II	DP
401. Carpenter, Samuel	Jeweler	Mauch Chunk		
473. Carter, Albert	Agent	Kidder Tsp. N. D.		
550. Carter, R. C.	Clerk	Beaver Meadow	Kelly	DC
548. Carter, T. H.	Book Keeper	Beaver Meadow		
449. Chapman, Joseph H.	Agent	East Mauch Chunk	F/Mk	Juror
75. Christman, Adam J.	Farmer	Towamensing	Doyle	CP
335. Christman, Daniel	Lumberman	Penn Forest		
578. Christman, Daniel	Farmer	Summit Hill		
570. Christman, Jacob	Carpenter	Summit Hill	Doyle	DC
482. Christman, Jacob	Inn Keeper	Kidder Tsp. S. D.	Donahue	DC
493. Christman, Peter F.	Butcher	Weatherly		
546. Clark, B. S.	Clerk	Beaver Meadow		
362. Clase, Nicolas C.	Clerk	Mauch Chunk		
577. Clauss, Nathan	Inn Keeper	Summit Hill	Donahue	DC
301. Clauss, Phaon	Tinsmith	Lehighton		
441. Cooke, E. R.	Merchant	East Mauch Chunk	Kelly	DC
592. Cooper, William	Moulder	Summit Hill		
461. Cortright, Butler	Laborer	East Mauch Chunk		
352. Cortright, N. D. Sr.	Coal Dealer	Mauch Chunk		
29. Craig, John	Merchant	Lower Towamensing		
24. Craig, William	Merchant	Lower Towamensing	Doyle	Excused
425. Crellin, John W.	Engineer	Mauch Chunk		
426. Crellin, Thomas R.	Coal Operator	Mauch Chunk		
434. Culver, Charles D.	Foreman	Mauch Chunk	Doyle	DP

*Jurors of Irish Heritage
**DP=Defense Peremptory
CP=Commonwealth Peremptory

DC=Defense for Cause
CC=Commonwealth Challenge Cause

EXHIBIT 1

574. Cunfer, Gideon	Farmer	Summit Hill		
225. Cunfer, Jacob	Farmer	Mahoning Tsp.		
332. Danner, Paul	Merchant	Penn Forest	Donahue	Juror
102. Davis, George	Machinist	Parryville		
583. Davis, John W.	Miner	Summit Hill	Kelly	DC
458. DeFrehn, William	Carpenter	East Mauch Chunk	Doyle	DC
201. DeLong, David	Farmer	East Penn Tsp.	Donahue	DP
215. DeLong, Griffith	Blacksmith	East Penn Tsp.	Donahue	Juror
302. Derhammer, George	Carpenter	Lehighton		
162. Dick, Charles	Gentleman	Weissport		
105. Diehl, Alvin	Farmer	Franklin Tsp.	Donahue	CC
226. Dilcher, Gabriel	Farmer	Mahoning Tsp.	Kelly	Juror
110. Dimmick, J. R.	Laborer	Franklin Tsp.	Doyle	DP
417. Dink, John	Moulder	Mauch Chunk		
531. Dodson, E. E.	Farmer	Packer Tsp.	Campbell II	Juror
303. Dollenmeyer, A. G.	Watchmaker	Lehighton	Campbell II	DP
275. Dolon, George	Laborer	Packerton		
400. Dolon, John C.	Jeweler/Jewler	Mauch Chunk		
140. Dorward, Thomas	Farmer	Franklin Tsp.		
26. Dorward, William	Boat Builder	Lower Towamensing		
342. Douglass, A. A.	Gentleman	Mauch Chunk		
304. Dreiblebeis, J. E.	Tanner	Lehighton		
57. Dreisbach, Charles	Farmer	Towamensing		
228. Dreisbach, G. W.	Farmer	Mahoning Tsp.	Campbell II	DP
108. Dreisbach, Lewis	Carpenter	Franklin Tsp.		
446. Dreisbach, Solomon	Clerk	East Mauch Chunk	Campbell I	CC
130. Dreisbach, William	Carpenter	Franklin Tsp.		
227. Drumbore, Alfred	Farmer	Mahoning Tsp.		
494. Drumbore, Lewis	Inn Keeper	Weatherly	Doyle	DC
561. Drumheller, Nathan	Foreman	Summit Hill		
429. Dutot, Thomas	Sugar Maker	Mauch Chunk		

*Jurors of Irish Heritage
**DP=Defense Peremptory
CP=Commonwealth Peremptory

DC=Defense for Cause
CC=Commonwealth Challenge Cause

EXHIBIT 1

112. Eaches, Adam	Carpenter	Franklin Tsp.		
306. Eaches, A. W.	Carpenter	Lehighton	Campbell I	Juror
495. Eadie, James G.	Merchant	Weatherly	Kelly	DC
502. Eadie, W. W.	Bartender	Weatherly		
305. Ebert, David	Merchant	Lehighton		
230. Eberts, Joseph	Farmer	Mahoning Tsp.		
70. Eckhart, Joseph D.	Farmer	Towamensing		
78. Eckhart, Reuben	Farmer	Towamensing		
69. Eckhart, William	Farmer	Towamensing		
551. Ely, Ezra B.	Book Keeper	Beaver Meadow		
163. Emery, George	Plasterer	Weissport	F/MC	CP
229. Ervin, Thomas	Farmer/Farmer	Mahoning Tsp.	Kelly	DC
399. Esser, George W.	Coal Operator	Mauch Chunk	Donahue	DP
347. Esser, John A.	Clerk	Mauch Chunk		
538. Eustice, Richard	Foreman	Nesquehoning		
545. Evans, Joseph	Blacksmith	Beaver Meadow		
164. Everitt, H. H.	Carpenter	Weissport	Kelly	Juror
280. Farren, John	Butcher/Laborer	Packerton		
536. Faust, John	Farmer	Packer Tsp.	Kelly	Excused
166. Faust, Michael	Laborer	Weissport		
165. Feist, Joseph	Inn Keeper	Weissport	Campbell II	DC
238. Fenstermaker, Stephen	Inn Keeper	Mahoning Tsp.	Campbell I	DC
397. Fidler, John	Carpenter	Mauch Chunk		
562. Fisher, Caleb	Carpenter	Summit Hill	Campbell II	DP
498. Fisher, Jeremiah	Carpenter	Weatherly		
437. Fister, James M.	Engineer	Mauch Chunk	Kelly	DC
463. Flick, Franklin	Farmer	Penn Forest	Campbell I	Juror
231. Flickinger, Daniel	Farmer	Mahoning Tsp.		
203. Flickinger, John	Laborer	East Penn Tsp.		
523. Fowler, N. D.	Inn Keeper	Audenried		
558. Fowler, Yoder	Clerk	Jeanesville		

*Jurors of Irish Heritage
**DP=Defense Peremptory
CP=Commonwealth Peremptory

DC=Defense for Cause
CC=Commonwealth Challenge Cause

EXHIBIT 1

235. Frantz, Jacob	Farmer	Mahoning Tsp.	Campbell I	DC
455. Freharn, David	Merchant	East Mauch Chunk		
205. Freyman, Edward	Farmer	East Penn Tsp.	Campbell I	DC
232. Freyman, John	Farmer	Mahoning Tsp.		
233. Freyman, Levi	Farmer	Mahoning Tsp.	Donahue	Juror
206. Friebie, Solomon	Farmer	East Penn Tsp.		
421. Frisbie, William E.	Shoemaker	Mauch Chunk		
236. Fritz, Charles	Farmer	Mahoning Tsp.	Campbell II	Juror
539. Fritz, Charles	Laborer	Nesquehoning	Doyle	DC
237. Fritz, Daniel S.	Farmer	Mahoning Tsp.	Kelly	Excused
202. Fritzinger, Charles H.	Farmer	East Penn Tsp.		
204. Fritzinger, Jacob	Laborer	East Penn Tsp.	F/Mc	Juror
234. Fritzinger, Levi	Laborer	Mahoning Tsp.		
521. Fuehrer, George	Clerk	Audenried	Kelly	DC
474. Fulmer, Christian	Inn Keeper	Kidder Tsp. N. D.	F/Mc	Juror
156. Gaumer, Reuben	Carpenter	Franklin Tsp.		
488. George, Christian	Laborer	Kidder Tsp. S. D.	Kelly	Juror
208. George, Elias	Farmer	East Penn Tsp.	Campbell II	Juror
288. Gerber, Nathan	Laborer	Packerton		
529. Gerhart, Jonas	Farmer	Packer Tsp.	Campbell II	Excused
489. Getz, William	Lumberman	Kidder Tsp. S. D.		
387. Ginder, Charles	Moulder	Mauch Chunk		
408. Ginder, Jacob Sr.	Laborer	Mauch Chunk	Campbell I	DP
207. Ginder, Lewis	Laborer	East Penn Tsp.		
516. Ginder, Philip	Foreman	Lehigh Tsp. P. Haven		
371. Glace, N. F.	Shoemaker	Mauch Chunk		
460. Glasser, John	Inn Keeper	East Mauch Chunk	Donahue	CC
555. Gould, Justice	Blacksmith	Jeanesville		
168. Graver, Andrew Jr.	Huckster	Weissport	Doyle	DP
167. Graver, Andrew Sr.	Boat Builder	Weissport		
307. Graver, Daniel	Merchant	Lehighton		

*Jurors of Irish Heritage
**DP=Defense Peremptory
CP=Commonwealth Peremptory

DC=Defense for Cause
CC=Commonwealth Challenge Cause

EXHIBIT 1

148. Graver, Edward	Farmer	Franklin Tsp.		
116. Graver, Jacob	Farmer	Franklin Tsp.		
114. Graver, Joshua	Farmer	Franklin Tsp.		
124. Graver, Owen	Laborer	Franklin Tsp.	Kelly	Juror
322. Graver, Samuel	Tin Smith	Lehighton		
308. Graver, William A.	Gentleman	Lehighton		
418. Green, John	Clerk	Mauch Chunk	F/Mc	DC
85. Greensweig, Benjamin	Farmer	Towamensing	Campbell II	Juror
67. Greensweig, H. F.	Carpenter	Towamensing		
25. Greensweig, Joseph	Farmer	Lower Towamensing		
126. Greensweig, Joseph Sr.	Farmer	Franklin Tsp.		
17. Greensweig, Reuben	Farmer	Lower Towamensing		
23. Greensweig, Samuel	Farmer	Lower Towamensing		
63. Greensweig, Samuel	Carpenter	Towamensing		
20. Grill, Nicholas	Gentleman	Lower Towamensing		
32. Grill, William	Teacher	Lower Towamensing		
151. Grum, Daniel	Farmer	Franklin Tsp.		
289. Grum, Levi	Laborer	Packerton	Campbell I	DP
239. Gumbert, Aaron H.	Mason	Mahoning Tsp.	Doyle	CC
240. Gumbert, J. H.	Farmer	Mahoning Tsp.		
292. Haagen, George	Inn Keeper	Packerton		
61. Hade, George	Farmer	Towamensing		
48. Hagenbuch, J. H.	Lock Tender	Lower Towamensing		
30. Hahn, Jacob	Farmer	Lower Towamensing		
91. Hahn, Joseph	Blacksmith	Parryville		
587. Halderman, John	Laborer	Summit Hill		
281. Hammann, Con. W.	Foreman	Packerton		
274. Hander, Josiah C.	Carpenter	Mahoning Tsp.		
381. Handwork, James	Clerk	Mauch Chunk		
174. Haney, Thomas	Laborer	East Penn Tsp.		
360. Harlan, Josiah H.	Laborer	Mauch Chunk	Donahue	CC

*Jurors of Irish Heritage
**DP=Defense Peremptory
CP=Commonwealth Peremptory

DC=Defense for Cause
CC=Commonwealth Challenge Cause

EXHIBIT 1

16. Harleman, Abraham	Gentleman	Lower Towamensing		
18. Harleman, Levi	Gentleman	Lower Towamensing		
503. Harleman, Samuel	Foreman	Weatherly	Doyle	DP
506. Hartz, Levi	Inn Keeper	Weatherly		
535. Hartz, Peter	Inn Keeper	Packer Tsp.	Donahue	DC
316. Hauck, John	Baker	Lehighton	Donahue	Juror
210. Haverman, Joseph	Farmer	East Penn Tsp.		
481. Hawk, Jacob S.	Lumberman	Kidder Tsp. S. D.		
364. Hazard, Fisher	Coal Operator	Mauch Chunk	Campbell I	DC
394. Heberling, James W.	Merchant	Mauch Chunk	F/Mc	DP
396. Heberling, Nathan	Merchant	Mauch Chunk		
312. Heberling, Samuel G.	Wheelwright	Lehighton	Doyle	CC
395. Heberling, Thomas J.	Merchant	Mauch Chunk	Doyle	DP
430. Heckman, John R.	Gentleman	Mauch Chunk		
248. Heilman, George	Laborer	Mahoning Tsp.		
310. Heilman, Moses	Merchant	Lehighton	F/Mc	DC
484. Heimbach, Harrison	Laborer	Kidder Tsp. S. D.	Campbell I	Juror
479. Heimbach, Joseph	Sawyer	Kidder Tsp. S. D.		
117. Heiney, Levi	Blacksmith	Franklin Tsp.	Doyle	DP
173. Heintzleman, Elias	Huckster	East Penn Tsp.		
349. Heist, Samuel	Merchant	Mauch Chunk	Campbell II	DC
571. Heister, George	Carpenter	Summit Hill		
145. Held, F. J.	Saddler	Franklin Tsp.	F/Mc	Excused
340. Henning, Charles	Farmer	Penn Forest	Campbell I	DP
339. Henning, Henry	Farmer	Penn Forest	F/Mc	Juror
137. Henry, Abraham	Huckster	Franklin Tsp.	Doyle	Juror
120. Hill, William	Carpenter	Franklin Tsp.		
575. Hobart, W. S.	Merchant	Nesquehoning	Donahue	DC
118. Hoffman, David	Carpenter	Franklin Tsp.		
243. Hoffman, J. D.	Farmer	Mahoning Tsp.	Donahue	Juror
209. Hoffman, Nathan	Farmer	East Penn Tsp.	Campbell II	Juror

*Jurors of Irish Heritage
**DP=Defense Peremptory DC=Defense for Cause
CP=Commonwealth Peremptory CC=Commonwealth Challenge Cause

EXHIBIT 1

309. Hofford, R. F.	School Supt.	Lehighton		
554. Hooven, E. T.	Machinist	Beaver Meadow	Doyle	CC
497. Hooven, Samuel	Merchant	Weatherly	Doyle	DC
244. Hoppes, Elias	Miller	Mahoning Tsp.		
245. Horn, Charles	Laborer	Mahoning Tsp.	Campbell I	Juror
448. Horn, Jacob	Foreman	East Mauch Chunk	Donahue	CC
122. Horn, Lewis	Farmer	Franklin Tsp.		
504. Horn, Reuben	Laborer	Weatherly		
246. Horn, Thomas	Farmer	Mahoning Tsp.		
247. Horn, William	Farmer	Mahoning Tsp.		
572. Houser, Nathan	Engineer	Summit Hill	Kelly	Excused
527. Hudson, S. B.	Foundryman	Packer Tsp.		
526. Hudson, S. W.	Foundryman	Packer Tsp.		
433. Hughes, Paul	Druggist	Mauch Chunk		
241. Hunsicker, John	Farmer	Mahoning Tsp.		
242. Hunsicker, Joseph	Farmer	Mahoning Tsp.		
314. Hunsicker, Reuben	Farmer	Lehighton	Campbell I	DP
581. Hyndman, W. P.	Agent	Summit Hill	Campbell I	Excused
90. Jones, Oliver	Farmer	Towamensing		
462. Keifer, John	Cab. Maker	Mauch Chunk	Kelly	DP
413. Keiser, Jerry	Inn Keeper	Mauch Chunk		
54. Kelchner, Charles	Farmer	Lower Towamensing	F/Mc	DP
534. Keller, D. R.	Farmer	Packer Tsp.		
86. Keller, E. F.	Laborer	Towamensing	Doyle	CP
485. Kelsey, Abel	Farmer	Kidder Tsp. S. D.		
318. Kemerer, Theodore	Carpenter	Lehighton		
251. Kemmerer, George	Gunsmith	Mahoning Tsp.	Doyle	CC
58. Kemmerer, J. J.	Farmer	Towamensing		
175. Kemmerer, Solomon	Laborer	East Penn Tsp.		
33. Kern, LaFayette	Teacher	Lower Towamensing		
6. Kern, Levi	Farmer	Lower Towamensing	Doyle	Excused

*Jurors of Irish Heritage
**DP=Defense Peremptory
CP=Commonwealth Peremptory

DC=Defense for Cause
CC=Commonwealth Challenge Cause

EXHIBIT 1

77. Kern, Peter	Laborer	Towamensing		
21. Kindt, Francis	Butcher	Lower Towamensing		
359. King, William T.	Laborer	Mauch Chunk		
508. Kinkle, Lewis	Shoemaker	Weatherly	Campbell II	DC
250. Kistler, David D.	Farmer	Mahoning Tsp.		
376. Kistler, Wilson	Boss	Mauch Chunk		
564. Klein, George	Merchant	Summit Hill	F/Mc	Juror
2. Kleintop, David	Carpenter	Lower Towamensing		
588. Kleppinger, Benjamin F.	Merchant	Nesquehoning		
311. Klotz, Ammon	Inn Keeper	Lehighton		
15. Klotz, Charles Jr.	Farmer	Lower Towamensing	Kelly	DC
584. Klotz, Nathan	Gentleman	Summit Hill		
405. Klotz, Robert	Gentleman	Mauch Chunk		
125. Klotz, William H.	Laborer	Franklin Tsp.		
464. Koch, Enos	Inn Keeper	Penn Forest	Donahue	DC
334. Koch, William F.	Sawyer	Penn Forest	Campbell I	Juror
423. Kocher, Conrad	Boat Builder	Mauch Chunk		
496. Kocher, David	Farmer	Weatherly	Doyle	CC
500. Koons, Joseph	Moulder	Weatherly	Doyle	DC
317. Koons, Thomas	Gentleman	Lehighton	Doyle	DC
169. Koons, William	Butcher	Weissport	Campbell II	DP
385. Kreider, Tobias T.	Carpenter	Mauch Chunk	Doyle	DP
119. Kresge, Daniel	Laborer	Franklin Tsp.		
83. Kresge, Paul	Merchant	Towamensing		
68. Kuchner, August	Mason	Towamensing		
524. Kuder, J. H.	Clerk	Audenried		
338. Kuebler, Emanuel	Inn Keeper	Penn Forest		
505. Kuehner, Daniel	R. R. Eng.	Weatherly	Doyle	DP
329. Kuehner, Levi	Distiller	Penn Forest	Donahue	Juror
453. Kuehner, Thomas	Coal Dealer	East Mauch Chunk		
40. Kunkel, Joseph	Mason	Lower Towamensing	Kelly	DP

*Jurors of Irish Heritage
**DP=Defense Peremptory
CP=Commonwealth Peremptory

DC=Defense for Cause
CC=Commonwealth Challenge Cause

EXHIBIT 1

491. Kunkle, Charles	Lumberman	Kidder Tsp. N. D.	Kelly	DP
12. Kunkle, George	Farmer	Lower Towamensing		
478. Kunkle, Henry	Foreman	Kidder Tsp. S. D.		
477. Kunkle, Harrison	Lumberman	Kidder Tsp. S. D.		
586. Kuntz, Edward	Carpenter	Summit Hill		
249. Kuntz, Elias	Inn Keeper	Mahoning Tsp.	Kelly	Juror
320. Kuntz, Richard	Laborer	Lehighton		
256. Lapp, John	Farmer	Mahoning Tsp.		
419. Lauber, Jacob	Shoemaker	Mauch Chunk		
253. Lauchner, Adam	Farmer	Mahoning Tsp.		
517. Lauderbach, James	Lumberman	Audenried		
525. Leisenring, E. B.	Supt.	Audenried		
254. Lentz, Alfred	Farmer	Mahoning Tsp.		
492. Lentz, George W.	Carpenter	Weatherly	Campbell II	CP
406. Lentz, LaFayette	Coal Operator	Mauch Chunk		
319. Levanway, H. C.	Gentleman	Lehighton	Doyle	DC
543. Lewis, Thomas H.	Miner	Beaver Meadow		
520. Lewis, William H.	Miner	Audenried	Donahue	DC
36. Lichtenwatler, Daniel	Farmer	Lower Towamensing		
341. Lilly, William	Coal Operator	Mauch Chunk	Kelly	DC
255. Long, Henry	Farmer	Mahoning Tsp.	Doyle	Juror
291. Long, James	Foreman	Packerton		
313. Long, Zackary H.	Merchant	Lehighton		
252. Longacre, David S.	Farmer	Mahoning Tsp.	F/Mc	Juror
290. Longcomer, Charles	Foreman	Packerton		
355. Luckenbach, E. F.	Painter	Mauch Chunk		
416. Lynn, Joseph	Printer	Mauch Chunk	Campbell I	DC
528. Mace, Jacob	Farmer	Packer Tsp.	Donahue	CC
579. Marcey, B. W.	Cashier	Summit Hill	Donahue	DP
142. Markly, Stephen	Shoemaker	Franklin Tsp.		
213. Maurer, George	Farmer	East Penn Tsp.		

*Jurors of Irish Heritage
**DP=Defense Peremptory
CP=Commonwealth Peremptory
DC=Defense for Cause
CC=Commonwealth Challenge Cause

EXHIBIT 1

466. Maybe, William H.	Blacksmith	Kidder Tsp. N. D.		
522. McCollum, Ephraim	Foreman	Audenried	Campbell I	DP
470. McCormick, William	Lumberman	Kidder Tsp. N. D.	Campbell II	DC
287. McDaniel, J. T.	Inn Keeper	Packerton	Doyle	CC
87. McDaniel, Robert	Carpenter	Towamensing		
422. McFadden, Dominic*	Clerk/Clerk			
380. McGinley, John*	Merchant	Mauch Chunk	Campbell II	DC
337. Meckes, Adam	Inn Keeper	Penn Forest	Campbell I	Juror
327. Meckes, Samuel L.	Lumberman	Penn Forest		
336. Meckes, Samuel W.	Farmer	Penn Forest	Kelly	Juror
13. Mehrkam, Adam	Merchant	Lower Towamensing	Kelly	DC
549. Meixsell, Stephen	Engineer	Beaver Meadow	Doyle	DC
135. Meixsell, William	Carpenter	Franklin Tsp.		
8. Mendsen, Charles	Farmer	Lower Towamensing		
375. Meyer, J. A.	Dentist	Mauch Chunk	Kelly	DC
259. Miller, Aaron D.	Laborer	Mahoning Tsp.		
260. Miller, Amos	Farmer	Mahoning Tsp.		
447. Miller, Charles E.	Carpenter	East Mauch Chunk	Campbell I	Juror
261. Miller, Daniel	Farmer	Mahoning Tsp.		
353. Miller, Henry	Mason	Mauch Chunk	Kelly	DP
123. Miller, J. H.	Butcher	Franklin Tsp.		
257. Miller, John	Shoemaker	Mahoning Tsp.		
258. Miller, Lewis A.	Laborer	East Penn Tsp.		
22. Miller, R. E.	Tanner	Lower Towamensing		
379. Miner, John	Moulder	Mauch Chunk		
177. Montz, F. R.	Farmer	East Penn Tsp.		
357. Moore, Hugh	Merchant/Grocer	Mauch Chunk		
391. Morris, Frank	Agent	Mauch Chunk		
345. Morris, W. C.	Clerk	Mauch Chunk		
563. Moser, Abraham	Carpenter	Summit Hill	Doyle	DC
372. Moser, F. H.	Merchant	Mauch Chunk		

*Jurors of Irish Heritage
**DP=Defense Peremptory
CP=Commonwealth Peremptory

DC=Defense for Cause
CC=Commonwealth Challenge Cause

EXHIBIT 1

262. Moser, Nathan	Carpenter	Mahoning Tsp.	F/Mc	Juror
176. Moyer, Abraham	Farmer	East Penn Tsp.		
76. Moyer, David	Laborer	Towamensing		
44. Muschlitz, Robert	Gentleman	Lower Towamensing		
591. Muser, Mark	L&WB Coal Co.	Nesquehoning	Doyle	DC
264. Musselman, Josiah	Laborer	Mahoning Tsp.	F/Mc	Juror
501. Musselman, Peter	Machinist	Weatherly	Campbell I	DC
265. Musselman, Thomas	Farmer	Mahoning Tsp.		
263. Muthart, Levi	Laborer	Mahoning Tsp.		
178. Neff, Reuben	Farmer	East Penn Tsp.		
580. Neiumiller, H. G.	Merchant	Summit Hill		
490. Nicholson, William	Lumberman	Kidder Tsp. S. D.		
582. Nisley, William	Assessor	Summit Hill		
179. Noll, Samuel	Farmer	East Penn Tsp.	Kelly	Juror
214. Nothstein, Henry	Inn Keeper	East Penn Tsp.	Donahue	Juror
180. Nothstein, Noah	Merchant	East Penn Tsp.	Kelly	Juror
600. Nusbaum, John T.	Saloon Keeper	Lehighton	Doyle	DC
436. Orr, George	Clerk	Mauch Chunk		
344. Osborn, John	Laborer	Mauch Chunk		
212. Osenbach, Christian	Laborer	East Penn Tsp.		
127. Oswald, August	Merchant	Franklin Tsp.		
565. Patterson, Nathan D.	Agent/Coal Agent	Summit Hill	Kelly	Excused
518. Patterson, Thomas W.	Merchant	Audenried		
181. Peter, Gideon	Farmer	East Penn Tsp.		
101. Peter, Jacob	Merchant	Parryville		
158. Peter, Joseph M.	Clerk	Parryville		
103. Phifer, Jacob	Supt.	Parryville	F/Mc	Juror
552. Price, J. M.	Clerk	Beaver Meadow		
519. Prince, Frank	Coal Engineer	Audenried		
487. Protzman, Francis	Sawyer	Kidder Tsp. S. D.		
27. Prutzmanm, Charles	Carpenter	Lower Towamensing		

*Jurors of Irish Heritage
**DP=Defense Peremptory
CP=Commonwealth Peremptory
DC=Defense for Cause
CC=Commonwealth Challenge Cause

EXHIBIT 1

51. Prutzman, Thomas	Farmer	Lower Towamensing		
348. Rader, John	Merchant	Mauch Chunk		
276. Raubenbush, Thomas W.	Clerk	Packerton		
480. Rauch, William	Laborer	Kidder Tsp. S. D.	Doyle	DC
598. Raudenbush, J. W.	Inn Keeper	Lehighton		
113. Reber, Edward	Farmer	Franklin Tsp.		
5. Redline, John	Carpenter	Lower Towamensing		
576. Reed, John W.	Inn Keeper	Summit Hill	Campbell II	DC
541. Reese, David	Mining Boss	Nesquehoning		
544. Reese, John	Gentleman	Beaver Meadow		
553. Reese, J. P.	Machinist	Beaver Meadow	Doyle	CC
457. Rehrig, Aaron	Carpenter	East Mauch Chunk		
152. Rehrig, Cornelius	Farmer	Franklin Tsp.		
186. Rehrig, Gideon	Farmer	East Penn Tsp.	Campbell II	Juror
149. Rehrig, Jacob	Farmer	Franklin Tsp.	Campbell II	Juror
266. Rehrig, Jonas	Farmer	Mahoning Tsp.		
597. Rehrig, Owen	Painter	Lehighton		
185. Rehrig, Reuben	Farmer	East Penn Tsp.	Donahue	DP
187. Rehrig, William B.	Laborer	East Penn Tsp.	Kelly	Juror
351. Reihl, John	Merchant	Mauch Chunk		
269. Reinsmith, Nathan	Laborer	Mahoning Tsp.	Kelly	DP
53. Remaley, Daniel	Teacher	Lower Towamensing	Doyle	Juror
94. Remaly, LaFayette	Carpenter	Parryville		
365. Remmel, Edward	Lime Burner	Mauch Chunk	Kelly	DP
366. Rex, C. A.	Merchant	Mauch Chunk	Kelly	DC
267. Rex, Daniel	Farmer	Mahoning Tsp.	Kelly	Excused
268. Rex, Moses	Farmer	Mahoning Tsp.		
133. Rickert, J. K.	Merchant	Franklin Tsp.	Kelly	DC
560. Rickert, John	Teamster	Summit Hill		
157. Rinker, Oliver	Engineer	Parryville		
367. Roberts, William H.	Foundryman	Mauch Chunk	Campbell I	Juror

*Jurors of Irish Heritage
**DP=Defense Peremptory
CP=Commonwealth Peremptory

DC=Defense for Cause
CC=Commonwealth Challenge Cause

EXHIBIT 1

182. Romig, Daniel Jr.	Laborer	East Penn Tsp.		
533. Romig, John	Farmer	Packer Tsp.	Donahue	CC
183. Ross, William	Farmer	East Penn Tsp.	Doyle	CC
285. Roth, William	Foreman	Packerton	Campbell II	DC
104. Rowland, J. P.	Professor	Parryville		
184. Ruch, Jacob	Carpenter	East Penn Tsp.		
121. Ruch, Josiah	Lime Burner	Franklin Tsp.		
415. Salkeld, J. H.	Machinist	Mauch Chunk	Kelly	DC
378. Sandel, Alexander	Carpenter	Mauch Chunk	Doyle	DP
388. Sandel, Jacob	Cabinet Maker	Mauch Chunk		
278. Sandel, John	Farmer	Packerton	Campbell II	Juror
382. Sandel, Josiah	Carpenter	Mauch Chunk	F/Mc	DP
82. Schaeffer, David	Laborer	Towamensing		
73. Schaeffer, William	Shoemaker	Towamensing		
590. Schneider, Anthony	Merchant	Summit Hill	Doyle	Excused
170. Schoch, Daniel	Lime Burner	Weissport	Kelly	DP
191. Schoch, Philip	Huckster	East Penn Tsp.		
435. Schultz, John	Laborer	Mauch Chunk	Kelly	DC
459. Schwab, Edward	Plasterer	East Mauch Chunk		
153. Schwab, John	Laborer	Franklin Tsp.		
465. Scott, W. W.	Boss	Kidder Tsp. N. D.		
409. Scott, W. W.	Laborer	Mauch Chunk		
326. Searfass, Benjamin	Sawyer	Penn Forest		
324. Searfass, Fribie	Lumberman	Penn Forest	Kelly	Juror
325. Searfass, Henry	Laborer	Penn Forest		
328. Searfass, Peter	Lumberman	Penn Forest		
333. Searfass, Wilson	Sawyer	Penn Forest		
271. Seidel, Charles H.	Merchant	Mahoning Tsp.	Doyle	Excused
147. Sensinger, Edwin	Farmer	Franklin Tsp.		
407. Sensinger, Ely	Shoemaker	Mauch Chunk	Donahue	DP
14. Serch, Owen	Miller	Lower Towamensing		

*Jurors of Irish Heritage
**DP=Defense Peremptory
CP=Commonwealth Peremptory
DC=Defense for Cause
CC=Commonwealth Challenge Cause

EXHIBIT 1

45. Serfass, Daniel Sr.	Sawyer	Lower Towamensing	Kelly	DC
192. Shaffer, Thomas	Farmer	East Penn Tsp.		
89. Shaffer, William K.	Farmer	Towamensing		
273. Shives, Jacob	Farmer	Mahoning Tsp.		
193. Shoemaker, Daniel	Farmer	East Penn Tsp.		
42. Shoenaberger, George	Inn Keeper	Lower Towamensing		
438. Siegfried, Henry J.	Contractor	East Mauch Chunk		
442. Siegfried, Thomas	Bottler	East Mauch Chunk		
279. Sitler, Charles	Farmer	Packerton	Kelly	DC
270. Sitler, William	Farmer	Mahoning Tsp.	F/Mc	Juror
343. Skeer, Charles O.	Coal Operator	Mauch Chunk		
330. Smith, Charles	Lumberman	Penn Forest		
194. Smith, Elias	Farmer	East Penn Tsp.	Kelly	Juror
331. Smith, Franklin	Sawyer	Penn Forest		
354. Smith, Isaac	Foreman	Mauch Chunk	Doyle	DP
47. Smith, John	Laborer	Lower Towamensing		
60. Smith, Nathan	Farmer	Towamensing		
190. Smith, Owen	Farmer	East Penn Tsp.		
64. Smith, Paul	Farmer	Towamensing		
80. Snyder, Anthony	Farmer	Towamensing		
95. Snyder, A. R.	Butcher	Parryville		
81. Snyder, Harrison	Farmer	Towamensing		
43. Snyder, Jacob	Farmer	Lower Towamensing	Campbell II	Juror
154. Snyder, Nathan	Merchant	Franklin Tsp.	Campbell II	DC
19. Snyder, Reuben	Blacksmith	Lower Towamensing	Kelly	Juror
88. Snyder, Simon F.	Farmer	Towamensing		
3. Snyder, Solomon	Miller	Lower Towamensing	F/Mc	DP
96. Snyder, Stephen Sr.	Farmer	Parryville		
4. Snyder, Washington	Laborer	Lower Towamensing	Donahue	Juror
443. Solomon, John	Carpenter	East Mauch Chunk		
146. Solt, Solomon	Huckster	Franklin Tsp.		

*Jurors of Irish Heritage
**DP=Defense Peremptory
CP=Commonwealth Peremptory
DC=Defense for Cause
CC=Commonwealth Challenge Cause

EXHIBIT 1

557. Spencer, George	Assist. Supt.	Jeanesville	Campbell II	DP
414. Stedman, John S.	Jeweler	Mauch Chunk		
272. Steigerwalt, Edward	Farmer	Mahoning Tsp.		
188. Steigerwalt, Jacob	Farmer	East Penn Tsp.		
189. Steigerwalt, T. W.	Farmer	East Penn Tsp.		
532. Steiner, Reuben	Farmer	Packer Tsp.		
84. Stemler, Nathan	Inn Keeper	Towamensing		
514. Stetler, George	Farmer	Lehigh Tsp. P. Haven	F/Mc	Juror
507. Stevenson, John	Laborer R. R.	Weatherly		
599. Sthare, Adam W.	Shoemaker	Mauch Chunk		
475. Stimson, George	Merchant	Kidder Tsp. N. D.		
410. Stockett, John T.	Supt.	Mauch Chunk	Kelly	DC
566. Storch, Henry	Stone Mason	Summit Hill		
195. Straub, David H.	Farmer	East Penn Tsp.		
34. Straub, Levi	Merchant	Lower Towamensing	Doyle	Juror
55. Straub, Samuel	Farmer	Lower Towamensing		
476. Streeter, William F.	Lumberman	Kidder Tsp. N. D.	Donahue	DP
424. Stroh, Abraham	Foreman	Mauch Chunk	Donahue	DP
386. Stroh, William H.	Foundryman	Mauch Chunk		
100. Strohl, Joel	Farmer	Towamensing	Doyle	Juror
74. Strohl, William	Farmer	Towamensing		
321. Stucker, Francis	Blacksmith	Lehighton		
284. Stucker, Thomas	Laborer	Packerton	Campbell I	CP
513. Swank, David S.	Engineer	Lehigh Tsp. P. Haven		
472. Swartz, H. E.	Lumberman	Kidder Tsp. N. D.	Doyle	CC
370. Tacey, Joseph P.	Barber	Mauch Chunk	Kelly	DC
402. Taylor, John	G. F. Agt.	Mauch Chunk		
39. Thomas, William	Painter Miller	Lower Towamensing		
440. Thompson, Elias	Carpenter	East Mauch Chunk		
358. Thompson, William	Sal.Keeper/Sal.Keeper	Mauch Chunk	Kelly	DC
537. Tilston, Eli	Powder Mercht.	Packer Tsp.		

*Jurors of Irish Heritage
**DP=Defense Peremptory — DC=Defense for Cause
CP=Commonwealth Peremptory — CC=Commonwealth Challenge Cause

EXHIBIT 1

374. Tobias, A. H.	Insurance Agent	Mauch Chunk		
445. Twirring, George	Supt.	East Mauch Chunk		
389. Van Horn, Alfred	Shoemaker	Mauch Chunk		
37. Wagner, David	Farmer	Lower Towamensing		
65. Wagner, Reuben	Farmer	Towamensing		
595. Wagner, William	Gentleman	Lehighton	Doyle	DC
143. Walk, Augustus	Carpenter	Franklin Tsp.		
141. Walk, Solomon	Farmer	Franklin Tsp.		
383. Walter, T. Frank	Coal Operator	Mauch Chunk		
361. Wanka, George Jr.	Carpenter	Mauch Chunk	Doyle	DC
373. Warg, John H. Jr.	Coal Dealer	Mauch Chunk	Donahue	DC
594. Warner, William	Huckster	Lehighton	Donahue	DP
596. Waterbear, William	Foreman	Lehighton		
567. Watt, James	Teacher	Summit Hill	Kelly	DC
277. Weaver, Thomas M.	Contractor	Packerton		
432. Webb, Charles H.	Clerk	Mauch Chunk		
509. Weeks, Charles	Machinist	Weatherly		
217. Wehr, David	Mason	East Penn Tsp.	Campbell I	DC
216. Wehr, Owen	Farmer	East Penn Tsp.		
46. Weidaw, Peter	Boat Builder	Lower Towamensing		
542. Weir, John	Supt.	Beaver Meadow		
282. Weiss, Charles B.	Blacksmith	Packerton		
59. Weiss, John H.	Inn Keeper	Towamensing		
92. Wentz, Daniel	Sawyer	Parryville	Campbell II	Excused
97. Wentz, Dennis	Farmer	Parryville	Doyle	Excused
93. Wentz, Harrison	Farmer	Parryville		
483. Wernert, Francis	Lumberman	Kidder Tsp. S. D.		
467. West, Isaac	Blacksmith	Kidder Tsp. N. D.	Donahue	Juror
469. West, Levi	Lumberman	Kidder Tsp. N. D.	Doyle	Juror
593. Wilford, Henry	Boiler Maker	Summit Hill		
363. Wilhelm, William H.	Foreman	Mauch Chunk	Kelly	DC

*Jurors of Irish Heritage
**DP=Defense Peremptory
CP=Commonwealth Peremptory
DC=Defense for Cause
CC=Commonwealth Challenge Cause

EXHIBIT 1

559. Williams, Thomas R.	Miner	Summit Hill	Doyle	CC
431. Williams, William	Carpenter	Mauch Chunk	Campbell I	CC
499. Wilson, Edward C.	Engineer	Weatherly	Kelly	DC
512. Woodring, George	Boss	Lehigh Tsp. P. Haven	Kelly	DC
398. Woodring, H. J.	Inn Keeper	Mauch Chunk		
412. Yaeger, Benjamin F.	Justice	Mauch Chunk	Doyle	Excused
411. Yaeger, Leonard	Cab. Maker	Mauch Chunk		
218. Yanser, James	Laborer	East Penn Tsp.	Donahue	Juror
172. Yeakle, Solomon	Merchant	Weissport	Campbell I	DP
315. Younkin, R. J.	Carpenter	Lehighton	Campbell I	Juror
171. Yundt, Francis	Merchant	Weissport		
456. Zelner, Charles	Teamster	East Mauch Chunk	Campbell I	Juror
28. Ziegenfuss, David	Carpenter	Lower Towamensing	Doyle	Excused
139. Ziegenfuss, John C.	Mason	Franklin Tsp.		
35. Ziegenfuss, Reuben	Farmer	Lower Towamensing		
150. Ziegenfuss, Thomas	Mason	Franklin Tsp.		
283. Zimmerman, Benjamin H.	Laborer	Packerton	F/Mc	DP

*Jurors of Irish Heritage
**DP=Defense Peremptory — DC=Defense for Cause
CP=Commonwealth Peremptory — CC=Commonwealth Challenge Cause

EXHIBIT 1

LIST OF JURORS SUMMONED AS TALESMEN IN CASE OF COMMONWEALTH VS. MICHAEL DOYLE, JANUARY SESSIONS 1876

NO.	NAME	OCCUPATION	RESIDENCE	VOIR DIRE RESULT**	
T1.	Albright, Daniel B.	Lumberman	Weissport		
T2.	Bachman, G. H.	Engineer	Weatherly		
T3.	Beck, H. L.	Merchant	Weatherly		
T4.	Belsner, Charles	Blacksmith	Mauch Chunk		
T5.	Brady, Peter T.	Tobacconist	Lehighton		
T6.	Brill, Joseph	Butcher	Weatherly		
T7.	Buehman, Adam	Carriage Man.	Lehighton		
T8.	Campbell, Henry	Merchant	Franklin	Doyle	DP
T9.	Cheeseman, Peter	Plasterer	Weatherly	Doyle	Juror
T10.	Croll, Samuel	Gentleman	Weatherly		
T11.	Eberts, David	Livery Keeper	Lehighton		
T12.	Fegley, Mathias	Clerk	E. Mauch Chunk		
T13.	Feist, Joseph	Inn Keeper	Weissport		
T14.	Fenstermacher, Reuben	Merchant	Lehighton		
T15.	Flickinger, S.	Laborer	Weatherly		
T16.	Freeman, H. F.	Carpenter	Weatherly		
T17.	Freyman, Daniel	Stone Mason	Weatherly		
T18.	Gangwere, Samuel	Carpenter	Weatherly	Doyle	DC
T19.	Graver, William	Bakery	Lehighton		
T20.	Hein, Peter	Shoemaker	Lehighton		
T21.	Hoffecker, A. B.	Machinist	Weatherly	Doyle	DC
T22.	Hoover, Frank	Clerk	Weatherly		
T23.	Jones, George H.	Moulder	Weatherly		
T24.	Kistler, John	Boatman	Mauch Chunk		
T25.	Knecht, William H.	Merchant	Weissport	Doyle	CC
T26.	Kocher, William	Butcher	Weatherly	Doyle	DC
T27.	Long, Drake H.	Clerk	Lehighton	Doyle	T28.r
T28.	Miller, Isaac	Seamster	Weatherly		
T29.	Morrow, David K.	Gardner	E. Mauch Chunk	Doyle	DC

EXHIBIT 1A

COMMONWEALTH VS. MICHAEL J. DOYLE

T30. Oswald, August	Merchant	Franklin Twp.		
T31. Peters, Thomas	Carpenter	Weatherly		
T32. Pryer, John W.	Moulder	Weatherly		
T33. Remmel, Edward	Lime Burner	Mauch Chunk		
T34. Rouse, H. D.	Livery Keeper	Weatherly	Doyle	DP
T35. Smith, Nelson	Blacksmith	Weatherly		
T36. Steigerwalt, Lewis	Shoemaker	Weatherly	Doyle	DP
T37. Stiles, Daniel	Merchant	Weatherly	Doyle	DP
T38. Williams, Thomas A.	Shoemaker	Lehighton	Doyle	Juror
T39. Yeakle, Solomon	Lumber Dealer	Weissport		
T40. Yundt, Francis	Lumber Dealer	Weissport		

EXHIBIT 1A

NEWSPAPER COVERAGE OF THE CASE OF COMMONWEALTH VS. MICHAEL DOYLE, JANUARY SESSIONS 1876

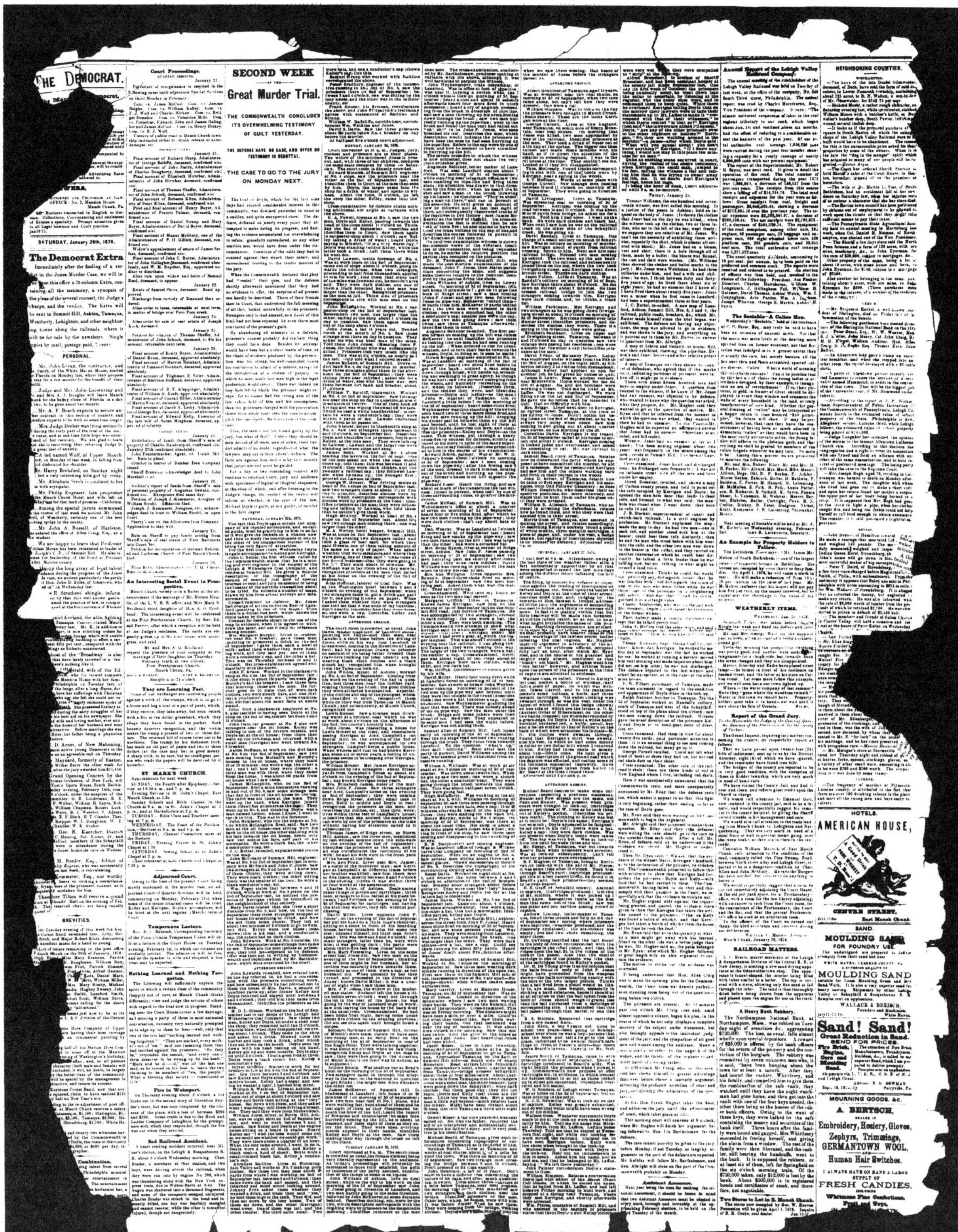

THE DEMOCRAT.

Court Proceedings.

SECOND WEEK

Great Murder Trial.

THE COMMONWEALTH CONCLUDES ITS OVERWHELMING TESTIMONY OF GUILT YESTERDAY.

THE DEFENSE HAVE NO CASE, AND OFFER NO TESTIMONY IN REBUTTAL.

THE CASE TO GO TO THE JURY ON MONDAY NEXT.

The Democrat Extra

PERSONAL.

BREVITIES.

WEATHERLY ITEMS.

Report of the Grand Jury.

RAILROAD MATTERS.

NEIGHBORING COUNTIES.

AMERICAN HOUSE,

MOULDING SAND

Sand! Sand!

EXHIBIT 2

VOIR DIRE OF JURY PANEL
COMMONWEALTH VS. MICHAEL J. DOYLE
JANUARY 16, 1876 - JANUARY 20, 1876

JUROR	VOIR DIRE INFO	ATTORNEY ACTION	COURT ACTION
1. Samuel Harleman	Dispatcher for Lehigh Valley R.R. - Read about killing of John P. Jones in newspapers - Can't say I formed an opinion	Defense Peremptory (1)	
2. Charles Fritz	Carpenter - Read about Jones killing in *Democrat* - Talked about it frequently - Heard it read from other newspapers - Has fixed opinion on guilt of prisoner - Would require evidence to change opinion	Defense Challenge for Cause	Sustained
3. William Bloss, Jr. #1	Heard and talked frequently about Jones murder - No opinion on guilt or innocence of prisoner - Understands German better than English	No Challenge	Juror Sworn
4. Jonas Beck #2	Heard of Jones killing but did not hear who killed him - "Have not made up my mind"	No Challenge	Juror Sworn

EXHIBIT 3

COMMONWEALTH VS. MICHAEL J. DOYLE

5. Mark Muser	Works for Lehigh & W. B. Coal Company at Nesquehoning - Read about killing of Jones in newspapers - Overheard conversations about killing here in Court but did not participate in them - Have opinion and expressed it - Would require good evidence to change opinion	Defense Challenge for Cause	Sustained
6. H. E. Swartz	Opposed to capital punishment	Commw. Challenge for Cause	Sustained
7. Andrew Graver, Jr.	Read and talked about Jones killing frequently - Formed opinion from newspaper stories - "I threw opinion aside a few months ago"	Defense Peremptory (2)	
8. J. T. McDaniel	Against capital punishment - "Could not convict of 1st degree murder unless I saw it myself"	Commw. Challenge for Cause	Sustained
9. Daniel Kuehner	Stationary engineer for Lehigh Valley R.R. - Read about Jones killing and heard about it - Have not formed opinion as to guilt or innocence of defendant	Defense Peremptory (3)	
10. William DeFrehn	Heard about killing of Jones - "Formed opinion based on what I heard" - Would take evidence to change opinion - If evidence would not agree with my opinion, my opinion would influence my verdict	Defense Challenge for Cause	Sustained

EXHIBIT 3

COMMONWEALTH VS. MICHAEL J. DOYLE

11. Joel Strohl #3	Favors hanging - Heard talk of killing of Jones - Understands but does not read or write English - Not asked about opinion	No Challenge	Juror Sworn
12. Alexander Sandel	Has opinion about prisoner - Would require evidence to change it - Read newspaper accounts of murder	Defense Challenge for Cause Defense Peremptory (4)	Overruled
13. Adam J. Christman	Heard about case - Talked about it - Has no opinion	No initial Challenge Commonwealth Peremptory (1)	
14. E. F. Keller	Heard about murder through *Mauch Chunk* newspaper - Has not formed opinion about prisoner	No initial Challenge Commonwlth Peremptory (2)	
15. Charles H. Seidel	Has read about this affair and formed and expressed opinion - Was on grand jury which returned indictment		Excused
16. Tobias T. Kreider	Has opinion about prisoner and expressed it - would require evidence to shake it - could try case impartially - Read accounts of Kelly	Defense Challenge for Cause Defense Peremptory (5)	Overruled
17. Stephen Meixsell	Read account of murder in *Democrat* - Has formed opinion and expressed it about prisoner	Defense Challenge for Cause	Sustained

EXHIBIT 3

COMMONWEALTH VS. MICHAEL J. DOYLE

18. E. Mell Boyle	Publisher of the *Coal Gazette* - Does not think he expressed an opinion about prisoner - When shown article he wrote in September of 1875, said he expressed no opinion - If sworn he would base verdict on evidence and divert his mind from any opinion he has of prisoner	Defense Challenge for Cause Defense Peremptory (6)	Overruled
19. E. T. Hooven	Conscientious scruples against capital punishment	Commw. Challenge for Cause	Sustained
20. Daniel Boyer, Jr. #4	Heard of killing but not name of person killed - No opinion	Defense Challenge for Cause	Overruled Juror Sworn
21. Benjamin F. Yaeger	County District Justice		Excused
22. Thomas Koons	Read about killing - Talked about it - Formed an opinion which would require evidence to change	Defense Challenge for Cause	Sustained
23. Manasses Acker	Heard of killing and read about it - Formed no opinion - Trouble understanding English - Hearing Problem	Commw. Challenge for Cause	Sustained
24. Thomas J. Heberling	Read statements in the *Democrat* - Talked with many people about the murder - Has no opinion	Defense Peremptory (7)	
25. George Wanka, Jr.	Talked about case with others frequently - Has strong opinion - Would require evidence to change - Did not read newspapers	Defense Challenge for Cause	Sustained

EXHIBIT 3

COMMONWEALTH VS. MICHAEL J. DOYLE

26. James Beiber	Does not understand English	Commw. Challenge for Cause	Sustained
27. C. H. Bower	Read about case in newspapers - discussed case every day - Has decided opinion about prisoner - "Would influence me in jury box"	Defense Challenge for Cause	Sustained
28. Levi Heiney	Read about case in *Coal Gazette* - Has not formed an opinion	Defense Peremptory (8)	
29. A. J. Brodhead	Against capital punishment	Commw. Challenge for Cause	Sustained
30. Anthony Schneider	"Nicht Versteht"		Excused
31. Daniel Remaley #5	Does not understand English as well as he might - No opinion - Does not understand all that was said - Does not recall whether he read anything about killing - Heard & talked about it, though	No Challenge	Juror Sworn
32. Abraham Moser	Heard case talked about continually - Did not read about killing - Has opinion about prisoner - Would require evidence to change it - Works for L&WB Coal Co.	Defense Challenge for Cause	Sustained
33. George Kemmerer	Does not understand much English - Speaks Dutch	Commw. Challenge for Cause	Sustained
34. Isaac Smith	Read newspaper accounts of killing - No positive opinion about prisoner - No opinion evidence would not remove	Defense Peremptory (9)	

EXHIBIT 3

COMMONWEALTH VS. MICHAEL J. DOYLE

35. Thomas R. Williams	Worked in mine where Jones was Superintendent - Talked about killing daily - Read about killing - "Formed opinion from what I heard" which would influence verdict	Commw. Challenge for Cause	Sustained
36. Aaron H. Gumbert	Opposed to capital punishment	Commw. Challenge for Cause	Sustained
37. William Rauch	Talked about killing of Jones - Formed fixed opinion which would take evidence to change	Defense Challenge for Cause	Sustained
38. William Wagner	Read about Jones killing in newspapers - formed a decided opinion about prisoner - Would influence verdict	Defense Challenge for Cause	Sustained
39. Samuel G. Heberling	Does not understand English very much - Against capital punishment	Commw. Challenge for Cause	Sustained
40. Samuel Hooven	Read about Jones killing in newspaper - Talked about it - Formed opinion - Might influence my verdict	Defense Challenge for Cause	Sustained
41. Henry Beltz	Talked and read about murder of Jones - Has formed opinion and likely influenced by opinion	Defense Challenge for Cause	Sustained
42. William Craig	Brother of Allen Craig		Excused
43. William H. Arner	Fixed decided opinion - Read newspaper accounts	Defense Challenge for Cause	Sustained

EXHIBIT 3

COMMONWEALTH VS. MICHAEL J. DOYLE

44. David Kocher	Opposed to capital punishment - Could not render a verdict unbiased by opinion	Commw. Challenge for Cause	Sustained
45. William Ross	Doesn't understand English well - Talks German at home	Commw. Challenge for Cause	Sustained
46. Joseph Koons	Has formed opinion which he thinks would prejudice him - Would take good evidence to upset my opinion - Read & talked about murder	Defense Challenge for Cause	Sustained
47. John T. Nusbaum	Talked and read about murder - Formed an abiding opinion	Defense Challenge for Cause	Sustained
48. H. C. Levanway	Read about murder and formed an opinion - Thinks evidence might remove opinion	Defense Challenge for Cause	Sustained
49. Abraham Henry #6	Heard about this affair - Talked and read about it - Formed opinion - To remove opinion would require evidence - Thinks he could try case uninfluenced by opinion	Defense Challenge for Cause	Overruled Juror Sworn
50. Levi West #7	Heard about murder - Knows no names - Read nothing about it	No Challenge	Juror Sworn
51. Levi Kern	Cannot understand English		Excused
52. David Ziegenfuss	"Nicht Versteht"		Excused
53. Lewis Drumbore	Heard, read and talked about case - Formed opinion which would influence verdict	Defense Challenge for Cause	Sustained

EXHIBIT 3

COMMONWEALTH VS. MICHAEL J. DOYLE

54. Levi Straub #8	Does not understand much English - Would understand what witnesses say - Read nothing about murder - Heard about it from others - Had not formed opinion	Commw. Challenge for Cause	Overruled Juror Sworn
55. J. P. Reese	Opposed to capital punishment	Commw. Challenge for Cause	Sustained
56. Dennis Wentz	Excused for sickness		Excused
57. Charles D. Culver	Heard about case and formed opinion - Would require evidence to remove it - Could render verdict uninfluenced by present opinion	Defense Challenge for Cause Defense Peremptory (10)	Overruled
58. Henry Long #9	Speaks German - Does not think he could understand everything - Never formed any opinion about case - Heard about murder at Church - Thinks that murderers should be hanged	Commw. Challange for Cause	Overruled Juror Sworn
59. J. R. Dimmick	Runs express & freight line business - Only heard man was shot and three arrested - No opinion	Defense Peremptory (11)	
60. Jacob Christman	Works at Lansford car shop - Talked about case and read about it - Formed opinion - Would take considerable evidence to change opinion - Could try case uninfluenced by opinion	Defense Challenge for Cause	Sustained
61. William H. Knecht	Could not vote for death penalty unless I saw act committed	Commw. Challenge for Cause	Sustained

EXHIBIT 3

COMMONWEALTH VS. MICHAEL J. DOYLE

62. William Kocher	Talked about murder of Jones and heard accounts of it read from newspapers - Formed strong opinion on Defendant's guilt	Defense Challenge for Cause	Sustained
63. Daniel Stiles	Read and talked about case but formed no opinion - Suggests Judge controlled his statement on "conscientious scruples"	Defense Peremptory (12)	
64. A. B. Hoffecker	Works as draftsman for Lehigh Valley R.R. - Read about case - Formed an abiding opinion	Defense Challenge for Cause	Sustained
65. Lewis Steigerwalt	Heard and talked about case - Formed opinion - Would take evidence to remove it - Thinks he could decide case uninfluenced by opinion	Defense Challenge for Cause Defense Peremptory (13)	Overruled
66. Samuel Gangwere	Carpenter for Lehigh Valley R.R. - Heard and read about case - Has strong fixed opinion	Defense Challenge for Cause	Sustained
67. Henry Campbell	Heard, read and talked about case - No opinion	Defense Peremptory (14)	
68. Peter Cheesman #10	Spoke, read and heard about case - No opinion - Should be governed by evidence	No Challenge	Juror Sworn
69. H. D. Rouse	Traveling salesman - Read and talked about case - Formed fixed opinion - Doesn't think opinion would influence verdict - Require "good evidence" to overcome	Defense Challenge for Cause Defense Peremptory (15)	Overruled

EXHIBIT 3

70. Thomas A. Williams #11	opinion	No Challenge	Juror Sworn
71. David K. Morrow	Read & Heard of murder - No opinion - Could enter jury box unbiased	Defense Challenge for Cause	Sustained
72. Drake H. Long #12	Talked and read about case frequently - Has strong opinion which might influence verdict - Would require very strong evidence to change opinion	No Challenge	Juror Sworn
	Heard and read about case - Never formed an opinion		

EXHIBIT 3

VOIR DIRE OF JURY PANEL
COMMONWEALTH VS. EDWARD KELLY
MARCH 29, 1876 - MARCH 30, 1876

JUROR	VOIR DIRE INFO	ATTORNEY ACTION	COURT ACTION
1. Dr. J. A. Meyer	Had opinion on guilt or innocence of prisoner and "would take strong evidence to change my mind" - Read evidence in *Carbon Democrat* and *Gazette* - Attended Doyle trial	Defense Challenge for Cause	Sustained
2. Nathan D. Patterson	Read about case in local newspapers - Expressed opinion about case - Ill health		Excused
3. Christian George #1	Read about Doyle case in local newspapers - Heard people talk about case - Does not understand English too well - Hard of hearing - No opinion formed	No Challenge	Juror Sworn
4. H. H. Everitt #2	Read about Doyle case in newspaper - Has no opinion	No Challenge	Juror Sworn
5. Elias Kuntz #3	Understands some, not much English - Read a little about killing - No opinion formed	No Challenge	Juror Sworn
6. John Keifer	Attended some of Doyle trial - Read about case in newspapers - No fixed opinion	Defense Peremptory (1)	

EXHIBIT 4

COMMONWEALTH VS. EDWARD KELLY

7. John T. Stockett	Has opinion about prisoner based on newspaper reports - Would be influenced by that opinion - Attended Doyle trial and witness at Doyle trial - Superintendant	Defense Challenge for Cause	Sustained
8. Gabriel Dilcher #4	No opinion - Read only Allentown paper	No Challenge	Juror Sworn
9. James G. Eadie	Attended Doyle trial - Read newspapers - Formed strong opinion	Defense Challenge for Cause	Sustained
10. Edward Remmel	Attended part of Doyle trial - Read newspaper - Formed opinion, but would not carry opinion into jury box.	Defense Challenge for Cause Defense Peremptory (2)	Overruled
11. J. H. Salkeld	Attended part of Doyle trial - Read newspaper - Formed opinion which would require convincing evidence to overcome	Defense Challenge for Cause	Sustained
12. Henry Miller	Would require strong evidence to change mind - Attended Doyle trial and heard one constable witness	Defense Peremptory (3)	
13. Charles Kunkle	Gets the *Mauch Chunk Democrat* newspaper but did not read articles about murder or trial - Never talked with anyone about cases	Defense Peremptory (4)	
14. Daniel Rex	"Nicht Versteht"		Excused

EXHIBIT 4

COMMONWEALTH VS. EDWARD KELLY

15. W. W. Blakeslee	Attended Doyle trial for 2 days- Has fixed opinion which would influence verdict - Read about case	Defense Challenge for Cause	Sustained
16. William Thompson	Attended Doyle trial - Has opinion and would require much evidence to change it	Defense Challenge for Cause	Sustained
17. C. A. Rex	Attended Doyle trial - Formed opinion which would require evidence to change - Read about case in newspaper	Defense Challenge for Cause	Sustained
18. Noah Nothstein #5	No opinion - Reads the *Advocate* but did not read anything about evidence in Doyle case - Heard case talked about	No Challenge	Juror Sworn
19. Nathan Houser	Opposed to hanging - No opinion - Refused to answer prosecutor's questions - Engineer		Excused
20. James Watt	Formed opinion about prisoner since Doyle trial - Read newspaper reports - Would require clear evidence to change mind	Defense Challenge for Cause	Sustained
21. Reuben Snyder #6	Reads a little English - Can understand some English - No opinion - Heard others talking about Doyle case - Did not understand questions asked	No Challenge	Juror Sworn

EXHIBIT 4

COMMONWEALTH VS. EDWARD KELLY

22. John W. Davis	Attended Doyle trial - Has fixed opinion about defendant and would require evidence to change mind - read about evidence in Doyle trial	Defense Challenge for Cause	Sustained
23. Charles J. Klotz, Jr.	Was member of grand jury that returned indictment against prisoner	Defense Challenge for Cause	Juror Withdrawn
24. James M. Fister	Attended Doyle trial - Read newspaper reports of Doyle trial - formed opinion from what I heard and read - would require evidence to change opinion	Defense Challenge for Cause	Sustained
25. Daniel S. Fritz	"Nicht Versteht" - Does not understand English		Excused
26. R. C. Carter	Read newspapers - Attended Doyle trial - Formed and expressed fixed opinion of guilt of defendant - Require evidence to change it	Defense Challenge for Cause	Sustained
27. Daniel Serfass, Sr.	I think prisoner should be hung - Read newspapers *Coal Gazette*, *Mauch Chunk Democrat* - Has fixed opinion	Defense Challenge for Cause	Sustained
28. Adam Mehrkam	Formed opinion - Could not try prisoner uninfluenced by opinion - Read newspaper reports of Doyle case	Defense Challenge for Cause	Sustained
29. George Woodring	Formed fixed opinion - Could not try prisoner uninfluenced by opinion - Read newspapers - Attended Doyle trial	Defense Challenge for Cause	Sustained

EXHIBIT 4

COMMONWEALTH VS. EDWARD KELLY

30. Samuel Noll #7	Has no knowledge of case	No Challenge	Juror Sworn
31. Joseph P. Tacey	Attended Doyle trial - Read evidence in newspapers - Fixed opinion about defendant	Defense Challenge for Cause	Sustained
32. John Bittner	Could not try prisoner unprejudiced by present opinion - Read newspaper reports of Doyle case	Defense Challenge for Cause	Sustained
33. Fribie Searfass #8	Has no opinion - Did not read or talk about case	No Challenge	Juror Sworn
34. Daniel Schoch	Heard some talking about Doyle case - No opinion	Defense Peremptory (5)	
35. Owen Graver #9	Does not read newspapers - No opinions formed - Heard some talking about killing	No Challenge	Juror Sworn
36. Elias Smith #10	Did not read about Doyle case - Thinks he could understand testimony - Does not understand English as well as he ought to - No opinion	No Challenge	Juror Sworn
37. Edward C. Wilson	Has fixed opinion about prisoner - Read evidence in newspapers	Defense Challenge for Cause	Sustained
38. George Fuehrer	Has opinion about prisoner from reading newspapers - Would not be unbiased	Defense Challenge for Cause	Sustained

EXHIBIT 4

COMMONWEALTH VS. EDWARD KELLY

39. Joseph Kunkel	I can make out English - Did not respond when asked whether he heard / read about cases - No opinion	Commonwealth Peremptory (1)	Sustained
40. Charles Sitler	Formed opinion about prisoner from newspapers	Defense Challenge for Cause	Sustained
41. George Beer	Objects to capital punishment	Commonwlth Challenge for Cause	Sustained
42. Nathan Reinsmith	Read about Doyle case - Works for Lehigh Valley Railroad - No opinion now, (had opinion, but gave it up)	Defense Peremptory (6)	
43. E. R. Cooke	Has fixed opinion and would require evidence to change - Read newspapers - Attended Doyle trial	Defense Challenge for Cause	Sustained
44. J. K. Rickert	Has fixed opinion - Attended part of Doyle trial - Read newspapers	Defense Challenge for Cause	Sustained
45. John Schultz	Formed opinion from reading newspapers	Defense Challenge for Cause	Sustained
46. Thomas Ervin	Has fixed opinion about prisoner - Did not read any evidence on Doyle	Defense Challenge for Cause	Sustained
47. William H. Wilhelm	Has opinion about prisoner from what was in newspapers which I presume is true - Foreman	Defense Challenge for Cause	Sustained
48. Daniel G. Bertsch	Read newspapers - Pretty fixed opinion about prisoner	Defense Challenge for Cause	Sustained

EXHIBIT 4

COMMONWEALTH VS. EDWARD KELLY

49. John Faust	78 years of age and defective hearing		Excused
50. William B. Rehrig #11	Heard about Jones' killing - No opinion - Don't think I talked to anyone about case	No Challenge	Juror Sworn
51. Gen. William Lilly	Has opinion on case from reading newspapers and rumors circulating through the atmosphere - Attended part of Doyle trial - Coal operator	Defense Challenge for Cause	Sustained
52. Samuel W. Meckes #12	Did not read about Doyle case in newspapers - No opinion	No Challenge	Juror Sworn

EXHIBIT 4

VOIR DIRE OF JURY PANEL
COMMONWEALTH VS. ALEXANDER CAMPBELL
MURDER OF JOHN P. JONES
JUNE 21, 1876

JUROR	VOIR DIRE INFO	ATTORNEY ACTION	COURT ACTION
1. W. P. Hyndman	Might be witness in case		Excused by consent of parties
2. George F. Anthony	Read evidence of Doyle trial and Kerrigan confession in newspaper - Has strong opinion about defendant's guilt - "Would take strong evidence to change my opinion about defendant's guilt"	Defense Challenge for Cause	Sustained
3. Adam Meckes #1	Has not read anything about case - Heard Doyle and Kelly cases talked about in the Township - No opinion	No Challenge	Juror Sworn
4. Elias Berger #2	Works at Packerton shops - Read evidence of Doyle and Kelly trials in newspapers - Read Kerrigan's confession - "Formed opinion about prisoner from what I read" - Would take strong evidence to change opinion - Thinks he could render verdict uninfluenced by opinion when asked by court	Defense Challenge for Cause	Overruled Juror Sworn
5. Isaac Butz	Sick		Excused for Sickness

EXHIBIT 5

COMMONWEALTH VS. ALEXANDER CAMPBELL

6. Fisher Hazard	Member of Board of Managers of LC&N Company - Would scrutinize evidence very carefully - Read evidence of Doyle and Kelly cases and Kerrigan's confession in newspaper - "Formed strong opinion from what I read in Kerrigan's confession that was evidence that pointed to Campbell's guilt" - "Could not sit as juror as if I never heard about case" - Would require pretty strong evidence to change opinion -"There ought to be more hangings than there is"	Defense Challenge for Cause	Sustained
7. R. J. Younkin #3	Carpenter - Lives in Lehighton - Read evidence of Doyle and Kelly cases in *Carbon Advocate* and *Shenandoah Herald* - Read Kerrigan's confession - talked about case - said he did not form opinion	No Challenge	Juror Sworn
8. David Wehr	Reads a little English - Speaks and keeps accounts in German - Would not be able to understand witnesses, lawyers or judge	Defense Challenge for Cause	Sustained

EXHIBIT 5

COMMONWEALTH VS. ALEXANDER CAMPBELL

9. Charles E. Miller #4	Read evidence in Doyle and Kelly cases - Also read about cases in Pottsville - Read Kerrigan's confession - Has opinion about defendant's guilt - Heard case discussed frequently - When asked if opinion would influence verdict, juror said "I don't think it would. It might, I don't know"	No Challenge	Juror Sworn
10. Franklin Flick #5	Read nothing and heard nothing about case - No opinion - No knowledge of case	No Challenge	Juror Sworn
11. Reuben Hunsicker	Read the evidence in Kelly and Doyle case - Heard about Kerrigan's confession - No opinion about prisoner	Defense Peremptory (1)	
12. Asa R. Beers	Read Kerrigan's confession - Read evidence of Pottsville cases in *Miners Journal* - "Strong opinion about Defendant's guilt" - in Court to hear Doyle case	Defense Peremptory (2)	
13. Joseph Lynn	Owner and Publisher of *Mauch Chunk Democrat* - Read and published evidence in Doyle and Kelly cases - Also Kerrigan's confession - Wrote editorials expressing strong opinion on guilt of prisoner - Believes Campbell is guilty "of what he is accused of."	Defense Challenge for Cause	Sustained

EXHIBIT 5

COMMONWEALTH VS. ALEXANDER CAMPBELL

14. Solomon Dreisbach	"Against death penalty" - Entire discussion on this issue	Commw. Challenge for Cause	Sustained
15. Levi Grum	Works on railroad - Has opinion on prisoner's guilt which would require evidence to change - Heard case talked about	Defense Challenge for Cause Defense Peremptory (3)	Overruled
16. Jacob Frantz	Does not read/write English	Defense Challenge for Cause	Sustained
17. Solomon Yeakle	Read about Doyle and Kelly cases - Has opinion about guilt of prisoner	Defense Peremptory (4)	
18. Ephraim McCollum	Read evidence of Doyle and Kelly cases and Kerrigan's confession in newspaper - Thinks he could try defendant on evidence - Strong opinion about guilt of Defendant - Would require evidence to change	Defense Challenge for Cause Defense Peremptory (5)	Overruled
19. Daniel Christman	"Nicht Versteht"		Excused
20. Jacob Ginder, Sr.	Heard a good deal of talk about case and the Mollie Maguires - Thinks he could render verdict on evidence - formed opinion	Defense Challenge for Cause Defense Peremptory (6)	Overruled
21. A. W. Eaches #6	Read about Doyle and Kelly cases - Heard them talked about and talked about them - no opinion formed	No Challenge	Juror Sworn

EXHIBIT 5

COMMONWEALTH VS. ALEXANDER CAMPBELL

22. William H. Roberts #7	Read the confession of Kerrigan in newspaper - Heard a great deal of public opinion expressed about the guilt or innocence of Campbell in Mauch Chunk - formed "general opinion"	No Challenge	Juror Sworn
23. Thomas Stucker	Carpenter for Lehigh Valley R.R. - "Friend of Carroll's Brother" - no opinion	Commw. Peremptory (1)	
24. William F. Koch #8	Read confession of Kerrigan in *Carbon Democrat* - Has opinion of cases - Not very strong	No Challenge	Juror Sworn
25. Charles Horn #9	Stationary engineer for a tannery in Lehighton - Read evidence of Doyle case in newspaper - Heard opinion about guilt or innocence of defendant - No opinion	No Challenge	Juror Sworn
26. Jonas C. Beer	Works on a farm - Read some of Kerrigan's confession in the newspaper - Cannot understand everything in Court - Speaks mostly in German - Has opinion	Defense Challenge for Cause	Sustained
27. Peter Musselman	Machinist from Weatherly - Read confession of Kerrigan in newspaper - Formed opinion from what I read in Doyle and Kelly cases and Pottsville case - "I don't believe my opinion would be changed by evidence"	Defense Challenge for Cause	Sustained

EXHIBIT 5

COMMONWEALTH VS. ALEXANDER CAMPBELL

28. Stephen Fenstermaker	Read confession of Kerrigan and evidence of Doyle and Kelly cases in newspaper - Read McParlan's testimony in Pottsville case - "From what I have read, I think he is guilty"	Defense Challenge for Cause	Sustained
29. William Williams #10	Read Kerrigan's confession - Has opinion on guilt or innocence of prisoner - Believes he can render verdict on evidence - "Scruples about capital punishment"	Commw. Challenge for Cause	Overruled Juror Sworn
30. Jonas Beer	Read Kerrigan's confession - Strong opinion about Defendant's guilt - Could not be changed by evidence	Defense Challenge for Cause	Sustained
31. John Behler	Read Kerrigan's confession - Formed strong opinion about prisoner's guilt or innocence - Would require strong evidence to change it - Could not try case on the evidence -Strong opinion about Defendant's guilt	Defense Challenge for Cause	Sustained
32. Charles Henning	Read Kerrigan's confession and case in Pottsville - Read evidence in Doyle and Kelly cases - Partly formed opinion	Defense Peremptory (7)	
33. Edward Freyman	Does not understand English - Served as juror previously	Defense Challenge for Cause	Sustained

EXHIBIT 5

COMMONWEALTH VS. ALEXANDER CAMPBELL

34. James Belford	Read part of evidence of Doyle and Kelly cases and Kerrigan's confession in newspaper - Thinks he could try case according to the evidence - Has opinion	Defense Peremptory (8)	
35. Harrison Heimbach #11	No opinion of case - Heard a little about case	No Challenge	Juror Sworn
36. Charles Zelner #12	No opinion or knowledge of case	No Challenge	Juror Sworn

EXHIBIT 5

VOIR DIRE OF JURY PANEL
COMMONWEALTH VS. JOHN DONAHUE
OCTOBER 19, 1876 - OCTOBER 20, 1876

JUROR	VOIR DIRE INFO	ATTORNEY ACTION	COURT ACTION
1. Ely Sensinger	Does not understand what capital punishment means - Talked and read about case - No Opinion - "Was a witness in Pottsville in one of 'Molly Maguire' cases, so termed" - Heard that Donahue was a "Molly" - Read newspapers about Doyle and Kelly cases	Defense Peremptory (1)	
2. John Hauck #1	Lives in Lehighton - No feelings or prejudice against prisoner - No opinion about case - Never heard cases spoken of	No Challenge	Juror Sworn
3. Isaac West #2	Read some about trial - Has not talked about it - No opinion - "Thinks" he can render verdict according to evidence	No Challenge	Juror Sworn
4. John Glasser	Partly opposed to capital punishment - "I will not take what I cannot give"	Commw. Challenge for Cause	Sustained
5. John H. Warg, Jr.	Has opinion on guilt of prisoner - Would take evidence to change opinion - "may have heard something outside evidence" which would influence him	Defense Challenge for Cause	Sustained

EXHIBIT 6

COMMONWEALTH VS. JOHN DONAHUE

6. Francis Stucker #3	Read about case - Did not express any opinion about prisoner's guilt	No Challenge	Juror Sworn
7. James Yanser #4	Poor knowledge of English - did not understand Judge - Converses in German at home	No Challenge	Court refused to excuse juror because of poor knowledge of English - Juror Sworn
8. Levi Kuehner #5	Never heard of case - No opinion	No Challenge	Juror Sworn
9. Reuben Rehrig	Understands English well enough but not all - Heard nothing about case - Has not expressed any opinion about case	Defense Peremptory (2)	
10. William H. Lewis	Has opinion about defendant's guilt - Could not render verdict uninfluenced by opinion	Defense Challenge for Cause	Sustained
11. William Behler	Heard case discussed many times - Tavern keeper in Weissport - Read about case - No Opinion - "I guess I could decide case without prejudice"	Defense Peremptory (3)	
12. William Warner	Heard case talked about while at Courthouse - Has not formed opinion	Defense Peremptory (4)	
13. Paul Danner #6	"Heard talk about case since I'm here" - Has not read about case - Was present during perjury cases in Court - "in during perjury case" - No opinion	Defense Challenge for Cause	Overruled Juror Sworn
14. Jacob Christman	Spoke only German	Commw. Challenge for Cause	Sustained

EXHIBIT 6

COMMONWEALTH VS. JOHN DONAHUE

15. J. D. Hoffman #7	Understands some but not every word of English - Had not read anything or heard anything about case - No opinion about prisoner	No Challenge	Juror Sworn
16. Benjamin Becker	Does not understand English "as good as I ought to" - Does business in German - Does not write - Has opinion about defendant's guilt and expressed it - Heard "a good bit" about prisoners	Defense Challenge for Cause	Sustained
17. Abraham Stroh	Read and talked about case - Has not formed opinion - Foreman	Defense Peremptory (5)	
18. Joseph Anthony	Read and talked about case	Defense Peremptory (6)	
19. Josiah H. Harlan	Opposed to capital punishment	Commw. Challenge for Cause	Sustained
20. George W. Esser	Has opinion on guilt of prisoner - Would require evidence to change opinion - Would decide case on evidence	Defense Peremptory (7)	
21. John Romig	Understands very little English	Commw. Challenge for Cause	Sustained
22. Jacob Mace	Farmer - Cannot read or write - Does not understand English very well - Talks mostly German	Commw. Challenge for Cause	Sustained
23. Peter Hartz	Hotel keeper - Read and talked about case considerably - Could not render unbiased verdict	Defense Challenge for Cause	Sustained

EXHIBIT 6

COMMONWEALTH VS. JOHN DONAHUE

24. W. S. Hobart	Clerk for LC&N Co. - Read and talked about case - Has opinion about defendant's guilt - Heard defendant was connected with Powell murder - Would require evidence to change opinion - "I am considerably prejudiced"	Defense Challenge for Cause	Sustained
25. Alvin Diehl	Opposed to hanging - Understands only half of what is said in English - Could not vote guilty if penalty was death	Commw. Challenge for Cause	Sustained
26. Enos Koch	"Read and talked about these other Mollies" - "Could not render verdict uninfluenced by what I read" - Does not hear on left side and has difficulty hearing	Defense Challenge for Cause	Juror excused because of hearing problems
27. David DeLong	Cattle dealer in East Penn Township - Does not understand much English - Speaks and writes in German - Neighbors are all German - Heard about case	Defense Peremptory (8)	
28. Washington Snyder #8	No opinion formed or expressed about prisoner - Not asked if he had heard about cases	No Challenge	Juror Sworn
29. Griffith DeLong #9	Does not understand English very well - Would not understand what all the witnesses say - Has not heard or read anything about case - When asked if he could render verdict on evidence, answered "I guess I could" - No opinion	No Challenge	Juror Sworn

EXHIBIT 6

COMMONWEALTH VS. JOHN DONAHUE

30. B. W. Marcey	Read, heard and talked about case very frequently	Defense Peremptory (9)	
31. Jacob Horn	Hard of hearing - Foreman	Commw. Challenge for Cause	Sustained
32. Nathan Clauss	Has opinion about guilt of prisoner - Does not read or write English - Was witness for Commonwealth in Yost case in Schuylkill County	Defense Challenge for Cause	Sustained
33. William F. Streeter	Heard and read about case - Thinks he could render verdict on evidence - Has opinion	Defense Peremptory (10)	
34. Oliver Bloss #10	Has not heard or read about case - No opinion on guilt of prisoner	No Challenge	Juror Sworn
35. Levi Freyman #11	Heard and talked about case - Read a little about it - Has not formed opinion	No Challenge	Juror Sworn
36. Henry Nothstein #12	Does not understand English very well - Has a tavern in East Penn - Does business in Dutch & German - Guesses he could understand some of the evidence - Did not hear or read about case - No opinion	No Challenge	Juror Sworn

EXHIBIT 6

VOIR DIRE OF JURY PANEL
COMMONWEALTH VS. THOMAS P. FISHER & PATRICK MCKENNA
DECEMBER 5, 1876

JUROR	VOIR DIRE INFO	ATTORNEY ACTION	COURT ACTION
1. Joseph H. Chapman #1	No fixed opinion about guilt/innocence of prisoners - Read evidence about Donahue trial in newspaper - Not present while Donahue trial in progress	No Challenge	Juror Sworn
2. George Stetler #2	Read of the Powell case in newspaper - Read about evidence from Donahue trial in *Carbon Democrat* and *Gazette* - Conversed about case - Expressed no opinion about guilt/innocence of the two prisoners	No Challenge	Juror Sworn
3. James W. Heberling	Conversed about the evidence in the Donahue case - No fixed opinion on that evidence - Expressed opinion against the Mollie Maguires - Says he will be guided by evidence and not his prejudice	Defense Challenge for Cause Defense Peremptory (1)	Overruled
4. Henry Henning #3	Neither read nor heard about Donahue trial but heard talk about Powell killing - No opinion about defs' guilt/innocence - Feels sorry for the defs - Can only "get the meaning of" the witnesses	No Challenge	Juror Sworn

EXHIBIT 7

COMMONWEALTH VS.THOMAS P. FISHER & PATRICK MCKENNA

5. George Emery	Did not read about Donahue trial but talked about it - Cannot read well - No expressed opinion about defs' guilt/innocence - Would judge defendants based on evidence, whether or not it showed they commited a crime	Commonwealth Peremptory (1)	
6. Alexander Campbell #4	No opinion as to defendants' guilt/innocence - Read about Donahue trial in newspaper but claimed that would not influence him - Admits to prejudice against Mollie Maguires and that this prejudice would prevail if defendants were members connected with murder	No Challenge	Juror Sworn
7. G. W. Dreisbach	No opinion about defs' guilt/innocence - Heard talk about Campbell and Powell - Believed anyone belonging to the Mollie Maguires "ought to be punished"	Defense Challenge for Cause	Sustained
8. George Klein #5	Read evidence about Donahue trial in newspaper - No opinion about defs' guilt/innocence - No expressed bias against the Mollie Maguires	No Challenge	Juror Sworn
9. Benjamin H. Zimmerman	Read "pretty much all of" Donahue case in newspaper - No expressed bias against Mollie Maguires - No opinion as to defs' guilt or innocence	Defense Peremptory (2)	

EXHIBIT 7

COMMONWEALTH VS.THOMAS P. FISHER & PATRICK MCKENNA

10. Henry Bretney	Did not understand English well - 74 years old		Excused for age and insufficient understanding of English
11. John Green	Had opinion as to defs' guilt/innocence at time of their arrest - Expressed bias against anyone connected with Mollie Maguires - Could not separate evidence from connection to Mollies	Defense Challenge for Cause	Sustained
12. Moses Heilman	Read about Donahue case in newspaper - Prejudiced against Mollie Maguires - "I hardly think I could" try the case upon the evidence	Defense Challenge for Cause	Sustained
13. Charles Kelchner	Did not read about Donahue case but heard talk - Claimed no prejudice against Mollie Maguires - Foreman at Hazard's yard for Lehigh & Wilkes Barre Coal Co.	Defense Peremptory (3)	
14. William Roth	Claimed no opinion as to defendants' guilt/innocence - Heard about this case and the Donahue case, but did not read or form opinion about Donahue case - No expressed bias against the Mollie Maguires - Employed as car repairman at Packerton for the Lehigh Valley Road	Defense Peremptory (4)	

EXHIBIT 7

COMMONWEALTH VS.THOMAS P. FISHER & PATRICK MCKENNA

15. Jacob Boose	Read evidence about Donahue trial in newspaper and spoke with people about the case - Expressed a prejudice against the Mollie Maguires	Defense Peremptory (5)	
16. John McGinley	Expressed strong fixed opinion - Only "strong evidence" could change that opinion	Defense Challenge for Cause	Sustained
17. F. J. Held	Difficulty in understanding and writing English		Excused
18. Jacob Phifer #6	Ran a foundry for the Lehigh furnace at East Penn Junction - Knew "very little" about the case - No opinion about case and no expressed prejudice against the Mollies - Was here one day while Donahue was on trial	No Challenge	Juror Sworn
19. Josiah Musselman #7	Teacher for Mahoning Township - Read about Donahue trial in newspaper, but does not remember what he read - No expressed opinion about the defendants or bias against the Mollies	No Challenge	Juror Sworn
20. John Sandel	Served as juryman several times before - No expressed opinion - Heard about the Donahue case	Defense Peremptory (6)	
21. David S. Longacre #8	Read about Donahue case in newspaper - No expressed opinion	No Challenge	Juror Sworn

EXHIBIT 7

COMMONWEALTH VS.THOMAS P. FISHER & PATRICK MCKENNA

22. Josiah Sandel	Read about Donahue case, but claimed no opinion on it - "Rather prejudiced against the order"(Mollie Maguires) - No opinion on case	Defense Peremptory (7)	
23. Benjamin Greensweig	No expressed opinion about guilt/innocence of defendants - Heard but did not read about Donahue case - Understands what is said in court "pretty near" - Expressed feeling prejudice against some orders w/in the Mollies	Defense Peremptory (8)	
24. William Bittenbender	66 yr old farmer who was hard of hearing - Poor grasp of English		Excused
25. Christian Fulmer #9	Read about case in newspaper and heard talk about it - "Passed no opinion about it" - No expressed prejudice against the Mollies	No Challenge	Juror Sworn
26. Solomon Snyder	No expressed opinion about the case - Read nothing about this case, but did hear talk about the Donahue case - Lived near the Blue Mt. down below the gap	Defense Peremptory (9)	
27. William Koons	Weissport resident - No opinion about the guilt/innocence of the defendants' - Did not read about the case and heard "very little" about it	Defense Peremptory (10)	

EXHIBIT 7

COMMONWEALTH VS.THOMAS P. FISHER & PATRICK MCKENNA

28. Nathan Moser #10	No opinion about the guilt or innocence of the defs' - "Partly" read about Donahue case - Expressed no prejudice against the Mollies	No Challenge	Juror Sworn
29. Samuel Bradley	Machinist for Albright and Stroh - Read about Donahue case in newspaper - Expressed opinion	Defense Challenge for Cause Defense Peremptory (11)	Overruled
30. Jacob Fritzinger #11	Hard of hearing - Cannot hear when "they speak softly" - Heard talk about Fisher-McKenna trial, but expressed no opinion - Retired wagon and plow maker in good health - 79 years old	No Challenge	Juror Sworn
31. William Sitler #12	Heard of the case - Expressed no opinion - Understands "biggest part" of English, but not all words	No Challenge	Juror Sworn

EXHIBIT 7

VOIR DIRE OF JURY PANEL
COMMONWEALTH VS. ALEXANDER CAMPBELL
MURDER OF MORGAN POWELL
DECEMBER 18, 1876

JUROR	VOIR DIRE INFO	ATTORNEY ACTION	COURT ACTION
1. David Beltz #1	Expressed no opinion as to guilt/innocence of defendant - Not asked if he read/heard anything about defendent	No Challenge	Juror Sworn
2. Samuel Bradley	No objection to Capital Punishment - Only the Commonwealth's 1st question asked	Defense Peremptory (1)	
3. Jacob Boose	Fixed opinion about guilt/innocence of defendant - Admitted that his opinion would bias his decisions in trial	Defense Challenge for Cause	Sustained
4. George Berger #2	No opinion about guilt/innocence of defendant - Claimed no knowledge about case	No Challenge	Juror Sworn
5. Daniel Wentz	No opinion as to guilt/innocence of defendant - Read about case in newspaper - Could try case on the evidence, but could not "stand it for any length of time" - Excused for age/health		Excused

EXHIBIT 8

COMMONWEALTH VS.ALEXANDER CAMPBELL

6. Caleb Fisher	Strong fixed opinion - "It would take strong evidence to remove my opinion" - Not asked if he heard or read anything	Defense Peremptory (2)	
7. Samuel Heist	"Pretty strong" opinion - Would require evidence to remove	Defense Challenge for Cause	Sustained
8. E. E. Dodson #3	Does not know that he has formed or expressed an opinion - No information on whether he read/heard of case - Feels that he could go on the evidence	No Challenge	Juror Sworn
9. Jacob Snyder #4	No expressed opinion - Talked about the case - Could try case according to the evidence	No Challenge	Juror Sworn
10. Gideon Rehrig #5	No expressed opinion - Did not talk about the case	No Challenge	Juror Sworn
11. John W. Reed	Expressed fixed opinion - Would take strong evidence to remove it	Defense Challenge for Cause	Sustained
12. Robert Campbell	No opinion - Claimed that he knew nothing about the case	Defense Peremptory (3)	
13. Nathan Snyder	Fixed opinion - Would require strong evidence to change it	Defense Challenge for Cause	Sustained
14. Jacob Rehrig #6	No opinion as to the defendants guilt/innocence - Could go according to the evidence	No Challenge	Juror Sworn

EXHIBIT 8

COMMONWEALTH VS.ALEXANDER CAMPBELL

15. Edwin Andrews #7	No expressed opinion - Knew nothing about the case - Tended store for *Miles & Andrews*	No Challenge	Juror Sworn
16. William Roth	Fixed opinion - Would require strong evidence to remove it - Familiar with facts of case through newspaper	Defense Challenge for Cause	Sustained
17. George Spencer	Lived in Brisco - No other questions asked	Defense Peremptory (4)	
18. Josiah Andreas	No objection to Capital Punishment - Only the Comm.'s 1st question asked	Defense Peremptory (5)	
19. Benjamin Greensweig #8	Towamensing resident - No opinion - Knew nothing about the case	No Challenge	Juror Sworn
20. George W. Lentz	Objection to Capital Punishment	Commonwealth Peremptory (1)	
21. Lewis Kinkle	Expressed strong opinion - Would require evidence to remove it	Defense Challenge for Cause	Sustained
22. G. W. Dreisbach	Could not understand the Commonwealth's question regarding Capital Punishment	Defense Peremptory (6)	
23. Joseph Feist	Has formed and expressed strong opinion	Defense Challenge for Cause	Sustained
24. William Koons	Expressed no opinion - Talked with people about this case and all of the previous ones	Defense Challenge for Cause Defense Peremptory (7)	Overruled

EXHIBIT 8

COMMONWEALTH VS.ALEXANDER CAMPBELL

25. William McCormick	Maintains no opinion against Campbell in particular, but has fixed opinion about the Mollie Maguires - Did not feel he would be able to go by the evidence if Campbell was proven to be a member of the Mollie Maguires	Defense Challenge for Cause	Sustained
26. Jonas Gerhart	Opposed to hanging as a death penalty - Did not understand questions		Excused
27. Charles Fritz #9	Mahoning Valley resident - No expressed opinion about case - Claimed no knowledge about case	Defense Challenge for Cause	Overruled Juror Sworn
28. Nathan Hoffman #10	Understood English "pretty well" - No opinion as to the defendants guilt/innocence - No knowledge of case	No Challenge	Juror Sworn
29. John McGinley	Strong fixed opinion - Would require evidence to remove it - Heard Campbell's name associated with the Powell killing in the newspaper - Admitted to forming opinion from that newspaper article - Mauch Chunk resident	Defense Challenge for Cause	Sustained
30. John Sandel #11	No opinion as to guilt/innocence of the defendant - No information on whether he read/heard about case	No Challenge	Juror Sworn

EXHIBIT 8

COMMONWEALTH VS.ALEXANDER CAMPBELL

31. A. G. Dollenmeyer	No opinion as to guilt/innocence of defendant - Fixed opinion against Mollie Maguires based on "talk as talk goes"	Defense Challenge for Cause Defense Peremptory (8)	Overruled
32. Elias George #12	No opinion as to guilt/innocence of defendant - Heard talk about the case - Has not formed opinion against the Mollie Maguires	No Challenge	Juror Sworn

EXHIBIT 8

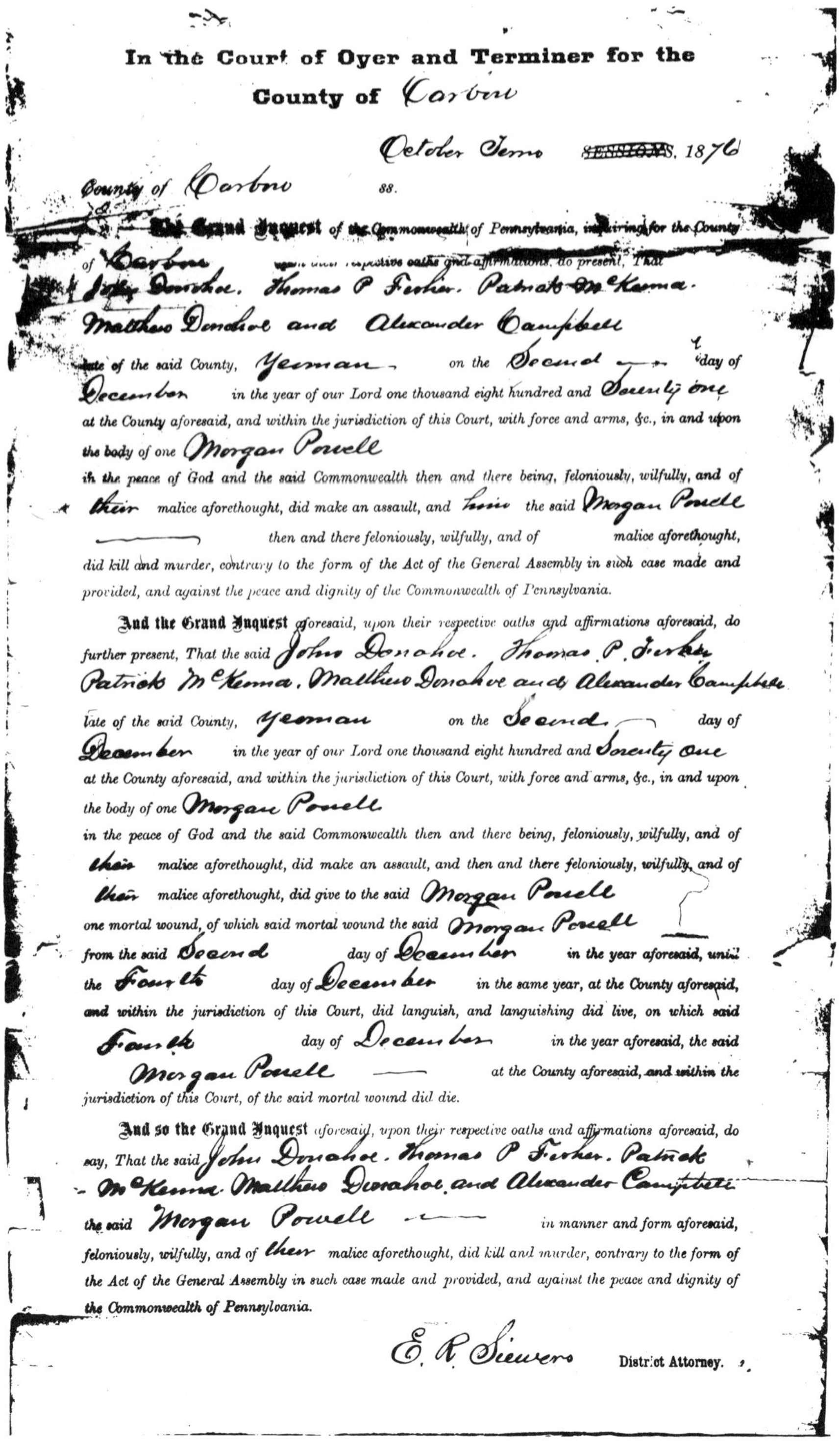

In the Court of Oyer and Terminer for the County of Carbon

October Term SESSIONS, 1876

County of Carbon ss.

The Grand Inquest of the Commonwealth of Pennsylvania, inquiring for the County of Carbon upon their respective oaths and affirmations, do present, That John Donahoe, Thomas P Fisher, Patrick McKenna, Matthew Donahoe and Alexander Campbell late of the said County, Yeoman, on the Second day of December in the year of our Lord one thousand eight hundred and Seventy one at the County aforesaid, and within the jurisdiction of this Court, with force and arms, &c., in and upon the body of one Morgan Powell in the peace of God and the said Commonwealth then and there being, feloniously, wilfully, and of their malice aforethought, did make an assault, and him the said Morgan Powell then and there feloniously, wilfully, and of malice aforethought, did kill and murder, contrary to the form of the Act of the General Assembly in such case made and provided, and against the peace and dignity of the Commonwealth of Pennsylvania.

And the Grand Inquest aforesaid, upon their respective oaths and affirmations aforesaid, do further present, That the said John Donahoe, Thomas P. Fisher, Patrick McKenna, Matthew Donahoe and Alexander Campbell late of the said County, Yeoman on the Second day of December in the year of our Lord one thousand eight hundred and Seventy One at the County aforesaid, and within the jurisdiction of this Court, with force and arms, &c., in and upon the body of one Morgan Powell in the peace of God and the said Commonwealth then and there being, feloniously, wilfully, and of their malice aforethought, did make an assault, and then and there feloniously, wilfully, and of their malice aforethought, did give to the said Morgan Powell one mortal wound, of which said mortal wound the said Morgan Powell from the said Second day of December in the year aforesaid, until the Fourth day of December in the same year, at the County aforesaid, and within the jurisdiction of this Court, did languish, and languishing did live, on which said Fourth day of December in the year aforesaid, the said Morgan Powell at the County aforesaid, and within the jurisdiction of this Court, of the said mortal wound did die.

And so the Grand Inquest aforesaid, upon their respective oaths and affirmations aforesaid, do say, That the said John Donahoe, Thomas P Fisher, Patrick McKenna, Matthew Donahoe and Alexander Campbell the said Morgan Powell in manner and form aforesaid, feloniously, wilfully, and of their malice aforethought, did kill and murder, contrary to the form of the Act of the General Assembly in such case made and provided, and against the peace and dignity of the Commonwealth of Pennsylvania.

E. R. Siewers District Attorney.

Photo of indictment of John Donahue, Thomas P. Fisher, Patrick McKenna and Alexander Campbell for the murder of Morgan Powell.

Coal Gazette

Friday, December 8, 1871.

ASSASSINATION.

THE FOREMAN OF THE MINES AT SUMMIT HILL SHOT IN THE STREETS.

The Murderers Escape--Arrest of Two Suspected Men---$1000 Reward for the Murderers.

The usually quiet mining town of Summit Hill was thrown into a frantic state of excitement, on last Saturday evening, by the discovery that a foul and cowardly murder had been committed within its boarders. For some months past there have been occasional exhibitions of lawlessness upon the part of some of the lower class, which has caused much alarm among the better portion of the people. But little attention was given the matter until a last awful crime has almost aroused the inhabitants to a frenzy.

THE SCENE OF THE MURDER.

Summit Hill is a large mining town, nine miles from Mauch Chunk. It is the headquarters of the Lehigh Coal and Navigation Company, that corporation having ten mines in the vicinity. It is the only town upon the famous Switch-Back Railroad, and, as its name indicates, it is situated upon the top of the mountain.

THE MURDERED MAN.

The victim is Morgan Powell, the Foreman of W. D. Zehner, Esq., Mining Engineer. Mr. Powell had been a very long time in the employ of the Company. He was considered a most valuable man, as he had a perfect knowledge of all the mines. He had risen from a common laborer to one of the first positions. For several years he was a miner and daily worked in his breast, but some time ago he was appointed Inside Boss at No. 2 Mine. He held this post until Mr. Zehner was appointed Engineer, when he became his Foreman. He was always a sober and industrious man, who had the respect of the community.

THE COURSE OF THE BALL.

The ball entered the left breast, taking a downward course, through the fifth rib, and striking the spine, the lowest part of the wounded man's body was at once paralyzed. He fell to the ground with a piercing cry, which brought Samuel Allen to the scene. Mr Zehner was soon at the side of his Foreman, and did all in his power to alleviate his sufferings. Dr. Thompson was called at once. His examination of the wound resulted in the discovery that it was fatal.

THE ESCAPE OF THE MURDERERS.

The murderers ran away immediately after the shot, in the direction of the No. 1 Plane. A man saw them a moment afterwards, but he failed to recognize any of them. It is rumored that the assassins were seen making their way to Tamaqua some time late on Saturday night.

THE CAUSE OF THE MURDER.

Why anybody should kill Morgan Powell is a mystery. He was at peace with all his neighbors and with the miners generally. There has for a long time been a spirit of jealousy existing between the Irish and Welsh at Summit Hill, and this is thought by many people to have prompted some scoundrel to do the deed. How true this rumor will prove can only be decided at the Coroner's inquest. The citizens of Summit Hill, to a man, condemn the cowardly murderers, and are doing all in their power to effect their arrest.

THE CORONER'S JURY.

The Coroner's Jury assembled on Monday, and, after taking some unimportant testimony, adjourned until Thursday.

POWELL'S DYING STATEMENT.

Mr. Powell made a dying statement in legal form before a Justice of the Peace. Owing to the extreme darkness he was not able to recognize the men who assaulted him. He was of the opinion, however, that Patrick Brislin and Patrick Gilday were in the party. These two were arrested and lodged in jail on Monday. The main evidence against them is Powell's statement, and this is not at all positive. They will be brought before the court next week.

THE PRISONERS.

The prisoners, Patrick Gilday and Patrick Brislin, are confident of proving an alibi. They are in comfortable quarters in the new prison, (price $125,000.) The Lehigh Coal & Navigation Company have offered $1,000, and the County Commissioners will probably offer $500 reward for the arrest and conviction of the murderers.

The people at Summit Hill are loud in their denunciations of the assassins. The better class are determined to put down the "buckshots," cost what it may. In their endeavors they will have the assistance of the people of the county. Summit Hill has been free from any rowdy element for many years, and ruffians cannot but expect to suffer if they make it their dwelling place.

THE DEMOCRAT.

The Mauch Chunk Democrat.

A POLITICAL AND NEWS JOURNAL.

Published Every Saturday Morning.

SATURDAY, September 4, 1875

Murder at Lansford!

A MAN KILLED IN BROAD DAYLIGHT!

THE ASSASSINS CAPTURED AT TAMAQUA.

Lansford and Ashton were thrown into the most intense excitement yesterday (Friday) morning by the murder of Mr. John P. Jones, one of the two inside bosses in the mines under Mr. Zehner.

Jones, who lives at Ashton, was going down the path to Lansford at seven o'clock to go to his work, when he was followed by two men who shot him through the back. He turned to run into the bushes at his left when they fired again and followed him. He staggered some ten or fifteen feet when they again fired twice, and then turned and fled up the hill.

Mr. John Weyhenmeyer, the train mas-ter, heard and saw the affair, and ran to the spot, he exclaimed, "My God, is this John P. Jones?" Jones said "yes." He asked him if he knew who his assassins were, to which he replied in the negative and immediately expired. The Body was re- moved to his residence, and an inquest was to be held yesterday afternoon by Justice Williams.

After committing the deed the men ran up the path to Ashton. Here Samuel Allen met them and asked "what's the matter?" to which they replied "nothing," and kept on. They made to the woods above Ashton and west of Summit Hill, and it was not long before hundreds of villagers were in pursuit. On entering the woods one of them placed his fingers to his mouth and gave a shrill whistle, as was supposed to accomplices who were concealed near.

The news of the murder having been telegraphed to Tamaqua, and that the murderers were escaping in that direction, men were on the lookout all morning for them. About noon Samuel Beard, of Tamaqua, who was looking from Cemetery Hill with a glass, saw parties in the woods near that place signalling to each other with handkerchiefs. The alarm was at once given and at twenty minutes past twelve the murderers were caught and brought into Tamqua. One Carrigan, of Tamaqua, who acted as guide to the men, and to whom signals were evidently given, was also arrested. The three men were brought to Mauch Chunk, securely ironed and guarded, arriving here about 6.30 o'clock. To avoid the crowd as much as possible, they were brought on a special engine, the people being kept in ignorance as to when they would arrive, the wisdom of which precaution was evident, as even then a large and excited crowd, which grew larger at every step, followed the prisoners and posse from the depot the jail, ready at the least opportunity to tear the prisoners limb from limb.

The men were seen at No. 5 tunnel Tuesday afternoon, and were overheard to say they wanted work. As Mr. Jones had entered the tunnel and they waited there about an hour, until the train came out, it is supposed that they were waiting for Jones to re-appear. He went from No. 5 to No. 4 before he came out, and so they missed him.

The men were well-dressed in dark clothing. One is a tall, strong-looking man with a heavy sandy moustache and chin whiskers, and those who saw him say, a villainous-looking face. The other was a smaller man with a smooth face, and wore a silk hat. Talk of lynching them was quite freely indulged in by the exasperated villagers.

Mr. Jones was a man about 43 years old, and has held his present position about three years. He was a steady, faithful man, and well liked by all. He was not unpopular with the men under him, and no cause can be given for the murder, unless, perhaps, in the performance of his duty to the company he may have discharged some worthless hand, who in revenge has procured his death. He leaves a wife and seven children, the eldest being thirteen years old and the youngest an infant of eight months, who were dependent upon him for support, he leaving no property of any amount.

Later Particulars.

The men arrived via L. & S. R. R. at 6:30, guarded, by a strong party of men armed to the teeth. The three prisoners were handcuffed together, and on being assisted from the open car, a procession was formed which was soon turned into a tumult of excited citizens, who, as the officers proceeded towards Esquire Yeager's office, excitedly demanded that they be hung. The crowd in a moment increased to several hundred and shouts of "hang them," "lynch the scoundrels" greeted the prisoners, who, notwithstanding the peril they were in, kept quite cool. The scene in front of the Squire's office on Broadway was exciting, the crowd demanding that they be lynched, while some of our prominent citizens appealed to the crowd to let the law take its course, which advice, backed by the carbines and drawn revolvers of the officers, was heeded, though it needed but a rope, and in a moment tho three would have been dangling from the awning in front of the justice's office.

Yesterday morning Mr. Frank Walters directed Constable Painter to summon a possee and proceed to Summit Hill to assist in finding the murderers. Messrs. Wm. Walters, Jeff Fister, Charles Armbruster and the constable went at once to Summit Hill, where they were directed to take the White Bear, or lower road to Tamaqua. Half way over they met a possee from Tamaqua, under charge of policeman Walton, who were also on the search. The Mauch Chunk possee went on to Tamaqua, the other party directing their steps to the mines and houses near Summit Hill. Arriving at Tamaqua our officers noticed a commotion and were informed that the supposed murderers were captured and were locked up in the station house. They were the parties looked for and Constable Painter demanded the prisoners, and after some parleying they were turned over to him.

A cordon of policemen was formed about the prisoners and they were marched to the depot, followed by an immense and excited throng who yelled "hang them," "hang them," and were it not for the officers surrounding and protecting them they would have been lynched. They were put on a flat car, hand-cuffed, the engine steaming off amid hideous yells. Nothing occurred until they arrived at Lansford, where fully five hundred people were awaiting the murderers to inflict summary vengeance upon them. Those in charge very prudently ran the train through without stopping to Mauch Chunk, where it not being generally known when they would arrive, not more than a hundred had gathered to see the desperadoes.

The men were fully identified in Tamaqua by parties from Lansford who saw them there, they being positive as to their identity. The men deny the charge but tell contradictory stories. The tragedy occurred within 75 yards of the Lansford depot where at least 20 men were standing. Mrs. Williams fully identified two of the men. When captured they were quite wet from perspiration and from wading the Little Schuylkill below Tamaqua.

The details of the capture are as follows: News having reached Tamaqua of the tragedy and that the murderers were making towards that point, a lookout was kept up and a little after 12 o'clock, noon, they were seen by parties with glasses and surrounded. They were found resting at a spring with a bottle of whiskey, but as soon as they discovered their pursuers they started to run, but were warned not to go farther or they would be shot, when they surrendered, and were marched to the town.

Policeman Brink, of the Coal and Iron Police, from the description sent him is of the opinion that Doyle is the man who killed the boss at Heaton's Colliery, Raven Run.

THE MURDERERS.

Edward Kelley, is a young man, about 20 years of age, smooth face, florid complextion, reddish hair, and wore a black railroad cap. He hails from Schuylkill County and is unknown at Summit Hill.

The principal, who is supposed to be the one who fired the fatal shot, gave his name as Michael Doyle, and his residence at Mt. Laffey, Schuylkill Co. He is about 28 years of age, a tall, heavy set fellow, dark moustache, and wears the countenance of a determined, villainous desperado. He wore a dark suit, no vest, white shirt, but no collar.

James Carrigan, the smallest of the three, who did the signalling to get his comrades out of harm's way, is a reputed hard case from the vicinity of Tamaqua, where he has an unenviable reputation. He is quite small in stature, has small and ill-looking eyes, and a countenance that would be signaled out in a crowd as that of a treacherous, cunning villain. His features are sharp, wears dark side whiskers, and appeared the most nervous of the three. He is older than a glance at him would indicate, evidently about 35 years of age.

John Weyhenmeyer, an employee of the Central R. R. Co., heard the shot fired, saw the smoke ascending and saw these two men fleeing from the direction where Jones was found. He is positive that Doyle and Kelley are the men.

District Attorney Siewers will do all he can to give them a speedy trial and in all probability theirs will be the first case presented to the Grand Jury on October 18th, when Court convenes. Gen. Albright will be associated with Mr. Siewers, he being the counsel for the L. & W. C. Co.

CHAPTER XVI

CARBON BAR -- 1993

Richard P. Abbott -b. Scranton, Pennsylvania May 6, 1961; University of Pittsburgh; University of Pittsburgh School of Law; adm. August 5, 1993; Carbon County District Court Administrator (1992-). Resident of Jim Thorpe.

David W. Addy -b. Abington, Pennsylvania July 23, 1957; Temple University; Villanova University School of Law; adm. January 5, 1987; Law Clerk to President Judge John P. Lavelle (1987-1988); Private Practice, Lehighton; Assistant District Attorney of Carbon County (1989-). Resident of Lehighton.

William H. Bayer -b. Lehighton, Pennsylvania February 8, 1922; Penn State University; University of Pennsylvania Law School; adm. January 1, 1950; Private Practice, Lehighton; Assistant County Solicitor; Solicitor, Lehighton Zoning Board of Adjustment; Lehighton Planning Commission, Central Carbon Industrial Development Corporation; Former Solicitor - Treasurer of Carbon County, Register of Wills of Carbon County. Resident of Lehighton.

Christie Ellen Schaffer-Bower -b. Somerville, New Jersey November 16, 1961; Rutgers University; Rutgers-The State University-School of Law; adm. January 5, 1987; Private Practice with Dyrda & Schaffer, Lehighton. Resident of Marshall Creek.

Randy Theodore Burch -b. East Stroudsburg, Pennsylvania September 22, 1964; East Stroudsburg University; Vermont Law School; adm. 1991; Private Practice with Charles C. Hansford & Associates, Palmerton. Resident of Reading.

John G. Cipko -b. Nesquehoning, Pennsylvania May 19, 1909; Dickinson College; Dickinson School of Law; adm. October 10, 1932; Private Practice, Lansford; President of the Nesquehoning School Board; Solicitor for Nesquehoning School District, Panther Valley School District, Panther Valley Authority, Kidder Township, Kidder Township Authority. Resident of Lansford.

Steven M. Cormier -b. Allentown, Pennsylvania February 3, 1958; Penn State University; Dickinson School of Law; adm. November 25, 1983; General Counsel, The Kovatch Companies; Summit Hill Zoning Hearing Board - Member, (1987-1991), Chairman (1989-1991). Resident of Summit Hill.

John DiBernardino -b. Philadelphia, Pennsylvania May 20, 1960; American University; Delaware Law School of Wiedner University; adm. December 1, 1986; Private Practice, Lehighton; Assistant District Attorney of Carbon County (1988-1989). Resident of Lehighton.

Dianne M. Dickson -b. Quakertown, Pennsylvania March 25, 1954; Lebanon Valley College; Dickinson School of Law; adm. January 1992; Private Practice with Worth Law Offices, Allentown and Jim Thorpe; Law Clerk to the late Honorable David E. Mellenberg (1979-1980) board member Lehigh County Drug and Alcohol Commission. Resident of Allentown.

Gary F. Dobias -b. Palmerton, Pennsylvania May 17, 1949; Franklin and Marshall College; Memphis State University School of Law; adm. November 22, 1974; Camp Cadet Troop "N", Financial Secretary/Treasurer; Assistant District Attorney of Carbon County (1978-1992) District Attorney of Carbon County (1992-). Resident of Palmerton.

John J. Dobosh -b. Lansford, Pennsylvania July 23, 1902; Catholic University of America; Dickinson School of Law; adm. 1932; Private Practice; Pennsylvania Department of Revenue Immigration Department. Resident of Lansford.

Thomas W. Durnin -b. Jim Thorpe, Pennsylvania February 18, 1910; Providence College; Dickinson School of Law; adm. 1952; Private Practice, Jim Thorpe; Solicitor of Banks Township; Borough of Jim Thorpe; Jim Thorpe School District; Kidder Township; Penn Forest Township; Jim Thorpe Municipal Authority; Borough of Nesquehoning Water Authority; Pennsylvania Motor Vehicle Hearing Inspector; County Detective, Carbon County (1943-1948). Resident of Jim Thorpe.

George T. Dydynsky -b. Philadelphia, Pennsylvania June 21, 1952; Villanova University; Villanova University School of Law; adm. October 2, 1980; Private Practice, Lehighton; Law Clerk to President Judge John P. Lavelle (1980-1982). Resident of Towamensing Township.

Cynthia Ann Dyrda -b. Bridgeport, Connecticut October 8, 1961; Penn State University; Dickinson School of Law; adm. October 7, 1988; Private Practice Dyrda & Schaffer, Lehighton. Resident of New Ringold.

R. Michael Edridge -b. Olean, New York July 14, 1943; Parsons College; University of Buffalo Law School; adm. November 8, 1978; Private Practice, Hansford & Strubinger, Palmerton. Resident of Bethlehem.

Jane F. Engler -b. Allentown, Pennsylvania November 17, 1943; Temple University; Delaware Law School; adm. May 6, 1981; Private Practice, Jim Thorpe; Solicitor, Register of Wills, Jim Thorpe Area School District; Vice-President Carbon County Economic Development, Advisory Board Member Carbon County Bureau of Economic Development; Task Force Member Dislocated Work Task Force. Resident of Jim Thorpe.

Jean A. Engler -b. Hazleton, Pennsylvania October 14, 1959; Villanova University; Villanova University School of Law; adm. November 18, 1985; Private Practice, Jim Thorpe; Assistant District Attorney Carbon County (1989-) Solicitor Prothonotary's Office Carbon County, Counsel for Child Support Complainants, Treasurer Carbon County Bar Association. Resident of Jim Thorpe.

Robin M. Fenick -b. New Brunswick, New Jersey December 3, 1965; Penn State University; Widener University School of Law; adm. December 18, 1993; Partner, Levy & Fenick. Resident of Palmerton.

Marc S. Fisher -b. Boston, Massachusetts November 18, 1957; Brandeis University; Villanova University School of Law; adm. January 1, 1992; Private Practice Worth Law Offices, Allentown and Jim Thorpe; Former Law Clerk to the Honorable Michael V. Franciosa Northampton County, Solicitor Upper Milford Township, East Penn School District. Resident of Allentown.

Michael J. Garfield -b. Waverly, New York August 1, 1948; University of Scranton; Duquesne University School of Law; adm. October 30, 1974; Private Practice, Jim Thorpe; Assistant District Attorney Carbon County (1975-1987) Solicitor Carbon County Solid Waste, Carbon County Railroad Commission, Agency on Aging. Resident of Jim Thorpe.

Joseph G. Greco, Jr. -b. Hazleton, Pennsylvania March 27, 1947; Mount St. Mary's College; University of Notre Dame Law School; adm. May 22, 1974; Private Practice, Greco & Greco, Nesquehoning; Secretary, Treasurer, and Borough Manager for Nesquehoning; Solicitor Nesquehoning Zoning Board; Current Secretary, Carbon County Bar Association. Resident of Nesquehoning.

Michael S. Greek -b. Lehighton, Pennsylvania April 20, 1963; Penn State University; Widener University School of Law; adm. December 18, 1993; Associate, Law Offices of William G. Schwab. Resident of Nesquehoning.

Charles C. Hansford -b. Philadelphia, Pennsylvania January 17, 1938; Private Practice, Palmerton; Villanova University; Villanova University School of Law; adm. 1988. Resident of Allentown.

Steven J. Hartz -b. Philadelphia, Pennsylvania August 28, 1941; University of Oxford; University of Oxford; adm. November 18, 1977; Private Practice, Palmerton; Solicitor for Bowmanstown Zoning Hearing Board; Law Clerk to the Honorable John P. Lavelle (1978-1979); Research assistant for supplement to Pennsylvania Vehicle Code Annotated. Resident of Bowmanstown.

Edmund J. Healy -b. Newark, New Jersey October 9, 1962; Rutgers University; Temple University School of Law; adm. December 23, 1991; Law Clerk to the Honorable Richard W. Webb, Carbon County Court of Common Pleas (1991-1993). Resident of Emmaus.

Holly A. Heintzelman -b. Lehighton, Pennsylvania January 9, 1957; Gettysburg College; Dickinson School of Law; adm. March 1, 1982; Private Practice, Lehighton; Assistant District Attorney, Carbon County, (1992-) Solicitor Mahoning Township, Lower Towamensing Township Zoning Hearing Board, Coroner's Office Carbon County; Board of Directors Gnaden Huetten Hospital. Resident of Mahoning Township.

Bradford E. Landon -b. East Bangor, Pennsylvania August 13, 1954; Dickinson College; University of Richmond-T.C. Williams School of Law; adm. 1978; In-House Counsel Lehigh County Authority; Jim Thorpe Area School District Board of Directors; Lehigh Valley Legal Services Board of Directors. Resident of Jim Thorpe.

K. Tucker Landon -b. Concord, New Hampshire August 11, 1951; Goucher College; University of Richmond-T.C. Williams School of Law; adm. 1978; Executive Director, Schuylkill County Legal Services, Inc.; Chairwoman, Jim Thorpe Zoning Hearing Board. Assistant District Attorney, Carbon County, (1980-1981). Resident of Jim Thorpe.

Colleen F. Coonelly-Lavelle -b. Philadelphia, Pennsylvania; Duke University; Vanderbilt Law School; adm. December 18, 1993; Associate, Pepper, Hamilton & Scheetz, Philadelphia, Pennsylvania (1991-). Resident of Wynnewood.

John P. Lavelle, Jr. -b. Lehighton, Pennsylvania May 12, 1963; Princeton University; Harvard University School of Law; adm. December 18, 1993; Law Clerk to the Honorable Thomas E. O'Niell, District Court Judge U.S. Court for Eastern District of Pennsylvania (1990-1991); Associate Counsel, Hangley, Connolly, Epstein, Chicco, Foxman & Ewing, Philadelphia, Pennsylvania (1991-). Resident of Wynnewood.

Marianne Shutack Lavelle -b. Nesquehoning, Pennsylvania September 19, 1933; Bucknell University; Dickinson School of Law; adm. May 6, 1959; Private Practice with Shutack & Lavelle, Lehighton; Solicitor, Weissport Borough (1978-1982) Weissport Sewer Authority; Lehighton Borough (1978-1981); Pennsylvania Deputy Attorney General (1966-1970); Secretary Carbon County Bar Association (1967-1985). Resident of Lehighton.

Lynne Kimberly Law -b. Horsham, Pennsylvania November 3, 1968; Lafayette College; Dickinson School of Law; adm. December 18, 1993; Law Clerk to the Honorable John P. Lavelle, President Judge of Carbon County Court of Common Pleas (1993-). Resident of Whitehall.

Paul J. Levy -b. Brooklyn, New York June 10, 1966; Lock Haven University; Widener University School of Law; adm. December 23, 1991; Private Practice, Lehighton; Counsel for Legal Services of Northeastern Pennsylvania. Resident of Palmerton.

Murray Mackson -b. Wilkes-Barre, Pennsylvania November 18, 1925; Penn State University; Dickinson School of Law; adm. October 5, 1959; Private Practice with Weaver, Mosebach, Piosa, Hixson & Marles, Allentown; Assistant District Attorney, Carbon County, (1967-1975); Past President, Palmerton Area Communities Endeavor; Former Tax Claim Bureau Solicitor; Mahoning Township; Solicitor Bowmanstown Borough; Gnaden Huetten Memorial Hospital. Resident of Allentown.

Karl J. Maehrer -b. Sommerville, New Jersey June 9, 1964; Muhlenberg College; Vermont Law School; adm. December 23, 1991; Private Practice with Thomas Turczyn, Allentown; Conflict Counsel for the Public Defender's Office Carbon County. Resident of Jim Thorpe.

Robert J. Magee -b. Norristown, Pennsylvania February 16, 1951; Kutztown State College; Temple University School of Law; adm. January 14, 1992; Private Practice with Worth Law Offices, Allentown and Jim Thorpe. Resident of Walnutport.

Joseph J. Matika -b. Lehighton, Pennsylvania April 5, 1962; King's College; University of Bridgeport School of Law; adm. July 14, 1988; Private Practice, Summit Hill; Solicitor, Rush Township Zoning Hearing Board, Summit Hill Planning Commission, Summit Hill Zoning Hearing Board, Carbon-Monroe-Pike MH/MR Program Carbon Office. Resident of East Penn Township.

Thomas S. McCready -b. Palmerton, Pennsylvania December 11, 1930; Dickinson College; Dickinson School of Law; adm. May 13, 1957; Private Practice, Lansford; Chief Public Defender of Carbon County (1969-1990). Solicitor, Lansford Borough, Summit Hill Borough, Nesquehoning Borough, Panther Valley School District, Mahoning Township. Resident of Summit Hill.

William E. McDonald -b. Coaldale, Pennsylvania January 29, 1953; Muhlenberg College; Dickinson School of Law; adm. October 17, 1977; Private Practice, Lansford; Assistant District Attorney for Carbon County, (1981-); Solicitor Lansford Borough, Nesquehoning Borough Authority, Carbon-Monroe-Pike Drug and Alcohol Commission, Inc. Resident of West Penn Township.

George T. McKinley -b. New York, New York June 20, 1922; Lehigh University; University of Pennsylvania Law School; adm. January 15, 1950; Private Practice with Ozalas & McKinley, Jim Thorpe; Solicitor Eastside Borough, Borough of Parryville, Lower Towamensing Township; Counsel for Palmerton Hospital; Counsel for Palmerton Library; Director for Probation Services; Former Assistant District Attorney Carbon County, (1967-1970) Assistant Solicitor for Carbon County (1992-). Resident of Palmerton.

Christine Mifkovich -b. Coaldale, Pennsylvania February 18, 1954; Lehigh University; Widener University School of Law; adm. January 29, 1981; Private Practice, Lehighton. Resident of Lehighton.

Daniel A. Miscavige -b. Mount Carmel, Pennsylvania May 23, 1952; Elizabethtown College; Dickinson School of Law; adm. October 27, 1977; Private Practice with Mylotte, David & Fitzpatrick, Hazleton; Carbon County Bar Association representative-Legal Services of Northeastern Pennsylvania; Solicitor Weatherly Area School District, Township of Kidder, Township of Packer, Weatherly Area Joint School Authority, Beaver Meadows Municipal Authority, Tax Claim Bureau of Carbon County, Tax Assessment Office of Carbon County. Resident of Weatherly.

Gregory L. Mousseau -b. Inglewood, California May 16, 1961; Brigham Young University; Brigham Young University-J. Reuben Clark Law School; adm. January 2, 1990; Private Practice with Shulman & Shabbick, Palmerton and Northampton; Former Law Clerk to the Honorable John P. Lavelle (1990-1991) Public Defender for Carbon County. Resident of Jim Thorpe.

James R. Nanovic -b. Palmerton, Pennsylvania July 10, 1960; University of Notre Dame; Dickinson School of Law; adm. November 25, 1985; Private Practice with Nanovic Law Offices, Jim Thorpe; Solicitor, Lehigh Township-3 years; Weatherly Borough-2 years; Lower Towamensing Township-1 year; East Side Borough-2 years; Carbon County Telecommunications Commission-3 years. Resident of Lehighton.

Roger N. Nanovic -b. Palmerton, Pennsylvania April 22, 1929; University of Notre Dame; Dickinson School of Law; adm. October 14, 1955; Private Practice with Nanovic Law Offices, Jim Thorpe; Solicitor, Carbon County (1967-1971); Solicitor, Lehigh Township, Franklin Township, Towamensing Township, Lower Towamensing Township, Borough of Weatherly, Penn Forest Township, Palmerton School District and Weatherly School District; Assistant District Attorney, Carbon County, (1960-1967). Resident of Palmerton.

Roger N. Nanovic, II -b. Allentown, Pennsylvania August 13, 1954; University of Notre Dame; Dickinson School of Law; adm. October 22, 1979; Private Practice with Nanovic Law Offices, Jim Thorpe; Solicitor, Carbon County (1992-); Borough of Jim Thorpe; Township of Lausanne; Carbon County Redevelopment Authority; Carbon County Industrial Development Authority. Resident of Bear Creek Lakes, Penn Forest Township.

Susan J. Nanovic -b. Palmerton, Pennsylvania August 16, 1965; University of Notre Dame; Dickinson School of Law; adm. November 4, 1993; Private Practice with Nanovic Law Offices, Jim Thorpe. Resident of Lehighton

Thomas S. Nanovic -b. Palmerton, Pennsylvania November 18, 1957; University of Notre Dame; Dickinson School of Law; adm. October 28, 1982; Private Practice with Nanovic Law Offices, Jim Thorpe; Solicitor, Towamensing Township; Franklin Township; Penn Forest Township; Mahoning Township Planning Commission and Zoning Hearing Board. Resident of Penn Forest Township.

Michael L. Ozalas -b. Palmerton, Pennsylvania July 18, 1949; Lafayette College; Villanova University School of Law; adm. August 4, 1976; Private Practice with Ozalas & McKinley, Jim Thorpe; Solicitor, Sheriff's Office Carbon County; Borough of Palmerton; Borough of Weissport; Former Solicitor for the Borough of Lehighton and Carbon County Children and Youth; Former Court Appointed Representative of Mentally Disabled Persons. Resident of Palmerton.

George C. Parrish -b. Houston, Texas July 4, 1965; Moravian College; University of Pittsburgh School of Law; adm. December 23, 1991; Law Clerk to the Honorable John P. Lavelle, President Judge Carbon County Court of Common Pleas (1991-1993). Private Practice with Ross, Negrete, & Schwartz, Bethlehem. Resident of Bethlehem.

Keith Richard Pavlack -b. McKeesport, Pennsylvania May 24, 1963; University of Pittsburgh; Widener University School of Law, Delaware Campus; adm. 1992; Private Practice, Lehighton. Resident of Allentown.

Jacob Philip -b. Palmerton, Pennsylvania October 4, 1909; Penn State University; University of Pennsylvania Law School; adm. June 22, 1936; Private Practice with Philip & Wimmer, Palmerton. Resident of Allentown.

Martin H. Philip -b. Palmerton, Pennsylvania; 1907 Penn State University; University of Pennsylvania Law School; adm. June 1931; Private Practice in Palmerton and Allentown; Resident of Palmerton.

William B. Quinn -b. Lansford, Pennsylvania January 27, 1923; Villanova University; Dickinson School of Law; adm. December 1950; Private Practice, Lehighton; Solicitor, Carbon County Area Vocational-Technical School; Carbon County Area Vocational-Technical School Authority; Kidder Township Zoning Hearing Board; Penn Forest Township Zoning Hearing Board; Borough of Lehighton Sewer Authority; Carbon County Mental Health Review Officer (1976-); Carbon County Custody Hearing Officer (1981-). Resident of Lansford.

Cynthia S. Ray -b. Hazleton, Pennsylvania January 18, 1960; Bloomsburg University; Dickinson School of Law; adm. December 23, 1991; Private Practice, Weatherly; Current Solicitor for Carbon County Treasurer, Co-Solicitor Carbon County Airport Authority. Resident of Weatherly.

George B. Richards -b. Lansford, Pennsylvania May 30, 1915; Temple University; Temple University School of Law; adm. May 15, 1942; Private Practice, Lansford; Administrator of the Magisterial System for Carbon County (1969-1972); Solicitor Carbon County Controller (1948-1955); Solicitor Lansford Board of School Directors (1955-1960); Lansford Borough Council (1964-1966); Carbon County Recorder of Deeds (1961-1975). Resident of Lansford.

George M. D. Richards -b. Lansford, Pennsylvania June 8, 1902; Penn State University; University of Pennsylvania Law School; adm. 1933; CPA with LyBrand Ross Bros. & Montgomery; Private Practice, Lansford; Solicitor, Lansford Borough, Carbon, Schuylkill Industrial Development Corporation; President, First National Bank of Lansford and Dime Bank of Lansford. Resident of Lansford.

Anthony Roberti -b. Queens Borough, New York, New York February 12, 1946; Swarthmore College; Boston College Law School; adm. April 3, 1973; Private Practice, Jim Thorpe; President, Carbon County Training Center, Inc. (1989-). Resident of Jim Thorpe.

William G. Schwab -b. Philadelphia, Pennsylvania January 16, 1951; Temple University; Temple University School of Law; adm. July 8, 1977; Private Practice, Lehighton; Solicitor East Penn Township; Lehighton Area School District; Continuing Legal Education Chairman, Carbon County Bar Association. Resident of East Penn Township.

Marvin O. Schwartz -b. Coaldale, Pennsylvania October 6, 1954; Temple University; Gonzaga University School of Law; adm. November 1985; Private Practice with Ross, Negrete & Schwartz, P.C., Bethlehem. Resident of Allentown.

William Z. Scott, Jr. -b. Coaldale, Pennsylvania July 15, 1952; Lafayette College; Dickinson School of Law; adm. September 27, 1979; Private Practice, Lansford; Former officer of Young Lawyers division of Pennsylvania Bar Association; Member of Professionalism Committee of Pennsylvania Bar Association; Co-Founder and member of Board of Directors of Pennsylvania Mock Trial; Member of Review and Certifying Board of Commonwealth of Pennsylvania. Resident of Mahoning Township.

Barry C. Shabbick -b. Spangler, Pennsylvania February 25, 1949; Lafayette College; University of Pittsburgh School of Law; adm. January 1, 1988; Private Practice, Shulman & Shabbick, Palmerton and Northampton; Former School Director Northern Lehigh School District (Treasurer 1991). Resident of Slatington.

David B. Shulman -b. Philadelphia, Pennsylvania April 15, 1949; Temple University; Rutgers-The State University-School of Law; adm. January 1, 1988; Private Practice Shulman & Shabbick, Palmerton and Northampton; Chairman - Lehigh Township Planning Commission (Northampton County). Resident of Cherryville.

George A. Shutack -b. Nesquehoning, Pennsylvania August 21, 1900; Georgetown University Law School -LL.B. 1923; adm. June 11, 1928; Private Practice; Balliet & Shutack - Shutack & Lavelle; Lehighton; Deputy Attorney General of Commonwealth; Deputy United States Attorney for Middle District of Pennsylvania (Land Damage Division) Solicitor, Beaver Meadows Borough; Mahoning Township; Lower Towamensing Township; Lehighton Water Authority (1955-1980) Member Carbon County Recreation Authority. Resident of Lehighton.

Arnold Sousa -b. New Bedford, Massachusetts March 7, 1933; Temple University; Temple University School of Law; adm. August 22, 1963; Private Practice, Jim Thorpe; Solicitor, Carbon County Sheriff, Carbon County Tax Claim Bureau, Jim Thorpe Zoning Hearing Board. Resident of Jim Thorpe.

Gerald F. Strubinger, Jr. -b. Palmerton, Pennsylvania April 19, 1966; College Misericordia; Widener University School of Law; adm. December 21, 1992; Private Practice with Charles C. Hansford & Associates; Palmerton. Resident of Palmerton.

Joseph John Velitsky -b. Coaldale, Pennsylvania November 4, 1944; Penn State University; Dickinson School of Law; adm. November 23, 1970; Private Practice, Summit Hill; Solicitor, Carbon County (1979-1991). Resident of Summit Hill.

Edward H. Vermillion -b. Hazleton, Pennsylvania April 15, 1947; Susquehanna University; Dickinson School of Law; adm. November 21, 1974; Private Practice, Lehighton; Assistant District Attorney, Carbon County (1976-1980) Solicitor Lehighton Water Authority, Parryville Zoning Board; Lehighton Area School District Board of Directors - member. Resident of Lehighton.

Stephen P. Vlossak, Sr. -b. Philadelphia, Pennsylvania August 23, 1946; Mount St. Mary's College; Temple University School of Law; adm. May 10, 1979; Private Practice, Palmerton; Carbon County Public Defender (1988-). Resident of Palmerton.

Carole J. Wildoner-Walbert -b. Lehighton, Pennsylvania November 3, 1956; Dickinson College; Villanova University School of Law; adm. December 3, 1981; Private Practice, Jim Thorpe; Law Clerk to President Judge John P. Lavelle (1985-1986); U.S. Commissioner-Delaware and Lehigh Canal National Heritage Corridor; Hearing Officer, Carbon County Domestic Relations Office, Master in Divorce (1987-). Resident of Jim Thorpe.

James A. Wimmer -b. Scranton, Pennsylvania February 13, 1941; University of Pennsylvania; University of Pennsylvania Law School; adm. November 22, 1965; Private Practice with Philip & Wimmer, Palmerton; Assistant District Attorney, Carbon County (1967-1975) Solicitor, Eldred Township (Monroe County) Palmerton Area School District. Resident of Allentown.

Wallace C. Worth, Jr. -b. Bethlehem, Pennsylvania March 26, 1922; Muhlenberg College; Dickinson School of Law; adm. January 1, 1992; First Assistant District Attorney (Lehigh County) Solicitor Prothonotary (Lehigh County); East Penn School District; Upper Milford Township. Resident of Zionville.

William A. Wyatt -b. Freeland, Pennsylvania April 22, 1927; Lafayette College; University Of Pennsylvania Law School; adm. February 12, 1954; Retired; Pennsylvania House of Representatives 1957-1958; President Lake Harmony Association; Advisory Board Hometown Nursing Center; Kidder Township Planning Commission. Resident of Lake Harmony.

Robert T. Yurchak -b. Palmerton, Pennsylvania September 17, 1955; Harvard University; Temple University School of Law; adm. December 3, 1981; Private Practice, Nesquehoning; Solicitor Beaver Meadows Borough, Banks Township, Carbon County Recorder of Deeds Office; Public Defender of Carbon County, (1983-). Resident of Nesquehoning.

Daniel F. Zeigler -b. Coaldale, Pennsylvania December 6, 1947; Penn State University; Duquesne University School of Law; adm. May 24, 1976; Private Practice, Jim Thorpe; Carbon County Domestic Relations Hearing Officer; Solicitor, Controller of Carbon County; Assistant Solicitor to the Carbon-Schuykill Industrial Development Corporation. Resident of Lansford.

Carbon County Bar Association -- 1993

First Row:
1. President Judge John P. Lavelle
2. Justice Peter Paul Olszewski
   (Superior Court of Pennsylvania)
3. Justice Stephen J. McEwen, Jr.
   (Superior Court of Pennsylvania)
4. Judge Richard W. Webb
5. Judge Richard D. Grifo
   (Senior Judge, Northampton County)

Second Row:
6. Joseph J. Matika, Esquire
7. William G. Schwab, Esquire
8. Edward H. Vermillion, Esquire
9. Michael J. Garfield, Esquire
10. George T. McKinley, Esquire
11. Edmund J. Healy, Esquire
12. Barry J. Shabbick, Esquire
13. Gregory L. Mousseau, Esquire
14. Gary F. Dobias, Esquire
15. Michael L. Ozalas, Esquire
16. David W. Addy, Esquire
17. George C. Parrish, Esquire
18. Marvin O. Schwartz, Esquire

Third Row:
19. James R. Nanovic, Esquire
20. Paul J. Levy, Esquire
21. Lance M. Gordon, Esquire
22. Robert T. Yurchak, Esquire
23. Joseph J. Velitsky, Esquire
24. James A. Wimmer, Esquire
25. Roger N. Nanovic, Sr., Esquire

Fourth Row:
26. Stephen P. Vlossak, Sr., Esquire
27. Thomas S. Nanovic, Esquire
28. Michael R. Edridge, Esquire
29. Roger N. Nanovic II, Esquire
30. Robert Magee, Esquire
31. Richard P. Abbott, Esquire
32. George T. Dydynsky, Esquire
33. William E. McDonald, Esquire
34. Michael S. Greek, Esquire
35. William H. Bayer, Esquire

Fifth Row:
36. Marc S. Fisher, Esquire
37. Donald B. Shulman, Esquire
38. William Z. Scott, Jr., Esquire
39. Lynne Kimberly Law, Esquire
40. Arnold Sousa, Esquire
41. William A. Wyatt, Esquire
42. William B. Quinn, Esquire
43. George B. Richards, Esquire
44. George A. Shutack, Esquire (Dean of the Bar)
45. Cynthia Ray, Esquire
46. K. Tucker Landon, Esquire
47. Holly A. Heintzelman, Esquire
48. Thomas S. McCready, Esquire

Sixth Row:
49. Susan J. Nanovic, Esquire
50. Jean A. Engler, Esquire
51. Jane F. Engler-Brogan, Esquire
52. Carole J. Wildoner-Walbert, Esquire
53. Christine E. Mifkovich, Esquire
54. Christie E. Schaffer-Bower, Esquire
55. Cynthia A. Dyrda, Esquire
56. Gerald F. Strubinger, Esquire
57. Dianne M. Dickson, Esquire
58. Marianne S. Lavelle, Esquire
59. Daniel F. Zeigler, Esquire

Seventh Row:
60. Charles C. Hansford, Esquire
61. Murray Mackson, Esquire
62. Joseph G. Greco, Jr., Esquire
63. Robin Fenick, Esquire
64. Anthony Roberti, Esquire (Chancellor of the Bar)
65. Martin H. Philip, Esquire

George Shutack as a World War I doughboy in 1918.

John Lavelle on duty with U.S. Army Communication Center in Livorno Italy in 1955.

Tom McKinley (third from right) with his B25 crew at Myitkyina Air Base in Burma flew 55 missions in 1943.

Captain George B. Richards returned to Lansford after serving on the battlefields of Europe to dedicate World War II memorial in 1946.

Tom McCready worked on a newspaper and TV productions as part of his naval duties at Little Creek, Virginia, Naval Base in 1956.

CARBON LAWYERS IN THE MILITARY

Attorneys	Rank on Discharge	Branch of Service	Years Served
1. H. B. Burnham	Colonel (Career Sol.)	Union Army	1861-1864
2. John D. Bertolette	Colonel	Union Army	1861-1865
3. William M. Rapsher	Private	Union Army	1861-1865
4. William H. Butler	Private	Union Army	1862-1863
5. Charles Albright	Brigadier General	Union Army	1862-1863
6. William G. Freyman	First Sergeant	Union Army	1862-1863
7. Wesley B. Leonard	Private	Union Army	1862-1864
8. John H. Kline	Captain	Union Army	1862-1865
9. Allen W. Craig	Infantryman	Union Army	1862
10. Raymond F. Smith	Private 1st Class	Army	1916-1918
11. James C. McCready	Staff Sergeant	Army	1917-1919
12. Alan S. Loose	Private 1st Class	Army	1918-1919
13. Frank X. York	First Lieutenant	Army	1918
14. George A. Shutack	Private 1st Class	Army	1918
15. George M. D. Richards	Captain	Army Air Corps	1942-1945
16. Martin H. Philip	Sergeant	Army	1942-1945
17. Frank D. Llewellyn	Tech Sergeant	Army	1942-1945
18. Joseph G. Greco	Technician 4th grade	Army	1942-1945
19. Michael S. Lukish	Tech Sergeant	Army	1942-1945
20. George B. Richards	Captain	Army Air Corps	1942-1945
21. George T. McKinley	Tech Sergeant	Air Force	1942-1945
22. William H. Bayer	Captain (Pilot)	Air Force	1942-1945
23. William B. Quinn	Corporal	Air Force	1942-1945
24. Albert P. Leonzi	Captain	Army	1942-1946
25. William Z. Scott	Captain	Army Infantry	1942-1946
26. Murray Mackson	Commander	Navy	1942-1946
27. George Kerestes	Staff Sergeant	Army	1943-1946
28. Robert Lazorchick		Navy (Seabees)	1943-1946
29. Thomas W. Durnin	Tech Sergeant	Army	1943-1946
30. W. Joseph Engler	Sergeant	Army	1944-1945
31. Donald L. McCay	Sergeant	Army Air Corps	1944-1945
32. William A. Wyatt	Seaman 1st Class	Navy	1944-1946
33. Russell Chaplinsky	Lieutenant	Navy	1950-1953
34. Robert W. Cunliffe	Corporal	Army	1951-1953
35. John P. Lavelle	Corporal	Army Signal Corps	1954-1955
36. Roger N. Nanovic	Sergeant	Army Artillery	1954-1956
37. Charles C. Hansford	Corporal	PA National Guard	1954-1958
38. Thomas S. McCready	Journalist 3rd Class	Navy	1955-1957
39. Stephen P. Vlossak, Sr.	Private 1st Class	Army	1968-1970
40. Anthony Roberti	Private	Army Reserves	1968-1972
41. Michael J. Piosa	Private 1st Class	Army	1969-1970

N.B. The information in this list was compiled from discharge records filed in the Carbon County Recorder of Deeds office or from the bar member where his discharge is not filed. Any errors or omissions are the result of misplaced or unattainable records.

CARBON COUNTY DISTRICT ATTORNEYS

(The year indicates the year of election)

James R. Struthers	1843
William H. Butler	1845
O. H. Wheeler	1848
Samuel McLean	1856
Allen W. Craig	1859
Wesley B. Leonard	1862
Wesley B. Leonard	1865
John D. Bertolette	1868
Edward C. Dimmick	1871
Edward R. Siewers	1873
Edward R. Siewers	1876
Edward M. Mulhearn	1879
Edward M. Mulhearn	1882
William M. Rapsher	1885
Joseph S. Fisher	1888
Joseph S. Fisher	1891
Eugene O. Nothstein	1894
Daniel W. Sitler	1897
Frank P. Sharkey	1901
George E. Gray	1904
George E. Gray	1907
Chester G. Setzer	1911
Chester G. Setzer	1915
Ben Branch	1919
Ben Branch	1922
David Davis	1925
David Davis	1928
David Davis	1931
David Davis	1934
Ben Branch (Appointed)	1935
Albert H. Heimbach	1935
Albert H. Heimbach	1939
Carl A. Niehoff	1943
Carl A. Niehoff	1947
Carl A. Niehoff	1951
Carl A. Niehoff	1955
George Kerestes	1959
George Kerestes	1963
John Deutsch (Appointed)	1965
John Deutsch	1967
John Deutsch	1971
Richard W. Webb	1975
Richard W. Webb	1979
Richard W. Webb	1983
Richard W. Webb	1987
Gary F. Dobias	1991

CHANCELLORS OF THE CARBON BAR

Allen W. Craig	1893 - 1899
Frank P. Sharkey	1918 - 1943
Nathan M. Balliet	1943 - 1951
Raymond F. Smith	Oct. 1951 - June 1959
George A. Shutack	June 1959 - June 1962
Daniel P. Dougherty	June 1962 - Jan. 1963 (Died in office)
Albert Prutzman	Jan. 1963 - June 1965
George M. D. Richards	June 1965 - June 1966
Eugene Edelstein	June 1966 - Feb. 1967 (Resigned)
Joseph G. Greco	Feb. 1967 - June 1968
Carl A. Niehoff	June 1968 - July 1969
Martin H. Philip	July 1969 - July 1970
John G. Cipko	July 1970 - July 1971
Jacob Philip	July 1971 - July 1972
W. Joseph Engler	July 1972 - July 1973
Carl A. Niehoff	July 1973 - July 1974
George B. Richards	July 1974 - July 1975
Sidney R. Webb	July 1975 - July 1976
John Deutsch	July 1976 - July 1977
George T. McKinley	July 1977 - July 1978
William H. Bayer	July 1978 - July 1979
William B. Quinn	July 1979 - Dec. 1979
Thomas W. Durnin	Dec. 1979 - Dec. 1980
Robert Lazorchick	Jan. 1981 - Jan. 1982
Roger N. Nanovic	Jan. 1982 - Jan. 1983
Thomas S. McCready	Jan. 1983 - Jan. 1985
Marianne S. Lavelle	Jan. 1985 - Jan. 1987
Arnold Sousa	Jan. 1987 - Jan. 1989
James A. Wimmer	Jan. 1989 - Jan. 1991
Richard W. Webb	Jan. 1991 - July 1991 (Resigned)
Joseph J. Velitsky	July 1991 - Aug. 1993
Anthony Roberti	Aug. 1993 -

APPENDIX C

ROSTER OF ATTORNEYS OF THE CARBON COUNTY BAR (1843-1993)

William H. Butler	December 18, 1843
Silas E. Buzzard	December 18, 1843
William Davis	December 18, 1843
John W. Hornbeck	December 18, 1843
J. Glancy Jones	December 18, 1843
Christopher Loeser	December 18, 1843
John D. Morris	December 18, 1843
Francis J. Osborn	December 18, 1843
John Shouse	December 18, 1843
James R. Struthers	December 18, 1843
O. H. Wheeler	December 18, 1843
George W. Yates	December 18, 1843
William H. Barton	February 19, 1844
Edward C. Dimmick	June 24, 1844
William H. Dimmick	June 24, 1844
John D. Stiles	June 24, 1844
William P. Miller	June 24, 1844
Thomas L. Foster	1844
B. S. Schoonover	June 1845
Joseph H. Siewers	December 8, 1846
Samuel E. Dimmick	August 20, 1849
Horace B. Burnham	November 14, 1849
Edmund Neff	June 4, 1850
Milo M. Dimmick	1852
Samuel McLean	1855
Charles Albright	1856
Paul R. Weitzel	June 2, 1856
Allen W. Craig	May 1858
Daniel Kalbfus	1859
Stephen E. Sites	1859
Wesley B. Leonard	1861
N. F. Handy	1863
Edward C. Dimmick	October 4, 1865
John D. Bertolette	1867
B. F. Kleppinger	1868
John C. Dimmick	1869
Francis A. Doney	1869
Jabez Alsom	1870
William M. Rapsher	January 3, 1871
Edward M. Mulhearn	June 20, 1873
Edward R. Siewers	October 21, 1873
William G. Freyman	October 23, 1873
Frederick Bertolette	June 17, 1874
James S. Loose	June 23, 1875
Joseph Kalbfus	October 1876
Francis P. Longstreet	1876
Samuel R. Gilham	June 19, 1879
Laird H. Barber	June 20, 1881
Joseph S. Fisher	June 9, 1885
Horace Heydt	June 12, 1885
Frank P. Sharkey	April 20, 1887
Michael Cassidy	June 15, 1888
Jacob C. Loose	January 14, 1890
Robert A. Heberling	January 18, 1892
Douglas S. Craig	April 8, 1893
Eugene O. Nothstein	April 8, 1893

Theodore A. Snyder 1895
Nathan M. Balliet . . . . October 17, 1895
Ira E. Seidle . . . . May 2, 1896
Gustave A. Hemm . . . . November 2, 1896
James M. Breslin . . . . October 12, 1896
Daniel W. Sitler . . . . November 12, 1896
Horace DeYoung Lentz 1896
William G. Thomas . . . . April 12, 1897
Leighton C. Scott . . . . June 13, 1898
James Smitham . . . . October 9, 1899
George E. Gray . . . . October 21, 1899
Philip M. Graul . . . . June 11, 1901
Harrison L. Geggus . . . . January 13, 1902
Ellsworth E. Scott . . . . January 13, 1902
Charles A. Hauck . . . . January 21, 1903
Chester G. Setzer . . . . October 10, 1905
Winfred D. Lewis . . . . February 4, 1908
Ben Branch . . . . October 24, 1910
Leighton R. Scott . . . . October 14, 1912
Raymond F. Smith . . . . January 10, 1916
David Davis . . . . April 10, 1916
Frank S. Riordan . . . . April 10, 1916
Eugene Edelstein . . . . April 8, 1918
Frank X. York . . . . June 10, 1918
James C. McCready . . . . . . September 11, 1922
Alan S. Loose . . . . October 20, 1925
Daniel P. Dougherty . . . . April 19, 1927
George A. Shutack * . . . . June 11, 1928
Martin H. Philip * . . . . November 6, 1931
Albert G. Prutzman . . . . March 12, 1932
John G. Cipko . . . . October 10, 1932
Nicholas B. Dobosh . . . . October 10, 1932
David G. Watkins . . . . October 10, 1932
George M. D. Richards * . . . . January 23, 1933
John J. Dobosh * . . . . April 19, 1933
Albert H. Heimbach * . . . . April 1, 1935
Jacob B. Philip * . . . . May 28, 1936
William Joseph Engler . . . . May 10, 1937
Donald L. McCay . . . . April 27, 1938
Frank D. Llewellyn . . . . May 4, 1938
Joseph G. Greco . . . . April 21, 1939
Michael S. Lukish . . . . April 21, 1939
Morris Moskovitz + ... April 14, 1941
Carl A. Niehoff . . . . May 2, 1941
George B. Richards * . . . . May 15, 1942
Albert P. Leonzi . . . . June 12, 1942
Sidney R. Webb . . . . October 6, 1942
George Kerestes . . . . October 16, 1942
Joseph J. Heimbach + ... May 17, 1943
William Z. Scott . . . . November 2, 1945
John Deutsch . . . . June 14, 1948
George T. McKinley * . . . . May 15, 1950
William H. Bayer * . . . . . . November 13, 1950
William B. Quinn * . . . . December 11, 1950
Thomas W. Durnin * . . . . . November 25, 1952
William A. Wyatt * . . . . February 8, 1954
Robert Lazorchick . . . . December 20, 1954
Roger N. Nanovic * . . . . October 14, 1955
Joseph H. Foster . . . . April 1, 1957
Russell Chaplinsky . . . . May 6, 1957
Thomas S. McCready * . . . . May 25, 1957
Daniel R. Minnick . . . . December 16, 1957

Robert W. Cunliffe .... January 31, 1958
Raymond F. Smith, Jr .... May 19, 1958
Marianne Shutack Lavelle * ...... May 6, 1959
Murray Mackson * .... October 5, 1959
John P. Lavelle * .... March 24, 1960
Howard R. Moore, Jr. .... July 13, 1961
Arnold Sousa * .... August 20, 1963
Karl P. Niehoff .... December 28, 1964
James A. Wimmer * ...... November 22, 1965
John M. Yarema .... January 2, 1968
Richard W. Webb * .... April 20, 1970
Michael J. Piosa .... June 4, 1970
Joseph J. Velitsky * ...... November 23, 1970
Anthony Roberti * .... April 3, 1973
John F. Gibbons .... February 6, 1974
Joseph G. Greco, Jr. * .... May 22, 1974
Edward H. Vermillion * ... November 21, 1974
Gary F. Dobias * .... November 22, 1974
Michael J. Garfield * ...... February 13, 1975
Steven J. Hartz * .... August 21, 1975
Daniel F. Zeigler * .... May 24, 1976
Michael L. Ozalas * .... August 4, 1976
William G. Schwab * .... July 8, 1977
William E. McDonald * ..... October 26, 1977
Daniel A. Miscavige * ...... October 27, 1977
Richard M. Edridge * ..... November 9, 1978
Stephen P. Vlossak, Sr. * .... May 10, 1979
Bradford E. Landon * .... July 26, 1979
William Z. Scott, Jr.* ..... September 27, 1979
K. Tucker Landon * .... October 22, 1979
Roger N. Nanovic II * ...... October 22, 1979
George T. Dydynsky * .... October 2, 1980
Anthony P. Sodroski ...... December 4, 1980
Christine E. Mifkovich * .... January 29, 1981
Steve M. Gordon .... March 9, 1981
Paul M. Curran .... October 5, 1981
Carole J. Wildoner-Walbert * December 3, 1981
Robert T. Yurchak * ...... December 3, 1981
Holly A. Heintzelman * .... March 1, 1982
Jane F. Engler * .... July 26, 1982
Thomas S. Nanovic * .... October 28, 1982
Susan M. Rooney-Saunders * November 14, 1983
Steven M. Cormier * ..... November 25, 1983
Jean A. Engler * .... November 18, 1985
James R. Nanovic * ...... November 25, 1985
Marvin O. Schwartz * .... November 1985
John DiBernardino * ..... November 13, 1986
David W. Addy * .... January 5, 1987
Christie E. Schaffer-Bower * .. January 5, 1987
Barry C. Shabbick * .... May 16, 1988
David B. Shulman * .... May 16, 1988
Joseph J. Matika * .... July 14, 1988
Cynthia A. Dyrda * .... October 6, 1988
Keith R. Pavlack * .... November 3, 1989
Gregory L. Mousseau * .... December 5, 1989
Cynthia S. Ray * .... December 23, 1991
Karl J. Maehrer * .... December 23, 1991
Edmund J. Healy *+ ...... December 23, 1991
George C. Parrish *+ ..... December 23, 1991
Paul J. Levy * .... December 23, 1991
Dianne M. Dickson * .... January 14, 1992
Marc S. Fisher * .... January 14, 1992

Robert J. Magee * . . . . January 14, 1992
Wallace C. Worth, Jr. * . . . . . January 14, 1992
Gerald F. Strubinger * . . . . . December 21, 1992
Richard P. Abbott * . . . . August 5, 1993
Susan J. Nanovic * . . . . November 4, 1993
Robin M. Fenick * . . . . December 18, 1993
Michael S. Greek * . . . . December 18, 1993
Colleen F. Coonelly-Lavelle* + December 18, 1993
John P. Lavelle, Jr. *+ . . . . . December 18, 1993
Lynne Kimberly Law * . . . . . December 18, 1993

* indicates a present member of the Carbon County Bar
\+ indicates a lawyer with a practice outside of Carbon County

NOTE WELL: Other attorneys lived for a few months to a year within the county without leaving records. The most eminent lawyers of Eastern Pennsylvania have practiced at the Carbon County Courts from time to time, and were members of its bar though not residents of the county.

CARBON COUNTY ASSOCIATE JUDGES

Asa Packer	Mauch Chunk	Dec	1843 -	Nov	1848
Jacob Dinkey	East Penn	Dec	1843 -	Dec	1845
Daniel Heberling	Weissport	Jun	1846 -	Sep	1851
Joseph Butler		Mar	1849 -	Sep	1851
Isaac T. Dodson	Mauch Chunk	Dec	1851 -	Sep	1856
William H. Cool	Banks Township	Dec	1851 -	Sep	1856
Dennis Bowman	Bowmanstown	Dec	1856 -	Sep	1861
John Lentz	Parryville	Dec	1856 -	Sep	1861
A. G. Brodhead	Mauch Chunk	Dec	1861 -	Oct	1866
Tilghman Arner	Mahoning Township	Dec	1861 -	Oct	1866
James Huston	Mauch Chunk	Dec	1866 -	Sep	1871
Herman Hamburger		Dec	1866 -	Sep	1871
John Leisenring	Mauch Chunk	Dec	1871 -	Mar	1872
James Huston	Mauch Chunk	Dec	1871 -	Oct	1876
Levi Wentz	Aquashicola	Oct	1872 -	Oct	1878
Rensselaer Leonard	Beaver Meadow	Jan	1877 -	Oct	1881
Charles Meendsen	L. Towamensing Twp.	Jan	1879 -	Oct	1888
Harry E. Packer	Mauch Chunk	Jan	1882 -	Jan	1884
James Heberling	Weissport	Apr	1884 -	Oct	1884
Rensselaer Leonard	Beaver Meadow	Jan	1885 -	Oct	1888
Charles H. Seidle	Mahoning Township	Jan	1889 -	Oct	1893
William H. Stroh	Mauch Chunk	Jan	1889 -	Oct	1889
Samuel B. Price	Mauch Chunk	Jan	1890 -	Oct	1894
Daniel Rouse	Weatherly	Jan	1894 -	Oct	1898
Jacob G. Zern	Lehighton	Jan	1895 -	Oct	1899
Eugene P. Williams	Weatherly	Jan	1899 -	Oct	1903
Edwin R. Enbody	Mauch Chunk	Jan	1900 -	Oct	1904

CHAPTER I WILLIAM PENN AND THE FIRST PENNSYLVANIA COURTS

Schwartz, Bernard. *The American Heritage History of the Law in America.* New York: American Heritage Publishing Co. Inc.

CHAPTER II BENCH AND BAR BEFORE CARBON COUNTY (1776-1842)

Eastman, Frank M. *Courts and Lawyers of Pennsylvania -- A History, 1623-1923 (3 Volumes)* New York: The American Historical Society, 1922.

Schrader, Michael C., Esq. *Two Hundred Years In The Life of Northampton County, PA.* Easton, PA: Mack Printing Co., 1976. Vol V.

CHAPTER III EARLY CARBON COUNTY COURTS AND LAWYERS (1843-1900)

Godcharles, Frederick A. *Pennsylvania, Political, Governmental Military and Civil.* New York: The American Historical Society, 1933, Governmental Volume.

Hydro, Vincent, Jr. "Just Ramblin'." *Valley Gazette.* May 1992.

Ibid. June 1992.

Ibid. July, 1992.

Keller, Robert Brown. *History of Monroe County, Pennsylvania.* Stroudsburg, PA: Monroe Publishing, Co., 1927.

Stevens, Sylvester K. *Pennsylvania, Birthplace of a Nation.* New York: Random House, 1964.

CHAPTER IV FIFTY-SIXTH JUDICIAL DISTRICT (1901-1943)

Hoben, Richard J. *Lansford -- The First Hundred Years*, 1976.

CHAPTER VI THE COURTHOUSES

A Walking Tour of Jim Thorpe. 1992.

Brenckman, Fred. *History of Carbon County, Pennsylvania.* Harrisburg, PA: James J. Nungesser, Publisher, 1913.

Carbon County Transit. March 26, 1843.

Ibid. March 28, 1843.

Ibid. June 10, 1843.

Ibid. May 16, 1847.

Hydro, Vincent, Jr. "Just Ramblin'." *Valley Gazette.* July, 1992.

Kreamer, Ralph. *Morning Call.* July 27, 1951.

Lenahan, Joseph. *Morning Call.* December 6, 1956.

Wagner, A.E. *History, Government and Geography of Carbon County, Pennsylvania.* Allentown, PA: Berkemeyer, Keck & Co., 1910.

CHAPTER VII CARBON COUNTY JAIL

Mathews, Alfred and Austin N. Hungerford. *History of the Counties of Lehigh and Carbon in the Commonwealth of Pennsylvania.* Philadelphia: Everts and Richards, 1884.

CHAPTER VIII PAST PRESIDENT JUDGES

Judge Nathanial B. Eldred

Carbon-County Transit. March 28, 1843.

History of Warren County.

Keller, Robert Brown. *History of Monroe County, Pennsylvania.* Stroudsburg, PA: Monroe Publishing, Co., 1927.

Mathews, Alfred and Austin N. Hungerford. *History of the Counties of Lehigh and Carbon in the Commonwealth of Pennsylvania.* Philadelphia: Everts and Richards, 1884.

Judge Luther Kidder

Downey, Edgar, Esq. *Publications of the Historical Society of Schuylkill County: The Law Courts and Law Judges of Schuylkill County.* Pottsville, PA: 1947, Vol. VI., No. 1.

Hemenway, Abbey Maria. *The Vermont Historical Gazetteer.* 1868, Vol. I.

Kulp, George B. *Families of the Wyoming Valley.* Wilkes-Barre, PA: E.B. Yordy Printer, 1890, Vol. III.

Pearce, Stewart. *Annals of Luzerne County.* Philadelphia: J.B. Lippincott & Co., 1860.

Pennsylvania Archives. 4th Series. Vol. 6.

Judge George R. Barrett

Aldrich, Lewis Cass, ed. *History of Clinton County, Pennsylvania.* Syracuse, NY: D. Mason & Co. 1887.

Mauch Chunk Gazette. May 12, 1853.

Ibid. October 4, 1855.

Carbon Democrat. April 30, 1853.

Ibid. May 21, 1853.

History of Clearfield County.

Judge James M. Porter

Mauch Chunk Gazette. October 6, 1853.

Ibid. October 20, 1853.

Heller, William J. *History of Northampton County (Pennsylvania) and the Grand Valley of the Lehigh.* New York: American Historical Society, 1920, Vol. II.

Schrader, Michael C. *Two Hundred Years Of Life in Northampton County, PA* 1976, Vol. V.

Judge Thomas S. Bell

Ashmead, Henry Graham. *History of Delaware County, Pennsylvania.* Philadelphia: L. H. Everts & Co., 1884.

"Death of Judge Bell." *Delaware County Republican.* June 14, 1861.

Futhey, J. Smith and Gilbert Cope. *History of Chester County, Pennsylvania.* Philadelphia: Louis H. Everts, 1881.

Garner, Winfield Scott, ed. *Biographical and Portrait Cyclopedia of Chester County, Pennsylvania.* Philadelphia: Gresham Publishing, 1893.

Mauch Chunk Gazette. October 4, 1855.

Ibid. October 11, 1855.

Judge Samuel S. Dreher

Coal Gazette Extra. June 30, 1893.

Commemorative Biographical Record of Northeastern Pennsylvania. Chicago: Beers, 1900.

Jeffersonian. June 29, 1893.

Keller, Robert Brown. *History of Monroe County, Pennsylvania.* Stroudsburg, PA: Monroe Publishing Co., 1927.

Mathews, Alfred. *History of Wayne, Pike and Monroe Counties, Pennsylvania.* Philadelphia: R. T. Peck & Co., 1886.

Mauch Chunk Coal Gazette. June 30, 1893.

Ibid. July 1, 1893.

Judge John B. Storm

Commemorative Biographical Record of Northeastern Pennsylvania. Chicago: Beers, 1900.

Mauch Chunk Coal Gazette. October 17, 1855.

Ibid. October 6, 1893.

Ibid. November 3, 1893.

Mathews, Alfred. *History of Wayne, Pike and Monroe Counties, Pennsylvania.* Philadelphia: R. T. Peck & Co., 1886.

Judge Allen W. Craig

Brenckman, Fred. *History of Carbon County, Pennsylvania.* Harrisburg, PA: James J. Nungesser, Publisher, 1913.

Keller, Robert Brown. *History of Monroe County Pennsylvania.* Stroudsburg, PA: Monroe Publishing Co., 1927.

Mauch Chunk Coal Gazette. November 1893.

Judge Horace Heydt

Brenckman, Fred. *History of Carbon County, Pennsylvania.* Harrisburg, PA: James J. Nungesser, Publisher, 1913.

Mauch Chunk Daily Times. November 5, 1913.

Mauch Chunk Times News. November 17 1934.

Judge Laird H. Barber

Mauch Chunk Times News. February 16, 1928.

Judge William G. Thomas

Times News. December, 1928.

Judge James C. McCready

Mauch Chunk Times News. August 11, 1947.

Ibid. January 16,1967.

Times News. December, 1928.

Judge Albert H. Heimbach

Times News. September 16, 1977.

Ibid. November 21, 1977.

CHAPTER X COURT ADMINISTRATION AND CASE MANAGEMENT

Lavelle, John P., P.J. *County of Carbon Judicial Report: 1978-79-80.* Lehighton, PA: Times News, 1980.

Ibid. *County of Carbon Judicial Report: 1981-82-83.* Lehighton, PA: Times News, 1983.

Ibid. *County of Carbon Judicial Report: 1984-85-86.* Lehighton, PA: Times News, 1986.

Ibid. *County of Carbon Judicial Report: 1987-88-89.* Lehighton, PA: Times News, 1989.

CHAPTER XII CARBON COUNTY BAR ASSOCIATION

Minutes of the Meetings of the Carbon County Bar Association, 1959-1993.

CHAPTER XIII NOTABLE MEMBERS OF THE BAR

Laciar, J.D. *Patriotism of Carbon County, Pennsylvania.* Mauch Chunk, PA: 1867.

Mathews, Alfred and Austin N. Hungerford. *History of the Counties of Lehigh and Carbon in the Commonwealth of Pennsylvania.* Philadelphia: Everts and Richards, 1884.

Mathews, Alfred. *History of Wayne, Pike and Monroe Counties, Pennsylvania.* Philadelphia: R. T. Peck & Co., 1886.

Thompson, Katharine Foster. *Chapter and Verse: The Annotated Diaries of Asa Lansford Foster (1798-1868).*, 1992.

CHAPTER XV THE "MOLLIE MAGUIRE" TRIALS (1876)

Aurand, A. Monroe, Jr. *Historical Account of the Mollie Maguires.* Lancaster, PA: Aurand Press, 1940.

Brenkman, Fred. *History of Carbon County, Pennsylvania.* Harrisburg, PA: James J. Nungesser, Publisher, 1913.

Broehl, Wayne G., Jr. *The Mollie Maguires.* Cambridge: Harvard University Press, 1964.

Campbell, Patrick. *A Molly Maguire Story.* Jersey City, NJ: Templecrone, 1992.

Devlin, Ron. "State pardons miner hanged in Schuylkill 100 years ago." *Morning Call.* January 16, 1979.

Kashatus, William C. *Pennsylvania Heritage.*

Lewis, Arthur H. *Lament for the Molly Maguires.* New York: Harcourt, Brace and World, Inc., 1964.

Miller, E. Willard. *Pennsylvania - Keystone to Progress.* Northridge, CA: Windsor Publications, 1986.

Quinn, Edward G. *Of Myths and Men, An Analysis of Molly Maguireism in 19th Century Pennsylvania.*

Schlegel, Marvin W. *Ruler of the Reading, The Life of Franklin B. Gowen (1836-1889).* Harrisburg, PA: Archives Publishing Company of Pennsylvania, Inc, 1947.

Shenk, Hiram H., LL.D., ed. and Ester Shenk, assoc. ed. *Encyclopedia of Pennsylvania.* Harrisburg, PA: National Historical Association, Inc., 1932.

The Great Mollie Maguire Trials in Carbon and Schuylkill Counties, PA. Pottsville, PA: Chronicle, 1876.

Times News. August 25, 1980.

ILLUSTRATION CREDITS

William Penn Historical Society of Pennsylvania, Philadelphia p. 1

William Penn publishes Frame Of Government Ceiling of Supreme Court Chambers, Harrisburg p. 3

Blackstone's Commentaries Ceiling of Supreme Court Chambers, Harrisburg p. 5

Northampton County Courthouse Northampton County Historical and Genealogical Society, Easton p. 8

View of Mauch Chunk Horsehead Resource Development Co. p. 12

Asa Packer Historical Society of Pennsylvania p. 14

Scaled Survey Map of Northampton County Michael Cabot Associates, Inc., Stroudsburg p. 16

Mauch Chunk in 1845 Mr. & Mrs. Charles E. Wildoner p. 18

Minutes of First Court Session George A. Harvan p. 19

Mauch Chunk and Mount Pisgah Horsehead Resource Development Co. p. 26

Mansion House Hotel Horsehead Resource Development Co. p. 28

Balliet and Seidle Testimonial Mrs. William O. Moyer (daughter of Ira Seidle) p. 35

County Officials at time of County Centennial *Mauch Chunk Times-News*, Dimmick Memorial Library p. 49

Alexander Campbell testifies at Mock Trial George A. Harvan p. 65

James McParlan sworn in at Mock Trial George A. Harvan p. 66

Defense lawyer Steve Vlossak cross-examines James Kerrigan at Mock Trial George A. Harvan p. 66

Judicial Sesquicentennial Logo Donald Abbott p. 70

Courthouse I Watercolor by David Price p. 72

Courthouse II Watercolor by David Price p. 76

Courthouse II -- 1876 Horsehead Resource Development Co. p. 78

Photo of Mauch Chunk in 1850 from Flagstaff Mountain Franklin E. Wehr p. 79

County Row Offices, Circa 1892 County of Carbon p. 80

Courthouse II, Circa 1893 County of Carbon p. 81

Courthouse III Watercolor by David Price p. 82

Courtroom II Richard L. Walp p. 86

Stain glass window depicting Lady Justice in Main Courtroom William J. Vogt p. 88

Main Courtroom after restoration in 1993 George A. Harvan p. 89

Carbon County Jail George A. Harvan p. 91

Graphics of Mauch Chunk Scenes *The Daily Graphic*, New York June 22, 1877 p. 93

Execution of Thomas P. Fisher Dimmick Memorial Library p. 94

Carbon Prison Cell George A. Harvan p. 99

James Madison Porter Skillman Library, Lafayette College, Easton p. 110

Civil War Monument Dimmick Memorial Library p. 131

"Pigeonholes" George A. Harvan p. 161

District Justices and President Judge Lavelle Paul J. Hadzick p. 168

Magisterial Districts established in 1993 Aileen Cassidy p. 169

District Court Justices Richard L. Walp p. 170

Case Docket Books George A. Harvan p. 175

Court computer system George A. Harvan p. 176

1938 Carbon Bar Carbon County Bar Association p. 180

Balliet welcomes Deutsch to Bar Katharine L. Bartholomew p. 182

Rules of Court George A. Harvan p. 200

Bar Association fetes wives in 1970 *Times News* p. 195

Principals in Mock Trial of Alexander Campbell George A. Harvan p. 200

Roberti accepts Pennsylvania Bar Award for "Mock Trial of a Mollie" Carbon County Bar Association p. 201

Thomas Lansford Foster John D. Gunsser p. 204

Milo Melancthon Dimmick Dimmick Memorial Library p. 205

Charles Albright MASS-MOLLUS/U.S. M.H.I., Carlise p. 206

John D. Bertolette John D. Gunsser p. 209

William M. Rapsher M6-22, Legislators Photo Album, Pennsylvania Historical and Museum Commission, Harrisburg p. 210

Edward M. Mulhearn *History of Carbon County (1913)*, Fred Brenckman p. 211

William G. Freyman *Lehigh, Northampton, & Carbon Counties,* Chapman Publishing (1894) p. 212

Frederick Bertolette Carbon County Bar Association p. 214

Frank P. Sharkey United States Post Office, Jim Thorpe p. 216

Jacob C. Loose John D. Gunsser p. 217

Nathan M. Balliet Katharine L. Bartholomew p. 219

Illustration Credits

Ira E. Seidle Mrs. William O. Moyer p. 221

Horace DeYoung Lentz Sts. Mark & John Episcopal Church, Jim Thorpe p. 225

George E. Gray *Pennsylvania Political, Governmental, Military and Civil*, Frederic A. Godcharles p. 226

James Smitham Princeton University Library, New Jersey p. 226

Philip M. Graul *History of Carbon County (1913)*, Fred Brenckman p. 227

Ellsworth E. Scott *History of Carbon County (1913)*, Fred Brenckman p. 228

Chester G. Setzer *History of Carbon County (1913)*, Fred Brenckman p. 228

Winfred D. Lewis Princeton University Library, New Jersey p. 229

Ben Branch *Pennsylvania Political, Governmental, Military and Civil*, Frederic A. Godcharles p. 230

David Davis Skillman Library, Lafayette College, Easton p. 231

Raymond F. Smith, Sr. Carl Hesse p. 232

George Kerestes Skillman Library, Lafayette College, Easton p. 247

William Herman Rau photo of Mauch Chunk, 1891 George A. Harvan p. 270

Rear view of Courthouse II in 1876 George A. Harvan p. 285

Sketch of Alexander Campbell on trial in Carbon County courtroom George A. Harvan p. 288

James Kerrigan Historical Society of Schuylkill County, Pottsville p. 289

Graphic of "Mollie Maguire" Trials Edmund J. Healy, Esq. pp. 324, 325

Indictment against alleged "Mollies" George A. Harvan p. 389

INDEX

COURT CASES INDEX

The Carbon Advocate.
INDEPENDENT—"Live and Let Live."
CARDS
Railroad Guide.
HOGS!
Dressed or Live Hogs
JOSEPH OBERT.
CHARLES W. LENTZ
THE LUNGS!
CONSUMPTION!
Syrup of Wild Cherry
Dr. Swayne's Compound Syrup of Wild Cherry
Wall Paper a Specialty!
FIFTY FOR COMPANY.
Itching Piles!
SWAYNE'S OINTMENT
SKIN DISEASES
Office of the Secretary of the Commonwealth.
Pennsylvania, ss:
I do hereby Certify, That the foregoing and annexed is a full, true and correct copy of the original Act of the General Assembly, entitled
"An Act
relative to the establishment
a law library in the County
Carbon"
RULES
FOR THE
REGULATION OF THE PRACTICE
IN THE
Court of Common Pleas
OF THE
FIFTY-SIXTH JUDICIAL DISTRICT OF PENNSYLVANIA, COMPOSED OF CARBON COUNTY
In force April 10, 1922
In the Court of Quarter Sessions of the Peace and Oyer and Terminer and General Jail Delivery OF CARBON COUNTY Pennsylvania
TRIAL LIST
for
JANUARY SESSIONS, 1953
JAMES C. McCREADY, Pres. Judge
CALENDAR
COURT OF COMMON PLEAS
OF CARBON COUNTY, PA.
TRIAL LIST
October Term 1949
COMMENCING MONDAY, OCTOBER 24, 1949
JAMES C. McCREADY, P. J.
CALENDAR
COURT OF COMMON PLEAS
OF CARBON COUNTY, PA.
TRIAL LIST
October Term 1936
COMMENCING MONDAY, OCTOBER 26, 1936
HON. WM. G. THOMAS President Judge
THE DEMOCRAT.
The Mauch Chunk Democrat,
A POLITICAL AND NEWS JOURNAL,
Published Every Saturday Morning.
SUBSCRIPTION RATES
Murder at Lansford
THE ASSASSINS CAPTURED